A Worker's Economist

A Worker's Economist

John R. Commons and His Legacy from Progressivism to the War on Poverty

John Dennis Chasse

LONDON AND NEW YORK

First published 2017 by Transaction Publishers

Published 2017 by Routledge
2 Park Square, Milton Park, Abingdon, Oxon OX14 4RN
711 Third Avenue, New York, NY 10017, USA

Routledge is an imprint of the Taylor & Francis Group, an informa business

Copyright © 2017 by Taylor & Francis

All rights reserved. No part of this book may be reprinted or reproduced or utilised in any form or by any electronic, mechanical, or other means, now known or hereafter invented, including photocopying and recording, or in any information storage or retrieval system, without permission in writing from the publishers.

Notice:
Product or corporate names may be trademarks or registered trademarks, and are used only for identification and explanation without intent to infringe.

Library of Congress Cataloging-in-Publication Data:
A catalog record for this title has been applied for.

ISBN: 978-1-4128-6539-5 (hbk)

To the Memory of Yngve Ramstad

Contents

Preface		ix
Introduction		1
1	Randolph County	9
2	Oberlin	21
3	Hopkins	29
4	Wesleyan-Oberlin	37
5	Indiana Beginning	41
6	Sociologist at Syracuse	53
7	Exile	71
8	The National Civic Federation	83
9	Wisconsin Labor History	97
10	Multitasking	111
11	The Wisconsin Idea	127
12	The Commission on Industrial Relations	143
13	Shattered Illusions	161
14	The Dominant Class	177
15	Croaking Cassandras	193

16	The Social Statesman and His Team	209
17	The Trailer Park and the Last Book	225
18	The Team's Last Stand	235

Appendix A to Chapter 12: Report and Dissent at the USCIR — 247

Appendix B to Chapter 14: *The Legal Foundations of Capitalism* — 257

Appendix C to Chapter 16: *Institutional Economics* — 273

Chronology — 281

Abbreviations — 285

Bibliography — 287

Index — 311

Preface

In 1980 David LeSourd and I decided to investigate the economics of occupational health. In our literature review, we discovered that many economists were arguing that worker compensation could create an incentive for workers to injure themselves in order to collect the payments. There were similar arguments against engineering solutions to occupational health problems.[1] We decided that we did not want to go there, and that would have been the end of it. But I grew curious about the thinking behind the original occupational health legislation, and that led me to John R. Commons and a whole different way of thinking.

After a few years, I received a small grant from the joint SUNY Foundation-United University Professions faculty development fund, and I traveled to the archives of the Wisconsin Historical Society where I met the chief archivist Harold Miller. He gave me a reprint of his article on the American Bureau of Industrial Research, guided me to the files on Commons's students, and told me about the microfilm editions of the Commons, Ely, and McCarthy papers.

In 1986, after my first article on Commons was published, I was surprised to receive a letter from Kenneth Parsons, Commons's last living student. He liked the article. I sent him my second article for comments. In his reply, he suggested that I might think about writing a biography of John R. Commons. I wrote some other articles about Commons, and when I retired, I decided to take Parsons's suggestion, and, in doing so, I became indebted to many people in addition to David LeSourd, Harold Miller, and Kenneth Parsons.

The book could not have been written without the assistance of Brockport's interlibrary loan sleuths, Bob Gilliam and Laura Emerson. Time and again, they proved themselves capable of the impossible, of finding and obtaining almost everything I ever requested. And they were typical of the archivists and librarians I encountered everywhere. The librarians at the local public libraries in Union City, Indiana, and in Winchester, Indiana, produced microfilms of the newspapers that were edited by John A. Commons over a hundred years ago. The archivist at the Indiana Historical Society introduced me to the broader history within which the histories of Wayne and Randolph Counties evolved. Louisa Hoffman, the Oberlin College archivist, in addition to making the Oberlin archives available, tipped me off to the Internet address of all the historical copies of the *Oberlin Review* where I discovered that John R. Commons was the editor during his senior year. The archivists at the New York Public Library helped me find my way around the papers of the National Civic Federation. When I contacted the archivist at the University of Indiana, he responded that there wasn't much, only a couple of letters which he sent me. Those letters explained why Indiana's president told Commons to go to Syracuse. At Syracuse the archivists made the papers of James Roscoe Day accessible. The Syracuse librarians went to their off-site storage to retrieve copies of *The University Forum* during the years that Commons was there. Robin Carlaw, a researcher at the Harvard University archives, sent me a copy of Alvin Hansen's paper, "The Contributions of John R. Commons to American Economics." And there is another librarian: my wife, Linda, who has patiently suffered through this whole thing, helping when she could.

In addition to the librarians and archivist, I must mention the members of the Association for Institutional Thought and the Association for Evolutionary Economics. The book would have been impossible without them. Through conferences, the *Journal of Economic Issues*, and online interchanges, they have maintained a lively dialogue, not just about current economic problems but also about all the ways of understanding and analyzing them—including the ways of John R. Commons and his students.

Finally, the book owes very much to the advice and editing of the enormously helpful anonymous reviewer and the editors at Transactions Press, Jeffery Stetz, Allyson Fields, and Carolyn Russomano. They improved the manuscript in myriad ways, though I am sure that my flaws were not completely erased. I only hope that the book will convince some readers to look more closely at the life and work of John R. Commons.

Note

1. John Dennis Chasse and David A. LeSourd, "Rational Decisions and Occupational Health: A Critical View," *International Journal of Health Services* 14, no. 2 (1984): 433–45.

Introduction

My point of view is based on my participation in collective activities,
from which I derive a theory of the part played by collective action
in control of individual action—Institutional Economics

In 1883 John R. Commons was supporting his education at Oberlin by setting type at the *Cleveland Herald* when, on the advice of an older printer, he started reading Henry George's *Progress and Poverty*. And in the very first chapter, Henry George introduced him to "The Problem," beginning with this sentence, "The present century has been marked by a prodigious increase in wealth producing power."

For two pages, George waxed poetic about the possible benefits of this "prodigious increase in wealth producing power." It could "make poverty a thing of the past . . . . Youth no longer stunted and starved, age no longer harried by avarice, the child at play with the tiger," and on and on. Then, on page three, George brought his reader down to earth.

> Now, however, we are coming into collision with facts which there can be no mistaking. From all parts of the civilized world come complaints of industrial depression; of labor condemned to involuntary idleness; of capital massed and wasting; of pecuniary distress among business men; of want and suffering and anxiety among the working classes. All the dull, deadening pain, all the keen, maddening anguish that to the great masses of men are involved in the words "hard times," afflict the world today.[1]

For a while, the book made John R. (as everyone called him) an obnoxious true believer in the whole Henry George doctrine—that land owners scooped off in rent all the surplus income created by workers and capitalists and that a tax on the site value of land would solve all problems. But George's book had more permanent effects. It would influence John R.'s decision "to become an educated man and to take the side of the workers."

An Oberlin teacher helped him "become an educated man" by securing financing for his graduate education at Johns Hopkins, where he learned that George had oversimplified everything. He learned that there was not one problem; but many—most without obvious solutions. But he remained committed to investigating this more complex form of George's problem and to seeking solutions for its many manifestations. This commitment got him in trouble, but it also put him in the company of social workers, labor leaders, politicians, and other reformers committed to solving the same problems. These were the people with whom he worked in the "collective activities" on which he based his "point of view."

Thus, the story of Commons's life becomes not just about him or his ideas but also about these "collective activities," about the people with whom he collaborated, about their efforts to realize what the historian Clarence Wunderlin has called "visions of a new industrial order," and about the powerful forces that opposed their efforts. And, if the story is extended to include the "collective activities" of his students, Commons's story merges with the larger story of social workers, labor leaders, politicians, and other reformers who struggled during the first sixty-five years of the twentieth century to understand and alleviate the damaging side effects of America's drive toward a mass consumption society. This alone might make his story worth telling.

But, there is more. Commons's name appears in histories of American social science, histories of American public policy, and histories of the progressive era.[2] Moreover, he wanted to "take the side of the workers" less as an activist and more as "an educated man"—a scholar and a teacher.

As a scholar, he sometimes called himself a sociologist, sometimes, an economist—never a labor historian, never a labor economist—though he helped create the institutionalist branch of labor economics, the discipline of industrial relations, and the "old labor history."[3] And, though his work crossed academic borders, he gained a level of recognition that surpassed respectable in more than one field.

Legal historians still credit his original contributions to jurisprudential theory.[4] Economists elected him president of the American Economic Association in 1917. Three recipients of the Nobel Prize for economics either acknowledged their debt to Commons or used his ideas.[5]

Once fired for bad teaching, he had by the end of his life gained the loyalty and affection of so many students that the number could compete for the Guinness Book of Records. Former students formed "Friday Night Clubs" in large cities, meeting weekly, sending him letters with signatures running off the page. "No other single scholar turned as many graduate students in the direction of labor studies as did Commons."[6] Six of his students were presidents of the American Economic Association.[7]

And it would be hard to find a teacher whose students exercised as much influence on public policy. John B. Andrews, the executive secretary of the American Association for Labor Legislation, oversaw the intellectual dialogue that became the "seedbed" for most labor and social legislation between 1907 and 1940.[8] Edwin Witte and Arthur Altmeyer worked on the design of the Social Security Act, and Altmeyer served as commissioner of Social Security until 1950. Wilbur Cohen under Presidents Kennedy and Johnson, oversaw the creation and implementation of Medicare, the Elementary and Secondary Education Act, the Civil Rights Act, and a host of Social Security amendments.

Finally, there is a growing interest in Commons's writings, especially in his two most theoretical books, *Legal Foundations of Capitalism* and *Institutional Economics*.[9] And, of course, he has been criticized—a reason for restoring the context that helps to set the record straight.

The following chapters try to restore the context, to tell the story of his life without losing sight of the path of his thought or of the policy tradition that his students carried into their various roles in government. It was possible, in doing this, to take advantage of primary and secondary sources unavailable to Lafayette Harter, who wrote the only other biography of Commons published in 1962. Harter's sources were limited by time and place. He did not have access to the work of historians who wrote after 1962, historians such as Dorothy Ross, Clarence Wunderlin, Christopher Cyphers, and many labor historians who explored the worlds in which Commons worked: the worlds of social science, higher education, public policy, and labor relations. Harter was limited to information he could find in Madison, Wisconsin, and Palo Alto, California. But there was much information, particularly about what Commons did before he got to Madison, in Syracuse, Cornell, New York City, Oberlin, Ohio, Indianapolis, and in the Indiana towns of his youth—Union City, and Winchester. Information about these early years permits a more accurate narrative of the interaction between his "habitual assumptions" and the almost accidental "collective activities" that turned his mind in new directions. This interaction between events

3

and habitual assumptions permits one to think of his life as moving through six stages.

The first stage, formation of his habitual assumptions, started with the unique culture of Randolph County, the subject of chapter 1, continued through his formal education at Oberlin (chapter 2), and at Johns Hopkins (chapter 3), and then through his informal education as a teacher at Wesleyan and Oberlin. Chapter 4 shows him still learning—by mistakes at Wesleyan where he was fired for poor teaching and by the books through which he took his classes at Oberlin—Böhm-Bawerk's *Theory of Positive Capital* and Alfred Marshall's *Principles.*

The second stage, the first of his professional life, started at Indiana (chapter 5), where he became a popular teacher and published his first major work, *The Distribution of Wealth.* He was still in this stage "at" Syracuse (chapter 6), where he was even more popular as a teacher and where he published *Proportional Representation.* At Syracuse he also spent a summer with the sociologist Lester Frank Ward, wrote a huge syllabus that appeared to be a long-run research plan, and also wrote two series of articles indicating that at this time "taking the side of the workers" meant political reform, and reform of prisons and the treatment of wayward youth. There was little mention of trade unions in this second stage.

Chapters 7 and 8 cover the "collective activities" that established a third stage. While working on the staffs of the United States Industrial Commission and the National Civic Federation, he developed a commitment to trade unions and collective bargaining. He also became acquainted with economists, journalists, and social workers who shared his concern for the problems of the working classes.

A fourth stage began with his arrival at the University of Wisconsin to work on an "interpretive history of labor." With two outstanding students, he amassed a monstrous collection of documents and produced eight volumes of the *Documentary History of American Industrial Society.* But the "interpretive history" was to play only a minor role in his professional life. It was delayed by competing demands, some introduced in chapter 10 and some in chapter 11. Chapter 10 covers his work in outside organizations and in the department where he developed close relations with more students and collaborated in the development of a problems approach to teaching and of a bargaining theory of wages.

Chapter 11 describes his work for the Wisconsin Industrial Commission where he learned about the legal notion of reasonable value,

Introduction

a notion that he would expand beyond its legal context to a theory of due process in policy formation. His experiences in those years led him to reflect on public administration, publishing first a series of articles and then a book *Labor and Administration*, published in 1913. That book introduced notions of "constructive democracy" and "constructive research."

Chapter 12 traces the tragic consequences of his appointment to the United States Commission on Industrial Relations in 1914. Before the commission collapsed in discord in 1916, Commons published with John Andrews *The Principles of Labor Legislation*.

Chapter 13 might be viewed as the beginning of a fifth phase, starting in 1917 with war and ending in 1919 with *Industrial Goodwill*, a book that proposed "collective democracy" in the workplace. In between he would become president of American Economic Association in 1917, and, in 1918, he would see the publication of the long-delayed first two volumes of the "interpretive history." After this, his writing would take a theoretical turn, and his "collective activities" would reach the national stage..

Chapter 14 finds Commons confronting the Supreme Court's hostility to unions, proposing an unemployment compensation bill, and publishing the *Legal Foundations of Capitalism*, the first volume of his theory of reasonable value. Chapter 15 begins with the death of Samuel Gompers in 1924, the decline of unions, and the development of labor economics. It moves to 1927 and 1928, to Commons's testimony on a bill to make price stability a goal of the Federal Reserve System. It notes the work of his student Ed Witte on an anti-injunction bill.

Chapter 16, beginning with the depression, might mark a final stage. Commons had achieved social statesman status while his students carried his principles to Washington. He published what he considered at the time to be his final books—four between 1934 and 1936—the last two volumes of the labor history, the fourth edition of the *Principles of Labor Legislation*, *Myself*, and *Institutional Economics*, his second volume on reasonable value. Chapter 17 recounts his daughter's death in 1936, his trip to a trailer camp in Fort Lauderdale, his work on his last book, his last major article, his summer seminars at Madison, his trip to Raleigh, North Carolina, in the spring of 1945, his death there on May 11, and the deaths in 1951 and 1957 of his sister and son.

The final chapter starts with *The Economics of Collective Action* and the conservative political climate in which it was published. It follows three Wisconsin students, who brought Commons's traditions into the design of Lyndon B. Johnson's "War on Poverty."

In all this, there was an effort to keep track of John R. Commons the human being while sketching the path of his thought. To avoid unnecessary complexity in the respective chapters, three appendices were added. An appendix to chapter 12 argues that his commission dissent had much in common with the staff report from which he appeared to be dissenting, that it could be read more as a supplement than as an open critique, and that, combined with the staff report, and with *The Principles of Labor Legislation*, the dissent laid out a comprehensive program for labor and social reform. An appendix to chapter 14 illustrates the necessity of imposing one's own organization on Commons's most theoretical works. It shows three such organizations imposed on the *Legal Foundations of Capitalism*: the organization that Wesley Clair Mitchell imposed, the one that, legal scholars imposed, and one that stresses his approach to the wage bargain. An appendix to chapter 16 suggests an approach to *Institutional Economics* and illustrates the approach with two examples.

Notes

1. Henry George, *Progress and Poverty, an Inquiry into the Causes of Industrial Depression and the Increase of Want with the Increase of Wealth* (1879; reprint, with a preface by John Kieran, New York, 1942), 3–5.
2. Sidney Fine, *Laissez-Faire and the General Welfare State* (Ann Arbor: MI: University of Michigan Press, 1956), 210, 327–28, 379; Dorothy P. Ross, *The Origins of American Social Science* (New York: Cambridge University Press, 1991); 194, 202–3. Mary O. Furner and Barry Supple, *The State and Economic Knowledge* (New York: Cambridge University Press, 1990), 258–60; Theda Skocpol, *Social Policy in the United States, Future Possibilities in Historical Perspective* (Princeton, NJ: Princeton University Press, 1995), 148–50.
3. David Brody, "Reconciling the Old Labor History and the New." *Pacific Historical Review* 62 (February 1993): 1–18. The term "labor economics" never appeared in any of Commons's writings; see Paul McNulty, *The Origins and Development of Labor Economics: A Chapter in the History of Social Thought* (Cambridge, MA: MIT Press, 1980), 127.
4. Katherine, V. W Stone, "John R. Commons and the Origin of Legal Realism; or the Other Tragedy of the Commons," in *Transformations in American Legal History: Law, Ideology, and Methods: Essays in Honor of Morton Horwitz* vol. 2(Cambridge, MA: Harvard University Press, 2010), 326–43; Morton Horwitz, *The Transformation of American Law 1870–1960* (New York: Oxford University Press, 1977).
5. Herbert Simon, *Models of My Life* (New York: Basic Books, 1992), 87; Elinor Ostrom, *Governing the Commons: the Evolution of Institutions for Collective Action* (New York: Cambridge University Press, 1991), 51, 237; Oliver Williamson, *Markets and Hierarchies* (New York, Free Press, 1975) 4, 24, 254; *Economic Organization, Firms, Markets, and Policy Control* (New York: NYU Press, 1986), 175–76;Thomas Kemp, *Progress and Reform: The*

Economic Thought of John R. Commons (Saarbrucken: VDM, 2009) explores the connection between Commons and Williamson.

6. McNulty, *The Origins and Development of Labor Economics*, 151.

7. The six students were Harry Millis, Sumner Slichter, Alvin Hansen, Calvin B. Hoover, Theodore W. Schultz, and Edwin Witte. Theodore W. Schultz was the only Wisconsin graduate to receive the Nobel Prize in economics.

8. Clark Chambers, *Seedtime of Reform, American Social Service and Social Action* (Minneapolis, University of Minnesota Press, 1963); David A. Moss, *Socializing Security, Progressive Era Economists and the Origins of American Social Policy* (Cambridge, MA: Harvard University Press, 1996); J. Dennis Chasse, The American Association for Labor Legislation, An Episode in Institutionalist Policy Analysis," *Journal of Economic Issues* 25 (September 1991), 799–822.

9. To verify the growing current interest one need only consult references in current works such as Glen Atkinson and Steven Parschall, *Law and Economics from an Evolutionary Perspective* (Northampton, MA: Edward Elgar, 2016), or Romuald Dupuy, Philippe Roman and Benoit Mougenot, "Analyzing Socio-Environmental Conflicts with a Commonsonian Transactional Framework: Application to a Mining Conflict in Peru," *Journal of Economic Issues* 19 (December 2015), 895–921. The latter references a large number of books and articles in both English and French.

1

Randolph County

*Liberty, equality, and defiance of the fugitive slave law were
my birthright, and Hoosierdom my Education—Myself*

There was nothing impressive about him; he weighed just over a hundred pounds; his voice was soft, his face lined, and he always looked sick.[1] But John R. Commons should have felt good about himself. In 1932, more than two hundred former students had crowded into the Memorial Union Building for his seventieth birthday party. There had been speeches, jokes, and praise. The students had given him $1,300 with orders to spend it on a trip to England, and they had also ordered him to write his biography. So, sometime later, perhaps in 1933, he rose at about 4:00 AM, as was his habit, started a pot of weak coffee, picked up his pencil, and began. "I write this biography in sorrow and doubt."

So he did not feel good about himself. In 1927 his wife had died. In 1930 his son, the war hero whose troubles he had never comprehended, had driven off with the family car. His daughter was there, returned from a broken marriage and working on an anthropology degree at the University of Chicago. His half-sister Anna had come there after her husband had died. The old man reminisced a bit about his students, cheered up, and started again.

"My mother was a Presbyterian, my father a Quaker."[2] Well his mother was not a typical Presbyterian, and his father was not a Quaker, but the statement reflected his sense of deep roots. His father was an agnostic, but Quaker beliefs—in plainness and in the inner voice with its corollary that everyone deserves a hearing—ran deep in Randolph County where he grew up, and they ran deep in his father's extended family, starting with William and Sarah Scarlett Commons, Irish Quakers and weavers of fine linen who had carried those beliefs with them when, in 1755, they had come with their seven-year-old son Robert from County Kerry, Ireland, to Chester County, Pennsylvania.[3] In 1780,

Robert had married Ruth Hayes. Their oldest son, Isaac, was born in 1785. Other children followed, and the family moved around, settling at last in Virginia on the North Carolina border among Southern Quakers—a restless lot.

By 1800 all Southern Quakers had finally been convinced by Friends from England, Pennsylvania, and Delaware that slavery was a "moral iniquity." Then they had "found themselves" as the Quaker philosopher Rufus Jones put it, "in a social world in which they did not fit."[4]

So they had been ready in 1800 when Friends again visited their meetings and told them to go over the mountains and "northwest of the Ohio River to a place where there were no slaves held, being a free country." The Carolina Friends took this as a message "sent to call us out, as it were, from Egyptian darkness (for indeed it seemed as if the land groaned under oppression)." The message spread through meetings up and down the coast, and thus began the Quaker exodus from the Tidewater South, an exodus greater in numbers than the first exodus of Quakers from England to Pennsylvania.[5]

In 1802, Robert's son, Isaac, now seventeen years of age, set out, in the vanguard of that exodus with the David Hoover party from Randolph County, North Carolina. After five years and many adventures, the party reached the Whitewater River in Eastern Indiana and started carving out farms.[6]

David Hoover, the party's leader, would become a member of what Eric Voegelin has called the "Quaker aristocracy," the source of the democratic traditions of Randolph and Wayne Counties that so impressed Voegelin. Fifty years later, Hoover, by then a judge, recalled these early days. This was "the day," he wrote, "of the 'log-cabin' and log-rollings; and although we were in unbroken forest, without even a blazed pathway from one settlement to another, we yet enjoyed a friendship and neighborly exchange of kind offices which are unknown at this time."[7]

Quakers kept coming, and settlements multiplied. Towns appeared. And by November 19, 1809, Isaac Commons had found a wife, Mary Townsend. In 1812 Isaac and Mary met the steamboat bringing Robert and the rest of the family to Wayne and Randolph Counties.

John A. Commons

Mary bore ten children. Seven lived past childhood. One of the seven, John Alvin Commons, born on December 15, 1818, studied winters in the local country school, worked on Isaac's farm in spring and summer, and in every spare moment, he read anything he could get his hands on—William Shakespeare's plays, poetry, legal tomes, history books, novels, Herbert Spencer's *Social Statics*. Somewhere in all this reading, John A. began harboring doubts about the Quaker faith.

After leaving home, John A. taught school for a while. Then he traveled through Southern Wayne County selling leather goods. In 1847 he married Elizabeth Carlisle. She died in childbirth a year later. The little girl, Anna, lived and would remain a Quaker, even as John A. drifted from the meetings. (John A.'s son, John R., would later write of going to Quaker meetings with Isaac and Mary and of Quakers meeting in his home, where they prayed that John A. might return to the fold.)[8]

In 1856, John A. opened a harness shop in Hollandsburg, Ohio, a town bordering Randolph County, Indiana. In 1860, he moved his shop to Union City, Indiana, a railroad town on the edge of Randolph County, right next to Union City, Ohio. The people of Union City elected John A. Justice of the Peace in 1860, and they kept electing him until 1868. According to the Randolph County historian, John A. became "widely known and universally esteemed."[9] This contemporary account of John A. is more flattering than that of his son, John R., who complained that the old man was writing poetry when he should have been attending to business.[10] Most of John A.'s poems were "for the drawer" as poets say, but John R. kept one that his father had sent to Clarissa Rogers, a school teacher in Richmond, Indiana.

> No title high nor honored name
> To you my suit I bring
> No deeds of glory nor of fame
> Have I to boast and sing
> No gilded mansion towering high
> Where pomp and splendor shine
> Oh none of these to boast have I
> An humbler offering mine
> An honest heart's sincere devotion
> What ere thy fate may be
> Tis all I am—tis all I proffer
> Tis all I Pledge to thee.[11]

Clarissa

In 1860, John A. Commons married Clarissa Rogers. She was the great-great granddaughter of the Reverend John Rogers, the first Congregationalist Minister of Boxford, Massachusetts.[12] When Clarissa was eight, her family had moved from Fort Covington, New York, to Ashtabula,

Ohio, a port city on Lake Erie where her parents had enrolled her in the Ashtabula Academy and the Grand River Institute. At the age of sixteen, after a profound religious experience, Clarissa had become a Presbyterian.

She had attended Oberlin when Charles Grandison Finney was its president and its overpowering public personality. A fabled revival preacher with sharp features and piercing blue eyes, Finney could hold a thousand people spellbound. Traditionalist Presbyterians accused him of heresy because, as a revivalist, he implicitly rejected predestination by preaching that anyone could "see the light" and be "born again." Clarissa was a Finney Presbyterian.

Finney emphasized the virtue of usefulness in the Christian mission of building the "city on the hill." When Clarissa attended Oberlin, abolition of slavery was the paramount task for that mission. Finney encouraged students to join secular reform organizations such as abolition societies because they were more useful and effective than strictly religious ones.[13]

The Family

Clarissa had come to Richmond in 1858 to teach school where she met John A. Commons whom she married in 1860. Clarissa and John A. lived first in Hollandsburg. John R. was born there on October 13, 1862, four months before the Emancipation Proclamation. A year later, the family moved to Union City, Indiana, closer to John A.'s harness shop. Alvin was born in Union City in 1865 and Clara in 1867. The household also included Anna from John A.'s previous marriage, and a boarder or two. Anna maintained a quiet Quaker presence in the home and helped care for the children, all of whom became deeply attached to her. The family was not wealthy, but it was not unhappy. John R. did not recall his Presbyterian mother ever arguing with his agnostic father.[14]

In 1873, John A. traded his harness shop for a newspaper, the *Union City Times*. Four years later he traded the *Union City Times* for the *Winchester Herald*, and the family moved to Winchester, the county seat of Randolph County, Indiana.

His decisions to buy first the *Union City Times* and then the *Winchester Herald*, while consistent with his literary inclinations, also appear to have been related to the way that Union City's railroads connected Randolph County farmers to the world. Midwest American grain drove down world prices contributing to a complex of events that resulted in the collapse of Jay Cooke's investment firm, followed by the panic of 1873, which reduced the market for Randolph County grain—and for John A.'s leather goods. So he traded his harness shop for the *Union City Times.* In 1877, a railroad strike in Martinsburg, West Virginia, turned violent, and violence spread across the nation. There were riots in major cities—including Indianapolis. Many rioters were not strikers, but members of America's still unrecognized, underclass.[15] In 1878 John A. moved his family away from Union City, the railroad town, to Winchester, closer to the center of Randolph County, and he traded the *Union City Times* for the *Winchester Herald.*

Neither the harness shop nor the newspapers ever generated enough income to support the family, and Clarissa took in boarders to make ends meet. Years later, John R. recalled a "lady professor" at Oberlin who had graduated with Clarissa. This "lady professor" had told him that she was disappointed that Clarissa had not become "one of the prominent women in the country." John R. was "startled and humiliated. I could only say, in hesitation, that through all her married life she had kept boarders to support the family and educate the children."[16] If that was all he told her, he sold his mother short.

She did take in boarders, but she also wrote the temperance and Sunday school columns for the *Union City Times* and the *Winchester Herald.* She wrote about her revivalist vision of the "City on the Hill" and about the obstacles that remained after slavery's abolition. "The principles underlying the Levitical law—love to God and justice to man—would, if carried out, alleviate all the ills that afflict society while whisky shops, Sabbath breaking and vice, made attractive in every conceivable manner are educators in the direction of prisons."[17] She was a leader among local women. Seventy-five of them elected her president of the local Women's Crusade, and she led marches and demonstrations against the saloon society of the day, closing down some saloons.[18]

Clarissa taught her children to read with the Bible and *Foxe's Book of Martyrs.* Hoping that John R. might become a minister, she persuaded the local Presbyterian pastor to tutor him in Latin and Greek. And Clarissa was probably the source of the "thrilling stories" of the Underground Railroad "across my mother's Western Reserve and my father's Eastern Indiana."[19] The "Western Reserve" in the north of the "Middle Border" had been settled by New Englanders who carried their abolitionist convictions with them. Quaker settlements like those in Randolph and Wayne Counties were glaring exceptions to the "copperhead" culture of the Southern "Middle Border" where support for slavery before the Civil War and pressure for peace during it had remained strong.[20] The Northern Middle Border and Quaker settlements such as those in Randolph and Wayne Counties, had, before the Civil War, been hotbeds of defiance to the Fugitive Slave Act and the source of many thrilling tales.

In Ashtabula, when Clarissa was growing up, escaped slaves huddled in the basement of the Hubbard House until they could be smuggled aboard boats in Ashtabula Harbor for the trip across Lake Erie to freedom and safety. And in Fountain City, Indiana, not far from the Commons home, the National Trust for Historical Preservation has highlighted the Levi Coffin house, "the Grand Central Station of the Underground Railroad," with its hiding places and ingenious contraptions that Levi Coffin devised to conceal escaped slaves in wagons that carried them in the dead of night to the next stop on the underground railroad.

And, given Clarissa's Oberlin background, John R. must have heard about the "Oberlin Rescue."[21]

On September 13, 1858, on a country road outside of Oberlin, a bounty hunter accompanied by a deputy sheriff and a deputy United States Marshall captured John Price, an escaped slave who had been living in Oberlin. As they took him in their carriage toward Wellington where a train ran south toward Kentucky, they passed two young men. Price cried for help. One of the two, an ardent abolitionist, went into town and reported the incident. The entire population of Oberlin, it seemed, raced toward Wellington and surrounded the hotel where Price was held . . . After lengthy negotiation, a pair of students forced their way into the room where Price was held, and by trickery they got him out of the room and the hotel. The mob then escorted Price back to Oberlin where he was hidden in the home of an Oberlin faculty member until he could be smuggled safely across Lake Erie.

Vowing to uphold the Fugitive Slave Act, the Cleveland Federal. Attorney pressed charges against thirty-seven men who came to be called the Rescuers. He secured indictments in December. But On February, a Lorain County grand jury indicted four men, the three that had captured John Price, and a fourth that had planned the capture. The trial began in April. The prosecutor swiftly gained two convictions and seemed poised to gain more – to the consternation of the locals. On May 24, the people of Ashtabula, Clarissa's hometown, joined a noisy demonstration in Cleveland calling for the release of the rescuers.[22] But the Lorain County sheriff jailed the four kidnappers, as people called them. They were released on bail after eight days.

By July, with the trials about to resume after a recess, the kidnappers began to realize that they might face a Lorain County jury composed of abolitionists, and after a lengthy and protracted negotiation, there was a sort of exchange of prisoners the Lorain County authorities dropped charges against the kidnappers and the prosecutor dropped charges against the Rescuers.[23] And so it ended. Back in Oberlin a crowd of 3,000 celebrated the release of the rescuers and the local victory over the Fugitive Slave Act, a victory that may have had national repercussions as it illustrated the intransigent abolitionist opposition to the Fugitive Slave Act.

Such stories made "Liberty, equality, and defiance of the Fugitive Slave Law" part of John R's "birthright." But "Hoosierdom," John R. wrote, was his "education."[24]

He wrote that he "was brought up on Hoosierism" and that he "spoke Hoosier," a word of unknown origin applied to the dialect and culture of Indiana citizens. James Whitcomb Riley, "Indiana's Bobby Burns," celebrated Hoosier dialect in such poems, as "Little Orphant Annie," and in his tribute to his friend, Eugene Debs.

> "And there's Gene Debs—a man 'at stands
> And Jes' holds out in his two hands
> As warm a heart as ever beat
> Betwixt here and the Jedgment Seat."[25]

John A. was, of course, the family Hoosier, and many of John R's fondest memories of his father and of Randolph County came from his Winchester years where he developed his typesetting skills and witnessed cracker barrel conversations between John A. and his Hoosier cronies.

> They sprawled back on their chairs, with their feet on the table, squirting tobacco juice and drawling their words, lazily, but funny and keen. . . . He and his cronies talked politics and science. Every one of them, in that Eastern section of Indiana was a Republican, living on the battle cries of the Civil War, and everyone was a follower of Herbert Spencer, who was the shining light of evolution and individualism. . . . I was brought up on Hoosierism, Republicanism, Presbyterianism, and Spencerism.[26]

And, John R. fondly recalled his Winchester high school days with his two buddies, James Putnam Goodrich and James Eli Watson. Years later, when all had grown up, Goodrich would serve as Indiana's governor from 1917 to 1921. Then he would chair the committee that brought aid to drought-stricken Russia in 1922. And years later Eli Watson would be elected to Congress, serving as majority leader in the Senate from 1929 to 1933.

Together in high school, though, all three joined the Republican Artillery Club. John R. carried ammunition for the cannon that they fired to mark patriotic occasions and to greet visiting dignitaries. They also did the other things that teens do. John R. remembered the "old swimming hole" and "games of seven-up"—and the tobacco experiments—both smoking and chewing, but the chewing left John R. doubled over and vomiting into a creek.[27]

Their high school curriculum included geometry, trigonometry, higher algebra, Stoddard's Mental Arithmetic, literature, history, and Latin, culminating in the senior year with Vergil's Aeneid.[28] John R. would leave Winchester with a better academic background than is generally assumed.

Goodrich seems to have been the most mature of the group, and he may have been the sparkplug for the lecture series that they organized in 1880 to raise funds for their school library. They invited well-known Indiana citizens to give lectures for which they charged admission. The poet James Whitcomb Riley came and lectured in 1880 and 1881—even though the students never paid his usual fee.

Upon graduation in 1881, they all started teaching in one-room schools. Only Goodrich and his future wife survived. John R. recalled his failure.

> In passing the country slaughterhouse, on my four-mile walk once a week from Winchester to the school, I would get the butcher to give me an ox's heart, or eye or some other piece of anatomy, to demonstrate to the pupils the pictures we found in our textbook. But we never could identify a single valve or layer of muscle or anything else which we found so plainly pictured in the book. The pupils lost faith in me, tumbled me in the grass, pelted me with snow balls, and I had to resign in three months. They wanted something "for sure," handed down by the great authorities of the past, and I couldn't produce it. I vowed that never again would I teach.[29]

Financial problems at home troubled John R.'s high school years. John A. expanded the *Winchester Herald*'s circulation and popularity. He did not do as well on the cash flow side. He accepted bushels of potatoes or baskets of apples or similar produce as payment. John R. and Alvin proposed to their father that they take over the financial and technical parts of the paper, leaving the editorial work to him, but when the two went out demanding payment in cash, the old man insisted that they stop.[30] John R. attributed the problem to his father's inability to adapt to a money economy. There was also the ethic of "neighborliness" in which John A. had been raised. He probably empathized with the financial difficulties of his customers during the long depression that followed the 1873 crash. To ask his neighbors for cash would have been to betray his deepest instincts.

In any case, John R. seems to credit John A.'s cash flow problems for Clarissa's decision to take $100 from her own savings and send him with it to Oberlin. The next year Clarissa herself would come with Clara and Alvin, leaving John A. to dispose of the paper. So John R. left Randolph County and rented a "shack of a house" at 24 Main Street in Oberlin, Ohio, taking with him the presuppositions of Randolph County, Indiana.

For the philosopher Eric Voegelin, those presuppositions included the working model of participatory democracy created by the "Quaker aristocracy." "In Commons' concrete investigations and philosophical formulations, the pioneer society is always the first premise, and it is on this basis that the special problems he addresses have meaning." Moreover, "Commons' origin in the world of farmers and artisans links him with the goals of labor and enables him to understand them on the basis of a similar background."[31] Voegelin also mentioned the influence on John R. of John A.'s agnostic intellectual independence and curiosity.

The historian Robert Crunden emphasized Clarissa. He used Clarissa and John R. to illustrate his "paradigm for a progressive personality." "From its birth in the Middle West, a generation of intelligent youth, though remaining devoted to their parents, resisted efforts to compel them into the ministry or missionary work. Despite tension, uncertainty, and an occasional breakdown, these young progressives channeled their urges to help people into professions that had not existed for their mothers and fathers."[32] Crunden did not deal with specifics—with Finney's theology of usefulness, or the "city on the hill," or the revivalist belief in conversion. Nor did anyone mention the consequences of learning to read with *Foxe's Book of Martyrs* with its assumptions of Anglo-Saxon superiority.[33] But John R. carried all this with him as he left Randolph County.

Notes

1. Theresa McMahon, "My Story," in Geraldine Clifford, ed. *Lone Voyagers* (New York: The Feminist Press at City University of New York, 1989), 247.
2. Commons, *Myself*, 1, 7.
3. Andrew. Young, *History of Wayne County, Indiana from Its First Settlement to the Present Time with Biographical and Family Sketches* (1872; reprint, Knightstown, IN: Eastern Indiana Publishing Co, 1972), 327, Henry Clay Fox, *Memoirs of Wayne County and the City of Richmond Indiana* (Madison, WI: Western Historical Society, 1912), 461.
4. Rufus M. Jones, *Later Periods of Quakerism*, vol.1 (London: Macmillan, 1921), 378, 385.
5. Ibid. 338, 407; Hugh Barbour and J. William Frost, *The Quakers* (New York: Greenwood Press, 1988), 149; Daisy Newman, *A Procession of Friends: Quakers in America* (Garden City, NY, 1972), 83–84; there were, however, slave owners in the Northwest Territory. Governor William Henry Harrison had petitioned Congress to remove the antislavery clause in the Northwest Ordinance. The Quakers, when they arrived, formed a vociferous antislavery block in territorial assemblies. See James Madison, *The Indiana Way* (Indianapolis, IN: University of Indiana Press, 1990), 49–50. Jones 1921, *Later Periods*, vol. 1: 407; Newman, *A Procession* 1972, 83–84.
6. The earliest record found in Dr. John Plummer, *Reminiscences of the History of Richmond*, has two lists, one he compiled from many sources, the other from a manuscript kept by the Cox family. Jeremiah Cox came with the David Hoover party and was an early leader of the settlers. Isaac is not on the first list (pp. 11–12), but he is on the list kept by the Cox family (42) which is the oldest and probably the most accurate. Putting the two lists together places Isaac in the David Hoover party. Henry Fox, *Memoirs of Wayne County* (234), made Isaac Commons one of the first settlers; and Fox's timing is most consistent with the David Hoover party.
7. David Hoover, *Memoirs of David Hoover, Part I.*
8. Commons, *Myself*, 9.
9. Ebenezer Tucker, *History of Randolph County, Indiana*, 219.
10. Commons, *Myself*, 11.
11. John R. Commons *Papers* (Madison, WI,: State Historical Society of Wisconsin, 1982), microfilm, reel 1, frame 3.
12. Dodge, Esther, *Genealogy of John Rogers of Boxford Mass* (Manassas, VA: Esther Dodge, 1907), 23,25,29,30. It contradicts John R.'s statement that his "mother's people came by way of Vermont," but the 1907 editor, Esther Dodge, wrote on the first page that she was updating a genealogy compiled by Clarissa Commons, John R.'s mother. His grandmother, Ruth Saunders, came from Vermont.
13. Charles G. Finney, *Lectures on the Revival of Religion*, 404–5; James H. Moorhead, "Charles Finney and the Modernization of America," *Journal of Presbyterian History* 62 (Summer 1985), 95–110; Kenneth Wheeler, "How Colleges Shaped the Culture of Usefulness," in *The Center of a Great Empire: The Ohio Country in the Early Republic*, ed. Andrew R.I. Cayton and Stuart D. Hobbs (Athens Ohio, Ohio University press, 2005), 105–21.
14. Commons, *Myself*, 9.

Randolph County

15. Robert H. Wiebe, *The Search for Order 1877–1920* (New York: Hill and Wang, 1967), 10.
16. *Myself*, 11.
17. Clarissa Commons "Introduction Sunday School Department," *Union City Times* 4 (March 25, 1875), 2.
18. Ebenezer Tucker, *History of Randolph County*, 190–91.
19. Commons, *Myself*, 7.
20. The copperhead is a poisonous snake the color of fall leaves. Just as the snake can lurk unseen among fallen leaves, and then rise up in a deadly attack, so—according to their accusers—former slavery sympathizers lay hidden in the Southern Middle Border, ready to rise up and sabotage the Union cause. The reality was more complex, and historians still disagree about the merits of the accusations. See Charles Calhoun, "Fire in the Rear," *Reviews in American History* 35 (December, 2007): 530–37 and Jennifer Weber, *Copperheads: The Rise and Fall of Lincoln's Opponents in the North* (New York: Oxford University Press, 2006).
21. Nat Brandt, *The Town that Started the Civil War*. The entire account of this episode here depends heavily on Brandt's account, J. Brent Morris, *Oberlin, Hotbed of Abolitionism* (Chapel Hill, NC: University of North Carolina Press, 2014), 208-22.
22. Brandt, *The Town that Started the Civil War*, 139.
23. Ibid., 171, 222–37, Morris, *Oberlin*, 221.
24. Commons, *Myself*, 7.
25. Cited in James Madison, *The Indiana Way*, 227.
26. Commons, *Myself*, 8.
27. Ibid., 13–14, 16, 25.
28. Dana Starbuck, *The Goodriches: An American Family* (Indianapolis, IN: Liberty Fund, 2001), 24.
29. Commons, *Myself*, 27–28.
30. Ibid., 12.
31. Eric Voegelin, *On the Form of the American Mind, The Collected Works of Eric Voegelin*, trans. Ruth Hein, vol.1 (1928; reprint, Baton Rouge: University of Louisiana Press, 1995), 205, 219, 229.
32. Robert Crunden, *Ministers of Reform: Progressives in American Civilization 1899–1920*, 6-8, 14–33.
33. William Haller, *The Elect Nation: The Meaning and Relevance of Foxe's Book of Martyrs* (New York: Harper & Row, 1963); Jesse M. Lander, *Inventing Polemic: Religion, Printing, and Literary Culture in Early Modern England* (New York: Cambridge University Press, 2006).

2

Oberlin

The educated man should not become linked in an aristocracy of intellect, but should be a guide whom the army of the discontented may trust and follow—J.R. Commons, Oberlin Review

With the $100 that Clarissa had given him, John R. "rented a shack of a house" at 24 Main Street in Oberlin, Ohio, and, in the fall of 1882, he started his college career. Clarissa, Clara, and Alvin came a year later. Alvin enrolled as a freshman and Clara as a high school student at the Oberlin preparatory academy. They came in the middle of what the historian John Barnard has called Oberlin's transformation from "Evangelicalism to Progressivism."[1]

Much remained as Clarissa remembered it. The college still emphasized character. It did not allow smoking or drinking, and John R. stopped smoking. It still required chapel days and campus revivals. Its curriculum consisted mostly of required courses in the classical tradition, and it still preached Finney's usefulness in the cause of the "city on the hill." Slavery, or so people assumed, had ended with the Civil War. But other obstacles remained—saloon society, political corruption, limited suffrage, and a growing labor problem. "Slavery is gone," proclaimed the keynoter at the first convention of the Prohibition Party, "but drunkenness stays."[2] These things remained the same, but in other ways Oberlin was no longer the college that Clarissa remembered.

A different president, James Fairchild, had replaced Charles Finney in 1866. Fairchild shared Finney's faith and his commitment to social reform. (Fairchild was the faculty member who, after the "rescue," had hidden John Price in his home.) But Fairchild had never experienced an emotional conversion, and he was not "given to introspection." Barnard commented that Fairchild was "one of the few college presidents, even in that bucolic age who milked his own cow."[3] Even earlier, in 1860 Charles Henry Churchill, Oberlin's professor of mathematics and science, after reading Charles Darwin's *Origin of the Species*, had vigorously promoted evolutionism to the rest of the faculty. Oberlin theologians, with whom higher criticism was already popular, found no conflict between evolution and scripture properly interpreted. The school supported faculty members who studied under the German theologian Adolph Harnack.[4] And Oberlin, responding to changes in the broader academic climate, had introduced a few electives for the senior year.[5]

But there were darker changes. Before the Civil War when white students had asked Finney to sanction separate black and white tables in the cafeteria, he had refused and had taken an African American student into his home as an example.[6] But, when John R. reached Oberlin, blacks and whites ate at separate tables. Barnard described a contradictory consensus among white students—a faith in Americanism defined as Anglo-Saxon, rural, and Protestant accompanied by mistrust of immigrants and Roman Catholics, but paradoxically by sympathy for the poor and for the rising working classes.[7]

This complicated environment would have an influence, but, for John R., struggles and work experience were almost as important as the school. As at Winchester and Union City, Clarissa held the little family together by providing most of the income—from two boarding houses: one for boys and one for girls. John R. and Alvin helped with typesetting jobs. First they worked for the *Oberlin Review*. Later an Oberlin alumnus and former printer recommended John R. for a job at the *Cleveland Herald*, and in that job, John R. learned about union working rules.[8] Printers at the *Herald* belonged to the typographical union, and they distributed advertising copy by rules of fairness to which all agreed. (Printers could set advertising lines faster than ordinary news lines, and since printers were paid by the line, advertising copy was more lucrative.) A year later John R.'s brother Alvin got a job at a nonunion paper. The wages were the same in both shops, but, without union rules, foremen in the nonunion shop gave advertising copy to their cronies. John R. would recall this contrast for the rest of his life. He had experienced the benefits of union working rules.[9]

All this was interrupted in the spring of 1885. As John R. came out of a Greek examination, he felt "a fierce blow from outside" that "seemed to hit inside my head. I could hardly walk home."[10] It was the first of many breakdowns. Unable to concentrate, he wandered through the woods around Oberlin. When summer came, he traveled to Au Sable Michigan where Alvin was working as a printer. But he could not concentrate enough to set type. So he traveled back to Winchester, to the home of his half-sister Anna and her husband, George Best, a Standard Oil salesman. Their home stood on three acres, just on the edge of Winchester. George bought a second-hand incubator to hatch chickens, and by watching over the chicks in the incubator John R. regained his ability to concentrate—just in time to embark on an adventure with his father and brother in Leesburg, FL, where John A. owned thirty acres of land that he had gained in a previous trade.

Bankrolled at first by Clarissa, John A. and Alvin began working to turn the thirty acres into a successful farm. In October of 1885 John R. joined them. His father and brother had built a log cabin and started clearing land. But they had used up Clarissa's funds, and the farm was not producing much income, so John R. and Alvin got jobs setting type at a paper in Leesburg where, to take a term from Charles Finney, John R. backslid.

The printers at the Leesburg paper had a custom of pooling their funds on weekends to buy a gallon of bootleg gin for a little office party. John R. and Alvin joined right in. "We devoted ourselves Saturday night and Sunday, in the printing office, to a friendly consumption of this imported gin, and to plug cutting our own smoking tobacco in the Southern fashion."[11]

In spite of their weekend orgies, John R. and Alvin earned enough to give their father a big cash infusion for the farm. Prospects looked promising. They cleared the pine trees and planted orange trees.

In April, 1886, John R. returned to Oberlin weighing 160 pounds rather than his habitual 105—to which he returned. Then malaria felled both John A. and Alvin. Clarissa took the train down and escorted the two invalids back to Oberlin. She traded the Florida land for a lot in Oberlin which she sold for $500. Now the whole family depended for its subsistence on Clarissa's boarding houses.

A month after John R.'s return from Florida, on May 1, 1886, workers in Chicago struck for the eight-hour day. On May 3, police killed four picketers. The next day, May 4, to protest the shootings, a crowd of about 600 gathered outside the McCormick reaper factory in Haymarket square. As the last speaker was winding up his oration, a ragged phalanx of six police divisions came running toward the crowd. Just as the leader ordered the crowd to disperse, someone threw a bomb. In the subsequent melee eight policemen died, and a number of demonstrators were beaten and wounded. The *Chicago Tribune* reported that the crowd was composed of Poles, Bohemians, and Germans, that there were very few "*real* Americans" in the crowd. It called for action against "the aliens."[12]

The police obliged. For two months, they invaded and ransacked offices of anarchist newspapers, harassed immigrant communities, and arrested prominent anarchists. Few voices rose in protest.

One protesting voice belonged to a young economics professor from Johns Hopkins University, Richard T. Ely, who happened to be in Chicago at the time. Ely vehemently condemned this "period of police terrorism" and called for its end.[13]

In the fall, in the October 1886 issue of *The Nation*, John R. read a review of Ely's recently published book, *The Labor Movement in America*. The review was unsigned, but everyone knew who wrote it—Simon Newcomb, astronomer, mathematician, and pioneer mathematical economist. Newcomb accused Ely of economic ignorance and of "bias and bitterness toward all classes of society except one," a bias "for which it would be hard to find a parallel elsewhere than in the ravings of an anarchist or the dreams of a socialist." John R. read the review and decided that he wanted to study under Ely.[14]

Clarissa meanwhile had been drawn back into her crusade against saloon society by Howard Russell, a former lawyer and Republican politician who had come to Oberlin to study theology. Russell argued that the Prohibition Party with its array of proposals was not the right organization to take on the "Whiskey Trust." A nonpartisan organization with a single objective could appeal to a broader public and lobby both political parties on the single issue of prohibition. Russell started the Oberlin Anti-Saloon League in 1887, but he left almost immediately for Kansas City's urban ministry, and Clarissa took over. John R., returning from his gin-fueled weekends in Florida, joined Clarissa's crusade against liquor. They organized the Lorain County Anti-Saloon League, wrote a constitution, and secured funding from local merchants.[15] They published a semimonthly paper, *The Temperance Herald*. At one meeting, John R. proposed that they adopt business methods and create a "temperance trust." People could buy shares in this temperance trust and the funds so raised could support a boycott of the Whiskey Trust.

The Commons family's participation in the anti-saloon league came to an end in 1888 when Clarissa's rheumatoid arthritis crippled her so badly that she could no longer operate her boarding houses. The financial collapse forced the little family into a tragic triage. Since John R. was in his senior year, they decided that he should go on to graduation. Clara, a freshman, and Alvin, a junior, had to leave Oberlin for good. Alvin went to Michigan where he worked as a typesetter. Clara got a job at the Ohio State Home for the feeble-minded. How Clarissa, John A., and John R. survived is not clear. Most probably Clara and Alvin contributed to their support. This experience may have sobered John R. and burdened him with a sense of responsibility that may explain the decisions he made in his senior year. Or those decisions may have resulted from his interactions with Professor Monroe.

Professor James Monroe, the teacher of John R.'s senior year elective—political science, modern history, and political economy— would exercise an outsize influence on John R.'s career for the next ten years. It could be argued that John R.'s career would have been impossible without James Monroe.

Monroe was no ordinary teacher. In 1841, young James Monroe had been so moved by oratory at a meeting of the Connecticut Anti-Slavery Society that he had volunteered full-time for the abolitionist movement and had developed bonds of friendship with abolition's leading lights—William Lloyd Garrison, Wendell Phillips, Frederick Douglass, and others. When Monroe decided to go to college, Amasa Walker, the MIT economist had talked him into going to Oberlin rather than to Yale. Monroe had graduated from Oberlin with a bachelor's degree in 1848, and a year later had earned his theology degree. In 1856 he had won a seat in the Ohio State House of Representatives where he had introduced a habeas corpus bill to protect escaped slaves from the Fugitive Slave provisions of the Compromise of 1850.

Monroe, during a state Republican convention, had insisted on a resolution ordering the Ohio delegation to introduce at the national convention a platform plank demanding repeal of the Fugitive Slave Act. This plank and the Southern reaction to it might have justified the title of Nat Brandt's book, *The Town that Started the Civil War.*

In 1859 John Brown, Jr. had visited Oberlin and had recruited three students—Lewis Sheridan, John A. Copeland, and Shields Green—for his father's raid on Harper's Ferry, Leary had died from wounds suffered in the raid. Copeland and Green had been captured and hanged. Since free blacks were not allowed in Virginia, Copeland's parents asked Monroe to travel there and retrieve the bodies of Leary, Copeland, and Green. Monroe went, but when he arrived, he discovered that students from the local medical school had dug up Copeland's body within an hour of his execution. Presumably the other bodies had met the same fate. Monroe went to the school and requested the bodies, but the students objected violently, and faculty members begged Monroe to desist lest violence spread into the community. So Monroe returned empty handed. He was limited to delivering a stirring oration at the memorial service.[16]

In 1862 Monroe went to Rio de Janeiro as the US Consul to Brazil. He returned in 1869, and in 1870, he won the right to represent Ohio's 19th congressional district and served five terms. In 1881, anticipating a position in James Garfield's administration, he resigned his seat. But after Garfield's assassination, Monroe lost interest in politics. In 1883 he returned to Oberlin and taught modern history, political science, and political economy. Monroe also started a political economy club, and, in a strange alliance with Henry George, Monroe started John R. on his life's mission.

An older printer at the *Cleveland Herald* had recommended George's *Progress and Poverty* to John R. in his freshman year, and by his senior year, John R. had mastered George's argument.

George summarized his view of capitalism's problem in his book's extended title: *Progress and Poverty: An Inquiry into the Causes of Industrial Depression and of Increase of Want with Increase of Wealth*. One would expect increasing wealth to decrease want. But, as George saw it, capitalism seemed to increase both while generating depressions. George attributed the problem to a single cause which implied a single solution.

He asked his readers to picture a patch of empty land in the prairie, purchased for pennies per acre by a speculator. Imagine, then, that industrialists came to that patch of land, that they brought machinery and built factories. Imagine that workers came and built homes. The workers and the capitalists would have increased the value of the land enabling the speculator to become wealthy by charging a high rent—not because the speculator did anything productive but because the laws of private property permitted him to scoop off in rent the extra value created by the capitalists and workers. The problem, George concluded, was not that the capitalists were exploiting workers, but that the law of property allowed landowners to sweep off in rent the increased value created by capital and labor in combination.[17] The single cause implied a single solution: a tax on the unearned rent. Such a tax would reduce the bargaining advantage that landowners held over capitalists and workers and at the same time generate revenue for public services to ease the lives of the workers.

John R. would later retreat from most of George's argument—with the exception of an attachment to site value taxation—but at Oberlin he became an annoying true believer.

He and eight other students organized a Henry George club. They met in "Mr. Commons' room on Main Street."[18] The club fizzled after six meetings. But John R. and his friends brought George's ideas into Professor Monroe's political economy club where they presented papers advocating the single tax.

Even though he disagreed with them, Monroe encouraged the students—to the point of helping them bring Henry George to campus for a talk and discussion. More importantly, Monroe would make it possible for John R. to study under Professor Ely, the author of that book reviewed in *The Nation.*

Monroe had realized earlier that Oberlin's practice of retaining some of its best students for faculty positions would not be enough to maintain the school's reputation. So he had started soliciting funds from Oberlin's major donors to finance promising Oberlin students at Johns Hopkins.

He may also have been influenced by two editorials that John R. wrote for the student newspaper. The editorials indicate—albeit naively—the direction that John R. had chosen for his life. He began the first by stating that in order to understand problems of poverty and alcoholism, one needed to get close to the people suffering from these ills, and he concluded with this declaration: "Reforms as well as revolutions have broken through society from below, and those whose conditions in life lead them to be satisfied with the 'existing order of things' have been pushed along or overwhelmed by these upheavals. The educated man should not become linked in an aristocracy of intellect, but should be a guide whom the army of the discontented may trust and follow."[19]

On April 3, in another editorial, titled "Preparation for Life's Work," he argued that graduate education was essential for students who wanted to be "effective in their future careers."[20]

There was a little juvenile hubris in these articles, but they predicted the direction his life would take, and he would repeat them later with less hubris. He would give up the part about guiding the discontented. But he would not become linked to "an aristocracy of intellect," and he would become someone that the discontented would trust. To begin, he would seek an education beyond the bachelor's degree, and Professor Monroe would help.

John R. was one of only eight students for whom Professor Monroe secured loans so that they could attend Johns Hopkins. Two Oberlin trustees Albert H. Johnson and William Sumner agreed to finance John R.'s education there, and in the fall of 1888, John R. Commons enrolled at Johns Hopkins University. His major professor would be Richard T. Ely, the economist who had raised a lonely cry of outrage at police treatment of foreigners after the Haymarket riot.

Notes

1. John Barnard, *From Evangelicalism to Progressivism at Oberlin College, 1866–1917* (Cleveland: Ohio State University Press, 1969).
2. Norman H. Clark, *Deliver Us From Evil* (New York: Norton, 1976), 70.
3. Barnard, *From Evangelicism to Progressivism*, 4–5.
4. Ibid., 48–49.
5. John S. Brubacher and Willis Rudy, *Higher Education in Transition: An American History: 1636–1936* (New York: Harper and Brothers, 1958), 96–115. Paul Westermeyer, *A History of American Higher Education* (Springfield, IL: Charles C. Thomas, 1985), 111–19.
6. Charles G. Finney, *The Memoirs of Charles G. Finney: The Complete Restored Text*, eds. Frank M. Russell and Richard A. G. D. Dupuis (1876; 1975, reprint; Grand Rapids, MI: Zondervan Press, 1989), 411.
7. Barnard, *From Evangelicalism to Progressivism*, 57–58.
8. Commons, *Myself*, 16–18.
9. Ibid., 17–20.
10. Ibid., 26.
11. Ibid., 22.
12. James Green, *Death in Haymarket* (New York: Pantheon Books, 2006), 6–7.
13. Ibid., 199. Earlier Ely had visited Chicago presumably on his honeymoon, but he had made it a working honeymoon. He had visited the acclaimed village that George Pullman had built for his workers. Ely had condemned the enterprise as hypocritical, implicitly forecasting the Pullman Strike of 1894. Richard T. Ely, "Pullman: a Social Study," *Harper's New Monthly Magazine* 70 (February, 1885): 452–66.
14. Commons, *Myself*, 40, Simon Newcomb, "Dr. Ely on the Labor Movement," *The Nation* 1110 (October 7, 1896): 293–94.
15. K. Austin Kerr, *Organized for Prohibition: A New History of the Anti-Saloon League* (New Haven, CT and London: Yale University Press, 1985), 78–79.
16. James Monroe, *A Journey to Virginia: Thursday Lecture*. www.oberlin.edu /archive/exhibit/john_brown_new/lecture.html.
17. Henry George, *Progress and Poverty* (1879; reprint, New York: Walter J. Black, 1941), 198–204.
18. Barnard, *From Evangelicism to Progressivism*, 62.
19. John R. Commons, "Abstract Studies and the World," *Oberlin Review* 15 (February 7, 1888): 111–12.
20. John R. Commons. "Preparation for Life's Work," *Oberlin Review* 15 (April 3, 1888): 158–59.

3

Hopkins

In fact, the law of rent cannot be understood without a profound insight into many other laws. I am glad that you did not lose confidence in me last year because I was so radical Commons to Monroe, May 14, 1889.

John R. liked to tell stories, but his stories could mislead, and this happened when he introduced his Hopkins years with stories about Professor Ely setting him "to work visiting the building and loan associations of Baltimore;" or sending him to a Charity Organization Society as "case worker" where he secured a pension for a tuberculosis weakened Civil War veteran.[1] The stories were undoubtedly true, but taken alone, they created the impression that John R. spent most of his time at Hopkins doing social work. Thus, when Lafayette Harter informed his readers that Richard T. Ely "set his students to field work without much formal training," he unwittingly contradicted everything that is known about Johns Hopkins, about Ely's teaching style, and about what John R. thought he was doing while he was there.[2]

The School

The unique nature of this university originated in the strange will of Johns Hopkins, the wealthy Quaker merchant who died on December 24, 1873 (Johns was the maiden name of his great grandmother). In his will Hopkins instructed twelve chosen trustees—seven Quakers and five lawyers—to use half of his seven-million-dollar fortune to found a hospital and the other half to establish "a different kind of college." No one could figure out what he meant by "a different kind of college." But the twelve old men, after three years of due diligence, concluded that the United States needed a university devoted primarily to research and to the education of students beyond the bachelor's degree.[3] To create that university, they hired Daniel Coit Gilman, founder of the Sheffield Scientific School at Yale University and president of the University of

California. They promised Gilman freedom from "shackles of political dominance," from any denominational influence, and from any "obstacles or captious objections on our part."[4] Their vision excited Gilman, and, after his official installation on February 22, 1876, he scoured universities in the United States and Europe looking for faculty, waving a checkbook, and promising complete academic freedom.

Gilman hired two faculty members that would exercise a significant influence on John R.'s education—Herbert Baxter Adams and Richard T. Ely. Adams held a PhD from Heidelberg with specialties in political science, public and international law, and political and cultural history. His major research interests were the history of education and the Anglo-Saxon origins of democratic institutions. His influence on John R. was not direct, though John R. took courses from him. Rather, Adams, as head of the department, influenced John R. through his design of seminars required of all student. The seminars communicated an ideal of generalized social science research that easily crossed disciplinary boundaries.

Professor Ely

Richard T. Ely exercised a more direct influence. He had graduated *summa cum laude* from Columbia University and had won a fellowship to study in Germany where he had changed his major from philosophy to political economy, studying under the great German historical economists, Johannes Conrad at Halle and Karl Knies at Heidelberg. Ely had graduated from Heidelberg with a PhD *summa cum laude.*

Ely had been there six years when, in the fall of 1886, John R. read that negative review of Ely's *Labor Movement in America*—with its ominous conclusion. "Dr. Ely seems to us to be seriously out of place in a university chair."[5] It really was ominous. Simon Newcomb, also a Hopkins faculty member, was actively agitating and scheming to have Ely fired.[6] Newcomb had succeeded earlier in dislodging Charles Sanders Peirce from the Hopkins philosophy faculty; so the threat was real.[7] Fortunately, in Ely's case, Gilman resisted, and Ely remained. Newcomb's attack, though, reflected a struggle among economists that would rage for decades.[8]

In that struggle, Ely and his allies called themselves the "new" economists to distinguish themselves from the "old" economists who, according to Ely and his allies, followed the simplistic doctrines of Frederic Bastiat and the social Darwinism of Herbert Spencer and Charles Sumner. The "new" economists argued for inductive inquiry, statistics, and economic history. Moreover, they insisted that economic history could be understood only in the context of social and political events and that economics could not be separated from ethics.[9] Ely helped found the American Economic Association (AEA) "to combat the Sumner–Newcomb crowd," and he was responsible for the conclusion of the first preamble: "We hold that the conflict of labor and capital has brought to the front a vast number of social problems whose solution is impossible without the unified efforts of Church, State, and science."[10] Ely wanted the new organization to actively promote solutions to social problems, a degree of activism that bothered even some of his allies—including the AEA's president, Francis A. Walker, who wanted to include the "old" economists in the organization.[11] In calling their opponents "old," the "new" economists were at least partially attacking a straw man.

The "other side" was more sophisticated than Bastiat, and it was not really old.[12] Newcomb himself contributed to advances in monetary theory and this was the era of the "marginalist revolution" in economic theory. The opponents of the "new" economists based their idea of economics on analogies with the physical sciences. They accused the "new" economists of fuzzy and incompetent thinking. They held that economics should rigorously separate "positive" from "normative" statements and attacked the ethical pretensions of the "new" economists as unscientific.

But, though he held to one side of that conflict, "that excellent German professor in an American skin," as Joseph Schumpeter called Ely, brought his students up-to-date on every aspect of economic thought at that time—including Jevons and the Austrians as well as the Germans.[13] According to Toyokichi Iyenaga, John R.'s Oberlin friend who had preceded him at Hopkins, Ely in his introductory course assigned readings from three textbooks: *Political Economy* by John Stuart Mill, *The Relation of the State to Industry* by Henry Carter Adams, and Ely's own *French and German Socialism*.[14] In class, though, Ely lectured on the relation between sociology and economics and on the history of political economy. He did not lecture on the assigned texts, but he gave monthly tests on them.

John R. at Hopkins

In his first year, John R. took Ely's courses in History of Political Economy, Special Economic Questions, and Elements of Political Economy. His letters to James Monroe in the Oberlin College archives reveal his enthusiasm, not only for Ely's classes but also for the historical and social science seminars. The letters also reveal that he was chronically short of money and that Ely found jobs for him, and that may explain the stories in *Myself.*

Most influential for John R., after Ely's classes, were two required seminars one in history, the other in social science. In these seminars faculty members and invited scholars lectured, led discussions, and commented on student papers. During John R.'s years, Woodrow Wilson lectured on the history of local governments in England, France, and Germany, and James Bryce, the British reformer and author of *The American Commonwealth,* lectured on history and reform.[15] John R.'s classmate, the sociologist, Edward Alsworth Ross, described the pressures of the seminar. "We were a dead-earnest group, for three thousand volumes in our field lined the walls and alcoves of the big seminary room silently reminding us how little we knew. Every one of us was working like a beaver on seminary report or doctoral thesis. Outstanding among us were David Kinley, James Albert Woodburn, John R. Commons . . . Two-thirds of that group achieved distinction, while a fifth of it won fame."[16]

Woodrow Wilson's lectures on comparative local government inspired John R. to add two subspecialties to his major in economics, and he asked Professor Monroe if that would be a good idea. "Professor Wilson is expounding the new local government act of 1888 which makes such sweeping changes in English county government. I am thinking of making Administration and United States Constitution my supplementary studies. Do you think these would make a good choice?"[17]

On May 12, Monroe approved the two new specialties. John R. referred to Monroe's response in a long letter covering many issues on May 14.

In that letter, John R. confessed that his first year at Hopkins had shaken his faith in Henry George's simple view of capitalism and in his simple solution to capitalism's problems.

> In addition to the land question and the free trade question to which my early economic ardor was limited I am seeing great things in such questions as child labor, arbitration, profit-sharing, co-operation. When one sees the immensity of the field and the variety of human interests, he begins to lose faith in a simple nostrum and sees that there must be reforms along a great number of lines. In fact the law of rent cannot be understood without a profound insight into many

other laws. I am glad that you did not lose confidence in me last year because I was so radical—my danger now is to become too conservative when I get bewildered with the multitudes of different problems.[18]

In the final letter of his first semester, John R. wrote to Monroe about money problems. Ely had promised to find enough employment for him to finance much of his second year, but John R. was concerned that such work would distract him from his studies and that he would not be able to learn as much as he wanted. That fear seemed prophetic for his second year.[19]

During that year, in addition to the required general seminars, John R. studied Money and Banking with Ely and German institutions with Adams. He also took two courses—the English Constitution and the History of English Law—from George Henry Emmot, a British barrister and later dean of the University of Liverpool law school.[20] There is an indication of John R.'s future work in his comment at the end of the year on Emmot's lectures.

> One very profitable course has been the study of English law of Real Property, beginning from the earliest times and continuing to the latest reforms. My instructor is an English barrister having practiced at Manchester for eleven years. The useful feature of the course is the gradual development of the idea of private property in land as influenced by custom and legislation.[21]

The high point of the next semester was Ely's seminar on political economy.

> [We] are reading the works of Ricardo. This is the most interesting and profitable work I have yet entered upon, for there are seven of us, and our talks are entirely informal. We take plenty of time in examining every point that comes up, and I go away from every meeting feeling that I have mastered some important principle. The question of utility and value is before us now, and we are hunting up Jevons and Clark and others who have discussed it.[22]

John R. must have made a strong impression because Ely suggested that John R. and the future sociologist Edward Alsworth Ross collaborate with him on a book. Ross published two articles, but abandoned the project when he turned from economics to sociology.[23]

Ely, as noted, appeared to understand John R.'s financial situation. He paid him to write lesson outlines and examination questions for a correspondence course offered by the Chautauqua Institute. He hired

John R. to read the proofs and write a bibliography, index, and study questions for his *Outlines of Political Economy*.[24] But, in spite of Ely's help and in spite of the loans that Monroe scrounged from the trustees, financial constraints grew tighter in John R.'s second year. Clarissa had come to Baltimore to see if the mineral baths could alleviate her arthritis. So he was supporting her as well as supporting himself and paying tuition. His letters to Monroe are filled with tales of small financial crises.

On January 14, 1890, John R. confessed that he needed $200 or he would not be able to pay tuition for the second semester of his second year at Hopkins.[25] Monroe seems to have asked him to try for funds at Hopkins. He tried and was turned down, but Clarissa somehow found $100, so John R. asked Monroe if he could scrape up the extra $100 that would permit him to finish the second year.[26] Monroe succeeded in getting an additional $100 from Mr. Albert Johnson, one of the trustees who had already loaned money to John R.[27]

Then, a failing grade on a history test destroyed all hope of either a Hopkins or an Oberlin fellowship. The money from Oberlin had run out. There was no hope of remaining at Hopkins for a third year to work on a thesis.

John R. left Hopkins without a degree, but, as Joseph Dorfman noted, he left "professionally trained and entirely ready to grapple with technical problems."[28] Dorfman was thinking of economics. But John R. also left Hopkins with backgrounds in jurisprudence, in constitutional history, and in public administration. This triple background would emerge again and again in the confusingly variegated intellectual career of John R. Commons.

Ely had recommended John R. for a position at Wesleyan University, but John R. does not seem to have realized that Hopkins demanded a third year of residency for a degree. He planned to finish his thesis on the history of land taxation in England and the United States while at Wesleyan and to return to Hopkins.[29] It was not to be. He would never return to Hopkins. His only degree would be a Master's from Oberlin.

Notes

1. Commons, *Myself*, 43.
2. Lafayette Harter, John R. Commons, *His Assault on Laissez-Faire* (Corvallis, OR: Oregon State University Press, 1962), 18.
3. Hugh Hawkins, *Pioneer: A History of the Johns Hopkins University 1874–1889* (Ithaca, NY: Cornell University Press, 1960), 3.
4. Ibid., 21.

5. Simon Newcomb, "Dr. Ely and the Labor Movement," *The Nation* (October 7, 1886): 293–94.
6. Hugh Hawkins, *Pioneer: A History of Johns Hopkins University*, 180.
7. Joseph Brent, *Charles Sanders Peirce: A Life* (Bloomington: University of Indiana Press, 1998), 139–59. Peirce was an easier target because he had been divorced and remarried. He may also have been bipolar and given to unacceptable behavior. Ely was an upright Episcopalian.
8. Yuval P. Yonay, *The Struggle Over the Soul of Economics* (Princeton, NJ: Princeton University Press, 1998).
9. Jürgen Herbst, *The German Historical School in American Scholarship: A Study in the Transfer of Culture* (Ithaca, NY: Cornell University Press, 1965), 135–36, Richard T. Ely, Edwin R.A. Seligman, Edmond J. James, F.W. Taussig, Simon Newcomb and others, *Science Economic Discussion* (New York: Science Company, 1886).
10. Benjamin G. Rader, *The Academic Mind and Reform: The Influence of Richard T. Ely in American Life* (Lexington: University of Kentucky Press, 1966), 33, 36.
11. Joseph Dorfman, *The Economic Mind in American Civilization*, vol. 3 (New York: Viking Press, 1949), 207–10.
12. Ibid., 83–87, 258–75.
13. Joseph Schumpeter, *History of Economic Analysis* (New York: Cambridge University press, 1954), 874n.
14. Iyenaga to Monroe November 26, 1887, James Monroe Papers, Oberlin College.
15. Edward A. Ross, *Seventy Years of It: An Autobiography* (New York and London: Appleton Century Company, 1936), 40.
16. Ibid.
17. Commons to Monroe, March 12, 1989, Monroe Papers, Oberlin College.
18. Commons to Monroe, May 14, 1889, ibid.
19. Commons to Monroe, May 23, 1889, ibid.
20. Commons to Monroe, October 23, 1889, ibid.
21. Commons to Monroe, June 7, 1889, ibid.
22. Commons to Monroe, October 25, 1889, ibid.
23. Ross, *Seventy Years of It*, 56.
24. Commons to Monroe, May 14, 1889, Monroe Papers, Oberlin College.
25. Commons to Monroe, January 14, 1890, ibid.
26. Commons to Monroe, January 28, 1890, ibid.
27. Commons to Monroe, February, 1890, ibid.
28. Dorfman, *The Economic Mind*, 178.
29. Commons to Monroe, October 11, 1890, Monroe Papers, Oberlin College.

4

Wesleyan-Oberlin

President Raymond notified me that I would not be needed the next
year because I was a failure as a teacher—Myself

By 1888, Wesleyan university had dropped its requirement that teachers be practicing Methodists and had hired Woodrow Wilson, a Presbyterian and a Hopkins graduate.[1] Wilson had been popular—a dynamic lecturer, a prolific writer, and an energetic part-time football coach.[2] But in 1890, Wilson had accepted an offer from Princeton, and even with Wilson's help the school had been unable to find a replacement.

Finally, in August, a Wesleyan agent contacted John R. about a positon as tutor.[3] Bradford P. Raymond, Wesleyan's president, asked Ely about John R.'s qualifications.[4] Ely must have replied in the affirmative because John R. got the job with a salary of $1,000—less than half the average Wesleyan faculty salary of $2,500.[5] Still, for John R., $1,000 was big money. It made him feel secure enough to think back to 1888 and Oberlin.

Ella Brown Downey

The *Oberlin Review*'s masthead for that year, his senior year, had listed John R. Commons as chief editor and Ella B. Downey as a literary society editor. Ella had come from Akron, OH, where her parents operated a small hotel. When John R. went to Hopkins, she remained at Oberlin as a tutor. But when they had been together on the *Oberlin Review*, the two editors must have conversed on topics unrelated to editing. Now, in 1890, John R. had a steady income.

So he and Ella Brown Downey were married on Christmas Day 1890. Ella, or Nell as John R. called her, seemed gifted with an emotional intelligence to match her literary intelligence. She would be a tower of strength for this overly serious chronically depressed little man, and she would get her first chance within three months—even though nothing seemed amiss at the time.

Things had started smoothly. In September John R. had written Ely that he was teaching two hours of political economy, an elective on currency and finance, and another elective in social science. The last course would include "the state, the family, pauperism and charitable, prisons."[6] In November John R. seemed upbeat. His students liked Ely's book on political economy.[7] He was preparing for a return to Baltimore where he could fulfill the requirements for a PhD.

Fired

Then, three months before the end of the year, Wesleyan's president told John R. that his contract would not be renewed because he was a "failure as a teacher." "That certainly should have been shattering news for my Nell, and a baby on the way. But she passed it off as a mistake on the part of the University. Always after, she was the same if I lost a job. She never worried, as far as I could see. Why should I worry?"[8]

The fear of losing a job was alleviated by a letter from Professor Monroe who, in December had announced his retirement and had suggested John R. for a replacement.[9] John R., though, seemed more intent on returning to Baltimore.

He did not tell Ely what Raymond had told him. Rather he wrote that President Raymond wanted "a name" and that the president had told John R. that he had been pleased with his progress. John R. wanted to return to Baltimore for a year, retake an examination, and finish his thesis under Ely. His decision to return to Baltimore was not final, however. He would not seek a fellowship because Professor Monroe had written that he planned to retire and had suggested John R. for a replacement. It was not certain, however, that Oberlin would agree to Monroe's suggestion.[10]

Ely was not much help. He had contracted malaria that summer, and he had not completely recovered by fall.[11] Moreover, Ely was growing impatient with the Hopkins administration's failure to approve a separate department of social sciences or political economy or to offer him the position and the pay that he thought he merited. By the fall of 1892, Ely had moved to the University of Wisconsin.

Professor Monroe and Oberlin

Meanwhile, at Oberlin, Professor Monroe had indeed announced that at the age of seventy he needed help devising and teaching his advanced social science courses. He had recommended that the school offer John R. a job as associate professor and that courses in political economy and history be divided between himself and John R.[12] In March John R. wrote to Monroe asking how that proposal was coming along.[13] The Oberlin administration took Monroe's advice and offered John R. a position.

As he reflected on his disappointing year at Wesleyan, John R. developed some guideposts for the future.. "I determined thereafter always to go for short hours of working instead of increase in salary; and to use whatever I happened to be investigating as material for my classes, regardless of logical sequence."[14]

Following this plan, John R. bargained for reduced teaching hours at Oberlin, and he received his first lesson in negotiational psychology.[15] Oberlin expressed empathy, but there was no reduction in teaching hours. With a family to support, a child on the way, and no alternative job offers, John R. was in no position to negotiate. On May 25, John R. accepted the position of assistant professor at $1,200 per year—and a teaching load heavier than the one he had borne at Wesleyan.[16]

"Nell and I slipped away before commencement. We were happy. We were coming back to our friendly Oberlin, and I was coming back to Father, Mother, and Sister, after three years of academic venture".[17]

John R. spent only one year at Oberlin, but it was a crucial year for his development as a teacher and for his intellectual evolution. He was teaching five hours of political economy to seniors and three hours in American institutional history. He used "the conference method" to bring a class of seniors through Alfred Marshall's *Principles of Economics* and Eugen von Böhm Bawerk's *Positive Theory of Capital.*[18]

He sent Ely a paper he had written on the distribution of wealth, and he asked for comments.[19] He mentioned the principle of diminishing returns and diagrams. This paper was the beginning of his first book.

In 1934, John R. looked back on his teaching at Oberlin as a happy time. He was close to his family again. He and his brother took turns caring for their mother and father. His son Jack was born almost as soon as he arrived, on September 13, 1891, but the little family had trouble making ends meet on $1,200 per year, and so, when Indiana University offered him $2,000, he took the offer.

He wrote that he was ashamed to abandon Oberlin after all that the school had done for him.[20] His departure had to be a disappointment to Professor Monroe. But John R. was now supporting both his mother and his father in addition to Nell and his new son, and so he moved, ending, in a way, two years of intellectual incubation.

Notes

1. David P. Potts, *Wesleyan University 1831–1910* (New Haven and London: Yale University Press, 1992), 118–60.
2. Ibid., 141.
3. Commons to Ely August 18, 1890 *Richard T. Ely Papers* (Madison, WI: Historical Society of Wisconsin, 1986), microfilm, reel 3, frames 376–77.
4. Raymond to Ely, August 19, 1890, Ibid., reel 3, frames 378–79.
5. Potts, *Wesleyan University*, 309, 67n.
6. Commons to Ely, September 2, 1890, *Richard T. Ely Papers*, microfilm, reel 3, frames 425–28.
7. Commons to Ely, November 22, 1890, ibid., reel 3, frame 560.
8. Commons, *Myself*, 45.
9. Commons to Monroe March 16, 1891, Monroe Papers, Oberlin College Archives.
10. Commons to Ely March 26, 1891, Ely Papers, reel 3; frames 911–17.
11. Benjamin Rader, *The Academic Mind and Reform* (University of Kentucky Press, 1966), 108–11.
12. John Barnard, *From Evangelicalism to Progressivism at Oberlin College 1866–1917* (Cleveland, Ohio: Ohio State University Press, 1969), 84–85.
13. Commons to Monroe, March 16, 1891, Monroe Papers, Oberlin Archives.
14. Commons, *Myself*, 45.
15. Commons to Monroe May 11 and May 18, 1891, Monroe Papers, Oberlin Archives.
16. Commons to Monroe, May 25, 1891, ibid.
17. Commons, *Myself*, 48.
18. Commons to Ely January 18, 1891, Ely Papers, microfilm, reel 4, frame 734.
19. Commons to Ely January 13 and 15, 1892, Ely Papers, microfilm, reel 3, frames 706–7, 722.
20. Commons, *Myself*, 49.

5

Indiana Beginning

*Does the powerful lobby—so powerful that it is called a third house—
does the lobby that attends our councils, legislatures, and Congress
labor in behalf of the hard working masses? ... Where can they look
for help but to the educated man?—Social Reform and the Church*

John R.'s professional life began in the fall of 1892 with his arrival at
the University of Indiana. At Wesleyan and Oberlin, he had, in a way,
merely been continuing his education. At Wesleyan he had learned that
he needed a new method of teaching. At Oberlin, he had further educated himself in economic theory by taking students through the latest
influential books. Now, at Indiana, he started the unique combination
of teaching, research, and "collective action" that would characterize
the rest of his life.

Welcome

With his new teaching method, he overcame the problems that had
forced him from Wesleyan. He involved students in his research
projects and "collective activities," taking them with him to meetings
of the Indiana charity organization where he served on the executive
committee,[1] and involving them in municipal affairs and penal reform.[2]
He produced his first major publication at Indiana, *The Distribution of
Wealth*. He would pay a price for "taking the side of the workers," but
that was in the future. In the fall of 1892, Indiana was where John R.
wanted to be.

He wrote that he and Nell "felt ashamed" about leaving Oberlin
after all the school had done for them.[3] But the Indiana salary was
$800 more than his Oberlin salary, and he was now supporting five
people—himself, Nell, young Jack, and his parents. And Indiana offered
more than the salary—a lighter teaching load and a research climate
that would support John R.'s research ambitions.

There were benefits for Nell too—beginning with the social life of a young active faculty. "Our life with these youngsters and their wives was like getting back to my graduate days at Hopkins." Nell enrolled in a graduate literature class. John R. bragged that she was the first family member to break into print with an article in *Munsey's Magazine*.[4]

There was sadness in the future. Between the fall of 1892 when the Commons family arrived and the summer of 1895 when they left, the Commons family would experience three deaths. Robert Sidney Commons, born on June 1, 1893, died on August 16. John A. died in 1894; Clarissa, a year later. The family was reduced to John R., Nell, and Jack. But, for most of the intervening years, they thought that they had found a permanent home in Indiana.

With James Woodburn, a political historian and friend from Hopkins, John R. attended meetings of the People's Party—the last in a series of parties organized by Western and Southern farmers in response to Congressional efforts after the Civil War to replace paper currency with currency backed by gold.[5] The first effort, the Contraction Act of 1865, was abandoned after the panic of 1867. The second effort to withdraw paper money, the Specie Resumption Act of 1874, moved farm groups to create the Greenback Party in 1876. When that party collapsed, farmers organized successor parties with other names—all preaching the Greenback gospel. In 1892 the Knights of Labor joined the farmers in the last successor to the Greenback Party—the Populists, or the People's Party. John R. attended local meetings of this party with his friend, Indiana's political historian, James Woodburn who, in his political history, told the story of the Greenbacks and the campaigns for a fiat currency.[6] By 1892, though, the populist party stood for much more than a fiat currency. Much of the populist platform—the famous Omaha platform—reads like a blueprint for reforms enacted over the next twenty-five years—the graduated income tax, the secret ballot, direct election of senators, female suffrage, the eight-hour day, and so on.[7] But the populist party would not implement any of these reforms.

Populists won some local and state races, but nationally, they were trounced by Grover Cleveland, a "gold Democrat." The party died, but its ideas took on new life when politicians from the South and West captured the Democratic Party in 1896. William Jennings Bryan, in his losing campaigns, popularized populist positions. And, in 1893, the Greenback–Populist influence was responsible for John R.'s first publications on monetary affairs.

Pressure from farmers and mining interests had resulted in the 1890 Sherman Silver Purchase Act—a compromise between free silver and hard money forces. The act ordered the Treasury to buy 4.5 million ounces of silver each month and to issue silver certificates redeemable in silver or gold. The price of silver fell for the next three years. But gold could be purchased at the old silver price with silver certificates. Treasury gold holdings plummeted. When the Treasury's gold fell below $100 million in August, 1893, President Cleveland declared an emergency and called a special session of Congress to save the gold standard.

John R.'s First Collective Activities

Albert Shaw, a former Ely student and editor of the *Review of Reviews*, asked John R. and eleven others to suggest appropriate policies. John R. proposed a National Monetary Commission charged with keeping commodity prices stable.[8] If prices were falling, the commission would buy silver bullion and issue silver bullion notes. If prices were rising, the commission would sell silver and retire the notes—to be redeemed only at market prices, not at some fixed ratio of silver to gold. Later, John R. wrote that his National Commission should monitor price stability with a wholesale price index.[9]

And in 1893, Ely drew John R. into one of his reform schemes. After the American Economic Association (AEA) had abandoned his reform agenda Ely had turned to Chautauqua and the Social Gospel movement.[10] He called for a meeting on July 19 and 20 at which the American Institute of Christian Sociology was created.[11] Ely was the first president, John R., the secretary, and the reverend George Herron, the "Principal of Organization." In 1894 Josiah Strong succeeded Ely as president, and in 1895 George Herron succeeded Strong. But Herron dominated the organization from the start, and that may explain why it died such an early death.

In *Myself* John R.—who avoided naming people he did not like— mentioned an "eminent minister of the gospel," referring unmistakably to Herron, Professor of Applied Christianity at Iowa (later Grinnell) College.[12] Admirers have called Herron "a modern Jeremiah," the "most influential and dramatic character in the Christian socialist movement—an intellectual leader of social Christianity during the last decade of the nineteenth century."[13] Dark-eyed, wiry, bearded, and intense, Herron spoke slowly and forcefully. His addresses drew huge crowds and denunciations from all the right people. But Herron did not impress John R.

The Times

Someone of Herron's temperament could easily have been driven to desperate rhetoric during the 1890s. In 1892, a conflict with steelworkers at Andrew Carnegie's plant in Homestead Pennsylvania had ended in disaster for the workers. A stock market crash on May 5 had set off the panic of 1893—thus the title of a history: "Democracy in Desperation."[14] Unemployment haunted great cities and small towns. Miners died in collapsing Pennsylvania coal mines. In April violent strikes broke out in Connellsville, PA and Columbus, OH. There were riots in Cleveland and other cities. On Easter morning in 1894, Jacob Coxey organized the most famous of over forty marches on Washington. "Coxey's Army" actually made it to Washington, demanding that the government print money and employ workers in road building and other projects. Police arrested the marchers for trespassing.

The disastrous ending of the Pullman strike symbolized the times.[15] John R. was close to that strike. In 1893 he had visited Eugene V. Debs at his home in Terre Haute where Debs had explained his plan for the American Railway Union, an industrial union of all railway employees. John R. was also in Chicago on May 11, 1894 when Pullman employees walked out after George Pullman had slashed their wages without reducing rent or prices in his company town.[16] By chance, the American Railway Union was holding its convention in Chicago. Over the objections of Debs, the members voted to support the Pullman workers. Switchmen refused to handle trains that included Pullman cars.

Rail traffic might have been only moderately disturbed if the railroads had simply left Pullman cars on sidings, but the railroad's General Managers' Association had decided to break the strike by making its effects more dramatic. The railroads attached Pullman cars to all trains including freight trains and mail trains. A young lawyer for the Northwestern Railway Company, Clarence Darrow, resigned in protest, but the scheme worked.[17] Rail traffic east of the Mississippi froze, and the union was blamed. The companies asked Judge William Howard Taft to issue an injunction. He obliged, ordering the strikers back to work. Debs may not have completely understood the nature of an injunction, because he ignored it. The railroads asked President Grover Cleveland to send in troops. Cleveland obliged—over the objections of the Illinois governor, John Altgeld, and the army commander for that region, General Nelson Miles. Until the troops came, the strike had been relatively peaceful, but the arrival of the army incited mobs that rioted, overturned rail cars, and started fires. The troops responded with bayonets and bullets. Debs was jailed for contempt of court.[18]

The Pullman episode after all the others was enough to drive Reverend Herron into greater heights of despairing inconsistent rhetoric. John R. was puzzled. "On one night of his series our lecturer identified Christianity with anarchism; on the next night he identified it with Communism. He identified each with the love of God. But I became mystified as to the meaning of Love itself ... Eventually, after many years, in working out my institutional economics; I made Duty and Debt, instead of Liberty and Love the foundations of institutional economics."[19]

Investigating Christian Socialism

To find out what Herron's Christian socialism was like, John R. visited the Amana settlement, a community that traced its origins to German pietists who had migrated in 1843 first to Western New York—and later to Amana, IA[20] Community members held all property in common. They farmed, sold handicrafts—and later manufactured goods. They ate meals in a common dining room, in silence, with men separated from women.

They elected trustees and elders to promulgate and enforce rules. Elders decided what occupations boys would enter, who could marry whom, and who would have contact with the outside world. Girls worked in kitchen gardens until they married. Then they worked in communal kitchens. Elders stood for election, and the entire community voted, but the same family names appeared among the elders year after year, creating what Diane Barthel-Bouchier called "an aristocracy of elders."[21]

Many praised Amana as a living example of Christian charity and socialism.[22] John R. was appalled—especially when he discovered that the community hired outsiders to perform menial tasks. He commented drily that successful communism required two prerequisites. It "must be based on religion; and the dirty work must be done by hired hands."[23]

Social Reform and the Church

In his own work for the American Institute of Christian Sociology, John R. wrote articles for its magazine, *The Kingdom*, and gave talks to ministers. He published six of those talks in *Social Reform and the Church* together with the speech he had given at the World's Fair on proportional representation, reprinted from the *Indiana Student*, and an article, "The Educated Man and Politics," also reprinted from the *Indiana Student*.[24]

In speeches to the ministers he emphasized the inadequacy of good intentions without knowledge and understanding. If they wanted to improve the lives of the workers, the ministers needed to investigate the actual problems that the workers faced and they needed to interpret those problems in the light of modern psychology and sociology. Love was not enough, he told them; they needed knowledge to guide that love.[25]

The article, "The Educated Man in Politics," reprinted from the *Indiana Student* was an extensive elaboration on a theme he had developed eleven years earlier at Oberlin—that the "educated man" should take the side of the workers.[26] He gave four reasons. First, wealthy people do not need help because their wealth buys influence, and they already control the government. Second, workers need others to plead their cause because they cannot afford a lobby. Third, wealthy people themselves lose when poverty damages the efficiency and morale of workers. Fourth, because of the declining marginal utility of money, "the burden of unjust laws and corrupt politics falls more heavily on the wage earning classes than on any other classes . . . the wealthy man can lose a thousand dollars and it means no more than cutting off a luxury or two; but with a poor man, it means the loss of his home and the breaking up of his family."

The American Institute of Christian Sociology was not John R.'s only cause during his Indiana years. He helped found and served as president of the Tax Reform Association of Indiana.[27] On August 11 and 12 of 1893 at the Chicago World's Fair he became one of the founding members of the American Proportional Representation League.[28] And *Social Reform and the Church* was not his major publication at Indiana.

The Distribution of Wealth

His major publication was *The Distribution of Wealth*. Joseph Dorfman may have been correct when he traced its immediate origin to the advanced economic theory course that John R. taught at Oberlin.[29] But the book also shows the influence of Henry George's *Progress and Poverty* and the effects of Johns Hopkins where John R. had concluded that George had underestimated the complexity of capitalism's problems and that any search for solutions would need to go beyond economics, to jurisprudence, and administration. In *The Distribution of*

Wealth John R. tried to address these problems from the perspectives of economics and jurisprudence.

He cited the Austrian economist Eugen von Böhm Bawerk as the inspiration for both perspectives—economics and jurisprudence. But he relied on him only for the economic perspective along with John Stuart Mill, Henry George, Simon Nelson Patten, and Alfred Marshal. For the legal perspective, John R. relied most heavily on the popular jurisprudential text written by Thomas Holland. But he also took ideas from German writers, especially Adolph Wagner.

The book's overarching argument started with a generic description of the social product. "Men do not work alone. It is impossible in these days to determine how much any individual contributes to the social product, because his contribution cannot be measured in goods but only in values. Society composed of associated and organized individuals and working as a unit produces goods in varied abundance. These goods are distributed among the members of society and the relative abundance for it, determines its value to all the members" (14–15).

After this broad definition of the social product, the argument moved to a careful definition of land value as pure site value. Rent, or income from land in this sense, depends not on any productive service performed by the landowners, but on the state's enforcement of the owners' rights to withhold their property unless they receive payment. John R. then added other "opportunities" that, just like the site value of land, yield a "rent" or "surplus," an income above and beyond any reward for productive activity. These "opportunities," like the site value of land, depend on legal rights enforced by the state. Examples of state-created "opportunities" include patents, copyrights, franchises, legal monopolies, and special legally sanctioned forms of organization such as trusts (159–160). Surplus value from these "opportunities" is pervasive. "Five sixths of the manufacturing in the United States is based on patents, and patents are simply exclusive rights to sell" (16).

John R. insisted that income from such "opportunities" should not be confused with capital income—payment for abstinence and the acceptance of risk. But, he qualified the distinction by noting that capital is always employed in combination with "opportunities" such as land or monopoly privileges and that income over and above rewards to labor, risk, or abstinence must be a surplus value (or rent) credited to "opportunities." This "rent" results not from any physical characteristic of capital or land, but from "social and legal relations" enforced by the police power of the state (159).

Thus, the major conclusion: "The so-called conflict between capital and labor is at bottom a conflict between capital and labor on the one hand, and the owners of opportunities on the other" (249). This conclusion echoed Henry George's conclusion—that the conflict is not between capital and labor but between land owners on the one hand and capital and labor on the other.[30] But the conclusion also departed from George in widening the meaning of rent to include excess income from "opportunities."

From Böhm Bawerk and Alfred Marshall, John R. had learned of the downward sloping demand curve, and it was a short step to define the area between the demand curve and a cost curve as a surplus similar to George's rent of land.

Within this broad argument John R. developed his economic, legal, and historical analysis of the distribution of income. His first chapter developed a subjective theory of value from concepts of diminishing marginal utility and rising incremental cost resulting from scarcity and costs of production. His theory of value included the diminishing marginal utility of money—an extra dollar of income is more useful for a poor man than for a rich man.[31] It may be worth noting that his treatment of marginal utility was unremarkably in the mainstream for that time.[32]

But, John R. modified this standard picture of the economy by noting that it assumed a legal environment enforced by the police power of the state and that the state was not enforcing "natural" universally recognized rights to life and property, but rules that had been first created and then modified over time to serve "the purposes of whatever may be the ruling political class at a particular time and in a particular country."[33] He did not assume that the ruling classes were totally self-interested. True, they responded to the incentive to "exploit other classes" and "to facilitate or suppress" certain industries, but they also entertained a desire "to realize certain ethical or political ideals."

Nevertheless, he emphasized the role of self-interest in the creation of "natural rights" by the dominant group. Thus, the right to life originated in the discovery by ruling classes that it was more profitable to enslave than to slaughter captives. The right to liberty emerged when landowners discovered that by abolishing slavery they could profit from the labor of free workers without the need to support them when they were not working.[34]

Over time, people came to grant an ethical value to the rights of life and liberty and to assume that those rights had always been universally recognized as "natural." John R. treated this as a social learning experience. Experience taught that it was better to accept these rights than to deny them. Rights to life and liberty by John R.'s time had gained such acceptance that he felt justified in arguing that these rights implied a right to a job.[35]

People need income to live, and in an industrialized society most people can earn income only through paid employment. So the right to life implies the right to paid employment. True, liberty has traditionally included a "right to industry," that is, a right to earn income either by starting a business or by farming. But the closing of the frontier limited the accessibility of farmland, and the rise of capital-intensive industry created financial barriers for most landless workers contemplating a new business. Consequently most people can exercise this "right to industry" only through paid employment.

John R. considered *The Distribution of Wealth* to have been a failure most likely because of negative reviews.[36] The best review, written by Richmond Mayo-Smith—who seemed to have actually read the book—complained that John R. had imported moral assumptions into what was supposed to be a value-free work and that John R. confused juristic with moral rights.[37] Adolph Miller, a UCLA economist, accused him of constructing "a disguised attempt to found a scientific basis for a theory of socialism."[38] Arthur Twining Hadley of Yale allowed dislike of Ely to creep into his review. Hadley attributed the book's assumed errors to "bad training in economics."[39]

In later years, however, readers found more fault with the critics. Joseph Dorfman pointed out that John R. clearly anticipated the nature of imperfect or monopolistic competition—forty years before Joan Robinson and Edward Chamberlain brought the notion into mainstream economics.[40] Lafayette Harter, while admitting that the book had flaws complained that "Commons' reviewers, preoccupied with the radicalism of his proposals, completely overlooked his analysis." Harter compared John R.'s analysis of monopoly with that of Cournot, and he continued "If Commons' work (or for that matter, Cournot's) had been understood by contemporaries, monopoly theory might have taken a prominent place in economic literature much earlier than it did."[41]

And if economists then (and perhaps later) did not know what to do with John R.'s jurisprudential analysis, historians of American jurisprudence recognized it as an anticipation of the legal realist literature of the 1920s and 1930s.[42]

His critics themselves made unbelievable errors. Both Mayo-Smith and Hadley argued strenuously that patents do not confer monopoly power. None of the reviewers admitted even the slightest possibility that imperfect competition might produce results that differed from those of a perfectly competitive model—and this in the age of Rockefeller, Morgan, and Carnegie. But, at that time, the reviewers appeared more credible than John R., and Adolph Miller's accusation of socialism troubled Joseph Swain, Indiana's new president.

The accusation came at a bad time. The violence and turmoil that followed the panic of 1893 were unsettling enough. There was also the wild socialist rhetoric of George Herron—representing an organization of which Commons was the secretary. Then, beginning on August 20, 1894, trustees of the University of Wisconsin opened the trial of Richard T. Ely on the charge of socialism.

In Indiana, some newspaper editors, local politicians, and conservative members of the university's board raised questions about John R.'s suitability for a state university.[43]

Indiana's President Swain might have been less concerned about what John R. wrote than about opposition from politicians or prominent individuals. Concerned politicians, egged on by prominent citizens, could burden the university with financial restrictions or damaging regulations. Swain was concerned enough to ask Jeremiah Jenks of Cornell and Henry Carter Adams of the University of Michigan whether Commons was "a dangerous man." Both assured him that Commons was not dangerous at all.[44] Jenks and Adams may not have completely allayed Swain's concerns. John R. might be safer as a sociologist.

In 1894, Swain hired Frank A. Fetter to teach economics. Fetter, born a year after John R. in Peru, IN, had interrupted his undergraduate education to run the family bookstore when his father fell ill. He eventually returned to college, earning his undergraduate degree at Indiana, and his PhD at Cornell. Fetter's arrival affected John R. in two ways. First, Fetter and John R. became fast friends. Fetter shared John R.'s enthusiasm for Böhm Bawerk, and he was interested in making economic theory consistent with the psychology of the day. Second, Fetter took over the economics classes, leaving John R. free to concentrate on sociology.

Then, like a *deus ex machina*, a miraculous solution appeared to John Swain's problem. One of John R.'s students was so impressed by his teaching that he wrote a glowing letter to his uncle, the historian W.H. Mace of Syracuse University—just when the university's chancellor was looking for someone to fill a chair in sociology. Mace suggested John R., and the chancellor offered John R. the position at $2,500, $500 more than he was receiving at Indiana. John R. did not want to leave Indiana, but he decided to tell Swain about the offer and negotiate for a higher salary at Indiana. John R. got his second lesson in negotiational psychology when Swain told him to "accept the offer at once."[45]

And so, the Commons family departed for Syracuse.

Notes

1. "Prof Commons," *Indiana Student* 19 (February 1893): 18–19.
2. James Woodburn, *History of Indiana University* (Bloomington: University of Indiana Press, 1940), 413
3. Commons, *Myself*, 49
4. Ibid., 49–50.
5. Ibid., 51.
6. James A. Woodburn, *American Politics, Political Parties, and Party Problems in the United States*, 2d ed. (New York and London: G.P. Putnam, 1914), 143.
7. American Social History Project. "The Omaha Platform: Launching the Populist Party," in *History Matters: The U.S. Survey Course on the Web* (New York and Fairfax, VA: CUNY Graduate Center and George Mason University, 1998), historymatters.gmu.edu/d/5361. accessed September 4, 2012,
8. John R. Commons, "What Should Congress do about Money," *Review of Reviews* 7 (August, 1893): 153.
9. John R. Commons, "Bullion Notes and an Elastic Currency," *Annals of Political and Social Science* 4 (September, 1893): 99–101.
10. The Chautauqua institute had started as a Methodist summer camp, but its offerings had been expanded to encompass all aspects of adult education. For the Social Gospel movement, see Robert Handy, *The Social Gospel in America 1870–1920* (New York: Oxford University Press, 1966); Howard Hopkins, *The Rise of the Social Gospel in American Protestantism 1865–1915* (New Haven, CT: Yale University Press, 1967).
11. John R. Commons, "The American Institute of Christian Sociology," *The Congregationalist*, 88 (July–December, 1893): 32.
12. Commons, *Myself*, 51.
13. Hopkins, *The Rise of the Social Gospel*, 184–200.
14. Douglas W. Steeples and David O. Whitten, *Democracy in Desperation: The Depression of 1893* (Westport, CN: The Greenwood Press, 1998).
15. David Ray Papke, *The Pullman Case: The Clash of Labor and Capital in Industrial America* (Lawrence: University of Kansas Press, 1999).
16. Commons, *Myself*, 150.
17. Papke, *The Pullman Case*, 46.
18. Commons, *Myself*, 150.
19. Ibid., 51–52.
20. Diane, L. Bartel-Bouchier, *Amana, from Pietist Sect to American Community* (Lincoln: University of Nebraska Press, 1984).

21. Ibid., 25.
22. Bertha Shambaugh, *Amana: The Community of True Inspiration* (1908; reprint Iowa City: Penfield Press, 1988).
23. John R. Commons, "Progressive Individualism, The *American Magazine of Civics* (June, 1895): 563.
24. Commons, "The Educated Man in Politics," *Indiana Student* 19 (March, 1893): 7–11; "How to Abolish the Gerrymander," *Indiana Student* 19 (April, 1893): 3–8.
25. John R. Commons, *Social Reform and the Church* (1894: reprint; New York: Augustus M. Kelley, 1967), 20–21.
26. Commons, "The Educated Man in Politics," *Indiana Student*, 7–8.
27. George Wilson, 'The Education Column," *Jasper (Indiana) Weekly Courier* (April 27, 1894), 1.
28. Clarence Gilbert Hoag and George Henry Hallet, *Proportional Representation* (New York: Macmillan, 1926), 187.
29. Joseph Dorfman, "Introduction," John R. Commons, *The Distribution of Wealth* (1894: reprint; New York: Augustus M. Kelley, 1963), v.
30. George, *Progress and Poverty*, 204.
31. Commons, *Distribution of Wealth*, 11–12.
32. Yuval P. Yonay, *The Struggle over the Soul of Economics* (Princeton, NJ: Princeton University Press, 1998), 32.
33. Commons, *The Distribution of Wealth*, 61–62.
34. This was not what he told the ministers. He told them that abolition resulted from the teachings of Christianity, Commons, *Social Reform and the Church*, 35–36.
35. Commons, *The Distribution of Wealth*, 79–84.
36. Commons, *Legal Foundations of Capitalism*, v.
37. Richmond Mayo Smith, "*The Distribution of Wealth* by John R. Commons," *Political Science Quarterly* 9 (September 1894): 568–72.
38. Adolph Miller, "*The Distribution of Wealth* by John R. Commons," *Journal of Political Economy* 2 (June, 1894): 462–64.
39. Arthur T. Hadley, "*The Distribution of Wealth* by John R. Commons," *The Yale Review* 2(February, 1894): 439–40.
40. Dorfman, "Introduction," *The Economic Mind in American Civilization*. vol. 3, xi–xiii.
41. . Lafayette Harter, *John R. Commons, His Assault on Laissez-Faire* (Corvallis: Oregon State University Press, 1962), 36–37.
42. Katherine Stone, "John R. Commons and the Origins of Legal Realism; Or the Other Tragedy of the Commons," in *Transformations in American Legal History: Law, Ideology and Methods: Essays in Honor of Morton Horwitz*, vol.2 (Cambridge, MA: Harvard University Press), 326–43.
43. Woodburn, *The History of the University of Indiana*, 440.
44. Jenks to Swain August 18, 1894, Adams to Swain, August 22, 1894, Swain Papers, University of Indiana Archives.
45. Commons, *Myself*, 52.

6

Sociologist at Syracuse

He answered to the effect: I do not care what you are if you are not an 'obnoxious socialist.' That settled it. I mistakenly thought I was not of the obnoxious kind—Myself

John R. came to Syracuse in the fall of 1895, two years after John D. Archbold, vice president of Standard Oil and president of Syracuse University's Board of Trustees, had insisted that the university offer the job of chancellor to his New York City pastor, James Roscoe Day. Day had accepted. And Day and Archbold had started transforming a small liberal arts college into a major research university, inaugurating "the Age of Day and Archbold."[1] The link between Day, Archbold, and Day's other wealthy parishioners accounted both for the beginning and the end of John R.'s sociology career at Syracuse.

It began when Day asked another wealthy parishioner, John S. Huyler, to fund a chair in sociology. Huyler obliged, and when Day sought suggestions for candidates to occupy the chair, William H. Mace, a Syracuse historian, volunteered the information that Mace's nephew had written enthusiastically to him about John R.'s classes at Indiana.

Day contacted John R. for an interview. At six feet, weighing more than 200 pounds and wearing a long black frock coat, the chancellor with his booming voice overwhelmed the diminutive Commons who overestimated Day's weight by almost 100 pounds. John R. wrote that he told Day "the whole truth." "I told him I was a socialist, a single-taxer, a free-silverite, a greenbacker, a municipal ownerist, a member of the Congregational Church. He answered to the effect: I do not care what you are if you are not an 'obnoxious socialist.' That settled it. I mistakenly thought I was not of the obnoxious kind."[2]

President Swain at Indiana had left John R. no alternative but to accept Day's offer. So John R. and Nell reluctantly came to Syracuse in the fall of 1895.

For a while their reluctance seemed misplaced. Life at Syracuse was as stimulating as it had been at Indiana. Day was hiring at breakneck speed. Nine new faculty members came with John R.[3] More came in the winter and spring. One who came in the spring of 1896, James Hamilton, had taken John R.'s class at Indiana. After graduation, he had gone to Halle in Germany where Joannes Conrad had predicted a bright future for him. Then, he had completed a PhD at Wisconsin, specializing in money and banking. Hamilton was a strong advocate of postal savings banks. Like Frank Fetter at Indiana, he became a close friend, a sounding board for John R.'s ideas; a collaborator on joint enterprises; and, like Fetter at Indiana, by handling economics courses, Hamilton freed John R. to concentrate on sociology.[4]

As Syracuse's sociologist, John R. continued his practice of mixing research with teaching, and "collective activities." He taught classes in anthropology, criminology, ethnology, juvenile delinquency, penology, poverty, municipal government, and political corruption.[5] He invited the citizens of Syracuse to attend his classes free of charge and addressed the Chamber of Commerce on political reforms. He led a series of discussions at the Plymouth Congregational Church and lectured at the South Avenue Congregational Church on the "Cooperative City." He invited the local clergy to his classes in social theory. And, even more than at Indiana, he brought his reform interests to the campus.[6]

He brought guest speakers to the campus and invited Syracuse citizens to their lectures. Edward W. Bemis, a fellow Ely student gave six lectures in March and April. Jane Addams of Hull House lectured and gave a chapel talk. Charlotte Wilkinson of Hartley House in New York, a student of New York's "sweating system," lectured John R.'s classes on that subject.[7]

In December of his first year, John R. proposed a "Settlement House Fellowship." The recipient would be paid $300 to spend a year in "one of the best settlements" with a view to returning to Syracuse and establishing a settlement house there.[8]

In the May issue of the student newspaper, John R. responded to student complaints about downtown prices by suggesting a cooperative organized according to Rochdale principles. In February of the next year the faculty approved the idea and appointed Hamilton and Commons as faculty advisors. Once the cooperative was up and running, Syracuse merchants complained so vociferously that many, including the student editor of the *University Forum*, argued for closing it down.[9]

The negative reaction did not reduce John R.'s popularity with the students who made his methods a source of institutional pride. In reporting on class trips to the Auburn prison, the Elmira reformatory, and the George Junior Republic, the editor of the *University Forum* commented that John R.'s method of teaching by "practical experience" was "very highly appreciated by the students and friends of the university." In September, 1897, the *University Forum* described "a new course in sociology" that would study "vice, crime, pauperism, charities, the criminal classes, asylums, reformatories and penal institutions." The class would supplement lectures and textbooks with "practical observations." The student reporter continued "the penetrating observer will not fail to notice that comparatively few institutions offer such a course at all and that in fewer still does it exist with anything like the importance which it has in Syracuse University."[10]

The George Junior Republic

John R.'s disorganized integration of research, teaching, and social action reached a sort of peak in the case of the George Junior Republic, founded by William Reuben George who had, at the age of fourteen gone with his parents to New York City from a farm in Tompkins County, Western New York State. Rejecting further schooling, George had gone to work—first for printers, then for importers. Eventually he started his own import business and prospered.[11] As he grew older, he grew more concerned about the children on the city's mean streets. He coached baseball teams and taught Sunday school.

Then starting in the summer of 1890, he brought increasing numbers of children to his former home in Tompkins County, imposing on his numerous—and reluctant—relatives for help in clothing, feeding, and housing the youths. Friends and neighbors complained about vandalism and stealing. All of George's efforts to rein in the vandalism failed until he hit upon the idea of trying troublemakers by a jury of their peers. Guilty verdicts meant time on a rock pile. At first, adults supervised the rock pile, but when George discovered that boys were tougher supervisors than adults, he replaced adults with boys. In 1894, concerned about the debilitating effect on character of free food and lodging George initiated a work for pay system.

In the summer of 1895 George established a legislature, police force, civil service, a George Republic currency, and a bank president. And he started letting some boys stay all year. In 1896, George dismissed all adults except one, and the children elected a president. Over time, and little by little, the Junior Republic became a little free market democracy with printing, carpentry, and blacksmith shops, a bakery, hotels—even a jail—all operated by children By 1897, the number of permanent residents had risen to fifty-three.

John R. sent students to serve as counselors and mentors for the Junior Republic workshops. He took students on trips to visit the Junior Republic. And when George got in trouble, John R. came to his aid.[12]

In October, 1897 the *Buffalo Courier* reported that the State Board of Charities had condemned the George Junior Republic on the advice of a Professor Dodge of the University of Rochester who had visited Freeville and complained to the Board that "The buildings were in filthy condition and that the education of the children was almost wholly neglected." The State Board of Charities condemned George's Republic.[13]

John R. had probably started his study of George's Republic earlier, but in the winter of 1897–98 he published two articles that constituted a sort of refutation of Professor Dodge's complaint and may have been instrumental in bringing George back into the good graces of the State Board of Charities.

The two articles appeared in successive issues of the *American Journal of Sociology*.[14] The student editors of the *University Forum* reviewed the first article, concluding that John R. had effectively refuted Professor Dodge's condemnation and had restored the reputation of the Junior Republic. They added that the article clarified how someone like the Rochester Professor who merely "glances upon it" can develop an unfairly negative impression of the Junior Republic.[15]

For John R., the Republic was an experimental alternative to the reform schools and orphanages of the day. The two articles are a fun read—reaching a *Lord of the Flies* quality as John R. described how one group, the permanent residents, edged the other, the summer residents, out of political power. The articles also recorded an economic experiment of a market system in a representative democracy. John R. documented monopolies, inflations, and a widening income gap.

But John R. studied the Junior Republic mainly as part of his quest for humane and effective alternatives to reformatories and orphanages whose depersonalizing regimentation repulsed him. And he definitely found George's system superior to others. He admitted problems. "It is sometimes questioned whether the strong emphasis in the Republic on money getting may not induce self-aggrandizement and those very qualities of selfishness which reformatory work should overcome.

There have been symptoms." But John R. concluded that positive effects outweighed any negative effects. "The Republic is based upon the wage system. This is a system of indirect coercion grounded upon the necessities of the wage-earners for food, clothing, and shelter. Traditional educational methods of coercion through corporal punishment and despotic control are based on the slave system. The indirect system is far more efficient both as an individual stimulant and as an educational device."

And John R. fastened on another positive result of George's political experiments. It would return as a minor motif in almost everything that he wrote—the effect on behavior of "the dignity of citizenship, the privileges and responsibilities of full membership in a democratic community." He contrasted this sense of dignity with the indignity of pauperism.[16]

The Research Plan

John R. may have envisioned the two articles as part of the larger inquiry into law and education that he had described earlier in a letter to Richard Ely.

> I am planning my work to center around the legal aspects of sociology—expanding the doctrines in my *Distribution of Wealth*. I am moved to it especially by the curious productions of Patten and Giddings, neither of whom in their treatises on sociology gives more than passing notice to the two great features of society, law and education.[17]

That plan took on a detailed shape after John R. spent the summer of 1897 in Chicago with Lester Frank Ward.[18]

Ward, the "Father of American Sociology," a Darwinian evolutionist, and an outspoken critic of Herbert Spencer's philosophy—which he refused to dignify with the title of "Social Darwinism"—agreed that much human history can be explained by random variation and natural selection. But at some stage of evolution, the human brain reached a capacity that enabled people to understand the forces of nature and to harness them to human purposes—to make sailing ships, water wheels, compasses, and telescopes. Humans learned to breed desirable traits into plants and animals as Darwin noticed by devoting his first chapters to artificial selection.

Thus, Ward conceived of history as the story of two forces interacting, one, the force of random variation and natural selection, purposeless, slow, and cruel; the other, the force of artificial selection, intentional, swifter, and more humane.[19] And just as people could learn laws of physical nature and use them for their own purposes, so they could learn laws of social forces, and then, through representative democracies, control and direct these forces to reduce poverty, ignorance, disease, and social scourges of the human race.

Ward's influence on John R. seems to have been immediate and wide. Ward, a militant atheist, probably influenced John R.'s decision "to omit modern religion from sociology and stick only to ethnology."[20] And the influence of Ward is clear in two detailed syllabi that John R. created for a summer school on sociology and economics that he designed in 1898 with James Hamilton.[21]

The syllabi take up over eighty pages, and the lectures in the syllabi reflect both the influence of Ward and a research program that was remarkably consistent with the plan that John R. had described in that letter to Ely.[22]

The syllabi also clarify the passage in *Myself* where John R. wrote that, after visiting the Amana community, he began to harbor doubts about love as the basis of society and that, many years later after reading Giuseppe Mazzini's "The Duties of Man," he substituted duty and debt for liberty and love as a basis for social reform.[23]

He took up Mazzini's "Duties of Man" toward the end of the syllabus in a section titled "personal aim" discussing ethics, both individual and social.[24] After reviewing literature, beginning with Aristotle, and emphasizing T.H. Green and John Dewey, John R. settled on an ethic of self-realization and the full development of individual capabilities but he found the notion of unmodified self-realization to be dangerously individualistic. Individual A seeking self-realization could come into conflict with individual B. John R. found the link between individual self-realization and the common welfare in the "Duties of Man" written by Mazzini in 1879 at the age of sixty-five and reprinted many times.[25]

Mazzini

The old revolutionary was addressing workingmen and asking why the revolutions that he had encouraged—even joined— had failed ultimately to really liberate ordinary people. He answered his question by pointing to an omission in the Declaration of the Rights of Man. It left out society when it defined individual rights, and, as a result, it neglected the problem of conflicting rights, a problem that could be solved only by associating duties with rights. The business classes, who benefitted from the revolutions, used the power of the state to advance what they considered their rights, but they ignored the rights of other classes—rights that implied correlative duties on the part of the business classes.

Mazzini argued partly from scholastic natural law and partly from historical descriptions. He started with the history of civilization and the way that the capabilities of each generation rest on the accumulated knowledge of past generations. Then he pointed out how the state enables individual self-realization by enforcing rights of citizenship. Families, by education and emotional support, enable the self-realization of children growing to adulthood, and so for other forms of collective action.[26] This notion—that collective action liberates individuals as it constrains them—would become a major theme in John R.'s later work.

Proportional Representation

In 1898 though, John R. was asking questions about laws. Who creates them? Why do they create them? In *The Distribution of Wealth* he had written: "Law is the expression not of the whole society, but of the sovereign element or social class. It is imposed simply by virtue of the *might* residing in government. . . . At the same time, laws are not the fortuitous and blind coercion of nature. There are always human purposes underlying the enactment of laws and these are the purposes of whatever may be the ruling political class at the given time and in the given country."[27]

For John R. at this time, the problem was one of enlarging the ruling class to include formerly excluded classes so that all points of view would be considered in the deliberations that resulted in laws. He addressed this problem in the two major works that he produced at Syracuse: *Proportional Representation* and *A Sociological View of Sovereignty.*

Proportional Representation appeared in print while John R. was at Syracuse, but he had started working on it earlier, before his address to the founding conference of the American Proportional Representation League during the Chicago World's Fair.[28]

He appealed to a widely held conviction at that time that legislative bodies at all levels of American government—municipal, state, and national—had become so dysfunctional that mayors, governors, and presidents were encroaching on legislative terrain and that judges were making legislative decisions.

These problems, according to John R., resulted from winner-take-all elections in geographical districts. In these districts, a strong candidate representing any single group was unelectable because such a candidate would alienate other groups in the same district. Since winning candidates cannot offend anyone, they do not stand for much of anything. A legislature composed of such candidates is easily captured by well-financed and well-organized special interests.

After analyzing and rejecting a number of alternative solutions to this problem, John R. reasoned to a modified system of proportional representation. If such a system were to exist, for example, in New York State and if a labor party in Western New York were to gain 30 percent of the votes for Congress, the labor party would have 30 percent of the representatives from Western New York. These representatives would be able in public deliberations to defend the interests of the people who voted for them. They would know how to compromise without betraying their constituents—where to yield and where to stand firm. The result, supposedly, would appear in laws that would more effectively represent the values of the citizens.

John R.'s next foray into the problem of representative government showed the influence of Lester Ward and of John Dewey who was at Chicago when John R. spent the summer there.

A Sociological View of Sovereignty

Eight articles, all titled "A Sociological View of Sovereignty," appeared in the *American Journal of Sociology* between July 1899 and July 1900. John R. probably planned to edit the articles into a book.[29]

The articles reveal wide reading in psychology and philosophy as well as in sociology. And jurisprudence references went beyond Thomas Holland's text, his major source of jurisprudence in *The Distribution of Wealth*. Here, he added John Austin and Sir Henry Maine. In *The Distribution of Wealth,* he had tried to combine Holland's jurisprudence with economic theory—a difficult task. The task was easier with sociology because many sociologists, such as Durkheim, identified legal evolution with social evolution.

John R.'s articles addressed Dewey's objection to standard interpretations of John Austin's definition of sovereignty: the power "of compulsion without limits."[30] Dewey cited a number of passages in which Austin assumed that this power was in fact limited by moral principles—most likely Jeremy Bentham's utilitarian principles. But Dewey accused Austin of inconsistency in his assumption about the proper way for a republic to create those limits. Austin seemed to assume that a small group of Platonic guardians imposed these limits on the sovereign power. Dewey argued that assigning the limiting power to a small group was inconsistent with the ideals of representative democracies. Consistency with these ideals, he argued, required looking for these limits, not in some group of people, but in the governing organs of representative democracy.[31]

In *A Sociological View of Sovereignty*, John R. addressed this issue— the source of limits on the theoretically unlimited coercive power of the state.[32] He would approach the issue as a sociologist, not as a lawyer, a political scientist, or a philosopher. Philosophers seek general principles, valid across space and time. Sociologists, on the other hand, seek genetic explanations—historical descriptions of the way that social institutions evolved over time.

To develop his genetic explanation, John R., followed the lead of Herbert Spencer, Lester Frank Ward, and Émile Durkheim. He started in a hypothetical past when there were so few people that small groups scattered sparsely over the land hardly ever came into contact with each other. When natural reproduction increased the volume and density of the original groups and brought them into communication, conflicts arose over scarce resources.[33] The strong looted the weak and protected their loot by threats of violence. Eventually the predators, to justify their positions, invented the notion of a natural right to property. In the Darwinian evolution of societies, those that defended this right survived. Thus, conquest was the origin of sovereignty and property.

Condensing centuries of warfare and barbarism into a few paragraphs and basing his conclusion on the Darwinian sociologies of Herbert Spencer and Lester Frank Ward, John R. reasoned to a climax of despotism. The rise of great empires was consistent with Ward's analogy between monopolization of power by human predators and of space by invasive plants. The development of organization and administration was consistent with Spencer's principle that centralization and structure accompany increased mass. Within their domains, despots made violence a sovereign power by depriving others of the right to use it. John R. insisted that, because there were no institutional checks on the despots, their empires were not true states. Everything and every person within the empire was the property of the despot.

He modified this a bit. Coercion was not the only source of despotic control. Even despots need love. Autocratic rule rested at some level on the willing acquiescence of subjects. Beliefs unique to each culture permitted persuasion, a better way than coercion to maintain the unity of purpose that is essential to the survival of organizations. Still despots could always force obedience by unchecked torture and murder.

Checks on despotic power could emerge only when rising productivity permitted the growth of reflective consciousness—a necessary, but not sufficient condition for the emergence of order and right—the limits on sovereign powers that convert autocracies into states. To describe reflective consciousness, John R. deserted Spencer and Ward for Émile Durkheim, Gabriel de Tarde, the psychologist James Mark Baldwin, and the philosopher William James.[34]

Baldwin placed the rise of reflective consciousness in psychological time—approximately the time when children reach the age of six. John R. placed it in social time—the time when productivity frees at least some people from the need to think only of survival. To further specify the meaning of reflective consciousness, John R. supplemented Baldwin's biological conception with William James's distinction between empirical and abstract thought and Gabriel de Tarde's distinction between imitation and innovation. Finally, John R. defined reflective thinking as "skeptical, critical, introspective, individualistic, at first iconoclastic, later inventive and constructive."[35] For examples of reflective consciousness, John R. cited the political and philosophical debates in ancient Greece and the Italian City States.

But reflective thinking, though necessary, was not sufficient to transform an autocracy into a true state. Reflective thinking had not deposed autocrats in Japan, China, India, or Russia as it had in England and France. Consequently, to see what else was needed, it was necessary to turn from world history to the histories of England and France.[36]

John R. started with English history. The English barons had leisure to develop reflective self-consciousness—the necessary condition. They could also organize and cooperate. And cooperation enabled them, in 1215, to force King John to sign the Magna Carta. It gave barons a share in the sovereign power, but it did not create limits on that power.

Circumstances permitted other groups to organize. Serfs gained freedom and moved to towns where they became skilled workers, merchants, and manufacturers. Townsmen gained leisure to reflect, innovate, and criticize; they gained the right of assembly under protection of the king who wanted to counterbalance the power of nobles. Craftsmen organized guilds, companies, and associations. Using their wealth, they lobbied and gained a share in the structure of government in 1688, and again in 1832. Government evolved from monarchy to aristocracy to plutocracy. Conflict between aristocrats and plutocrats in England resulted in universal suffrage. In the United States universal suffrage resulted from ideology and "the desire to attract immigrants" (49).

John R. drew conclusions about limits on the sovereign power. The House of Lords and House of Commons in Britain and Congress in the United States restrained the capricious will of the sovereign with the limit of order which controls violence by imposing due process.

Freedom to organize gave successive groups enough strength to force their way into the coalition that controlled the sovereign power. New institutions emerged to grant a voice to each group that forced its way into the ruling coalition. The institution of the House of Lords changed despotism to aristocracy. The House of Commons changed aristocracy to plutocracy. But the right to vote was extended to working classes without any institutional changes, and this absence of any institutional change created a political contradiction between voting rights that appeared to create political democracy and government structures that empowered a plutocracy (50–51). All men could vote, but institutional structures prevented the voters from gaining adequate representation. Reform movements to overcome this contradiction had been only partially successful. Nevertheless the emergence into power of other groups had established order as a limit on the capricious exercise of sovereign power. But order must be complemented by the other check on sovereign power: right.

"Right" proceeds from beliefs about moral perfection shared by all groups. By appealing to these shared beliefs, excluded classes can successfully challenge dominant groups. Such shared beliefs ground the optimism that keeps excluded classes struggling against the superior powers of groups that control the coercive power of the state.

Rather than accepting Austin's assumption that educated elites are responsible for the limit of right, John R. distinguished three empirical types of right—popular, legal, and moral. Popular rights result from propaganda created by dominant classes to justify their privileges. When propaganda makes some popular rights universally acceptable, they become legal rights enforced by the state. The divine right of kings and the rights of slave owners are examples of legal rights. Moral rights, on the other hand, stem "from belief in moral perfection."

To distinguish more carefully between popular, legal, and moral rights, John R. returned, this time more critically, to Holland's definition of right— "one man's capacity of influencing the acts of another by means not of his own strength but of the opinion and force of society." This definition was adequate for popular and legal rights—but not for moral rights. Rather than offering an alternative definition though, John R. returned to Giuseppe Mazzini's formula for seeking the moral right in any place or time. "In order to know the law of God," wrote Mazzini, "you must interrogate not only your *own* conscience, but also the conscience and consent of humanity" (55–56).

This description implied two conditions for the emergence of moral rights. First, society must have reached the state of "reflexive consciousness." Second, there must be dialogue and communication between groups. If any group is omitted from the dialogue, then the conscience of humanity has not been completely consulted. Only when people have been freed from a continual preoccupation with basic survival and only when all groups in society are free to communicate in public deliberations can one speak confidently of the conscience of humanity. As more groups make their way into the state's ruling coalition, broadening the dialogue about moral right, the state becomes the institution specializing in coercion controlled by order and right.

> We thus have the three constituents of sovereignty—coercion, order, right. Coercion originates as private property. The struggle for existence causes this to survive in the form of monopoly and centralization. Order emerges as a constituent of sovereignty in place of caprice only when sovereignty has been extended over wide areas and when subordinate classes have earned the veto power in determining the sovereign will. Right takes its place as the moral aim of sovereignty when freedom has displaced material and competitive necessity (61).

In examining the relation of the state to other institutions, John R. returned to coercion and its control. The sovereign, beginning in the age of despotism, gradually deprived other institutions of access to coercive powers, and this freed them to more effectively develop unique persuasive powers. With freedom to punish limited by law, families could more effectively channel sex drives and nurture children. Disestablishment of religion freed churches to more effectively explore the nature of moral perfection and to deal constructively with consciousness of guilt and moral right.

The abolition of involuntary servitude, however, did not deprive industrial institutions of access to coercion. Industrial institutions materially support the other institutions by producing "food, clothing, and shelter for wife and children; weapons and munitions for the state; cathedrals for the church; ballot paper for political parties."

The major contemporary industrial institution, the corporation, emerged by natural selection in the world of private commerce—with some help from the state—and corporate survival depends on forms of coercion still in use— "privative sanctions . . . expectations of social penalties: the dispossession of property, fines, the reduction or discharge from position in case of disobedience (21,76)."

Within the corporation, the law that gives a vote to each share of stock permits major stockholders to coerce other stockholders. The existence of these forms of coercion is evidence that the state has not yet been able to deprive corporations of all coercive power. Cooperatives organized on the basis of one person–one vote would be more democratic. But state-sponsored cooperatives have not survived in the Darwinian world of commerce—illustrating the difficulty of direct interference into processes of natural selection without careful attention to social forces.

John R. then described a few ways that the state might be able to inject order and right into a world of corporations. On the side of the stockholders, the state might pass laws that protect the rights of minority stockholders. On the side of the workers, the ultimate aim would be to deprive the corporation of all coercive ability, leaving it only the power of persuasion unique to the industrial sector, appeal to the "love of work." While that aim is unachievable, the state might begin by protecting the rights of employees which "turn especially upon the right to freedom from capricious employment and discharge, that is, to the introduction of order and right into the structure of the institution. In general, this may be designated as the right to employment (75, 82–83)."

In a concluding chapter John R. listed three problems that every institution must solve. The first, the technical problem, common to all, can be solved by skill and ability in the same way by all institutions (95–97).The second, the persuasive or administrative problem is unique to each institution. In families, persuasion rests on tact and love; in churches, on eloquence and personal character. Even in states, successful administration depends on persuasive skills that when exercised reduce the state's dependence on coercion.

The third problem, the political problem, is primarily ethical; it is the problem of the size and share of the joint product of collective action. Here single individuals are helpless. Only by organizing can they influence laws that determine their income from the products that they help to produce. If the machinery of government supports freedom of assembly, and the ability of classes to share in the government, they can attain their ends without resort to riot or rebellion.

So John R. reasoned to the importance of freedom of assembly in the process that places moral restraints on the sovereign access to the incentive of violence.

It is reasonable to assume that these articles were just the beginning of something more ambitious. But there is no way to know what that something was because of reactions to events at the 1898 annual meeting of the American Economic Association (AEA).

The End

At that meeting, Arthur T. Hadley, the president of the AEA and an old opponent of Richard T. Ely, asked in his presidential address why economists had so little influence on the decisions of politicians.[37] He reviewed the history of economic thought from Aristotle forward, noting that economists had made great strides in their understanding of economic activity, but that their language had grown more abstract and technical. He concluded that economists, standing back from partisan politics, with their vision of the good of society as a whole, had much to contribute to public debates, but, in order to do so, they needed to translate their insights into simpler language so that politicians would understand them.

In the discussion that followed Hadley's address, John R. argued that economists had never represented society as a whole.

"The political economy of the classical economists was the economy of the capitalist and banking classes. The other classes listened to these economists because they were able to show that the interests of the capitalist class were in harmony with the interests of the nation. The great influence of Adam Smith was due to the fact that his arguments were directed against the aristocratic and agricultural classes and were in harmony with the commercial classes. . . ." John R. concluded. "But a man cannot represent society as a whole. If he claims to do this, he really means that he wishes to have things as they are. To-day it is Henry George and Karl Marx that have the large influence, because they represent the radical classes that are acquiring power."[38]

Slightly less than a month later, on January 24, 1899, the university trustees held their semiannual meeting. John D. Archbold, the president of the trustees was not there and a second vice president called the meeting to order. The following resolution was introduced and modified. "It was moved that the matter of discontinuing the services of Professors in the University be referred to the executive committee with power." "Seconded."

"It was moved as a substitute that a permanent committee of five, of which the Chancellor shall be chairman, be appointed by the Chair of Faculties and courses of study. Seconded and carried."[39]

The following March, the chancellor called John R. Commons into his office and fired him.

> He said that the trustees, at their preceding meeting in December, had voted to discontinue my chair in sociology . . . He explained that when he went out on his trips to obtain money for the university from hoped for contributors, they refused as long as I held a chair at the university. Also at a recent national meeting of college presidents which he attended, all had agreed that no person with radical tendencies should be appointed to their faculties. Therefore I had no hope for another college position. He was convincing and I never tried to get another teaching job.[40]

The previous meeting had been in January, not December, but John R. remembered the basics. He decided to leave quietly without complaint, and Day praised him publicly.

Upon hearing of the dismissal, the faculty met and voted a resolution praising John R. for "teaching, scholarship, and manly character."[41] The trustees had changed the by-laws to remove all faculty influence on future appointments.

Notes

1. Francis W. Galpin, *Syracuse University, Volume I: The Pioneer Days* (Syracuse, NY: Syracuse University Press, 1952), vii.
2. Ibid., 10, Commons, *Myself*, 53.
3. Syracuse University, *The University Forum* 1 (Supplementary Number) (September 2, 1895): 3–4.
4. *The University Forum* 1 (April 26, 1896): 332.
5. Galpin, *Syracuse University* 1952, 24; Commons, *Myself*, 53.
6. *University Forum* 3 (October 13, 1897): 45.
7. *University Forum* 1 (March 3, 1896), 294; 1 (March 24, 1896): 283. Bemis had been fired by the President of the University of Chicago in a notorious academic freedom episode. See Harold Bergquist, "The Edward Bemis Controversy at the University of Chicago," *AAUP Bulletin* (Winter, 1972): 384–93.
8. *University Forum* 1 (December 25, 1895): 2–3.
9. Ibid., 1 (May 5, 1896): 338; Galpin, *Syracuse University*, 339. The strength of the opposition convinced Commons that cooperatives could not replace corporations because of the power of the limited liability corporation. Commons, *Myself*, 55–56.

10. Ibid., 2(April 20, 1897) 376; 3 (September 21, 1897): 498.
11. William R. George, *The Junior Republic: Its History and Ideas* (New York: Appleton Co., 1909), 2–3.
12. *University Forum* 2 (October 20, 1896), 53; 2 (April 20, 1897), 376.
13. *University Forum* 3 (October 27, 1897), 67.
14. John R. Commons, "The George Junior Republic," *American Journal of Sociology* (I) 3 (November 1897): 281–96; (II) 3(January, 1898): 433–48; *University Forum* 3(October 13, 1897).
15. *University Forum* 3(December 1, 1897): 128.
16. Commons, "The George Junior Republic," I (November 1897), 294; II (January, 1898), 438–40, 441–43.
17. Commons to Ely March 3, 1896, cited in Dorfman, *The Economic Mind in American Civilization*, vol.3, 285.
18. *University Forum* 2 (May 18, 1897): 449; 3 (September 9, 1897): 12.
19. J. Dennis Chasse, "The Alternate Conception and John R. Commons," *Journal of Economic Issues* 46 (September 2012): 589–613.
20. Commons, *Myself*, 56.
21. The summer school is described at length in two issues of the *University Forum* (February 16, 1898), 298 and (April 6, 1898): 307–8. It is interesting that Hamilton covered economics, including trade unions. For Commons at this time "taking the side of the workers" meant reforming prisons and the political system.
22. Commons papers Madison, State Historical Society of Wisconsin (1982) microfilm; reel 15, frames 321–508. The syllabi are also available from the New York State Library, Albany, NY.
23. Commons, *Myself*, 51–52.
24. Commons papers, reel 15, pages 50–55 of the syllabus.
25. Giuseppe Mazzini, *The Duties of Man and Other Essays.* (1907; reprint. New York: Macmillan, 1961), 7–122.
26. Ibid., 41–50.
27. Commons, *The Distribution of Wealth*, 61–62.
28. Clarence Hoag and George Hallett, *Proportional Representation* (New York: Macmillan, 1926), 126.
29. The eight issues of the *American Journal of Sociology* also contained Edward Alsworth Ross's articles on social control. It is reasonable to assume that John R. was planning to revise his articles as Ross revised his. Joseph Dorfman collected the articles in a book—John R. Commons, *A Sociological View of Sovereignty* (1899–1900; reprint, New York: Augustus M. Kelley, 1967). References here will be to the book.
30. John Dewey, "Austin's Theory of Sovereignty," *Political Science Quarterly* 9 (March, 1894): 31–52.
31. Ibid., 37.
32. Commons, *A Sociological View*, 1–3.
33. He referenced Émile Durkheim, *The Division of Labor in Society*, tr, George Simpson (1893 reprint. New York: Free Press, 1933), 336. For Durkheim's influence on John R., see Jean Jacques, Gislain, "American Institutionalism and Durkheimian Positive Economics," *History of Political Economy* 31 (1999): 273–96.

34. Durkheim, *The Division of Labor in Society*, 202. James Mark Baldwin, *Social and Ethical Interpretations in Moral Development* (1897; reprint, New York: Arno Press, 1973). Baldwin was famous for his experiments on children that verified and confirmed the work of G. Stanley Hall, proving that children do not think like small adults. Baldwin's work influenced Jean Piaget and Jacques Lacan.

35. Commons, *A Sociological View of Sovereignty*, 34

36. Ibid., 36. From the context, one might suspect that he was planning to follow British history with French history. Some references in his later work strengthen that suspicion. The truncation of his career at Syracuse, though, leaves it just a suspicion.

37. Arthur Hadley, "The Relation Between Economics and Politics," *Economic Studies* 4 (February, 1899): 7–28.

38. John R. Commons, "Discussion of President Hadley's Address," *Economic Studies Supplement* 4 (April 1899): 111–12.

39. Syracuse University Archives, *Minutes of the Board of Trustees February 22–24, 1870 to June 6, 1907* (Syracuse, NY: Syracuse University, 1909), 303. The meeting was in January, not December as Commons remembered it. He attributed the firing to an earlier episode when he had supported workers who wanted to play baseball on Sunday. This is credible, given Chancellor Day's famous letter to President Theodore Roosevelt, but the timing is wrong. Day did not fire him then. Day also mentioned a meeting of college presidents in February at which it was decided "that no person with radical tendencies should be appointed to their faculties." That would be the founding meeting of the Association of American Universities. Hadley, who was also the President of Yale, was a convener of that meeting.

40. Commons, *Myself*, 58

41. Galpin, *Syracuse University*, 25.

7

Exile

I named it 'constitutional government in industry'—Myself

In 1934 John R., reflecting on his "dismissal from Syracuse," declared it a "fortunate happening."[1] He could not have considered it fortunate when it happened in 1899. His sociology career was ruined; his work on the jurisprudence and the sociology of education, truncated. Chancellor Day was the third university president to have judged him unfit for college teaching. Nell still believed in him. But these years would be tough on her. She was pregnant when Chancellor Day sent John R. into the ranks of the unemployed. On borrowed money they moved to Mount Vernon, NY, near his sister Clara who worked with "difficult" boys for the New York City school district. Nell's third child, Rachel, would be born there on July 26, 1899. But other children would die during this exile. Especially hard would be the death of Julia Margaret on March 7, 1901—a little over two weeks before her fourth birthday. John R. wrote that "Nell turned to psychics and I thought of God as a big cat leading me on to intensity of love for my little girl and then suddenly snatching her away." John R. mentioned no other deaths, but on March 30, 1903, Nell would bear twins, Rose and Frank. Rose would die immediately; Frank, on July 4. Jack who had been born in Indiana would be nine in 1900. So, when John R. ended his career as a working economist, his family consisted of four members: John R., Nell, Jack, and Rachel. And though the family suffered little actual unemployment during that time, the nagging fear of it convinced John R. to make "unemployment the biggest foe of the capitalist system."[2]

In spite of all this, in retrospect, when time had dimmed the pain, he called those years fortunate for two reasons: First, the "dismissal . . . drove me out for five years to live in the struggles of human beings"; second, those "Five Big Years" gave him "stories to tell" at Wisconsin.[3] He might have added that during those years he developed a network of remarkable friends and that while participating in historic investigations, he gained his first glimpse into what the historian Clarence Wunderlin called *"Visions of a New Industrial Order."*[4]

And he was spared actual unemployment. Before he left Syracuse, a man he did not know, George Shibley, appeared mysteriously with a job. John R. wrote that he "had not been acquainted with" Shibley, but that Shibley had attended the 1893 Chicago World's Fair meeting at which John R. had presented his paper on proportional representation.[5] But Shibley did not hire John R. for anything related to proportional representation. He hired him to construct a price index that would support Shibley's book on bimetallism. Shibley wanted to influence the election of 1900, to show politicians that the 1890s deflation would continue as long as the United States remained on the gold standard.[6] The economy, though, would not cooperate with Shibley. The long depression of the 1890s was ending. And John R., by tracking this uncooperative economy, would undermine Shibley's argument.

The American Bureau of Economic Research

Shibley financed an assistant for John R.—N.I. (Nahum Isaac) Stone, a graduate student in statistics at Columbia University. Ed Bemis, the Ely student fired from the University of Chicago, came to help and financed himself.[7] They called themselves the American Bureau of Economic Research (ABER) and they published their first index during the first week of July.[8] The forty-page bulletin contained an introduction to index number theory and two commodity price indexes: one, a simple average of price relatives, the other, a weighted averaged, weighting each commodity by its share in total production. The base for the indexes was the average for the years from 1879 to 1889. Annual data showed the influence of gold discoveries, with a lumpy decline in prices from a high in 1881–82 to a trough in 1896–97, and then, as new gold discoveries made their way into world markets, the index started to climb—marking the end of the 1893 depression. It did seem, though briefly on a weekly basis, that prices were beginning to fall between 1897–98 and 1898–99, but then in September, they resumed their climb. In October, the group published their second bulletin which confirmed the end of the deflation.[9] Shibley could not believe it. At first, he told John R. to check his numbers. Then he told him to look for another job. Fortunately, the Honorable Thomas Wharton Phillips had created one.

The United States Industrial Commission

Phillips represented Pennsylvania's oil country in Congress. An oilman himself—and a sworn foe of John D. Rockefeller—Phillips had, in 1894, introduced a bill establishing a commission to study "the trust problem."[10] The bill failed, but Phillips kept revising and resubmitting it until 1898, when a new bill created the United States Industrial Commission (USIC) with five members from the House, five from the Senate and nine appointed by the President. The bill had accumulated new goals as it passed through revision after revision, and in its final form, it ordered the commission to "investigate questions relating to immigration, to labor, to agriculture, to manufacturing, and to business"—an unwieldy set of goals according to the commission's secretary, E. Dana Durand.[11]

But all those goals had justifications. Durand referred to one. "By what may seem an ironical turn of the economic history of the United States, the very period during which the Industrial Commission was investigating trusts was one of great activity in the formation of new industrial combinations."[12]

The industrial combinations did not resemble anything that had ever happened before or that has ever happened since. The captains of industry were merging, in staggering numbers, firms that produced the same product.[13] Over one thousand eight hundred firms disappeared. In the most symbolic transaction, a group led by J.P. Morgan bought out Andrew Carnegie, creating United States Steel, the largest corporation in the world—replacing a single empire builder with a complex web of debts, boards of directors, and Wall Street bankers.

In labor, the symbolic Pullman strike and boycott that tied up the country's railroads was only one notable event. The labor historian Bruno Ramirez emphasized sheer numbers. The recorded number of strikes increased from 1,096 in 1896 to 3,493 in 1903. The number of workers involved in strikes rose from 183,813 in 1896 to 531,682 in 1903.[14] Union memberships quadrupled in those years. And immigration changed the composition of the labor force—partly because firms sent contractors to foreign countries to recruit strike-breakers—but also because poor and persecuted people in Eastern and Southern Europe responded to tales of opportunity in the New World.

The final factor making those years uniquely problematic was the farm problem created by the long deflation of the 1890s with bankruptcies and heartbreaking auctions and prairie homes empty to howling winds as former farmers fled to crowded city tenements and labor markets.

Durand combined all these issues into a single multi-faceted "industrial problem." "The object of these inquiries has been to look upon the labor question as part of the whole industrial question in all its phases including its relation to agriculture, manufacturing, mining and transportation, and including influences on labor of foreign competition, domestic competition, immigration, technical and mechanical improvements, consolidation of business undertakings and state and national legislation."[15]

To develop a plan for all this, the commissioners called on Carroll D. Wright, the commissioner of Labor. Wright outlined a two-part strategy: the first followed the tradition of public hearings; the second called for a staff of social scientists to dig up statistics, to go on fact-finding missions, and to integrate their findings with the testimony of witnesses who would instruct the commission on reasons for mergers and acquisitions, and on the financial and planning techniques—such as cost accounting—first developed for the railroads and then adapted to management problems in other corporations.

The commissioners hired Jeremiah Jenks of Cornell University to implement the strategy. Jenks had written his dissertation under Joannes Conrad at Halle on the national economics of Henry Carey. He had preceded John R. at Indiana, then had moved to Cornell where he had studied Michigan's salt cartel, the Whiskey Trust, and trusts in general. In these studies Jenks developed a theory that foreshadowed the structure–conduct–performance framework of later industrial organization literature.[16]

Jenks hired Durand, his former graduate assistant, to be the commission's secretary. Before going to Cornell, Durand had taken John R.'s class on advanced economic theory at Oberlin.

As the commission secretary, Durand built an outstanding staff. By the time John R. appeared as a witness in 1900, the staff had filled five volumes with testimony and analysis of labor problems— covering prison labor, labor legislation, labor in manufacturing and business, labor problems in Chicago, and labor in agriculture.[17] Jenks, Durand, and Charles Edgerton, another Jenks student, had already described a solution to the labor question, embodying what Wunderlin has called "visions of a new industrial order" in which organized workers would bargain collectively with organized employers.[18]

John R. Before the Commission

John R. appeared before the commission on November 12.[19]He was still with the ABER. When asked about the ABER, he telegraphed insecurity. "That [the American Bureau of Economic Research] is largely a hope, a prospect. Four or five persons like myself have joined together with the idea of taking up any line of political or economic research for which there seemed to be a demand in New York City, giving information and making it of a scientific character as nearly as we could make something reliable. We have been organized about a year, but we have not done very much yet."

Then, he proposed creation of an institutionally neutral US commission patterned after the superior labor councils in France, Belgium, and Austria. To illustrate the advantages of such a body, he cited the record of state charity organizations governed by nonpartisan boards.[20]

Then, he described the French Superior Labor Council and used an example to show how such a board had actually improved labor legislation. The council was composed of forty-eight members—sixteen chosen by employer groups, sixteen by trade unions, and sixteen appointed by the government. In the example that John R. used, "the question of the prevailing rate of wages on public contracts was before the Parliament of France." Parliament asked the council for help. The council asked the bureau of statistics for information about rules in other countries. After receiving the information, the council deliberated for several days and forwarded to the parliament a proposal which the parliament passed without much debate or change because—and this was John R.'s point—the council had already considered the issue from all relevant points of view.

John R. continued that labor legislation in the United States suffered from the lack of such an institution. Because presidents appointed Labor Commissioners, they opened the Bureau of Labor to accusations of political bias. To forestall such accusations, the Bureau limited its activities to gathering and interpreting information. This limitation kept it from giving the type of specific policy guidance of which French, Belgian, and Austrian Superior Labor Councils were capable.

He moved to the problem of cyclical unemployment, using some of his ABER research to make his points. He introduced two charts. The first showed a negative relation between wholesale prices and unemployment in England between 1887 and 1900.[21] Admitting that correlation is not causation and that cyclical unemployment has many causes, John R., nevertheless, concluded that "there can be no permanent remedy for unemployment which does not involve the stability of the currency and the tariff." His second chart related wholesale prices to immigration in the United States between 1879 and 1900.[22] It was clear that immigration increased during expansions and declined during contractions. In both cases, immigration made things worse. During expansions, increased immigration prevented wages from rising. And during contractions, unemployed immigrants crowded slums in Eastern cities— increasing urban unemployment and burdening charity agencies.

Then, in a broad ranging question and answer period, he advocated publicly operated employment agencies, government labor colonies that would teach useful skills, and agricultural extension services that would reduce rural-to-urban migration by making farm life more attractive. He concluded his testimony in conversations with the committee members about arbitration, mediation, and injunctions.

Jenks hired John R. and a social worker, Kate Claghorn, to complete the report on immigration. They found an office in the Bible House, the headquarters of the American Bible Society. Claghorn remained in New York City. John R. traveled the country, stopping first at Hull House in Chicago where he met Abram Bisno, a Russian immigrant cloak-maker and organizer for the garment workers' union. With Bisno as guide, John R. visited garment districts in large cities, staying in flop houses and cheap hotels. John R. gave Bisno substantial credit for teaching him about sweatshops, Marxism, syndicalism, and the real world of union organizing. He almost admitted that Bisno deserved the credit for John R.'s report on sweatshops.[23]

His experiences with Bisno allowed John R. to increase the stock of stories that made his five years "big." In New York, he watched Emma Goldman address a crowd of strikers numbering in the thousands. Back in Chicago, he moved out of Hull House to get a closer view of sweatshops and trace the development of the garment industry. "Scattered over the city were Polish shops, Bohemian shops, Norwegian shops, other shops, and Italian women finishing garments with needles in their tenement homes. I took a room and boarded in one of these homes and wrote a complete report of the sweatshop system." Years later, he described the system, the gradual replacement of the home sweatshops by factories, and the formation of a textile workers' union in 1919.[24]

He followed his tour of the garment industry with trips to various union headquarters so he could find out how union leaders viewed immigration. On one of these trips, he witnessed a collective bargaining session between bituminous coal mine operators and United Mine Worker (UMW) representatives.

> I was struck by the resemblance to the origins of the British Parliament. On one side of the great hall were nearly a thousand delegates from the local unions, an elected representative body. On the other side were about seventy employers appearing directly, without election, as owners of the coal mines. It was evidently an industrial House of Commons and House of Lords, but without a King. I named it "constitutional government in industry," which the editor of the *Review of Reviews* changed to the newspaper title, "a new way of settling labor disputes."[25]

His work for the USIC eventually introduced John R. to every facet of the complex problem at the heart of the commission's mandate—not just labor and immigration, but—trusts, railroads, tariffs, farms. This complex introduction reached its final stage when the Commons family left Mount Vernon for Washington, DC, where the entire staff assembled to produce the final report. John R. "found," there, "the most interesting collection of young economists whom I had known since my Johns Hopkins days."[26] At the suggestion of Max West, the commission's "tax expert," they pooled their funds, rented a big house, and moved in together with their families. Nell, with skills honed in her parents' Akron hotel, managed the entire operation—in a "no nonsense" manner. Durand called Nell "a dictator." She "certainly worked," wrote John R. And the work was therapeutic. John R. and Nell had buried little Julia Margaret in March. The minister who officiated at the funeral, Owen Lovejoy, took them home with him for lunch and prescribed "hard work" as the best therapy for grief. Their Washington stay was therapeutic for more than the work.

The Washington "crowd" was "congenial and brilliant." In addition to their informal interactions, they followed procedures that educated everyone. Each staff member read a first draft of his report to the commission as a whole, then revised it before its final inclusion in the report.[27]

John R. and Kate Claghorn wrote the introductory chapter to the final volume: "Progress of the Nation." John R. collaborated with Durand and Charles E. Edgerton on the labor chapter. And John R. wrote the chapter on immigration by himself.[28]

Richard T. Ely praised the labor chapter as "the best text-book yet written on labor problems."[29] Ely was most impressed by conceptual advances over previous treatments of the labor problem. Unfortunately, the conceptual advances that Ely praised were most obvious in their admissions of failure. To estimate shares of capital and labor, the staff developed a "net product" concept equivalent to today's value-added. But, they ran into trouble getting appropriate statistics. They finally settled on 44 percent for labor's share and essentially gave up on estimating the return to capital—though they used John R.'s data from the ABER to form their admittedly inadequate final estimate. They also used his data to follow wage and price changes between 1869 and 1900 and to relate wage changes to price changes. Wages in general had increased faster than prices over those years, but wages had changed more slowly than prices on cyclical upswings—creating problems for wage-earners in times of inflation.

They argued that unions were a natural and beneficial response to industrial combinations. Unions emerged naturally in Britain and the United States along with the growth of capitalistic enterprises, and unions had survived efforts to destroy them. Prosecution as "conspiracies in restraint of trade" did not halt their growth. "The evolution of industrial society had proved too strong for legal fetters."[30] "It is readily perceived," they wrote, "that the position of a single workingman, face to face, with one of our great combinations, such as the United States Steel Corporation, is in a position of very great weakness. The workman has one thing to sell—his labor." Even a highly skilled worker needs capital equipment to be productive. But a "single legal person," the corporation, controls the capital equipment, and this control gives the corporation enough power "to dictate to the workingman upon what terms he shall make use of them." Workers can correct this bargaining disadvantage only by bargaining as a group organized in a trade union.[31] This argument was perhaps the most influential result of John R.'s participation in "collective activity" on the staff of the USIC. But there were other memorable experiences.

After all the official summaries had been completed, John R. had one more task. Congressman Phillips, who had set the entire operation in motion, wanted to write a dissent, and he recruited John R. to help him. Phillips agreed with the report's general conclusion—that Federal Government policies should concentrate on publicity and on curtailing socially harmful activities of large corporations—but he thought that the report had been too easy on John D. Rockefeller and his ilk—that its recommendations had been too vague and general. Phillips introduced John R. to life in the gilded age. "It was a great life. I dined with him every evening at the Shoreham Hotel. He was a bulky, florid individual, some seventy years of age; rather lethargic but bitter. Our dinner lasted about two or three hours, before I could read to him what I had written during the other fifteen or so. We had two bottles of champagne. You place them in a pail of ice and water on the floor at the right side of the host, while a waiter lifts out a bottle with a napkin and, pointing away from you—pop—the cork is out and the contents bubble up in a stemmed glass before you—Oh! My! Ain't it grand! Never before nor since have I known anything like it. Also we had fifty-cent cigars, moose meat, lobsters and other inspiring delicacies for the rich."[32]

It is worth noting that John R. worked fifteen hours before the two-hour dinner. This left only seven hours out of twenty-four for sleep and family.

John R.'s Reflections

John R.'s own reflections on his experience in the USIC were complex. After witnessing the testimony of the Rockefellers, Carnegies, and Morgans of the world, John R. came to admire them for their personal abilities and initiative, but he developed reservations about concentrations of economic power.[33]

He summarized these complex conclusions in a symposium on the concentration of wealth published in *The Independent*.[34] He admitted that economies of scale and advances in management could justify concentrations of capital. But he quickly added that individual initiative and creativity were the sources of progressive economic change and that those who control large aggregations of capital have access to "special privileges" with which they can legally block or crush the efforts of creative individuals. These "special privileges," he added, were "always supported by law or sprang from defects in the law." By interpreting "defects in the law" broadly, he could advocate changes that would prevent managers of concentrated capital from crushing initiatives of creative individuals; that is, changes in the laws could prevent some practices uncovered in the investigations of the USIC.

He advocated a central bank to remove from concentrated "money interests" the ability to crush new firms by denying credit or raising interest rates. He advocated railroad rate regulation to remove from railroads the ability to support the kind of rate discrimination that helped Rockefeller crush small oil producers. He advocated land taxes high enough to prevent monopolists from keeping others from access to raw materials. And he repeated Henry George's argument against big city landlords.

Though John R. dealt largely with dangers that the commission had uncovered, there were some inklings of a macro perspective in this article. Toward the beginning of the article, he introduced his argument for a central bank by assuming a federal government budget surplus which would be deflationary. Without a central bank, these surplus funds would be deposited in banks controlled by the concentrated "money interests." And the "money interests" could, by withholding credit or raising interest rates, crush the innovations of creative individuals. Then, at the end of the article, after showing that neither farm prices nor wages had kept up with the rate of inflation, he pointed out that total farm and worker spending could not buy everything that had been produced. Managers of concentrated firms would try to sell on export markets. But foreigners could not buy the goods without foreign exchange earned from selling to Americans. But Americans would not have the income to buy foreign goods. So, in a primitive manner, John R. had covered the components of aggregate demand—government spending, investment by creative individuals, consumer spending by workers and farmers, and foreign spending.

After the commission had finished everything, John R. collaborated for a time with William English Walling, a journalist who wanted to make the USIC's major findings available to the general public in a single easily understood volume. But fifteen-hour days had taken their toll, and John R. broke down. Walling, the kindly and independently wealthy heir of an old Kentucky family, packed the entire Commons family off to a farm in the Shenandoah Valley where they stayed until John R. had recovered.[35] Then John R. went to see Ralph Easley.

Notes

1. Commons. *Myself*, 60.
2. Ibid., 74–75, 67.
3. Ibid., 60,65.
4. Clarence E. Wunderlin, Jr. *Visions of a New Industrial Order: Social Science and Labor Theory in America's Progressive Era* (New York: Columbia University Press, 1992).
5. Commons, *Myself*, 63.
6. George Shibley, *The Money Question. The 50% Fall in General Prices, the Evil Effects; the Remedy, Bimetallism of 16 to 2 and Government Control of Paper Money in Order to Secure a Stable Measure of Prices—Stable Money. Monetary History 1850–1896* (Chicago: Stable Money Publishing Co., 1896).
7. Commons, *Myself*, 65.
8. American Bureau of Economic Research, *Quarterly Bulletin of Economic Research* 1 (July, 1900).

9. *Quarterly Bulletin of Economic Research* 2(September, 1900) (Both on reel 15 of the microfilm edition of Commons's papers). Irving Fisher told John R. this was the first monthly index of wholesale prices in the United States. It was among the first. There was the Faulkner index in 1897 and the Bradstreet index of 1893, updated in 1900, but that was it. See Christopher Hanes, "Prices and Price Indexes," *Historical Statistics of the United States.* Vol.3 of 5, ed. Susan B. Carter, Scott S. Gartner, Michael R. Haines, Alan L. Olmsted, Richard Sutch, and Gavin B. Wright (New York: Cambridge University Press, 2006), 3-247-3-157.
10. See Hans Thorelli, *Federal Antitrust Policy: Organization of An American Tradition* (Baltimore, MD: Johns Hopkins, 1955), 510–12, Clarence Wunderlin, *Visions of a New Industrial, Social Science and Labor Theory in America's Progressive Era* (New York: Columbia University Press, 1992), 28–29.
11. E. Dana Durand, *Memoirs of E. Dana Durand* (Washington, DC: Durand, 1954), 564–65. United States Industrial Commission *Final Report of the United States Industrial Commission* vol.19 (Washington, DC: Government Printing Office, 1902), viii.
12. Durand, Memoirs, 136.
13. Later merger waves were more marked by acquisitions in which large firms acquired smaller firms or by mergers of different kinds of firms. In this wave, many similar firms producing the same product merged. Naomi Lamoreaux, *The Great Merger Movement in American Business 1895–1904* (New York: Cambridge University Press, 1985), 1–2, There were two previous merger waves, on in the 1880s and one starting in 1889, but neither compared in size with this merger wave. Alfred D. Chandler, *Scale and Scope: The Dynamics of Industrial Capitalism* (Cambridge, MA: Harvard University press, 1990), 73–75.
14. Bruno Ramirez, *When Workers Fight: The Politics of Industrial Relations in the Progressive Era 1898–1916* (Westport, CN: Greenwood Press, 1978), 9–11.
15. United States Industrial Commission, *Final Report*, vol.19, 723.
16. John H. Brown, "Jeremiah Jenks: A Pioneer Industrial Economist," *Journal of the History of Economic Thought* 26 (March 2004): 69–89.
17. United States Industrial Commission *Reports*, vols. 3, 5, 7, 8, 10.
18. Wunderlin, *Visions of a New Industrial Order*, 47–48.
19. United States Industrial Commission, *Report* vol. 14, 32–48.
20. Ibid., 32, 33.
21. Ibid., 35.
22. Ibid., 36, 37, 42, 43.
23. Ibid., vol.15, 319–24, Commons, *Myself*, 68–69.
24. John R. Commons and Associates, *History of Labor in the United States* vol.3 (1935; reprint, New York: Macmillan, 1966), xviii.
25. Commons, *Myself*, 72.
26. Ibid., 75.
27. Ibid., 75–77.
28. E. Dana Durand, "The United States Industrial Commission: Methods of Government Investigation," *Quarterly Journal of Economics* 16 (August 1902): 572n.

29. Richard T. Ely, "Report of the Industrial Commission. I. Labor," *Yale Law Review* 11 (November, 1902): 229–50.
30. United States Industrial Commission, *Report*, 19, 794.
31. Ibid., 800.
32. Commons, *Myself*, 78–79.
33. Ibid., 143.
34. John R. Commons, "Symposium on Concentration of Wealth: Its Dangers," *The Independent* (May 1, 1902): 1040–45. There were eighteen articles in this symposium. John R.'s followed a stout Darwinian defense by William Graham Sumner.
35. Commons, *Myself*, 79–80.

8

The National Civic Federation

I spent five months with John Mitchell. . . . I agreed with a prominent lawyer who said to me that 'Mitchell made the coal operators look like thirty cents—Myself

Six years before he offered John R. a job, Ralph Easley, an energetic and gregarious newspaperman, distressed by Chicago's inadequate response to the panic of 1893, had concluded that the city needed a single organization to coordinate and focus its resources on its most pressing problems. He had consulted William Stead, a liberal British clergyman who was writing a book about Chicago.[1] Stead, enthusiastic enough to claim credit for the idea, had whipped up enough enthusiasm to recruit most of the city's influential citizens who organized the Chicago Civic Federation (CCF) to battle "the vicious elements of Society and slum conditions, to relieve the poor, and to work for industrial conciliation." Easley became secretary and "sparkplug" of the new organization.[2] The CCF created an unemployment relief system, raised $135,000 for homeless shelters, organized reform committees in all of Chicago's wards, and established a Bureau of Associated Charities to coordinate the city's organizations.[3]

Then, in 1894, at Easley's urging, the CCF mobilized a committee to seek a peaceful solution to the Pullman strike. Before the committee could act, President Grover Cleveland sent in the army. Troops fired on strikers in Kensington near Chicago, killing at least two, probably more, and wounding many.

The National Civic Federation

To learn how to prevent such tragedies, Easley organized a conference on industrial arbitration and conciliation. It went so well, that Easley started organizing conferences on other topics. In 1899, with the help of Jeremiah Jenks and Edwin R.A. Seligman of Columbia University, he organized a conference on trusts. At that conference a committee was organized to design a National Civic Federation (NCF). The NCF emerged a year later with Ralph Easley as executive secretary, Mark Hanna as president, and Samuel Gompers as vice president.[4] Jenks remained on the executive board, and since the NCF and the USIC were concerned with the same issues, it was natural that the USIC staff would become acquainted with the NCF.[5]

John R. had served as the secretary for the NCF's Conference on Taxation and Public Ownership in 1901. It was probably then that Easley offered him a job.

So, in 1902, John R. became Ralph Easley's general assistant. He later praised Easley as "the most illustrious combination that I had known of executive ability, astute insight, critical acumen in holding down to actual facts and boyish enthusiasm." John R. defended him from radical critics. And there were many. The labor leaders in the NCF tended toward the conservative end of the movement, and the president of the NCF, Mark Hanna, had masterminded the financing of William McKinley's campaign, the campaign that used massive funding and public relations tricks to defeat William Jennings Bryan. Moreover, Easley was a rabid anticommunist associated with all the most reprehensible excesses of the first red scare.

In his defense, John R. asserted that Easley simply sought nonviolent solutions to conflicts and that he was always conciliatory.[6] Easley was indeed rabidly anticommunist. But he was also rabidly critical of the National Association of Manufacturers. It might be true that the business members of the NCF moved it too far in one direction. But John R.'s defense of Easley was also a defense of cooperative solutions to the problems of capitalism.

Shortly after Easley hired him, John R. was drawn into labor problems by a threat to a labor pact in the Midwestern bituminous fields, the result of three years of strikes and negotiations. Veins of coal near the surface made it easy to open a mine there, and ease of entry set the stage for what Henry Carter Adams had called "the competitive menace"—the tendency for the least ethical employers to drag others down to their level. To gain an advantage, one firm would reduce wages and prices. Other firms would follow. Eventually, after all firms had reduced wages, the first firm's advantage would disappear but wages would remain lower for all firms.[7]

Miners had responded to this constant downward wage pressure by organizing the United Mine Workers (UMW) in 1890. A strike in 1897 had resulted in a joint interstate conference in Chicago in 1898 which had established an eight-hour day, uniform pay rates, and a wage increase of ten cents per ton. The miners and workers had agreed that this "industrial parliament" should meet every year in January or February. Negotiations were complex, and scale committees composed of worker and employer representatives would often negotiate for months, with the core objective of assuring that operators could sell at a reasonable profit while maintaining decent working conditions and paying decent wages.[8]

The Anthracite Strike

For this agreement to last, the UMW had to neutralize the "competitive menace" of the low-wage anthracite mines. It would not be easy. Unlike mines in the relatively competitive bituminous industry, anthracite mines were owned by railroads connected by interlocking directorates, and, unlike the bituminous mines spread over many states, the anthracite mines were confined to five counties in Pennsylvania. The veins lay deep below the hills. Coal extraction required extensive capital equipment so entry barriers were high. The owners, all railroad companies, had—as John R. had documented in the dissent he wrote for Phillips—used discriminatory rates to drive competitors out of the anthracite fields. They colluded to charge a monopoly price, and since railroads controlled the anthracite industry, they could hide coal profits in railroad charges.[9] To hinder union organization, the anthracite operators had "flooded the fields" with immigrants from fourteen different countries, speaking fourteen different languages.[10]

The president of the UMW, John Mitchell, was the youngest union president in history—just twenty-eight. The product of an unhappy childhood with a fairytale wicked stepmother, Mitchell had gone to work in the mines at the age of twelve. He had educated himself in his spare time by reading avidly and studying coal industry data, growing skilled enough to know more than company negotiators about market conditions and balance sheets. Mitchell believed in negotiation and conciliation. He opposed violence and did not have much confidence in strikes. As a member of the NCF, he hoped that he could reach a peaceful agreement with the anthracite operators.

While UMW organizers entered the little Pennsylvania coal towns, Mitchell sought meetings with the mine owners. But in spite of frantic efforts by Easley and Hanna, Mitchell met open resistance in the few meetings that he obtained. As a result, Mitchell coordinated what observers have considered an almost perfectly managed strike and a turning point in the history of American labor policy.[11]

On May 12, 1902, 150,000 immigrant Poles, Slavs, and Italians joined traditional miners of Scotch, Irish, and Welsh descent and walked out of the mines. On May 15, at a boisterous convention, and against Mitchell's advice, union delegates voted to make the strike permanent.

Easley and Hanna asked President Theodore Roosevelt for help. On June 8, 1902, Roosevelt sent Carroll D. Wright, the commissioner of Labor, to investigate. Wright called representatives of all parties to New York, interviewed them, and sent a report to Roosevelt together with recommendations. But the Attorney General Philander Knox told Roosevelt that there was no constitutional way for him to intervene.[12] The coal operators argued that intervention was unnecessary; the miners would not be able to hold out and would soon return to work.

John R. Interviews Miners

Easley sent John R. and Walter Weyl to the coal region to investigate. Weyl had studied at the Wharton School, writing his PhD thesis for Simon Patten, an Ely ally. Unlike John R. who had been forced from university life, Weyl could not stand it, and he left university life permanently in 1899.[13] He worked for a while with Carroll Wright's Labor Bureau, but he did not like bureaucracy either. Then he traveled to Puerto, Rico, Mexico, France, and Russia— "rudderless" in the words of his biographer. Weyl was at the New York University Settlement House when he read about the coal strike and decided to offer his services to John Mitchell. Weyl would later help Mitchell write his defense of conservative unionism, and Weyl would write an iconic philosophical brief for the progressive movement—in which he acknowledged his intellectual debt to Simon Patten.[14] Weyl, friendly, articulate, and a good listener, was the right companion for John R. Commons as they set out for the coal towns of Pennsylvania.

For some reason, they went under assumed names. John R. was a reporter named "Campbell" working on a magazine article.[15]

The trip gave John R. many stories to tell his students. One related to newspapers and violence. To prevent violence, Mitchell had ordered all locals to form "peace committees" with the mission of cooling hotheads and preventing confrontations. There were, nevertheless, reports of violence on both sides. Two men were shot by company guards as they approached a mine. A hardware store owner was beaten to death by a mob in Shenandoah.[16] UMW officials claimed that many reports of violence were false. Mitchell denied that the miners were involved with the mob that killed the owner of the hardware store.[17] Clergymen testifying before the Anthracite Commission accused large urban papers of exaggerating union violence. The newspaper of one small Pennsylvania town, the *Tamaqua Register*, denounced the "dime novel" fabrications of the large urban papers.[18] John R. recounted one "dime novel" fabrication.

> At Shenandoah, Pennsylvania, a Polish town, we visited on Sunday morning "John the Pollock." He spoke English and Polish from childhood—a huge intelligent piece of manhood. The same afternoon we sat on the hillside surrounding the mine pit, along with a thousand of the strikers and their families dressed up for Sunday, looking down upon the mining property surrounded by a picket fence and protected inside by armed guards in uniform. One of the strikers somehow broke into the enclosure, evidently drunk, and waved his arms and threatened the guards. Immediately from the other side came John the Pollock. Admitted to the enclosure, he took the drunken striker by the shoulder and gently led him out to the crowd on the hillside.
>
> The next morning, I received a telegram from my wife in New York asking if I were alive and safe. She had read in the New York Sunday Paper of the bloody riot of the mine-workers at Shenandoah, of the shootings of strikers and guards, of dead and wounded. Is it any wonder that thereafter I seldom believed the news concerning strikes that I read in the capitalistic press?[19]

On his mission for Easley, John R. reported that merchants and bankers in Scranton had assured "Campbell" that, if allowed to vote, 75 percent of the miners would opt to end the strike. But when "Campbell" talked to the miners, they told him that they could easily hold out for a year, and they seemed unanimous in their determination to hold out. They were all "placing great hope" in the likelihood that the bituminous miners would strike in sympathy with them and they seemed confident that John Mitchell would call out the bituminous miners.[20] The miners were English, Slavic, and Italian, and they were determined to hold out. "Especially the foreigners have implicit confidence in Mitchell & will do exactly what he says. Yet the Slavish fellows said they would not let Mitchell dictate to them."[21] In late August, John R. wrote that the miners were still holding out.[22] John R. met Mark Hanna for the first and only time in his life when he went with Easley to give Hanna his report.[23]

If the strike was less violent than most, it had its moments of color. Mitchell had hired Mother Jones as an organizer. Many of her strategies involved organizing miners' wives and daughters into mop, broom, and dishpan brigades. Her biographer, Richard Cordery, has described a number of such episodes. On September 22 she "led a long line" of women, and girls so armed along with "250 miners, and a band to the mines at Beaver Meadow and Coleraine," urging the miners there to join the strike.[24] Cordery described her last march on October 6, when "she led eight hundred miners and six hundred women for twelve miles over a narrow mountain pass to the mines at Lattimore, PA." At one point in that demonstration, "a thousand strikers charged down the hill" to keep strikebreakers from entering the mines. The sheriff refused orders to fire on the strikers. Fearing that the next sheriff might not hold his fire, Mitchell ordered Mother Jones to stop the marches and hold rallies. Like the anthracite miners, Mother Jones hoped that the bituminous coworkers would go out in a sympathy strike, and many bituminous miners were more than willing.[25]

The prospect terrified the NCF industrial committee. A sympathy strike might alienate the public and risk progress in the bituminous fields. Members of the committee fanned out over the bituminous fields visiting union locals and arguing against a sympathy strike.[26] At the convention, Mitchell convinced the delegates that it would be better to send financial support so the anthracite miners could hold out longer. The union set up a system, taxing bituminous locals for funds which were sent to anthracite locals which organized social assistance committees to supervise distribution of funds. A complex auditing system kept track of sources and uses of funds.

Theodore Roosevelt Intervenes

By September, the strike was radicalizing Pennsylvania and creating problems for the Republican Party. Coal shortages together with skyrocketing prices threatened winter hardships—and losses in the November elections. On October 3, 1902, President Roosevelt called Mitchell and the coal operators to the White House. Roosevelt, recovering from a carriage accident, faced the group from a wheelchair. Mitchell, polite and conciliatory, said he would agree to binding arbitration. The operators turned the idea down and vilified Mitchell with an arrogance that infuriated Roosevelt. Roosevelt wrote that Mitchell, the union leader, "behaved with great dignity and moderation. The operators, on the contrary, showed extraordinary stupidity and bad temper."[27]

On October 13, Elihu Root, Roosevelt's Secretary of War, met with J. Pierpont Morgan on his yacht, the Corsair, and told him that unless an agreement could be reached, Roosevelt was prepared to send the army into the mines. Two days later, Roosevelt had a paper signed by all the coal operators signifying their willingness to accept binding arbitration from a commission. After haggling from both sides, Roosevelt appointed the commission with the Labor Secretary Carroll D. Wright as recording secretary.

On October 21, 1902, union delegates accepted the arbitration offer. On October 23, the strike ended. The challenge for the union now became one of presenting their best case to the arbitrators.[28] Walter Weyl helped Mitchell design a strategy. John R. and Jenks joined the UMW research team. John R. spent five months with Mitchell in his New York hotel. He quoted a lawyer (most likely Clarence Darrow) who said that "Mitchell made the coal operators look like thirty cents."[29] Henry Demarest Lloyd, the famous author of *Wealth against Commonwealth* came to help. The corporations had their teams of lawyers, but Clarence Darrow, by now the most famous defense attorney in the United States, came to help the miners.[30]

Mitchell, as Craig Phelan noted, anticipated the arguments of the owners and instructed the staff to pursue issues such as drunkenness in the mining camps and age of marriage.[31] But Commons and Jenks developed their own arguments. They attacked the antiunion bias of labor laws and courts, and they argued for legalization of a long list of union tactics including secondary boycotts.[32]

On March 22, 1903, the commission issued its final report—with an arbitration decision that contradicted the report. The report did not recommend union recognition, but the arbitration decision created a board to mediate further disputes; the board was composed of three management and three labor representatives.

Resorting to booster language, John R. hailed the report "as the most important document ever issued on the modern labor question. . . . It frames a constitution for the government of a great industry." He pointed out inconsistencies between the decision and the report. The report found no reason for granting a wage increase; the decision granted one. The report argued against recognizing a union; the decision recognized the union in fact. The report opposed a trade agreement; the decision in fact granted a trade agreement. John R. seemed most enthusiastic about the machinery for settling disputes with a board containing both worker and employer representatives. On the other hand, though not obvious from this article, he was less enthusiastic about the report's condemnation of the closed shop which he would always defend. He seemed to think that over time "a voluntary trade agreement will in due time commend itself to both sides."[33] But within a year, he was criticizing the agreement "as interpreted by Colonel Wright."[34]

Theodore Roosevelt made the strike historically significant. As Jonathan Grossman, chief historian of the US Labor Department, explained it, previous administrations had brought the police power of the state to the aid only of employers; Roosevelt had introduced the notion of the public interest as the justification for a government role in labor disputes—the role of government as "peacemaker" rather than "strikebreaker."[35] Samuel Gompers called it the most significant event in the history of labor.[36]

Questioning the Commission's Report

Clarence Darrow questioned the rosy assessments. He condemned the commission's report as "a most cowardly document."[37] As time passed, events and the reflections of historians increased the credibility of Darrow's verdict. The miners had won, but the commission had nullified the win without addressing the underlying issues that caused the strike. The miners had gained only a 10 percent increase in wages and a 10 percent reduction in working hours. Moreover, the commission had introduced issues that, in years to come, would undermine principles developed so painstakingly by the USIC and the NCF.[38] At a time when the trade agreement philosophy was gaining extensive public support, the commission refused to endorse a trade agreement between the operators and the UMW—even though its recommendation of a conciliation board contradicted that refusal. By condemning the closed shop, the commission set the stage for an advertising assault on unions by the National Association of Manufacturers, an assault that would shatter Easley's dreams of trade agreements and labor peace and an assault on the vision of Jenks, Durand, and Commons of a "new industrial order."[39]

After the Anthracite strike and the report of the Arbitration Commission, Easley sent John R. to mediate a number of disputes—street railways, subways building trades, steel factories. John R. claimed that his experiences as a mediator led him to his "Malthusian" view of human nature—applied to both workers and employers—pigheaded, stubborn, "stupid and passionate."[40]

But before all this, even as John R. had been approaching Easley for a job, Richard T. Ely had been scheming to bring him to the University of Wisconsin.

In 1902 the Carnegie Foundation had agreed to fund a history of American labor unions under the direction of Carrol D. Wright. Ely had sent Wright a proposal that went nowhere. Undaunted, Ely had started raising funds for his own labor history project. He had worked hard to persuade the university's president to hire John R. And he had finally succeeded.

When Wisconsin's job offer became definite, John R. asked Easley to let him leave the NCF at the beginning of 1904 to work on a research project for the Department of Labor. This project originated in a proposal to investigate output restrictions by unions and firms. John R. had pointed out that firms and unions used the same tactics with different names. For example, publishers, wholesale druggists, and railroads used their ability to withhold orders in same way that unions withhold purchases during boycotts. He had urged that public authorities should refrain from blanket suppression of such activities, investigate their social consequences, and find ways "to preserve their benefits and prevent their excesses."[41]

His final report ran to 921 pages. With the exception of the introduction and a study of the typographical industry written by John R., the report contained case studies of output restriction in different industries written by others. John R. edited the entire volume. He did not hit it off with the Labor Commissioner. Thirty years later, John R. was still grousing about Wright.[42] The sour relations with Wright might have reflected the strain of John R.'s last six months. Nell bore twins that died during those months. Those tragedies alone must have clouded the optimism at the time about his "five big years." But, perhaps by historical accident, those years were indeed "big."

He had participated in the work of the United States Industrial Commission—the most ambitious and influential economic inquiry ever attempted up to that time in the United States, an "epic making . . . keynote of the progressive period."[43] The USIC's nineteen-volume report inspired the trust-busting campaigns of Theodore Roosevelt and William Howard Taft, and it provided the foundation for Thorstein Veblen's *The Theory of Business Enterprise.*[44]

Moreover, while working for the NCF, John R. had become a participant observer in the 1902 Anthracite strike—historic for its size, for its conduct, and—perhaps most significantly—for the response it elicited from Theodore Roosevelt who abandoned the history of anti-labor federal interventions for an intervention explicitly guided by a public purpose.

But what remained most significant was what Clarence Wunderlin insightfully labeled "visions of a new industrial order," visions of an order that would preserve the dynamic efficiencies of a capitalist society while controlling its negative side effects.

This vision was based largely on the conclusions that Jeremiah Jenks drew from his research on corporate power. Jenks's view can be contrasted with two others. The most famous, embodied in the theory that Thorstein Veblen drew from the records of the USIC, condemned the capitalist system as hopelessly inefficient because it operated on incentives for pecuniary rather than for technically efficient objectives. Though Veblen did not do so, others used his analysis to support extensive government planning or some type of moderate socialism. The second view, rested on the labors of John Bates Clark who reasoned his way to the model of the purely competitive system. The lawyer and Supreme Court Justice, Louis Brandeis, represented this view. It emphasized the need to break up large concentrations of economic power in an effort to create the utopia of the purely competitive system.

Jenks's view was more agnostic.[45] He readily admitted the socially destructive side effects of capitalist evolution. But he also pointed out that the rapid economic growth of the late nineteenth century was associated with the emergence of these giant corporations. In some cases, economies of scale justified large size. In others, Jenks was not really sure. He had concluded that frontal attacks on combinations would be futile and that the better solution lay in publicizing corporate behavior and in regulating specific antisocial practices as they were discovered. He would play an active role in the formulation of the Erdman, Hepburn, and Clayton Anti-Trust Acts. But he was already aware that their size endowed large corporations with socially harmful power in transactions with their employees. To correct this imbalance of power, Jenks had, with the assistance of John R. and Dana Durand, developed a conception of countervailing power.

John R. concurred in this general view. It was the view that Richard Gonce found in John R.'s articles and editorials written during these years.[46] Gonce also noted that during this period, John R. read *Industrial Democracy* by Sidney and Beatrice Webb. The Webbs advocated a degree of democracy within the workplace. Most significantly they wrote of working rules in trade agreements. John R., following Gustav Cassel, would later expand the notion of working rules beyond the labor-management context. The Webbs also emphasized supply networks, picturing the entire economy as a pyramid with consumers at the top and workers at the bottom. John R. would adapt this conception to his own view of the economy as a set of linked transactions.

John R.'s writings during the exile years marked a change of focus from political to economic democracy and working class power. He would maintain the NCF belief that such power could be exercised without violence. In spite of the booster language in his praise for the Anthracite Arbitration Commission, he would oppose most calls for binding arbitration and support the closed shop.

Notes

1. William Stead, *If Christ Came to Chicago* (Chicago, IL: Laird and Lee, 1894).
2. Marguerite Green, *The National Civic Federation 1900–1925* (Washington, DC: Catholic University, 1956), 5.
3. Christopher Cyphers, *The National Civic Federation and the Making of a New Liberalism* (Westport, CN and London: Greenwood Press, 2002), 21.
4. When union leaders suggested Hanna, Easley erupted "Hanna was the greatest buccaneer in the country" he would ruin everything (Green, *The National Civic Federation*, 40), but Hanna supported unions and principles of collective bargaining. "New" labor historians saw the NCF as an instrument of corporate liberalism, a technique for preventing worker unrest. See James Weinstein, *The Corporate Ideal in the Liberal State 1900–1918* (Boston, MA: Beacon Press, 1968), xv and Philip S. Foner, *History of the Labor Movement in the United States*, vol.3 (New York: International Publishers, 1975), 61–110. Cyphers, *The National Civic Federation*, 61, disagreed, finding its motive in "its belief in the inherent capacity of liberalism conceived as a cooperative compact among all Americans to advance the cause of freedom and liberty." Bruno Ramirez, *When Workers Fight*, 70, argued that the NCF filled a need for nationwide responses to national problems when the American fiscal federal system prevented federal government action.
5. Green, *The National Civic Federation*, 36, Commons, *Myself*, 82.
6. Commons, *Myself*, 83–85.
7. Ramirez, *When Workers Fight*, 19. Henry Carter Adams, *Relation of the State to Industrial Action and Economics and Jurisprudence, Two Essays by Henry Carter Adams*, ed. Joseph Dorfman (New York: Columbia University Press, 1954), 89–121.
8. Commons, *Myself*, 72–73, Commons, Brandeis, and Lescohier, *History of Labor*, vol.3, xv.
9. United States Industrial Commission, *Report* vol.19, 654.
10. Jonathan Grossman, "The Coal Strike of 1902—A Turning Point in U.S. Policy," *Monthly Labor Review* 98 (October, 1975), 21–29.
11. Craig Phelan, *Divided Loyalties: The Public and Private Life of John Mitchell* (Albany, NY: State University of New York, 1994), 154–63, Green, *The National Civic Federation*, 8, Robert J. Cornell, *The Anthracite Strike of 1902* (1957; reprint, New York: Russell & Russell, 1971), 60–92, Grossman, "The Coal Strike," Ramirez, *When Workers Fight*, 400.
12. Knox based his opinion on the American Sugar Trust Case (*United States v E.C. Knight Company* 156 U.S. 1 (1895). In that case the Supreme Court

ruled that the government could not stop the American Sugar Company from acquiring the E.C. Knight Company because manufacturing was not commerce, hence not subject to the interstate commerce clause.

13. Charles Forcey, *The Crossroads of Liberalism: Croly, Weyl, Lippmann and the Progressive Era* (New York: Oxford University Press, 1961), 56–70.

14. John Mitchell, *Organized Labor: Its Problems, Purposes, and Ideals, and Present and Future Wage Earners* (Philadelphia, PA: American Book and Bible House, 1903), Walter Weyl, *The New Democracy: An Essay on Certain Political and Economic Tendencies in the United States* (New York: Macmillan, 1912)

15. Commons to Easley June 8, 1902, NCF Papers. New York: New York Public Library, Box 2, Folder 6, microfilm reel 2; Wunderlin, *Visions of a New Industrial Order*, 76.

16. Cornell, *The Anthracite Strike*, 143–44, 152–55.

17. Ibid., 249.

18. Ibid., 155–57.

19. Commons and Associates, *History of Labor in the United States*, vol.3, xvi.

20. Commons to Easley June 18, 1902, NCF Papers microfilm reel 2.

21. Commons to Easley June 20, 1902, ibid.

22. Commons to Easley August 21, 1902, ibid.

23. Commons, *Myself*, 83.

24. Simon Cordery, *Mother Jones: Raising Cain and Consciousness* (Albuquerque: University of New Mexico Press, 2010), 68–69.

25. Phelan, *Divided Loyalties*, 166.

26. Green, *The National Civic Federation*, 49–50.

27. Grossman "The Coal Strike of 1902," 24.

28. Phelan, *Divided Loyalties*, 191.

29. Commons, *Myself*, 91.

30. Wunderlin, *Visions of a New Industrial Order*, 83.

31. Phelan, *Divided Loyalties*, 192, citing Mitchell to Commons October 29,1902, from Mitchell Papers.

32. Green, *The National Civic Federation*, 54–55, Wunderlin, *Visions of a New Industrial*, 83–84.

33. Commons, "The Anthracite Coal Strike Award," *The Independent* (March 26, 1903): 13.

34. Commons, "Causes of Union Shop Policy," *Publications of the American Economic Association*, 3rd series, vol.6 (1905): 140–50.

35. Grossman, "The Coal Strike of 1902," 29.

36. Samuel Gompers, *Seventy Years of Life and Labor* vol.2 of 2(New York: E.P. Dutton, 1926), 117, 126–27.

37. Cornell, *The Anthracite Coal Strike*, 258.

38. Ramirez, *When Workers Fight*, 42–45.

39. Phelan, *Divided Loyalties*, 198, 242–46.

40. Commons, *Myself*, 89.

41. Commons, "Combinations of Capital and Labor," *National Civic Federation Review* 3 (September 1903), 113–14.

42. Commons, *Myself*, 93–94.

43. Dorfman, *The Economic Mind in American Civilization*, vol. 3, 309; Wunderlin, *Visions of a New Economic Order*, 70.

44. David Hamilton, "Veblen, Commons and the Industrial Commission," in *The Founding of Institutional Economics: Leisure Class and Sovereignty*, ed. Warren Samuels (London and New York: Routledge, 1998), 3–1; John R. Commons, *Institutional Economics*, ed. Malcolm Rutherford (1934: reprint, New Brunswick, NJ: Transactions Press, 1990), 649–51.
45. Jeremiah Jenks, "The Trusts: Facts Established and Problems Unsolved," *Quarterly Journal of Economics* 15 (November 1900): 46–74.
46. Richard Gonce, "John R. Commons's 'Five Big Years' 1899–1904," *American Journal of Economics and Sociology* 61 (October 2002): 755–77.

9

Wisconsin Labor History

*I was born again when I entered Wisconsin after
five years of incubation—Myself*

Madison is picture book town nestled between lakes in Southern Wisconsin. On his first day at the university, there in the fall of 1904, John R. found himself in a secular revival. Charles Van Hise, the university president, in his inaugural address, spoke about the justification for and goals of a state university. Van Hise insisted that a faculty member's "greatest service is in his own creative work and the production of new scholars in the laboratory and the seminary . . . I hold that the state university, the university that serves the state, must see to it that scholarship and research of all kinds, whether or not a possible practical value can be pointed out must be sustained." But, he added that a state university, because it was a state university owed a debt to all the people of the state, to support the state government and to bring knowledge to all the people of the state through extension services and other services. Then, in the evening at a rally in the gymnasium, Robert M. ("Fighting Bob") La Follette, Wisconsin's governor proclaimed that he would make the state government "a people's government." And so, John R. felt "born again."[1]

Van Hise and Wisconsin were, in many respects, ideally suited for John R.'s own sense of mission. Van Hise, an internationally recognized geologist, an early conservationist, had offended the business community by opposing, on conservation grounds, the construction of a dam. He would not buckle to outside pressure.

The American Bureau of Industrial Research

Van Hise had helped Ely develop the financial plan that brought John R. to the campus. A new organization, the American Bureau of Industrial Research (ABIR), would pay John R.'s salary for the first half of the school year; the university would pay for the second half. During the first half of the year (including summers) John R. would work on an "interpretive history of labor" for the ABIR. During the second half he would teach in the Department of Political Economy. After three years, John R. would become a full-time faculty member in the Department of Political Economy. In March 1904, Ely and John R. signed the contract that created the ABIR.

The contract called for a one- or two-volume "interpretive" history of American industrial society to be completed by October 1909.[2] Ely was responsible for the period before the Civil War, socialism, and "great thought currents"; John R. for events after the Civil War and "the organization of industry and labor"; and Ulrich Phillips, a historian recommended by Frederick Jackson Turner, for the Southern states.

The contract would not be fulfilled on time or in the form prescribed for a number of reasons. The meaning of the word "interpretive" was never clear. John R. and Ely held different conceptions of their respective responsibilities. There were competing priorities for both of them—in the department and in the larger society. Relationships that John R. had developed during his exile years would distract him. Relationships from Ely's past would distract them both. The funding was less secure than it seemed. So there would be crises and delays and misunderstandings. Nevertheless, "ultimately," Harold Miller would conclude that in a broader sense, "the ABIR would accomplish almost all its goals."[3]

Work started smoothly. John R. recruited two gifted assistants, Helen Sumner and John Andrews—both talented, both committed to the worker side of the labor problem, and—most exceptionally— both able and willing to keep up with John R.'s impossible work schedules.

John Andrews, born in South Wayne, Lafayette County, WI, in 1880, had gone from a bachelor's degree at Wisconsin to a master's in economics from Dartmouth, and had returned to Madison for his PhD. Helen Laura Sumner, born in Sheboygan, WI, in 1876, had, at a young age, moved with her family to Denver where her father had been appointed a federal judge. She had graduated from Wellesley and had come to Wisconsin in 1902. She was Ely's secretary when John R. arrived.

Now, in the fall of 1904, she started out with John R. and John Andrews on an exhaustive search for documents, toiling from early morning till ten o'clock at night.[4] They placed ads in magazines, scoured used book stores, visited union offices, libraries, courthouses, and attics of old homes. They talked with fabled labor leaders—or with widows or heirs. Andrews described their labors.

> Such work, if done conscientiously, leads one into damp Chicago cellars, through dusty newspaper offices in Washington, Philadelphia and New York, and into stifling attics in Boston. It means days and nights of fruitless searching—disappointments only here and there brightened by real "finds"—but it also means meeting with men in every city who struggle hopefully or in spite of obstacles—men who have that "vision" without which "we perish," though finally weakened in body, they do not wither at the top. (underlining in original)[5]

John R. recruited his sister Clara who lugged her typewriter into homes and libraries, sometimes over objections of librarians.[6] When they could not take away actual documents, they typed copies and double-checked them for accuracy. By the spring of 1905, John R. realized that they were finding more documents than they had anticipated, and he suggested the first change in the ABIR plan—publication of a documentary history. Ely agreed—provided that they find new funding. Henry Farnam at the Carnegie Foundation promised $1,500 and Van Hise promised $3,000 more from university funds.[7]

In the winter of 1906, though, relations between Ely and John R. began to fray. John R. asked for a leave of absence so that he could spend the summer with a committee investigating municipal utilities for the National Civic Federation. Ely exploded.[8] He claimed that this kind of work makes one unfit for academic inquiry. He accused John R. of dodging his share of the department's administrative load. He complained that there was too much delay in publishing the interpretive history. A week later Ely fired off another letter complaining that John R. and his assistants were spending too much money. John R. cited his long hours of work and disagreed with Ely about the academic value of "real world" experience. They patched things up, but tempers simmered.

Then, a series of unfortunate events threatened the entire project. In 1907, a Wisconsin Court struck down as unconstitutional Van Hise's promise of $3,000. The strain of these events may have led to a new eruption at the end of 1908. During a meeting on January 18, 1909, Ely accused John R. of cavalier attitudes toward money. He also complained about the time John R. spent on activities unrelated to the history project and about his concentration on the documentary history at the expense of the interpretive history. John R. responded with a barrage of cruel and half-true accusations against his old benefactor. He asserted that Ely had not done his share of the work, had sought credit for the work of others, was planning to appropriate royalties for his own use, and intended to sell for financial gain the documents they had collected. Moreover, Ely himself had been responsible for outside activities since he had dragooned John R. into accepting the job of secretary for the American Association for Labor Legislation. Van Hise intervened, cooled temperatures, brokered an agreement, and forced a handshake.[9]

Shortly after this blow-up, a way out of the financial crisis began to emerge. On February 20, 1909, Carrol D. Wright died. Wright had been director of the Carnegie Foundation's labor history project when Ely first developed his ABIR proposal, and Wright had rebuffed Ely's requests for funds. Wright's replacement, Henry Farnam, knew and liked both Ely and John R. Farnam asked John R. to take over the Carnegie labor history project. John R. and Farnam worked out a plan. The Carnegie Foundation would finance publication of the Documentary History, and John R. together with Helen Sumner would complete the Carnegie labor history project. Ely objected that the ABIR plan for an interpretive history had been abandoned. Van Hise intervened again and brokered another compromise. The Carnegie history could be written in a way that would fulfill the ABIR plan. The Carnegie project could take the form of an "interpretive" labor history.[10]

The Documentary History

The *Documentary History of American Industrial Society* started rolling off the presses in 1910.[11] The first two volumes, covering the American South, were the work of Ulrich B. Phillips. It should be emphasized that John R. was not involved in the first two volumes. Phillips has become identified with the benign view of slavery. He had been suggested by Frederick Jackson Turner. He was not part of the Ely–Commons enterprise.

The next eight volumes were the work of Commons, Andrews, and Sumner. The third and fourth volumes covered labor conspiracy cases between 1806 and 1842. To deal with legal issues in these volumes, John R. recruited an editor from the university's law school, Eugene A. Gilmore.[12] Volumes five through ten chronicled labor movements, beginning with the earliest documents and ending about 1880.

The Interpretive Introductions

And though the full interpretive history lay in the future, the documentary history carried interpretive introductions in all odd numbered volumes, beginning with the third. Commons, Sumner, and Andrews created long- and short-term economic frameworks for organizing the documents; they introduced a philosophy of reform through democratic experimentalism; and they explored in specific contexts the relations between economic events, intellectual movements, and reform proposals.

The American Shoemakers

For the long-term framework in the introduction to volumes three and four, John R. introduced a slight revision of an earlier article, "The American Shoemakers."[13] That article became noted and praised—especially by John R.'s students—for its attribution of class conflict to expanding markets rather than to technical change in the Marxist tradition. This emphasis on a simple anti-Marxist theme could be misleading. John R. carefully qualified the difference. "Perhaps the difference is only one between the immediate and remote causes, but at any rate, so far as concerns the characteristic features of the labor movement as we find them in the documents at our command, it is the extension of markets rather than the technique of production that determines the origin of industrial classes, their form of organization, their political and industrial policies and demands, and their fate."[14]

Emphasis on disagreements with Marx can distract attention from reasoning that documented the processes by which expanding markets erode the bargaining power of workers and increase the bargaining power of financial and credit interests.

A table preceding the article divided history into seven stages. Puzzlingly, the text ignored the table, though the table anticipated the thrust of the argument. There is a column for industrial classes that becomes divided over time. It shows how functions performed by a single shopkeeper early in the evolution would be performed later by different specialized classes. There is a column titled "competitive menace"—a term introduced by Henry Carter Adams to indicate the tendency for the least ethical competitors to drag everyone else down to their level. The implication in the table is that the competitive menace changes form and that economic power moves around as markets expand.

John R. developed his argument using shoemaker organizations as "interpretive" representatives of more widespread stages in the evolution of markets. In differentiating the stages he focused on unique forms taken by each of three characteristics: the "competitive menace," the type of market, and the source of bargaining power

For his first stage, John R. chose, as typical of early guilds, "The Company of Shoemakers" chartered in Boston in 1648. The "competitive menace" was the "bad ware" of poorly trained traveling cobblers who made shoes in the homes of their customers. There was just one market based on personal relations—at which the traveling cobblers were at a bargaining disadvantage because they depended on homeowners for food, lodging, workplace, and leather. Consequently, John R. inferred, the traveling cobblers could not charge a price that covered the full cost of production.

The members of the "Company," however, had more bargaining power. All members performed three functions—merchant, master, and journeyman. As merchants, they set prices and bargained with customers; as masters, they organized production and regulated quality; as journeymen, they made the shoes and boots. Their complete control of raw materials and labor gave the guild members enough bargaining power to shift all costs of production to the consumers.[15]

For the next stage in the evolution of markets, John R. chose two organizations—"The Society of Master Cordwainers" and the "Federal Society of Journeymen Cordwainers." They clashed in a strike and lockout that resulted in an 1805 court case.[16] Documents from that case revealed four markets: a "bespoke market" for custom-made shoes, a "shop work" market for shoes sold in the shops, a "public market" which seemed to be a place in Philadelphia where shoes were sold at a discount (John R. lumped this market with the market created by advertising), and, finally, an export market in other cities where the masters sold their shoes at prices established in those cities. Since the masters could charge higher prices in the "bespoke market," they could pay higher wages for work done for that market, but the journeymen wanted wages to be the same for the same work no matter where shoes were sold. The "competitive menace" of shop work, public, and export markets became intense enough to motivate an opposing organization only for masters who sold in the export market.

A third stage was reached by 1835, when the "United Beneficial Society of Journeymen Cordwainers" struck for a ten-hour day. By that time, an expanded banking system had enabled merchant capitalists to buy large stocks of shoes and boots on credit. Highways, canals, and steamships had given these merchant capitalists a national market. Now retailers bought goods from merchants who bought them from producers who hired workers. The single price bargain between the

Boston shoemaker and his customer had been replaced by a string of price bargains: employer–capitalist, capitalist–retailer, retailer–consumer—and one wage bargain. Because workers had the least bargaining power in this supply chain, they bore the cost of "waiting" between the time that credit was granted and the time that goods were sold. And, at this the stage, competition forced wages down to the level paid by the least ethical employer.

In the final stage, the factory with steam power replaced skilled boot and shoe craftsmen with "green hands," the final competitive menace, against which the Knights of St. Crispin struggled in vain. "Its membership mounted to forty thousand or fifty thousand, whereas the next largest unions claimed only ten thousand to twelve thousand. It disappeared as suddenly as it had arisen, a tumultuous, helpless protest against the abuse of machinery."[17] This was the stage that stripped all bargaining power, not only from individual workers, but also from workers in craft organizations.

> It is enough to note that in the shoe industry . . . [the factory system] . . . was established in substantially its present form in the early part of the eighties; that detailed piece work has taken the place of team-work and hand-work; that the last vestige of property-right has left the worker; that the present form of labor organization, the Boot and Shoe Workers' Union, has endeavored, since 1895, to bring together all classes of employees, men and women, in a single industrial union rather than a partial trade union; and that the two classes of protective organizations have asserted their political power for protection against low levels of competition, the merchant-manufacturer against free trade in foreign products, the wage-earner against foreign immigrants, prison labor, child labor, and long hours of labor.[18]

In a final section, John R. implicitly rejected the value of consumer welfare as the ultimate ethical touchstone for a market society.

> The conflict is ultimately one between the interests of the consumer and the interests of the producer. Wherever the consumer as such is in control, he favors the marginal producer for through him he wields the club that threatens the other producers. Consequently the producers resort either to private organizations equipped with coercive weapons to suppress the menacing competition, or else they seek to persuade or compel the government to suppress him. In this way the contest of classes and interests enters the field of politics, and the laws of the land, and even the very framework of government, are outcomes of a struggle both to extend markets and to ward off their menace.[19]

John R. used the stages he had described to organize the document collection into four sections: a colonial period that lasted until 1820, a period from 1820 to 1840, 1840 to 1860, and 1860 to 1880, the last marking the emergence of the factory system. To this long-run economic framework of expanding markets, John R. and Helen Sumner, in the introduction to volumes four and five, added a short-run economic framework.

The Short Run

They introduced this short-run framework with a chart of wholesale prices. Based on that chart and on the business cycle, they divided post-colonial history into three periods—conveniently the same twenty-year intervals that John R. had worked out from his expansion of markets. Each period began and ended—roughly speaking—with a cyclical trough. For example, the first period ended with the "seven distressful years" between 1837 and 1843. The second period "includes . . . the vigorous uprising of 1850 to 1856 . . . The third period beginning with the paradoxical prosperity of the Civil War includes the collapse and depression from 1873 to 1879."

"Thus it is," they concluded, "that questions of money, banking, and credit have determined our three great periods of industrial history; and it is not an extravagance to claim, after contemplating also the wider political and social agitations accompanying the industrial movement, that the curve of prices here outlined is the backbone of American history."[20]

While the backbone analogy is a little difficult around which to wrap one's mind, the short-run framework is fairly straightforward. When prices start to rise on the upswing of the cycle, profits and the demand for labor increase, but the cost of living increases faster than wages; workers respond by organizing and agitating for higher wages and shorter hours; union membership increases; strikes increase. Employers organize; prices fall; and in the depression, employers succeed in crushing the unions.[21] Thus, before turning to details of the period from 1820 to 1840, Sumner and Commons added to the long-term framework of market expansion, the short-term framework of the business cycle, managing to create the same stages with both frameworks.

Constructive Democracy

In the introduction to chapters seven and eight John R. considered the role of ideas in social change. He found the years from 1840 to 1860 to be an ideal period for examining the role of ideas in social change—It was "the golden age of the talk-fest, the lyceum, the brotherhood of man—the 'hot air' period of American history."[22] The period ended with the passage of two laws: the compromise of 1850 and the Kansas–Nebraska Act of 1854. The first strengthened the fugitive slave law; the second allowed settlers of new territories to vote for slavery. These acts provoked an abolitionist reaction intense enough to drive all other issues from minds of reformers and end the "hot air period." But the intellectual ferment of that period allowed John R. to introduce his notion of "constructive democracy" which he first distinguished from "negative democracy."

"Negative democracy" removes obstacles to individual freedom. As an example of "negative democracy," John R. cited Andrew Jackson's destruction of the Second United States Bank without proposing a "peoples' bank" to replace it, initiating the panic of 1837 and seven years of a brutal depression. "Political democracy went bankrupt when the industrial bankruptcy of 1837 exposed its incapacity. It had vindicated equal rights, but where was the bread and butter? The call of the time was for a new democracy."[23]

This new democracy had to be "constructed" by social inventors. There was a caveat. Social inventors face threats that other inventors can ignore. Inventors of new machines or medicines need to experiment, and many of their experiments fail. The public, though, knows nothing of the failures—only the glowing final success. The failures of social inventors, however, are public, opening their authors to ridicule. Nevertheless, insights for "constructive democracy" can come only from trial and error, from an experimental method that must risk publicly ridiculed failures.

Of course the trials must rest on some prior likelihood of success. So where does this prior likelihood of success come from?

It comes from ideas. For a case study of this relation of ideas to social innovation or "constructive democracy," John R. turned to Horace Greeley.

He summarized Greeley's life, noting how Greeley experienced "a struggle through all the economic oppressions of his time." He was born on a farm in 1811. When he was eight, during the panic of 1819, his father lost the farm and spent the rest of his life as a dawn-to-dusk laborer barely making a living, moving periodically to avoid the debtors' prison. As a teen, Horace Greeley apprenticed himself to a printer and eventually, after many adventures, he became editor of the *New York Tribune*. Under his editorship, the *Tribune* became the largest and most influential newspaper in the nation earning John R.'s praise as "the first and only great vehicle this country has known for the ideas and experiments of constructive democracy."

Greeley was a man of many causes. He opposed slavery and capital punishment. He was a vegetarian. He helped found the Republican Party. His London correspondent was Karl Marx. But John R. concentrated on only two sets of Greeley's ideas.

The first set sprang from the American transcendentalist movement and from the French philosopher Charles Fourier. Greeley attached himself to the transcendentalist movement early in life. He became a Unitarian. He helped Henry David Thoreau and other transcendentalists publish their books. And, it was as a transcendentalist that Horace Greeley supported Brook farm, Fourier communities, and other utopian communities. It was not so much the core transcendentalist emphasis on intuition that led to Brook farm, but supplementary beliefs in the unity of mankind, in persuasion, and in cooperation—and distress at the devastating side effects of a capitalist depression from 1837 to 1842. The founders of Brook farm thought that there had to be a better way to organize economic activity. So they created an example of organization based on cooperation. The settlements based on principles developed by Charles Fourier had the same objective. They became failed experiments in collective action.

The second set of ideas that Greeley supported came from the labor movement and its apologists. This set of ideas, expounded in the debates at first convention of the National Labor Union and propounded in the various labor journals of the time, connected surplus labor with the monopoly of land speculators.

The solution, free land, had a long intellectual tradition based on the assumption of a natural right to land—a limited right for each person because one person's right to land could not imply a denial of another person's right. A grant of 160 acres seemed about right. The state could grant 160 acres to anyone who applied, with the stipulation that the grantee develop the land. When a New York Congressman died, Greeley was appointed in his place. Greeley introduced a homestead act that did just that. It went nowhere at the time. During his three months in Congress Greeley also alienated many fellow Congressmen by writing about their corruption in the *Tribune*, but he made one friend, an Illinois Congressman named Abraham Lincoln. Twenty years later, on May 20, 1862, Abraham Lincoln signed the Homestead Act, a successful experiment in "constructive democracy."

Greeley also supported the ten-hour day. At first, he opposed any government regulation because he assumed that once employers saw the benefits of a ten-hour day, they would voluntarily drop the dawn-to-dusk requirement. When they did not, Greeley supported a ten-hour law. When employers flouted the law, Greeley supported stronger enforcement. Perhaps because he changed his positions in response to evidence, Greeley served as an example of John R.'s "constructive democracy" based on ideas and experiments.

John R.'s reasoning was more complex and detailed. He reviewed at length the writings that justified the Homestead Acts. They assumed that there was a natural right to land. And even though he did not believe in the existence of any such right, John R. praised what he considered to be an erroneous belief in a natural right to land because it had inspired a successful experiment in "constructive democracy."

These experiments in "constructive democracy" were ended, in John R.'s view, by the aggressive insistence of slavery forces on the extension of their peculiar institution into new territories. This insistence provoked a reaction so intense from Greeley and other abolitionists that the slavery problem swept other social problems from their minds.

These were intellectual events unique to the United States, and John R., in collaboration with John Andrews, referred to their consequences in the introduction to volumes nine and ten.

> Certainly the observant American of to-day, whose span of life permits his memory to recall the events of the sixties, is not disturbed by the assertions of an increasing class struggle; for he remembers the time when the economic struggle was bitter and unrelieved by public opinion. And to the speculative reader or historian, who has followed the wave of humanitarianism and social reform through our volumes of the thirties and forties, and there seen it suddenly disappear in the slavery contest, the question must occur: what might have been the present condition of American democracy if there had been no race issue and its irrepressible conflict? For he could but have observed that, notwithstanding the absorption of Americans in the struggle for wealth, there was emerging in the forties a class of idealists and a spirit of progress more promising even than those of other nations.[24]

Commons and Andrews located this postwar period in their long- and short-run frameworks.

In long-run framework, they located the period in the "middleman stage," the stage in which the most powerful capitalists did not produce anything. They bought "the finished product" from "scattered manufacturers" and sold it to retailers. The middleman's power derived from "intangible capital"—goodwill, trade connections, and access to credit. Without this intangible capital—access to supply networks and credit provided by middlemen—farmers, manufacturers, and other producers could not get their products to market.

Within the short-run framework, Commons and Andrews followed the business cycle upswing associated with the Civil War and the issuance of greenbacks, the inflation, then, after the war, the subsequent deflation and recession when the Treasury began to retire the greenbacks, the reaction to the deflation and recession.

To illustrate resurgent concerns about the problems of capitalism, they chose the labor leader Ira Steward's crusade for the eight-hour day, Henry George's single tax, and the Greenback movement.

They praised the reasoning of Ira Steward, the president of the National Labor Union, for rejecting the wages-fund theory and the craft union tactic of reducing the number of workers in order to increase average wages. Steward assumed that wages depended in some sense on production and on the accepted customary standard of life. He reasoned that if workers could get the eight-hour day, their customary standards of life would rise, and consequently wages would follow. So he initiated the first eight-hour day campaign in the United States.

Steward and Henry George, continued Commons and Andrews, were both thinkers "with one idea." They were complementary, not contradictory. "Indeed, modern economics, with its 'diminishing increments,' its 'marginal laborers,' and its 'marginal uses of land,' is endeavoring more or less to reconcile them."[25]

Commons and Andrews spent considerable time on the Greenback Party. They criticized the logic of its proponents and they emphasized its uniqueness by comparing it to the European schemes of Marx, Proudhon, Lassalle, and Louis Blanc.[26] The Greenback movement, of course, reflected conditions unique to the United States: the predominance of small farmers and the effects of the postwar deflation.

Thus ended, in these introductions with their compressed reasoning, the only "interpretive history" that John R. and his students would produce for eight long years. They would eventually return to it, but for many years, other priorities—the needs of the department, the NCF municipal utility study, the American Association for Labor Legislation—would force delays in the completion of the interpretive history.

Notes

1. John Bascom, the president when Van Hise and La Follette were students, originated this idea. See Merle Curti and Vernon Carstensen, *The University of Wisconsin: A History 1848–1925*, vol.2 (Madison: University of Wisconsin Press, 1949), 549–50, see also 11–13, 20–23, 87, Commons, *Myself*, 9.
2. Harold L. Miller, "The American Bureau of Industrial Research and the Origins of the 'Wisconsin School' of Labor History," *Labor History* 25 (Spring 1984): 173.
3. Ibid., 187. See also Rader, *The Academic Mind and Reform*, 166–70. This account of the ABIR depends heavily on Miller in many respects, only some of which permit precise references.
4. Commons, *Myself*, 134, Miller, "The American Bureau," 175–79.
5. John Andrews, *American Bureau of Industrial Research Leaflet no.3* (Madison, WI: ABIR, 1907); *John R Commons Papers* (Madison: State Historical Society of Wisconsin, 1982) microfilm; reel 1, frame 170.
6. The communication between John R. and his sister is extensive. Commons *Papers*, microfilm, reel 1 frame 43 and frame 67.
7. Miller, "The American Bureau of Industrial Research," 174.
8. Ely to Commons January 1, 1906, Richard T. Ely Papers, Wisconsin Historical Society Archives, Madison, Box 32, folder7.
9. Miller, "The American Bureau," 179–84. Miller examines the disagreements in detail. In most cases, the accusations hurled back and forth were baseless. The founding of the American Association for Labor Legislation will be covered in chapter 10.
10. The agreement was more detailed, with the specifics spelled out in a memo of understanding dated April 8, 1909, in a letter to V. Everit Macy, the secretary of the ABIR and copied to John R.: Ely to Macy December 8, 1909, Commons Papers microfilm; Reel 1, frames 804–10.
11. John R. Commons, Ulrich B. Phillips, E.A. Gilmore, H.L. Sumner and J.B. Andrews, *A Documentary History of American Industrial Society.* 10 vols. (Cleveland, OH: Arthur H. Clark Co., 1910–1911). All volumes are available at www.hathitrust.org.
12. Gilmore of Wisconsin's Law School became Governor General of the Philippines from 1922 to 1930, and later president of the University of Iowa. He also offered legal advice for John R.'s worker compensation and public utility laws.
13. John R. Commons, "American Shoemakers 1648–1895, A Sketch of Industrial Evolution," *Quarterly Journal of Economics* 34 (November 1909): 39–83. Commons et al., *A Documentary History*, vol.3, 18–58.
14. Ibid., 28.
15. Ibid., 24–25.
16. Ibid., 30–39.
17. Ibid., 52.
18. Ibid., 54–55.
19. Ibid., 56.
20. John R. Commons and Helen L. Sumner, "Introduction to Volumes 5 and 6," in Ibid., vol.5, 20.
21. Ibid., 17–20.

22. John R. Commons, "Introduction to Volumes 7 and 8," in Ibid., vol.7, 20.
23. Ibid, 23.
24. John R. Commons and John B. Andrews, "Introduction to Volumes 9 and 10," in ibid., vol.9, 19.
25. Ibid., 28–29.
26. Ibid., 33.

10

Multitasking

I came to Wisconsin in 1904 to write a history of labor in the United States. My above mentioned work with the legislatures in 1905 and 1907 was outside this field—Myself

The "interpretive history" was fated to fall behind because both John R. and Ely had higher priorities. For Ely, there was the department; and there was his search for an organization that would do what he had wanted the American Economic Association to do. For John R., there were relationships and intellectual issues remaining from his "five big years." So between 1904 and 1910 when they were working on the documentary history, John R. went on the disputed trip to investigate municipal utilities; they both participated in the founding of the American Association for Labor Legislation; they worked in the department; John R. worked on an early social science study of the city of Pittsburgh—the Pittsburgh Survey; and he published his worst book.

Ely had frowned on John R.'s municipal utility junket partly because it would draw him away from the department as well as from the "interpretive history," but partly also because Ely really believed that the role of an academic in social reform should be limited to research and publication. John R. did not agree, and so he went.

The Municipal Utility Study

The disputed junket was part of an NCF effort to inform debates raging at the time— about ownership and operation of municipal utilities such as waterworks, street car lines, and gas works. Private corporations owned and operated most utilities, but some cities ran their own. Publicity about corporate misbehavior generated arguments for municipal ownership. Publicity about political corruption generated demands for private ownership. Debates raged on the streets, in the press, and on the college debate circuit. Each side battled with anecdotes, some true, some urban legends. Neither side could assemble a strong argument because neither had access to accurate information.[1]

Seeking ways to inform the debates, Ralph Easley and the NCF leaders, in October, 1905, organized a one-hundred-member Commission of Public Ownership of Public Utilities. That commission chose a smaller investigating subcommittee to collect and analyze data and to make recommendations. Half of its members were to visit cities in the United States and half to visit cities in England. John R. was in the half that went to England, and on May 6, 1906, he boarded the steamer *Cortania* for England.

To insure "objectivity," the NCF assigned two committee members to each issue, one for each side of the debate. John R. and James W. Sullivan were to investigate issues of labor and politics as they related to public utility ownership. Sullivan, the conservative editor of *The Clothing Trades Bulletin*, had been an official in New York City's typographical union.

After their return from England, John R. and Sullivan worked happily together on a joint report.[2] But they disagreed on the basic issue. John R. supported municipal ownership and operation, Sullivan insisted forcibly on private ownership.[3] They wrote separate reports which they had agreed to exchange before either was published. John R. received Sullivan's report, but Sullivan never received John R.'s.[4] In his report John R. had criticized some of Sullivan's statements, but Sullivan had no way to respond before both reports were published. Infuriated, the old union leader dashed off an angry pamphlet attacking John R.'s professionalism and ethics.[5] The attack stung. Feeling threatened and guilty, John R. rushed back to Madison where Nell rescued his ego. "I met my wife at the door, exclaiming to her that all was over, that I was ruined. As soon as I could tell her what had happened, she replied merely that I had forgotten. She did not know exactly what I had forgotten, but she went through all of my correspondence, made out her memoranda, and packed it in a suitcase for me to take to the New York headquarters to ask for an investigation by the Civic Federation."[6] The investigation revealed that the coordinator's clerk had neglected to forward John R.'s article to Sullivan. John R. was relieved; Sullivan was not appeased. (Copies of John R.'s apology and of Sullivan's response are in the Library of Congress copy of Sullivan's pamphlet.) In spite of John R.'s fears, the episode had no effect on his reputation.

The commission's final three-volume report, issued in August 1907, recommended municipal ownership of utilities that affected the public health—such as water works and sewerage. It allowed, but did not dictate, private ownership of utilities unrelated to public health. Doubts about public ownership rested on evidence of corruption and inefficiency in American cities. Commission members had witnessed efficient operation of publicly owned utilities in England, but they attributed this efficiency to a strict separation of utility management from political interference. Such a separation would have been impossible for most American cities at that time. To prevent collusion between city officials and utility managers, the commission recommended state regulation of utilities, and to insure uniformity of state regulations, the NCF developed a model bill. Later, John R. would begin with that model bill when the governor asked him to write Wisconsin's public utility law.

As a result of his experience with this "collective activity," John R. developed a public utility course which he taught for a year or two before turning it over to one of his best students, Martin Glaeser. So, one could argue that John R.'s junket was consistent with Ely's priorities. And one could argue on stronger grounds that Ely's work for the American Association for Labor Legislation (AALL) was consistent with John R.'s priorities.

The American Association for Labor Legislation

Ely's role in the founding of the AALL resulted from his affiliation with the "new economists" (now a bit older). One of those "new economists," Dr. Adna Weber of the United States Department of Labor, in October, 1905, sent a letter to Ely and others calling for a meeting at the December convention of the American Economic Association. Weber wanted to create a branch of the International Association for Labor Legislation (IALL) which had been founded in Paris in 1900. At the December meeting five people were appointed to organize the new association. The five—Clinton Rogers Woodruff, Henry W. Farnam, Henry R. Seager, and Richard T. Ely—met on February 15, 1906, in Madison and organized the AALL with Richard T. Ely as president, Adna Weber as secretary, and Isaac N. Seligman as treasurer.[7]

The AALL would become a bit too aggressive for Ely's tastes, but it would do what the American Economic Association and the American Institute of Christian Sociology had not done. The AALL would foster the type of "scientific" inquiry that Ely considered essential for any permanent solutions to the social problems of the American economy.[8] Ironically, Ely's interest in the organization would wane, and, in spite of his complaints, John R.'s interest would grow over the years, partly because he was less opposed than Ely to the AALL's activism, and partly because his student John Andrews became its executive secretary.

When Adna Weber resigned as secretary, Ely persuaded John R. to replace him. John R. delegated two students—John Andrews and Irene Osgood— "to do all the work." Andrews married Osgood. (John R. prided himself on his cupid role with graduate students.)[9] In 1909, Henry Farnam, another German educated economist, with Mayflower ancestors, and the wealthy heir of a railroad fortune, offered Andrews a salary of $5,000 to come to New York as permanent executive secretary of the AALL. Andrews came and immediately completed a path-breaking study of phosphorus poisoning in the match industry. Match industry executives had claimed that their sanitary policies protected workers from the harmful effects of white phosphorus. Andrews documented hundreds of cases of "Phossy jaw" and other phosphorus-related diseases. With the help of AALL lawyers, he wrote a law that imposed a prohibitive tax on phosphorus matches, convinced John J. Esch, a Wisconsin Congressman, to propose the law, and lobbied it through Congress—even bringing a "Phossy jaw" victim into a congressional hearing.[10]

For the next thirty years, the lives of John B. and Irene Osgood Andrews would be the life of the AALL. In discussions at its annual meetings, in informal communications, and in its journal, the *American Labor Legislation Review*, the AALL would create the intellectual basis for almost every social reform that became law—from its founding right through the New Deal.[11]

The Department, The Bargaining Theory, and the Team

In addition to complaining about John R.'s municipal utility Junket, Ely had complained that John R. was not devoting enough energy to the department. And the department was Ely's highest priority. With open corruption and incompetence rampant at every level of government, Richard T. Ely wanted his department to do for civil society what West Point was doing for the military.[12] He wanted interdisciplinary research centered on the social problems of the day; he wanted the results of that research made public; and he wanted to produce students who would bring competence and integrity to all levels of government.

With Andrews and Osgood running the AALL from his office, John R. could increase his attention to Ely's department—teaching classes, participating in the labor seminar, and supporting the initiatives of other department members, including the initiatives of Thomas Sewall Adams.

Adams had specialized in taxes at Johns Hopkins, and he is best known as the architect of President Wilson's progressive income tax. But, at Wisconsin, Adams made a pedagogical contribution to the department. He originated the problems–solutions method of teaching economics and statistics, and he standardized the curriculum. John R. would later write of Adams that: "He was the first to put our teaching of labor, taxation, and statistics on a sound and thrilling basis to which our economics department always looks back for its standards."[13]

In 1905, Adams and Helen Sumner published a book on labor problems that would remain the standard labor problems text well into the 1920s.[14] In the first part of the book they described "evils," and in the second part, "remedies." In his review, Henry Seager of Columbia praised the book for filling a need in the undergraduate curriculum, but he faulted it for dividing "evils" from "solutions," and for mixing them together in its actual discussions.[15] He also criticized the book for an absence of theory. Paul McNulty, though, found a bargaining theory of wages in the book, with the actual wage landing between a lower bound: "determined by the [laborer's] standard of life of his time and trade," and the upper bound by "the net value which the laborer is capable of adding to the output of the establishment." They added that in times of unemployment the lower bound could fall.[16]

John R. edited a book of readings to go with the text.[17] This book would also go through many editions.

And, of course, John R. taught classes—during second semesters until 1908—then during both semesters. The magic that had drawn undergraduates to his classes at Syracuse now seemed reserved for graduate students. Van Hise required all faculty members to teach undergraduates. But most undergraduate classes were held in large lecture halls with up to a hundred students. John R., small, soft-spoken, and disorganized, did not do well there. Nevertheless, he developed strong personal relationships with a number of undergraduates.

It was the practice at Wisconsin for teachers to recruit graduate assistants from the most promising graduating seniors. John R. seems to have recruited some of the more promising. Many became members of what might be called John R.'s "team." Like John R., they "took the side of workers," and they kept in touch with him and with each other in one way or another throughout their professional lives. In addition to Helen Sumner and John Andrews, at least four other students in these first years joined the "Commons team": William Leiserson, John A. Fitch, Selig Perlman, and David Saposs.

William (Billy) Leiserson was born in April 1883 in Revel (now Tallinn), Estonia. His father Mendel had been active in the underground opposition to the Czar and had planned to bring the family to America, but Mendel had disappeared, and his wife Sarah, after trying to support the little family as a peddler, and escaping from a harrowing time in a forced labor battalion, had managed to bring her four children to New York's East Side. By day, the Leisersons worked in the garment industry. By night, the children studied at the Cooper Union. Billy had attended a lecture there by John R. during John R.'s exile years, and when he learned that John R. was going to Wisconsin, Billy decided to follow him. The Madison registrar, an obstacle at first because Billy did not have a high school diploma, was no match for lower East Side chutzpah, and Billy Leiserson enrolled as a freshman in the same year that John R. arrived. John A Fitch grew up on a farm in South Dakota, graduated from Yankton College in 1904, and after a brief stint teaching high school came to Wisconsin for graduate study.

Another promising student came by the way of William English Walling, the journalist with whom John R. had planned to write an easy-to-read summary of US Industrial Commission reports.[18] In 1906 Walling and the socialist poet Anna Strunski had decided to marry in Europe, and Anna had hired a seamstress to create a wardrobe. The seamstress told Anna about her nephew in Italy. Upon arrival, they looked the boy up—Selig Perlman, a precocious teenager from Bialystok, Poland. Barred as a Jew from local universities, Perlman had gone to Italy for an education. An ardent Menshevik at the time, Perlman had read *Das Kapital* in the original German. William and Anna, delighted to find such a source on Marx, spent long hours with him. Walling eventually hired Perlman and brought him to New York City, but Perlman grew bored there. So Walling sent him to Wisconsin, and Selig Perlman graduated with a bachelors' degree in 1910.

David Saposs was born to Isaak and Shima Saposnik in Kiev where Isaak was a peddler. When David was five, Isaak and Shima came to Milwaukee and changed their name to Saposs. They were too poor to support David through school so he left in the fifth grade for a job in a brewery. In 1906, at the age of twenty, he was elected shop steward of the brewery workers' local. A year later, he entered the university. He graduated in 1911. Even before he graduated, though, John R. seems to have recruited David for the labor history project.

John R.'s students exhibited an affection and loyalty so intense as to seem incomprehensible. His tiff with Ely showed that he could be difficult. He could also be judgmental, as when he wrote that of the three students he took with him on the Pittsburgh Survey only two "did the work." "The third was not interested."[19] Nevertheless, he developed lasting personal relationships with an incredible number of students.

David Saposs described a "shabby and ascetic appearance" . . . and a "reserved air [that] would be likely to discourage and even unintentionally repel those not aware that this forbidding exterior sheltered a sensitive genius who warmheartedly overflowed with inspiring ideas and sympathetic appreciation of the trials and tribulations of novitiates."[20]

One of his first students Theresa McMahon may not have been typical, but in 1958, interviewed in a nursing home, she recorded this memory. "Commons was a kindly, sweet, gentle sort of man, a man you just loved; he possessed a most attractive smile, was soft-spoken and looked as if he suffered from chronic ill-health."[21] Harold Groves, another student wrote that "As a teacher he had a profound influence on those with whom he worked, and he had a positive genius for team work with graduate students."[22]

Mark Perlman, Selig's son, painted a less flattering portrait. His father, he said, had a strained relationship with John R., though he admired him professionally. Mark Perlman depicted John R. as somewhat vindictive and a stern taskmaster with his graduate assistants. He also discerned traces of anti-Semitism in some of John R.'s remarks.[23] As evidence for the assumption of anti-Semitism, Mark Perlman cited *Races and Immigrants*[24] which will be discussed later in this chapter. On the other hand, there were redeeming aspects even in the Mark Perlman interview.

For example, when John R. learned that Selig was concerned for the safety of his parents in Bialystok, he doubled Selig's salary so that he could bring them to the United States.[25] In addition John R. worked on good terms with Leiserson, Saposs, and later with Elizabeth Brandeis and Wilbur Cohen—all Jewish students. When he was working with the USIC he had traveled and worked with the Jewish cloak-maker Abraham Bisno whom he praised highly. He would later write a glowing tribute to the Jewish labor leader, Samuel Gompers. It is hard to square all this with anti-Semitism.

Though it is hard to pin down precisely, there is enough evidence to support the belief that his wife Ella (Nell) was a source, not only of John R.'s psychological security, but also of the warm personal relationships that he developed with many students. Helen Sumner often sent respects "to Mrs. Commons and Rachel." Ira Cross, who studied as an undergraduate at Madison and went to Stanford for graduate school, addressed letters to "Momma and Poppa Commons." Mark Perlman, Selig Perlman's son, commented, perhaps with some exaggeration that "actually my father's partisan really was not Commons, but someone else . . . it was Mrs. Commons."

Finally, of course, the way that John R. involved students in his projects generated untypical student–teacher relationships—beginning with Helen Sumner and John Andrews in the history project. Edwin Witte wrote that he did not get his ideas "from what Commons said in class or from his writings, but from working with him on the practical problems in which he was interested." Witte described him as "ever modest and always giving credit to his students even for ideas which really came from him, he inspired his students to work on the practical problems assigned to them with a devotion and intensity they did not develop in any other courses."[26]

The Pittsburgh Survey

The Pittsburgh Survey offers a case study of students "working with him on practical problems."

The survey's impetus came in March 1906, when Mrs. Alice Montgomery, the chief probation officer of the Allegheny Juvenile Court, read an article in the magazine *Charities and Commons* about "Neglected Neighborhoods in the Alleys, Shacks, and Tenements of our Nation's Capital."[27] In a letter to the magazine's editor, Paul U. Kellogg, Mrs. Montgomery wrote that conditions in Pittsburgh were just as bad as those in Washington, and she asked him to come and see. Kellogg came, saw, recruited an advisory committee, and raised funds for a study.[28]

Kellogg asked John R. to work on the survey; John R. agreed, but limited his work to summer vacations. He took three students with him. Following his practice of not naming people he disliked, he named only two: William Leiserson and John A. Fitch. The unnamed student, John R. claimed "was not interested" and the other two "did the work." He told Leiserson and Fitch to spend a month watching him interview people. Then he sent them out on their own. "We three ate and lived together, reviewing their own and my interviews. We arranged a scheme of 4×6 cards in triplicate, one to go to the Russell Sage Foundation, one to me and one kept by the interviewer."[29]

Their data on wage rates was published in the Survey volume titled *Wage-Earning Pittsburgh*.[30] But John R. seemed less impressed by his own work than by that of two others: Crystal Eastman and Florence

Kelley. Eastman investigated industrial health and Kelley, factory inspection.[31] Kelley was responsible for an experience that burned itself so deeply into John R.'s consciousness that he wrote about it twice.

She told him that, after the workers lost their union, they were subjected to twenty-four hour shifts in the mills. John R. did not believe her. So one night, he persuaded a former strike-leader to spirit him into the steel mill. And he found men working twenty-four-hour shifts. "One of them was a heater, who worked with blistered face and arms, and against a furnace that reminded me of hell, for twelve hours a day and twenty-four hours every other Sunday when the day and night shifts changed. He had come on that Sunday morning at about seven o'clock; it was now eleven o'clock at night and he had another eight hours to go."[32]

This demonstration of the raw management power over unorganized workers strengthened John R.'s support for unions.

The Pittsburgh experience affected his student John Fitch in another way. Fitch remained in Pittsburgh. John R. described Fitch's conversion to the labor side. "Fitch was from the prairies of South Dakota and thought that labor leaders had the horns which he had known in action on the farm. He was surprised to find out that the principal labor leader was a Sunday school superintendent. Others were Christian gentlemen. He remained in Pittsburgh for a year, and the Russell Sage Foundation published his book on *The Steel Workers.*"[33] Paul Kellogg renamed his magazine *The Survey* and hired Fitch as an associate editor.

Races and Immigrants

Races and Immigrants, published in 1905, was an edited collection of articles that John R. had written earlier for the Chautauqua Institute. It addressed the problems for American society created by new entrants unaccustomed to the demands of citizenship in a representative democracy. Commons based much of his treatment on ideas about race that were prominent at the turn of the century, but that have since been discredited. So the book is out of date. It plays no role in the development of Commons's thought, and it could be neglected but for the fact that its stereotypes and positions repulsive to modern readers made it a happy hunting ground for writers interested in exercising what E.P. Thompson has called "the enormous condescension of posterity"[34] So, it becomes necessary to show why writers who conduct such exercises with this book overstate their case by passing over Commons's criticisms of conventional wisdom and by ignoring policy proposals inconsistent with the positions that these writers ascribe to him. Two examples illustrate these points: his critique of conventional wisdom is illustrated by his treatment of Francis Walker's "race suicide" thesis, and his policy prescriptions that contradict positions attributed to him are illustrated in his chapter on "The Negro."

Walker's thesis, which he had proposed in 1890 and which had, by 1900, become an article of faith among America's immigration opponents, stated that immigrants from Southern and Eastern Europe were the cause of declining birth rates in America's preexisting population. Citizens descended from Anglo-Saxon and Scotch Irish colonists were committing "race suicide" because they were unwilling to bring children into a world where they would be condemned to compete with immigrants from Southern and Eastern Europe and to live with their revolting life styles.[35]

In *Races and Immigrants*, John R. demolished Walker's thesis.[36] American birth rates did decline as immigration increased, but increasing immigration did not cause the decline which was associated rather with increasing incomes and urbanization. Increasing incomes raised living standards, and people took steps to control family size in order to preserve and pass on to their children these higher standards of living. Urbanization affected birth rates because farm children were assets while city children were liabilities. So as incomes and urbanization increased, birth rates declined. So John R., though he kept the term "race suicide," refuted the conventional wisdom of the Walker thesis.

On the other hand, in his chapter "The Negro," John R. followed, for some pages, turn-of-the-century conventional wisdom. He repeated the now discredited African history story: that tropical climates resulted in genetically indolent races, and he repeated the equally discredited Southern narrative of the reconstruction era: that African Americans uneducated and unprepared for government had created chaos in Southern state governments until whites regained control by "intimidation, murder, ballot-box 'stuffing' and false counting"; and that Southerners kept control by literacy tests "with such adroit exceptions that white illiterates may vote but Negroes whether literate or illiterate are excluded from voting."[37]

But, then, John R. departed sharply from the contemporary consensus in a way that was completely overlooked by Ramstad and Starkey, intent as they were on depicting him as a raving racist.[38] He condemned the Southern disenfranchisement of African Americans. He made the case for a Northern intervention to undo that disenfranchisement. By depriving blacks of the right to vote, Southern whites had gained undue influence in national elections because African Americans are counted as citizens when seats are apportioned for the House of Representatives. Thus Southern white votes counted more than Northern votes.

In place of the Southern literacy test that excluded African Americans, John R. proposed a rational education test administered in the same way to whites and blacks and added that the state must make "an honest and diligent effort to equip every man to pass the test." And, by noting that the former slave states were spending "$2.21 per child for educating Negroes, and $4.92 per child for educating whites," he implied that Southern states were not making that effort.[39] So work must begin, he implied, by spending enough on education to qualify Negroes to vote and to fulfill the responsibilities of citizenship. Commons's recommendation implied that he considered African Americans capable of learning the three qualities that he considered necessary for citizenship in a democracy: intelligence or the ability to understand and discuss issues of public import; manliness, the old Roman virtue, or assertiveness; and the ability to cooperate—thus, he did not assume that they were genetically incapable of acquiring these qualities as Ramstad and Starkey implied. After describing, from the white point of view, the assumed technical backwardness of African Americans, he continued "With the more recent developments of Hampton and Tuskegee and their emphasis on manual training and property accumulation, it is to be expected that these basic qualities of intelligence and independence will receive practical and direct encouragement."[40]

When he looked for evidence that African Americans could cooperate, organize, and participate in democratically governed organizations, he found a "most hopeful indication of progress for the Negroes is the large number of voluntary religious, beneficial, and insurance societies whose membership is limited to those of their own color."[41]

Having sketched the nature of the education that he considered necessary, he insisted that African Americans should be allowed to vote. Many were already well enough educated to exercise the rights and duties of citizenship. "To exclude such individuals from suffrage is to shut the door of hope to all."

He urged opening higher education to African Americans to educate leaders that could represent African Americans in their struggle for equality. True leaders must be African Americans because only African Americans could understand their total situation and only African American leaders could inspire confidence. "Not a social class nor a struggling race can reach equality with other classes and races until its leaders can meet them on equal terms. It cannot depend on others, but must raise up leaders from its own ranks."[42] This implies the need for a broad education that prepares people for leadership. Commons would not have made these recommendations if he held the biased beliefs that Ramstad and Starkey ascribed to him.

Further, after again citing white worker and employer sentiments about the inefficiency of African Americans, Commons added that he had "made a comparison of two gas works in Southern cities—the one employing Negro stokers at 11 cents an hour, the other whites at 22 cents an hour." He found no differences between the two groups, either in efficiency or in the efforts.[43] So, though he repeated the conventional wisdom about the long-term genetic effect of the tropics, he could not have meant what Ramstad and Starkey claimed that he meant. Such a position would be inconsistent with his policy prescriptions.

Finally, Ramstad and Starkey admitted that they had searched through Commons's major works, including the labor volumes, for passages suggesting ill will toward Negroes, "and had been unable to find even 'one sign of enmity.'"[44] They found one passage that they interpreted as referring to African American inferiority. It was a passage about conflicts with white workers when African Americans were brought up as strike breakers. Whether that passage indicated such a belief can be debated. But the fact that they found so little further evidence for their position did not cause Ramstad and Starkey to reassess it.

And, one could argue that it was not the crazy science of the time that was to blame, but something else, a sort of Freudian blind spot, as John R.'s friend, William English Walling wrote in 1908. [We] "have closed our eyes to the whole awful menacing truth—that a large part of the white population of Lincoln's home, supported largely by the farmers and miners of neighboring towns, have initiated a permanent warfare on the Negro race ... Yet who realizes the seriousness of the situation, and what large and powerful body of citizens is ready to come to their aid?"[45] If John R. was to blame, it was not for what he wrote, but for what he, along with the entire white population, did not do, for his blind spot. That said, *Races and Immigrants* is a bad book, worth reading only for practitioners of the "enormous condescension of posterity."

The same cannot be said for the results of John R.'s initiation into the Wisconsin Idea.

Notes

1. Christopher Cyphers, *The National Civic Federation 1900–1915 and the Making of a New Liberalism* (Westport, CT: Praeger 2002), 127–35. This treatment depends heavily on Cyphers in ways that cannot be fully documented.

2. John R. Commons and James W. Sullivan, "Labor and Politics," in *Municipal and Private Ownership of Public Utilities: Report of the National Civic Federation*, vol.2 (New York: National Civic Federation, 1907), 1–112.

3. Cyphers, *National Civic Federation*, 140.

4. James W. Sullivan, "Labor," in *Municipal and Private Ownership of Public Utilities*, vol.1, 60–87, John R. Commons, "Labor and Politics," in *Municipal and Private Ownership of Public Utilities*, vol.1, 88–112.

5. Sullivan, *Municipal and Private Operation of Public Utilities, Relative to the Report of the National Civic Federation Commission on Public Ownership and Operation* (New York: Bible House, 1908).

6. Commons, *Myself*, 119.

7. American Association for Labor Legislation, *Proceedings of the Second Annual Meeting: Madison Wisconsin, December 30–31, 1907* (Madison: University of Wisconsin, 1908), 3, Rader, *The Academic Mind and Reform*, 168.

8. John R. and Ely revealed their different assumptions about the proper role of research in public policy creation when they responded differently to a change in the AALL's constitution. The constitution originally listed three objectives. – "(1) To serve as the American branch of the International Association for Labor Legislation, the aims of which are stated in the appended Article of its Statutes.— (2) To promote the uniformity of labor legislation.— (3) To encourage the study of labor legislation." (American Association for Labor Legislation, *Proceedings of the First Annual Meeting December 29–30, Madison, Wisconsin* (Madison: University of Wisconsin, April, 1908), 6.
   In 1911, a phrase was added so that the third objective became "To encourage the study of labor legislation with a view to promoting desirable labor legislation" (*American Labor Legislation Review*, 2 (1912), Commons and Ely both voted against the amendment, but Ely withdrew from the organization while Commons remained.

9. Commons, *Myself*, 138–39.

10. Alton R. Lee, "The Eradication of Phossy Jaw: A Unique Development of Federal Police Power," *The Historian* 29 (November, 1966): 1–21. John Dennis Chasse, "The American Association for Labor Legislation: An Episode in Institutionalist Policy Analysis," *Journal of Economic Issues* (September, 1991): 799–828.

11. Clarke A. Chambers, *Seedtime of Reform: American Social Service and Social Reform 1918–1933* (Minneapolis: University of Minnesota Press, 1963), David A. Moss, *Socializing Security: Progressive Era Economists and the Origins of American Social Policy* (Cambridge, MA: Harvard University Press, 1996).

12. Robert J. Lampman, ed., *Economists at Wisconsin 1892–1992* (Madison, WI: Board of Regents of the University of Wisconsin System 1993), 11.

13. Cited in Lampman, *Economists at Wisconsin*, 25.

14. Thomas Sewall Adams, Helen L. Sumner, and Richard T. Ely. *Labor Problems: A Textbook*, 241–42, Paul McNulty, *The Origins and Development of Labor Economics: A Chapter in the History of Social Thought* (Cambridge, MA: MIT Press, 1980), 157.

15. Henry R. Seager, "*Labor Problems: A Text-Book* by Thomas Sewall Adams and Helen L. Sumner," *Political Science Quarterly* 20 (September, 1905): 562–65.

16. Thomas Sewall Adams. Helen L. Sumner, and Richard T. Ely, *Labor Problems: A Textbook* (New York and London: Macmillan, 1905), 241–42, see also McNulty, *The Origins and Development*, 156.

17. John R. Commons, *Trade Unionism and Labor Problems* (New York: Ginn & Company, 1905).

18. Leon Fink, "A Memoir of Selig Perlman and His Life at the University of Wisconsin: Based on an interview of Mark Perlman Conducted and Edited by Leon Fink," *Labor History* 32 (Fall 1991): 503–25. Time may have distorted some of Mark Perlman's memories. For example, he said that both John R. and Frederick Jackson Turner offered his father assistantships in 1910. But Turner went to Harvard in 1910. He could not have offered Perlman an assistantship. There were other discrepancies with recorded facts. His description of Commons's personality clashes with every other description I have been able to find.

19. Commons, *Myself*, 143.

20. David Saposs, "The Wisconsin Heritage and the Study of Labor Works and Deeds of John R. Commons" an address at the Selig Perlman Memorial Dinner on November 20, 1959," cited in Harter, *John R. Commons, His Assault on Laissez-Faire*, 6.

21. Theresa McMahon, "MY Story," in *Lone Voyagers*, ed. Geraldine Joncich Clifford (New York: The Feminist Press at the City University of New York, 1989), 238–80.

22. Groves to Charles M. Sullivan, February 11, 1957, Harold M. Groves Papers, Wisconsin Historical Society, Archives, Box 3, folder16.

23. Fink, "A Memoir of Selig Perlman," 513.

24. John R. Commons, *Races and Immigrants in America*, 2d ed. (1920: reprint. New York: Augustus M. Kelley, 1967).

25. Fink, "A Memoir of Selig Perlman," 513, Commons, *Myself*, 81. Mark Perlman's description of Commons's personality conflicts with every other description that I have been able to find. It is also inconsistent with the fact that so many students expressed their affection for him. One explanation may lie in the fact that Mark Perlman was born in 1923. He was only seven when Commons retired. The interview was in 1990. There may have been distortions in memory.

26. Edwin Witte, "Institutional Economics as Seen by an Institutional Economist," *Southern Economic Journal* 21 (October 1954): 131.

27. Clarke A. Chambers, *Paul U. Kellogg and the Survey: Voices for Social History and Social Justice* (Minneapolis: University of Minnesota Press, 1971), 33.

28. Ibid., 37.

29. Commons, *Myself*, 141.

30. John R. Commons and William Leiserson, "Wage-*Earners of Pittsburgh*" in *Wage-Earning Pittsburgh*, ed. Paul U. Kellogg (1914: reprint. New York: Arno Press, 1974), 113–88.

31. Crystal Eastman, *Work Accidents and the Law* (New York: Charities Publication Committee, 1910), Florence Kelley, "Factory Inspection in Pittsburgh, in *Wage-Earning Pittsburgh*, 190–216.

32. Commons, *Myself*, 144, *The Economics of Collective Action* (New York: Macmillan, 1950), 141. The Amalgamated Association of Iron and Steel Workers, a former union, had been crushed in 1892 during the Homestead lockout.

33. Commons, *Myself*, 141.

34. John R. Commons, *Races and Immigrants in America* 2d edition (1920; reprint, New York: Augustus M. Kelley, 1967); E.P. Thompson, *The Making of the English Working Class* (New York: Pantheon Press, 1963), 12.

35. Francis Amasa Walker, "Immigration and Degradation," *The Forum* 11 (August 1891): 634–44. In 1896, Walker added further reasons for restricting immigration in "Restriction of Immigration," *Atlantic Monthly* 77 (June 1896): 199–208.

36. Commons, *Races and Immigrants*, 199–208.

37. Ibid., 43–44.

38. Ibid., 44–45; Yngve Ramstad and James Starkey, "The Racial Theories of John R. Commons," in *Research in the History of Thought and Methodology*, vol. 15 (Greenwood, CN, 1995), 1–74.

39. Commons, *Races and Immigrants*, 45.

40. Ibid., 49.

41. Ibid., 50.

42. Ibid., 51–52.

43. Ibid., 139.

44. Ramstad and Starkey, "The Racial Theories of John R. Commons," 52; John. R. Commons, ed. *Trade Unionism and Labor Problems* (New York: Ginn & Co, 1905), 32.

45. William English Walling, "The Race War in the North," *The Independent* 65 (September, 1908): 529, 534. For Freudian blind spots see B. J. F. Lonergan, *Insight: A Study in Human Understanding* (New York: Harper & Row, 1978), 191–203.

11

The Wisconsin Idea

So it was when magazine writers wrote articles on 'a university governs a state.' I could never see it that way. I was never called in except by Progressives, and only when they wanted me. I never initiated anything—Myself

In 1905, John R. met the man who wrote the book about the "Wisconsin idea."[1] Historians have dismissed the Wisconsin idea—an oversold claim of academic influence on state policies.[2] But for Charles McCarthy, the man who wrote the book, it was the university's essence, grounded in history and essential for real democracy. McCarthy traced its roots to the Northwest Ordinance of 1787 which had called for creation of universities "to promote practical knowledge of benefit to citizens," to the Morrill Land-Grant Act of 1862 which had set aside land for universities to "promote the study of agriculture and the mechanical arts," and finally to a Wisconsin University tradition which had identified "the boundaries of the public university" with "the boundaries of the state."[3] For Charles McCarthy, the Wisconsin Idea was essential for democratic government, an intellectual check on the corrupting influence of big business.[4]

And if John R. was less enthusiastic about the "Wisconsin Idea," he still learned much from McCarthy—about the intricacies of constitutional law and about much else identified with McCarthy's unique personality, which was indeed unique.

Charles McCarthy

His parents John McCarthy and Katherine O'Shea, potato famine fugitives from County Kerry, had met and married in Brockton, MA, where Katherine ran a boarding house and John tended machines in a textile mill. Charles was born on June 29, 1873. His high school advisors channeled him into a terminal rather than a college prep program. But Charles McCarthy could run—faster than almost anybody in the state of

Massachusetts—and his speed drew the attention of Brown University's football coach who offered him an athletic scholarship. As Brown's star running back, McCarthy—at a weight of only 135 pounds—won All American nominations every year that he played. He also began—what seemed to him anyway—a lifelong friendship with the team's assistant manager, John D. Rockefeller, Jr. McCarthy's academic record was mediocre with the exception of history where he shone. His insightful papers surprised and impressed John Franklin Jameson, the eminent constitutional law historian. After graduation, McCarthy coached the University of Georgia football team for a year. Then Georgia cancelled football. McCarthy secured a loan from his friend Rockefeller, hopped a freight train, and made his way to Wisconsin where, with Jameson's glowing recommendation, he was accepted in the graduate school.

In 1901, McCarthy earned a PhD in constitutional history and political science with strong endorsements from Frederick Jackson Turner, Homer Haskins, and Paul Reinsch—but they hesitated to recommend McCarthy for a teaching position. They described him as "rough." What they meant is not clear. Gaelic was the first language of both parents, and McCarthy spoke with a strong Irish brogue. Moreover, a childhood bout with scarlet fever had left his throat permanently scarred, giving his voice a slight rasp. Mark Perlman said this about McCarthy: "His incapacity to speak English in other than an Irish brogue typed him, in the world of his time as 'low class.' His English improved but he never got the Irish out of it. I assure you that was a handicap in the better circles in Wisconsin."[5] Then, a job opened up that seemed made just for Charles McCarthy.

In 1902, the Wisconsin Free Library Association moved government documents from the capitol to the Wisconsin Historical Society's new building and advertised for someone to develop a library in the state capitol. McCarthy applied, got the job, and created something so new and useful that his Legislative Reference Library became a model, studied and copied by states across the country and finally by the Federal Government.[6]

McCarthy was concerned that laws often failed to attain the purposes for which they were written because they contained unintentional loopholes, or were unenforceable, or were unconstitutional. He organized the library to help legislators write laws that overcame these obstacles. He collected and catalogued all possible information on all previous bills and their histories, as well as on similar bills in other states. He collected and indexed newspaper clippings on all topics in which the legislators might be interested—making it possible to trace the legislative and popular history of any issue. When legislators asked his help, McCarthy assembled all information on the legislator's topic and assigned a trained assistant to help in the technical details of bill drafting. He kept lawyers on his staff to check bills for legal acceptability. McCarthy was always there to comment, and he loved talking. Since a large number of inexperienced legislators were elected with Wisconsin's progressive governors, they could not, without McCarthy, have made Wisconsin a leader in progressive legislation.

And so, in 1905, McCarthy piled resources on John R.'s desk and assigned an assistant to help him write Governor Robert La Follette's civil service bill. In 1907, McCarthy did it again to help John R. write a public utility bill for La Follette's successor, James O. ("Yim") Davidson. In each case, John R. learned something from McCarthy. But John R. learned most when he wrote the public utility bill. Without careful wording, that bill could have fallen into the trap of unconstitutionality. McCarthy gave John R. a room, piled his desk high with resources, and assigned M.S. Dudgeon of the library's legal staff to assist him.[7] Dudgeon introduced John R. to the constitutional pitfalls and urged him to consult a constitutional lawyer. John R. went first to a Wisconsin Supreme Court justice who sent him to Harry Butler who was—according to McCarthy's biographer—one of the country's outstanding constitutional lawyers.[8] Butler introduced John R. to the concept of reasonable value and to a string of Supreme Court cases, the "Granger cases," that dealt with the constitutionality of railroad and grain storage regulation. And McCarthy stayed involved. "Most of all his stubborn criticism of every detail in my work, his participation in our conferences, and his fertile suggestions forced me to the most careful self-criticism that I had ever known except during my apprenticeship with Easley."[9]

With all that help, John R. designed a law that fulfilled constitutional requirements for due process and reasonable valuation. Starting with the NCF model bill, John R. designed a law that created a commission, specified uniform accounting systems, and allowed corporations to substitute indeterminate permits for franchises.[10]

The law's success, though, mattered less to John R. than his introduction to the legal notion of reasonable value. That notion would percolate through his mind for the next ten years moving from law to economics and back again, and then it would emerge in a major work.

John R. wrote the utility law for governor James (Yim) Davidson, Wisconsin's first Norwegian governor who had succeeded La Follette after the latter became a senator. Described as "genial and easygoing," Davidson made peace with La Follette's Stalwart opponents, even as he continued La Follette's reform tradition—not enough to satisfy La Follette though.[11]

In 1910 La Follette supported Francis McGovern who became governor in 1911. As Milwaukee's crusading district attorney, McGovern had gained twenty-two convictions for corruption. Though a Republican, he had developed his progressive positions independently of La Follette in the Milwaukee Municipal League where he had worked with Victor Berger, the socialist newspaper publisher, and Emil Seidel, the socialist mayor. While La Follette represented farmland reformers, McGovern represented the urban working class. And McGovern's reforms surpassed anything accomplished by La Follette or Davidson. Arthur Altmeyer, one of John R.'s students and later "Mr. Social Security," marveled that "The sweep of legislation enacted in the 1911 legislature was 'literally breath-taking.'"[12]

And McGovern drew John R. most deeply into the "Wisconsin Idea"—though for legislation that originated before McGovern took office in 1910.

The Wisconsin Industrial Commission

Earlier, in 1909, the legislature had created a special committee to study workers' compensation.[13] Evidence for the unfairness of the existing system was overwhelming. An injured worker's only hope for redress lay in the courts where common law traditions had created powerful defenses for employers. If an employee was injured or died, the employer—or lawyers for the employer's insurance company—could argue that the employee willingly accepted the risk when hired, that the employee was negligent, or that a fellow worker, not the employer, was at fault. Crystal Eastman in her work for the Pittsburgh Survey had tracked 212 cases of worker death in Pennsylvania. Of those cases, only forty-eight families received more than a single year's wages, and in forty cases, the compensation was less than $500. Harry Weiss later cited similar statistics from other states.[14]

In 1910 while the Wisconsin legislature was collecting data on worker compensation in other countries, the New York State Court of Appeals struck down, as unconstitutional, New York's worker compensation law.[15] So the constitutional problem loomed large in

Wisconsin. McGovern highlighted the problem in his first address to the legislature.[16] Then he asked John R. for help.

John R. was already responsible for all his academic duties. In addition, Milwaukee's mayor had asked him for help; so he was spending every spare moment with Milwaukee's Bureau of Economy and Efficiency.[17]

Fortunately, he had a capable student assistant, Francis E. Bird, a graduate of Dartmouth University. He put Bird in charge of his labor problems class and assigned him a dissertation topic on the Belgian Superior Council of Labor as described in Hector Denis's *Histoire des Systémes économiques et socialistes.*[18] The administrative structure of the Superior Labor Council would form a pattern for the administrative structure that John R. would eventually propose for the Wisconsin Industrial Commission.

Bird divided the labor problems class into groups, each responsible for the labor laws of a different country. The class made charts of all these laws and hung the charts on the walls of a large lecture hall. John R. called the class "a miniature world-wide council of capital and labor."[19] In 1911, John R., Bird, McCarthy, and McGovern met in the reference library, and, after reviewing all of Wisconsin's labor laws "going back to 1867, they devised a general strategy."[20]

They gave the new law two parts: a safety regulation part and a worker compensation part. Each part had to pass two constitutionality tests: a reasonableness test and a due process test.

The New York decision increased the urgency of finding a way to pass the due process test: that is, to give a constitutional answer to this question: When is it permissible to take property from A and give it to B?[21] The Fifth and Fourteenth Amendments to the Constitution set down the requirements for a constitutional answer. The New York State Court of Appeals had ruled that New York's law took property from the employer and gave it to the injured employee without due process.

The legal concept of reasonableness posed another problem. Judges had always interpreted "reasonable" to mean "average" or "ordinary." This interpretation would prevent the issuance of regulations designed to improve workplace health or safety beyond average practices at the time. John R. gave the impression that at first the problem seemed insuperable, and he gave Bird credit for the solution. "After many conferences he [Bird] came forward with the definition that reasonableness should mean the *highest* degree of safety, health, wellbeing of employees, etc., that the nature of the industry or employment would *reasonably permit.*"[22]

"Reasonable" was thus redefined as the practice of the safest firms that could survive in competitive conditions. This was an empirical concept, and it implied a "ratchet" strategy for occupational safety and health. Safety inspectors could report on the practices of firms, and in their reports they could describe the practices of the safest surviving firms—firms above the average in their safety practices. These practices could be spread to all firms by regulations. But since some firms would do still better, their practices could be found empirically and applied again, and so forth.

The 1911 law combined responsibility for workers' compensation with factory inspection by dissolving all separate labor agencies and entrusting their duties to a single industrial commission. In place of specific regulations, the law simply laid down general goals of public health and safety and empowered the commission to issue specific rules that bound with the force of statutory law.[23] The structure of the Belgian Superior Labor Council became a pattern for the commission's administrative structure. There were three commissioners appointed by the governor with the advice and consent of the Senate. The commission's staff, hired and promoted on merit, was insulated from political interference by civil service regulations. To address the problem of reasonableness and due process, all new regulations would be developed in consultation with outside advisory boards whose members would be suggested by organizations representing groups affected by the regulations. Legally, the commission appointed the members of the advisory boards and the voluntary organizations suggested the names. But this was enough to assure that rules resulted from a process that considered all the facts from all interested points of view. To further satisfy the due process requirement and assure reasonableness, parties objecting to rules as unreasonable could present their cases before the commission. If still unsatisfied, they could appeal to the courts. But they could present in the court only information that they had first presented to the commission.[24]

To forestall the constitutional objection that the workers' compensation bill deprived employers of property without due process, the legislature made participation voluntary, but it made things difficult for firms that failed to "volunteer." It removed two of the common law defenses that employers had used to avoid legal liability for injuries to their employees. Employers could no longer argue that employees voluntarily assumed risk when they contracted for employment. They could no longer blame a fellow employee.

After the law was passed, McGovern appointed John R. as one of the three commissioners. The terms were staggered—at two, four, and six years. McGovern appointed John R. to the two-year term. Salaries were fixed at $5,000 per year.

John R. conducted the investigations that produced rules on workplace safety and health. He contacted interested organizations, assigned research topics to staff members, and organized meetings in which advisors developed rules to be issued by the commission. His notion of consulting "all interested parties" went beyond simple labor-management principles; he contacted experts, workers, and managers when contemplating a new rule. For example, he assembled both sawmill employees and sawmill managers when devising rules for buzz-saw safety.

In 1913, the legislature amended the workers' compensation act to make life even harder for employers who failed to "volunteer." Rather than asking employers to apply for membership, the law automatically enrolled all employers in the system. Employers who did not want to be covered were required to explicitly apply to leave the system. In addition, the legislature removed the last common law defense of contributory negligence. Employers, if sued by injured employees, could no longer avoid liability by claiming that an injury resulted from employee negligence. On February 1, 1913, insurance companies raised their liability premiums to the level of worker compensation premiums, and the number of employers "voluntarily" joining the system more than doubled.[25]

John R.'s two years ended in 1913, and McGovern offered to reappoint him to a six-year term, but John R. wanted to return to the university. "I gained a reputation for declining a six-year appointment at $5,000 and returning to an appointment of $3,500 at will of the University Regents. But my reputation was undeserved. I had approached my friend, Charles R. Crane [who] gave me $2,500 per year, $1,000 for myself and $1,500 for a secretary."[26] John R.'s departure ended for a long time his association with the Wisconsin Idea—none too soon for some.

As early as 1911, some newspapers had editorialized against the high taxes associated with participation of university professors in the state government. Some state officials joined the newspapers, accusing the university faculty of conspiring to take over the government and impose socialism. "We have hell in our legislative halls and hell in our university," complained one public official. A farm magazine, *The National Equity News* denounced John R. by name for his statements on unemployment and proposed that the state cease funding the university until farmers received a better deal.[27]

To make things worse, conflicts in the 1912 presidential primary carried over into mutually destructive battles between Wisconsin progressives.[28] The battles ruined McGovern's political career and set the stage for the election in 1914 of a Republican Stalwart, Emanuel Philipp.

Philipp had campaigned on a platform of "reining in" the university, firing McCarthy, and abolishing the Legislative Reference Service. McCarthy, however, turned on his Irish charm, and persuaded Philipp to break this campaign promise. A bill introduced in the legislature to abolish the Legislative Reference Service died a lonely death.[29] But the "Wisconsin Idea" was mothballed for a very long time.

Still, John R. returned to the university with benefits from his exposure to the Wisconsin Idea— a financial benefit, and more significant intangible benefits.

The financial benefit, the commissioner's salary of $5,000, enabled John R. and Nell to engage the architect Cora Tuttle to design a home on a hill outside of town, with a forty foot second-story porch looking out over the prairie onto Lake Mendota. John R. and Nell called it Ho-Chee-Ra, the Winnebago word for welcome. Ho-Chee-Ra would offer John R. a place of refuge where he and Nell could welcome students—especially for the Friday Night dinners.

The intangible benefits were more significant. He had learned much from Charles McCarthy and from the constitutional lawyers who introduced him to reasonable value and due process. And he had learned much "on the job," designing and administering laws as a commissioner of the Wisconsin Industrial Commission.

Labor and Administration

These intangible benefits were evident in his 1913 book, *Labor and Administration*—a collection of previously published articles. The book's first sentence defined two problems. "The history of labor laws and strikes has this in common to both—laws become dead letters; the victories of strikes are nibbled away."[30] There were articles on different topics, but most of them converged on these two problems.

The first—McCarthy's problem: ineffective laws—occupied the beginning and the end of the book. The second—John R.'s problem: threats to union effectiveness—occupied most of the middle.

To solve McCarthy's problem—to assure that laws do more than create abstract rights and empty ideals—John R. proposed "constructive research": "that sort of investigation that goes along with administration and is designed to improve it."[31] Unlike academic research which seeks truth with no concern for practical application, or journalistic research which exposes problems without exploring solutions, "constructive research" diagnoses problems, develops solutions, and measures results.

John R. found examples of "constructive research" in the cost accounting departments of the great trusts, in research laboratories, and in the agricultural experiment stations of the university's extension department.[32]

In the case of accidents and occupational diseases, "constructive research" "should tell us whether the damage to the employee is public in nature, requiring legislation, or only private, requiring exhortation. It should reveal the nature and cause of the injury, its cure and the practicability of prevention. It should lead to such administration of the law that those enjoined to obey it would respect and support it."[33]

John R. emphasized the importance of selecting the right staff and protecting its members by civil service status. Pay should be competitive with private sector salaries. Staff members should have a background that enables them to understand the practical difficulties of implementation. In the case of occupational safety and health, these would be people with experience as shop technicians or as insurance claims agents. Technical experts could be hired as temporary consultants when a specific problem demanded skills not possessed by the staff. "But the selection of proper staff is not enough to assure practicality."[34] To assure "practicality" and reasonableness, an advisory board appointed by outside organizations is necessary. By representing all affected interests, the members of these boards assure that the "constructive research" fulfills the conditions for reasonableness—considers all the facts from all relevant points of view.

This "constructive research" makes the commission an essential supplement for the traditional three branches of government. Designed for a static agricultural society, the three branches could not cope with the challenges of a rapidly changing capitalist society. Legislatures operate slowly, sending bills through committees and then debating them before they are passed. While the legislature is debating its dangers, a technology can become obsolete and be replaced by a new technology with different dangers. But, once a commission has been created, the legislature can create a general rule and empower the commission to make specific applications. With its research capabilities, the commission can investigate new technologies and respond quickly.

To assure reasonableness, the commission's decisions can be appealed, first to the entire commission and then to the courts. And in this way commissions supplement the judicial branch. Judges apply legal principles to cases. But to apply principles correctly, judges must understand the facts of the case. If lawyers fail to adequately inform judges about the facts, then judges fall back on "common knowledge" which is almost always inaccurate. The system of commissions and appeals can correct the problem of judicial ignorance. Plaintiffs can only offer information in court that was first offered to the commission, and the commission's "constructive research" becomes available to inform judges about the implications of technical details, making reasonable decisions more likely. "It requires that all of the facts be considered and weighed 'as may be just and right in each case.'"[35]

So John R.'s answer to one of the problems with which he had started the book—Charles McCarthy's problem: that "laws become dead letters"—began with "constructive research" and expanded to a discourse on reasonableness and the place of commissions in a representative democracy.

The second problem—that "victories of strikes are nibbled away" was especially urgent for John R. These were troubling times for the visions that John R. had shared with his friends on the staff of the United States Industrial Commission (USIC)—visions of organized employers and organized workers bargaining with each other in semi-legislative sessions.

The visions had made sense in 1900. Union membership had more than doubled in the four years from 1897 to 1901, from 440,000 to 1,058,000, and membership had almost doubled again to 2,077,000 in 1904.[36] So facts had supported the vision then.

But the facts had changed. Union membership had dropped in 1905 and had remained stagnant until 1909 when it dropped again, and it kept dropping for a reason.

Even before the USIC staff had assembled to write their final reports, J. Pierpont Morgan and Elbert S. Gary, the creators of US Steel, had decided to crush the remnants of the Amalgamated Iron Workers' Union.[37] In 1901, in Dayton, OH, a group of employers had organized an "open shop" campaign. Unionized firms had closed and reopened as "open shops" hiring only nonunion workers. In 1903, these same Dayton employers had organized a coup at the annual meeting of the National Association of Manufacturers (NAM) unseating founders who had supported collective bargaining. The original founders had organized the NAM to lobby Congress on trade issues. But the men who had displaced them used the NAM to convert the open shop campaign into a national crusade. In cities across the nation employers began closing union plants, reopening them, and forcing former employees to reapply for their old jobs without union protection.[38] Heavy expenditures on propaganda portrayed antiunion employers as patriotic Americans and unions as criminal organizations. The propaganda worked.[39] Unions lost public support. Large employers abandoned Ralph Easley's utopia of trade agreements and collective bargaining for the open shop movement, undermining the credibility not just of Easley's vision but of John R.'s.[40] For workers, the open shop campaign strengthened the case for a more radical unionism to battle this radical capitalist assault.[41]

John R. addressed the problem in two parts. One part dealt with the large trusts, the other with the smaller unionized industries.

Trusts, with their cost accounting and efficiency studies, were creating a class-conscious workforce ripe for unionization. But there were no successful unions in those industries because management had so many weapons. They could promote local union leaders into management positions, hire detectives to spy, and fire active union members. They could raise wages when a strike is imminent and cut them later. They could close a plant and reopen it as an open shop. "It does not seem possible under such conditions that organization will get a footing in the great consolidated industries."[42] John R. still considered the trade agreement the only path to a permanent and equitable industrial peace.[43] But the power of the trusts stymied him.

Though, he generally opposed direct union political action, he saw some hope in a labor party. Such a party could represent at most a third of the voting population, but it could increase its political effectiveness if it could recruit allies by appealing to a universal "instinct of justice." Recalling American and British history, John R. expressed hope that such a strategy might work. It would then be possible to undo legislation that imposed burdens on the working classes and propose new legislation that could lighten their burdens. "It is not merely blind economic evolution that provokes economic classes into existence. It is class legislation in the past."[44] "[T]he thing that is equally plain is the infinite capacity of stocks and bonds to absorb every gain from the efficiency of labor."[45] Corrective legislation might include an excise tax on firms with inhumane workplace policies.[46]

The strategies of surviving unions had resulted from a history of experimentation. Gains from strikes had proved temporary unless the union remained in existence and bargained with employers. So the preservation of the union was essential.[47]

And on this basis, John R. defended the closed shop which he carefully defined as an agreement requiring employers to hire only union workers while allowing anyone to join the union. He defended it as the only alternative available to workers for protecting strike winnings against the employer tactic of bringing in low-wage workers recruited in foreign countries and firing union workers.

He also anticipated a version of the "free rider argument." He dismissed the "sentimental" version: that nonunion workers benefit from the sacrifices made by union workers. Everybody benefits in some way from the efforts of others. But he affirmed the more forceful version.

> There are always selfish and short-sighted members in unions. If they see a non-unionist enjoying the same privileges with themselves without the expense of union dues, and especially if the foreman shows a preference for the non-unionist, they too demand exemption from union burdens. Thus the union disintegrates, and a cut in wages or a stretch of hours cannot be warded off. Experience is a hard teacher and has taught this lesson thoroughly. It is not a mistake that the persistent non-unionist in private employment should be looked upon generally as a menace.[48]

In a sense, the publication of *Labor* and *Administration* marked the end of an era in John R.'s life. It summarized positions reached by 1913 in his search for solutions to Henry George's problem. He seemed to believe that he could best continue as a university teacher. And there was much to do at the university, both in research and in teaching especially in the labor seminar which needed updating.

The research agenda included a book with John Andrews that would summarize information on labor legislation and social security. And, still, there was the "interpretive history"—the deadline for its completion now four years in the past. Ely was complaining about the Carnegie contract.[49] Collaborators on the Carnegie Labor project had rejected John R.'s plan to publish student dissertations as individual volumes in an interpretive history series. Any volumes financed by the Carnegie Foundation had to be published under John R.'s name.[50]

John R. had recruited six former students to work on the history— John B. Andrews, Helen Sumner, E.B. Mittelman, Henry Hoagland,

Selig Perlman, and David Saposs—but only two remained in Madison—Perlman and Saposs. The rest were scattered around the country.[51] As he wrapped up his work on the Industrial Commission, John R. was arranging to bring all six together in Madison for an intensive two-month summer session to work on coordination problems.

He planned to devote much of his labor problems seminar to a new type of labor organization: The International Workers of the World (IWW). To prepare for this, he had set up an appointment for an interview in Chicago with Vincent St. John, the IWW executive secretary.

In 1901, as president of the miner's local in Telluride, CO, St. John, at the age of twenty-five, had led a strike that won wage hikes for the miners and enemies for him. An attempt to frame him for murder had backfired when the person he was supposed to have murdered showed up alive.[52] A hired assassin had missed his heart but had hit St. John's right arm shattering the bone. St. John was elected executive secretary in Chicago on June 27, 1905, at the meeting that created the IWW and initiated the tragic history of the "Wobblies"—the history of some of the most colorful, persecuted, and misunderstood personalities in American labor history. They included Elizabeth Gurley Flynn, Big Bill Haywood, and the song writer Joe Hill. They included a Catholic priest in Texas, the Reverend Thomas Hagerty. To railroad envoys sent to order him to cease his support for Chicano track workers, Hagerty had responded: "Tell the people who sent you that I have a brace of Colts and can hit a dime at twenty paces."[53] His bishop was not amused. Hagerty wrote the IWW constitution and edited its magazine. Years later, some old Wobblies discovered Hagerty in a flophouse on Chicago's skid row eking out a bare existence by giving Spanish lessons. In 1915, Hill was executed by a firing squad in Utah. Haywood and Flynn would flee the country and die in Russia.

The IWW was merely the most organized response of workers disillusioned with the philosophy and strategy of Samuel Gompers and the American Federation of Labor, and the disillusionment was related to the inability of the AFL to effectively combat the onslaught of employers who rejected the vision that Jenks, Commons, and Durand had written into their reports for the USIC.

But the event that would drag John R. back into the fray was not IWW rhetoric but a conflict between traditional unions and one of the most active open shop agitators in the nation, Harrison Gray Otis, publisher of the *Los Angeles Times*. And so the "interpretive history" would be delayed again.

Notes

1. Commons, *Myself*, 107. Charles McCarthy, *The Wisconsin Idea* (New York: Macmillan, 1912).
2. Robert Nesbit, *Wisconsin: A History* (Madison: University of Wisconsin Press, 1973), 426–28.
3. Lampman, *Economists at Wisconsin*, 21.
4. McCarthy, *The Wisconsin Idea*, 2, 17, 26.
5. Leon Fink, "A Memoir of Selig Perlman and his Life at the University of Wisconsin: Based on an interview with Mark Perlman Conducted and Edited by Leon Fink," *Labor History* 32 (Fall, 1991): 515.
6. Robert S. Maxwell, *La Follette and the Rise of the Progressives in Wisconsin* (Madison: State Historical Society of Wisconsin, 1956), 145, Robert M. La Follette, *La Follette's Autobiography* (1913: reprint. Madison: University of Madison Press, 1960), 15.
7. Maxwell, *La Follette and the Rise of the Progressives*, 156.
8. Edward Fitzpatrick, *McCarthy of Wisconsin* (New York: Columbia University Press, 1944), 118.
9. Commons, *Myself*, 109.
10. Fitzpatrick, *McCarthy of Wisconsin*, 119.
11. Maxwell. *La Follette and the Rise of the Progressives*, 83.
12. Arthur Altmeyer, *The Industrial Commission of Wisconsin* (Madison: University of Wisconsin Press, 1932), 16, the list of laws goes on for two pages in Robert C. Nesbit, *Wisconsin: A History*, (Madison: University of Wisconsin Press, 1973), 425–26.
13. Maxwell, *La Follette and the Rise of the Progressives*, 157, Altmeyer, *The Industrial Commission*, 25.
14. Crystal Eastman, *Work Accidents and the Law* (New York: Charities Publications Committee, 1910), 190. Harry Weiss, "Employer Liability and Workmen's Compensation," in *History of Labor in the United States*, ed. John R. Commons and Associates vol.3 (1935: reprint, New York: Augustus M. Kelley, 1966), 573.
15. *Ives v. South Buffalo Railway* (124 NY sup 920(1910).
16. Maxwell, *La Follette and the Rise of the Progressives*, 156.
17. J.E. Trelevan, "The Milwaukee Bureau of Economy and Efficiency," *Annals of the American Academy of Political and Social Science* 41(May 1912): 270–78, John R. Commons, *Labor and Administration* (New York: Macmillan, 1913), 195–218.
18. John R. claimed that he first came across the book in the University of Wisconsin library. But he had mentioned the superior labor councils in his testimony before the USIC.
19. Commons, *Myself*, 129–30.
20. Fitzpatrick, *McCarthy of Wisconsin*, 120. Selig Perlman in the oral histories was anxious that the legislative committee receive full credit for its contribution. See Lampman, *Economists at Wisconsin*, 24.
21. John Orth, *Due Process of Law: A Brief History* (Lawrence: University of Kansas Press, 2003), 52–53.
22. Commons, *Myself*, 155.
23. Altmeyer, *The Industrial Commission*, 17–18.

The Wisconsin Idea

24. Ibid., 18.
25. Ibid., 26.
26. Commons, *Myself,* 164.
27. Curti and Carstensen, *The University of Wisconsin, A History,* vol.2, 101–2, 142.
28. Maxwell, *La Follette and the Rise of the Wisconsin Progressives,* 173–94.
29. Ibid., 145.
30. Commons, *Labor and Administration, v.*
31. Ibid, 7.
32. Ibid., 9–14.
33. Ibid., 396.
34. Ibid., 405–6.
35. Ibid., 399.
36. Susan B. Carter, Scott S. Gartner, Michael V. Haines, Alan L. Olmstead, Richard Sutch, and Gavin Wright, *Historical Statistics of the United States,* vol. 2 (New York: Cambridge University Press, 2007), 2–336.
37. Philip Foner, *History of the Labor Movement in the United States: The Policies and Practices of the American Federation of Labor 1900–1909,* vol.3 (New York: International Publishers, 1964), 32–60.
38. Selig Perlman and Philip Taft, *History of Labor in the United States, 1896–1932,* vol.4 (1935. reprint. New York: Augustus M. Kelley, 1966), 129–37.
39. Ibid., 133–37, David Montgomery, *The Fall of the House of Labor: The Workplace, the State, and Labor, 1865–1925* (New York: Cambridge University Press, 1987), 269–75.
40. Ibid., 275.
41. Ibid., 281–93.
42. Commons, *Labor and Administration,* 80.
43. Ibid., 140.
44. Ibid., 79–83.
45. Ibid., 138.
46. Ibid., 350–57.
47. Ibid., 135–38.
48. Ibid., 153.
49. Ely to Commons January 25, 1913, Commons Papers, microfilm, reel 2 .frame, 464; Commons to Ely January 27, 1913, reel 2, frames 465–66.
50. Commons to Ira Cross November 7, 1912, ibid., F 366.
51. Miller, "The American Bureau of Industrial Research," 185.
52. Mary Martin, *The Corpse on Boomerang Road, Telluride's War on Labor 1899–1908* (Montrose, CO: Western Reflections Publishing Co., 2004).
53. Melvin Dubofsky, *We shall Be All: A History of the Industrial Workers of the World* (Chicago, IL: Quadrangle Books, 1969), 91.

12

The Commission on Industrial Relations

While the courts and law books have dealt with the labor contract as similar to other contracts, legislation goes behind the legal face of things and looks at the bargaining power which precedes the contract—Principles of Labor Legislation

In September 1913, John R. left the state capitol and returned to the campus facing a pile of plans and projects—the still unfinished "interpretive history," a planned book on labor legislation with John Andrews, and new topics for the labor problems seminars, including the philosophy and techniques of the IWW. He did not need another commission assignment. But such an assignment was coming, the almost accidental result of events that had occurred three years earlier and a continent away.

The Explosion in Los Angeles and the Reaction

On October 1, 1910, two bombs had exploded behind the *Los Angeles Times* building. Secondary explosions and a raging fire obliterated the building and killed twenty-three people.[1] Harrison Gray Otis, the building's owner, had been orchestrating an open shop campaign against union organizers from San Francisco. And Otis had blamed unions for the explosion. Samuel Gompers and other union leaders had angrily hinted at a conspiracy to discredit the unions.[2]

To aid local police, the mayor had hired the famous detective, William Burns who had fingered two brothers: John J. McNamara, secretary of the International Association of Bridge and Structural Iron Workers, and James McNamara, John's brother and fellow union member. Gompers and other union leaders, believing that the brothers had been framed, had called for Clarence Darrow. Darrow had come, but as he pursued his investigation, he had grown convinced that the brothers were guilty, that the prosecution had an airtight case. To save the brothers from execution, he needed a bargain with the prosecutors, and to get a bargain he needed to convince the brothers to plead guilty. Their guilty pleas shocked union leaders and wrecked the Los Angeles organizing campaign.

When news of the guilty plea reached New York City, Paul Kellogg, editor of *The Survey*, called a meeting in his office. He devoted the last issue of 1911 to the "Larger Aspects" of the case.[3]A short editorial by Kellogg preceded thirty invited pieces representing a variety of viewpoints. Finally, Kellogg printed a petition signed by twenty-eight people and presented to President William Howard Taft.

The petition called attention to a case larger than the McNamara case—a case before "the social conscience of the nation," the case of workers who "did not and would not use dynamite to attain their ends," but who remained victimized because the laws and institutions of the nation had lagged behind the social changes that accompanied "stupendous manufacturing developments," massive migrations of peoples, explosive growth of cities, and the reduction of workers to helplessness. "The workingman sees the club of the officer, the bayonet of the militia directed against him in defense of property, and he believes that the hand of the law, strong in protection of property, often drops listless whenever measures are proposed to lighten labor's heavy burden."[4]

The petition asked for a commission to investigate labor conditions, the economic and social costs of strikes, the rules of employer and employee organizations, the scope and effectiveness of state and federal labor departments, and alternative methods of labor organization.

The Commission on Industrial Relations

On December 30, 1911, President Taft received the petitioners graciously, and on February 2, 1912, in his State of the Union Address, Taft asked Congress to create that commission.[5] On August 23, 1912, Congress created the United States Commission on Industrial Relations (USCIR). Taft nominated nine men to serve on the commission. Three represented business; three, labor; and three, the public.

Liberals immediately attacked Taft's choices. All labor representatives came from conservative unions—no one from the IWW. One of the management representatives was an official in the hated "open shop" National Association of Manufacturers. Taft had not nominated any women. In the uproar, Congress rejected Taft's nominees, leaving the nominations to his successor, Woodrow Wilson. The petitioners had their own suggestions: For chairman, either Louis Brandeis or Father John Ryan, author of a book on the living wage. For labor, they wanted at least one member, such as "Big Bill" Haywood, to represent the IWW viewpoint, and they wanted a female representative, preferably Florence Kelley, president of the National Consumers' League. Wilson offered the chairmanship to Brandeis, but Brandeis turned him down. Wilson did not consider Father Ryan, but he huddled with his advisors.

John R., Frank Walsh, Florence Harriman

In June 1913, John R. was on a train returning from Manhattan, Kansas, to Madison when he was handed a telegram from Senator La Follette. La Follette wanted to know if John R. would be interested in the role of chairman.[6] John R. declined. Then, he left the train to visit friends at the *Kansas City Star*. Reporters there told him of a rumor that President Wilson had chosen Frank P. Walsh to chair the commission. With his newspaper friends, John R. went to Walsh's office, arriving in time to witness the arrival of a telegram offering Walsh the chairmanship. Walsh urged John R. to accept a position as public representative. John R. finally agreed on the condition that he could limit his commission work to vacations.[7]

Frank Walsh, a year younger than John R. and a child of potato famine immigrants, had grown up in St. Louis's infamous Kerry Patch. After his father died, Walsh had worked as a messenger during the day and had studied shorthand at night, and eventually he had become a court stenographer. He had used his court experience to study law, had passed the bar exam, had married Katie O'Flaherty, and had moved to Kansas City where his outstanding courtroom skills had earned him a wealthy corporate clientele. Then, in 1900, Walsh had dropped most of his corporate clients and had begun crusading against the corrupt Pendergast machine while defending people too poor to pay. Some cases made him famous. He successfully defended Jesse James Jr., and when a Pendergast prosecutor hauled the crusading editor of the *Kansas City Star* into court on trumped-up charges, Walsh got the conviction overturned by proving that the first judge had written his decision before the trial. Walsh was driven by a sense of justice so strong that it approached uncontrollable rage. And Walsh was one of the few progressives who rose to the defense of African Americans.[8]

On June 26, 1913, Wilson announced the names of the commissioners; three public representatives: John R. Commons, Florence Harriman, and Frank Walsh; three business representatives: Frederic

A. Delano, S. Thruston Ballard, and Harris Weinstock; and three labor representatives: James O'Connell, Austin R. Garretson, and John S. Lennon.[9]

Frederick Delano was president of the Wabash Railroad and uncle of Franklin Delano Roosevelt, the undersecretary of the Navy. Ballard, a Kentucky mill owner, had a reputation for paternalistic and humane employment practices. Weinstock, an immigrant from London who had built the largest department store in Sacramento, was known for "putting principles before profits." Weinstock would later play a major role in the organization of California farm cooperatives. The AFL had recommended all three labor representatives: James O'Connell, its vice president; John B. Lennon, its treasurer; and Austin Garretson, president of the railroad conductors' union. Critics assailed the conservative nature of the labor delegation. Wilson had ignored the suggestion of Louis Brandeis and John A. Fitch that someone like "Big Bill" Haywood should represent the anti-Gompers wing of the labor movement.

The third public member, Florence Harriman, disappointed those who wanted Florence Kelley, the president of the Consumers' League. But Harriman was not what she seemed. The daughter of a wealthy shipping magnate, she had attended special primary school with J.P. Morgan's children, had graduated from an elite finishing school, and had married J. Borden Harriman, a Wall Street financier and cousin of the railroad tycoon. She had founded the exclusive Colony Club for New York's society women. But, one night she had gone alone to a talk by Susan B. Anthony. That night had marked the beginning of an evolution. The conservative August Belmont considered her "safe" when he recruited her to head the Women's Welfare branch of the National Civic Federation (NCF). She proved more than he could handle. She was appalled at the working conditions she witnessed, and she turned her stubborn temper on managers who did not make corrections she suggested. Her NCF experiences had radicalized her a bit, and the USCIR would radicalize her even further.[10]

John R. erred by assuming that he could wall the USCIR off from his preoccupations at Madison, but he began by operating on that assumption. He informed John Andrews, Helen Sumner, and Henry Hoagland that the president had appointed him to the USCIR but that the appointment would not derail his plan to spend the summer of 1913 working with them on the interpretive history.[11] Those letters are some of the very few that mention the USCIR. Most of his letters for those years dealt with the history or with his classes. He participated

146

The Commission on Industrial Relations

in USCIR hearings and meetings, but his correspondence indicated that his mind was often elsewhere.

His prediction for that summer proved correct. The team gathered in Madison and worked together without interruption for two months. But the free summer was a grim omen. It would not have been free if Senator Hoke Smith of Georgia had not bottled up Wilson's nominations in committee.

Wilson had ignored Smith's request that he place one of Smith's friends on the committee. Smith now sought revenge. He found an ally in Senator James Reed of Kansas, an apparatchik of the Pendergast machine and a former prosecutor with a grudge against Frank Walsh. So, to "get even," the two kept Wilson's nominations tied up in committee all summer.

Wilson finally forced the bill into the full Senate which approved all nine nominees on September 10, 1913. And on October 23, the United States Industrial Commission (USCIR) held its first meeting and hired the first four members of its research staff: W. Jett Lauck, Basil Manly, Francis Bird, and Crystal Eastman Benedict.[12] Lauck, former staff director for the United States Immigration Commission, was given the same role for the USCIR. Manly came from the Bureau of Labor Statistics. Bird had helped John R. design the Wisconsin Industrial Commission. Eastman Benedict had written a path-breaking study of industrial hazards for the Pittsburgh Survey. By December 18, the commission had added Selig Perlman to the staff.[13]

The commission members divided responsibilities, with John R. responsible for the research staff, and Walsh, for hearings. John R. assembled a superb staff. It seemed like a dream combination, a superb research staff supported by one of the best trial lawyers in the country. But Walsh, perhaps because of his background, seemed incapable of understanding how the research staff could help him. And John R., focused on his work in Madison, left Jett Lauck to cope alone with the problem of coordinating top-flight but fiercely independent researchers and a tough-minded trial lawyer focused on hearings. Walsh would hold 154 days of hearings, call 740 witnesses, and explore every labor problem from the miserable working conditions of garment workers in New York to the grim lives of tenant farmers in Texas.

John R. probably arranged the first hearings in New York on December 29, 30, and 31 1913—"Suggestions of Expert Witnesses."[14] Before the first witnesses were called, Florence Harriman announced

147

that she had organized a women's advisory panel and that she had asked Florence Kelley to testify. The guys expressed doubts but Harriman held her ground. Kelley's name though does not appear in this session's witness list. The only woman who testified was Mrs. Raymond Robins, president of the National Women's Trade Union League.

John R. was not present on January 15, 1914, when the commission heard testimony on New York City's garment industry.[15] New York employers with union shop agreements that had been mediated by Louis Brandeis (the Brandeis protocol) were evading the agreements by sending work to nonunion shops in other cities such as Paterson, New Jersey.[16]

John R. attended the Paterson hearings on June 15, 1914, a year and a half after 800 angry workers had walked out of a silk mill.[17] Workers at other mills had followed, and by March the number of strikers in Paterson had swelled to 13,000. The walkouts had been spontaneous, but IWW leaders, Big Bill Haywood, Carlo Tresca, and Elizabeth Gurley Flynn, had come to help. Club-wielding police broke up meetings and arrested everybody including Haywood, Tresca, and Flynn—arresting even John Reed, drama critic for *American* magazine, permanently radicalizing Reed with his time in the vermin-infested "Sheriff Radley's Hotel."[18]

The Paterson strikers had already lost by the time of the hearings. As the strikers' resources ran low, Haywood had written IWW locals throughout the country asking for donations. Donations had come, but not enough. Reed had helped the strikers write a play that dramatized their plight. The play in Madison Square Garden had been an artistic success but a financial flop, and by the time of the commission hearings, the former strikers were straggling back to the mills.

Before the Paterson hearing however, at the beginning of June, Jett Lauck had resigned as staff director. Walsh and John R. asked Charles McCarthy to rescue the operation.[19] Like John R., McCarthy already had his hands full in Madison, but he agreed to work for the commission from June until the legislature opened in January.

In a rare rebuke to his old friend, McCarthy faulted both John R. and Walsh for failing to support Lauck, and he persuaded Lauck to remain on the staff. McCarthy divided the work into nine sections, set up a system of daily and weekly reports, and developed a method for creating running summaries of all reports. He handed day-to-day management to William (Billy) Leiserson. And he donated the time of a super-organized Wisconsin librarian, Miss Clara Richards.

McCarthy and Leiserson gave many of John R.'s students the types of projects that made them seek out John R.'s classes. David Saposs, John R.'s assistant, went to Lead, South Dakota; Butte, Montana; and the State of Colorado where he investigated corporate capture of local governments. Saposs met and corresponded with Big Bill Haywood and other luminaries of the IWW. Selig Perlman told his son Mark about a terrifying experience.

> Apparently Dad had been sent to Lawrence Massachusetts to investigate the development of IWW radicalism. There he had a frightening experience. He was sent to question a group of these IWW shoemakers who had been on strike . . . They thought he was a spy, and because they told him too much, he became convinced that they were really going to kill him. He said they were threatening to throw him out a window. They pulled out his wallet and made him empty his pockets. When he emptied his pockets they found a letter from William English Walling, starting "Dear Selig." They then figured that if he knew Walling, obviously, he could not be a spy. That letter, he said, saved his life.[20]

So with the Commons team engaged and the staff reorganized, McCarthy could consider the crisis resolved. But, in spite of McCarthy's rebuke, John R. had not changed his focus from Madison. That was all about to change with the advent of a new crisis.

The Breakdown

That crisis, caused by a series of three events, would finally force John R. to focus on his role in the USCIR.

The first event has generated tales, songs and rhetoric—"the most ferocious conflict in the history of American labor and industry" or "America's deadliest war."[21] East of the Rockies, in the foothills of the Sangre de Cristo Range, before the turn of the century, surveyors and geologists had found rich veins of lignite coal. Mining companies had recruited miners and had built little towns where they paid the miners in scrip that could be spent only at company stores or in company saloons. Mine fatality rates were twice the national average.

The United Mine Workers (UMW) had organized the mines in 1900, but they had lost a strike in 1903 when the companies had recruited trainloads of Greek, Serbian, and Croatian strikebreakers. The UMW sent organizers again, and by 1913, the former strikebreakers were UMW members. In September 1913, the companies ignored a list of demands sent by the unions to their corporate headquarters. The miners walked out, and the companies evicted them from the company towns.

The miners moved with their families into tent camps built in advance by the UMW which had leased lands at the ends of hollows where strikers could confront strikebreakers before they reached coal seams. One of those tent camps was at Ludlow, Colorado.

The employers hired the Baldwin–Felts Detective Agency and recruited strikebreakers from Mexico and Eastern Europe. Baldwin–Felts agents harassed the strikers, driving an armored car with a mounted machine gun around and through the camps, instigating violent responses from the strikers, some veterans of the Balkan wars. To prevent further violence, Colorado Governor Elias M. Ammons mobilized Colorado's National Guard. Guardsmen entered the camps on October 29. The striking miners met them with cheers, flags, and a band. On October 31, the Guardsmen disarmed the company guards and collected weapons from the strikers.

But, over the fall and winter, relations between the Guard and the strikers deteriorated. The original Guardsmen, "weekend warriors" from Denver, had returned home, to be replaced by new recruits. Many were former mine security agents. Then the governor changed his instructions. He had originally instructed the Guard to protect strikers and any miners who wanted to work—but not to escort imported strikebreakers into the mines. Then, under pressure from the state Chamber of Commerce and other business organizations, the governor ordered the Guard to escort strikebreakers into the mines. During the winter and into the spring, relations deteriorated. Accusing the miners of harboring weapons, Guardsmen periodically searched the tents, often stealing money and jewelry. The Guard commander, Major Pat Hamrock, had served in the US Cavalry during the Sioux wars that culminated in the massacre at Wounded Knee. Lieutenant K. E. Linderfelt had served in the Philippines. They both seemed to view the immigrant miners as "foreigners."

On April 19, 1914, the Greek community in the Ludlow camp celebrated Greek Orthodox Easter, wearing festive garments and putting on a show for their fellow strikers. The next day a trio of militiamen came to the tent colony, asking about a man that the miners were ostensibly holding hostage. The miners knew nothing about the man. Major Hamrock telephoned Louis Tikas, a leader of the Greeks, asking him to come to the Guard camp for a conference. Tikas responded that he would meet the major at an abandoned railroad building between the two camps. Before the meeting Major Hamrock ordered a machine gun brought up and placed halfway down a hill overlooking the camp. He ordered his troops to parade visibly on top of a hill.

According to Mrs. Pearl Jolly, the wife of a miner and a nurse in the camp, a band of Greek men, fearing an attack, filed ostentatiously out of the camp into a dry creek bed in order to draw fire away from the women and children.[22] When he saw the men filing into the dry creek bed, Lieutenant Linderfelt assumed that they might be preparing to fire on the troops on the top of the hill. He threw two small bombs toward the tents—a prearranged signal for reinforcements. Firing and maneuvering erupted immediately and went on all day with the machine gun continuously strafing the camp. Women and children took shelter in pits dug by the miners under the tents. At one point a railroad engineer stopped his train at the edge of the camp so that women and children could scramble into the open boxcars. Two Guardsmen climbed into the cab, held pistols to his head, and forced him to move. Later, Guardsmen swept into the camp, looting, pillaging, pouring coal oil on the canvas tents, and igniting fires that burned all afternoon and into the night.

The next day, a telephone lineman, going through the ruins, picked up one end of an iron cot, and beneath it in a trench, he saw the charred remains of eleven children and two women. There were more deaths—around twenty—but photos of the charred little bodies hit front pages across the nation. If this was not enough to enrage the officers of the UMW, there was the murder of Louis Tikas, an unarmed Greek strike leader who usually counseled patience and negotiation. Tikas, seeking a truce, had somehow managed to approach Lieutenant Linderfelt. Two Guardsmen had held Tikas while Linderfelt broke his rifle butt over Tikas's head. Tikas collapsed, and the Guardsmen pumped bullets into his prone body.

The UMW distributed rifles and ammunition to surviving strikers. And until President Wilson sent in Federal troops, war raged along a forty-mile front with strikers on one side and National Guardsmen and mine agents on the other.

These events shocked relations within the commission. McCarthy's old friend from Brown University, John D. Rockefeller Jr., owned 40 percent of the stock and controlled the Colorado Fuel and Iron Company (CFI), the biggest and most influential of the mining companies. The miners at Ludlow had been CFI employees. Moreover, CFI had one of the worst safety records in the country. There had been three disastrous mine explosions in Colorado in 1911—all preventable by standard safety procedures. Two of the three had racked CFI mines. The CFI also owned a steel mill in Pueblo, Colorado. John A. Fitch had visited that mill: "a steel plant more dangerous than any large steel plant that I had ever seen. And I have seen a considerable number of big ones."[23]

The second of the three shocks came from Congress. After Walsh had sent investigators to the Fulton Cotton Mills in Atlanta, the commission's old enemy, Senator Hoke Smith of Georgia, had rallied Southern senators and, with the help of Pendergast's Senator Reed, had tried to kill the commission by cutting off all its funds. Senator Borah of Idaho had led the fight that beat them back. But, in the course of debate and compromise, the Senate had drastically cut the committee's funds.[24]

William Leiserson saw what was coming, but John R. did not—another indication of John R.'s failure to really focus on the commission's troubles. On November 17, Henry Hoagland wrote to John R. that Leiserson had told him to accept another job offer should he receive one. John R. seemed surprised. He responded that he was sorry to hear that, but that Leiserson knew more than he. He suggested that Hoagland remain with the USCIR while he looked for another job.[25]

By late February 1915, funds were so low that Walsh had to set priorities. For Walsh the hearings were essential. They were the court in which he could plead the cause of the working classes. For McCarthy research was essential to generate the information that could ground permanent solutions. Walsh wanted to cut research. McCarthy wanted to curtail hearings. The clash between the two Irishmen reached donnybrook proportions. Then Walsh fired McCarthy—and the entire research staff.

McCarthy decided to take his case to the commission. He worked out what he considered an iron-clad case for reinstating the research staff and publishing the reports. He confided his plan to John R. They agreed that after McCarthy's presentation, John R. would move that the commission repeal Walsh's decision and reconsider the allocation of the remaining funds.

When the commission met, Walsh demolished McCarthy's arguments point by point. Then Walsh produced letters written by McCarthy to John D. Rockefeller Jr., the owner of the CFI. He accused McCarthy of ethical violations, of weakening the commission's case against Rockefeller, and of collaborating with Rockefeller's scheme to undermine the commission's effectiveness. The eight other commission members voted to reject John R.'s motion.

Rockefeller had appeared twice before the commission. In his first appearance, coached by his public relations consultant, Ivy Lee, Rockefeller had projected the image of a humane philanthropist deceived by dishonest managers.[26] But the commission's staff had already uncovered documents showing that Rockefeller had not only known, but had approved of every step taken by his managers.

And those managers had broken and ignored laws, terrorized miners, and corrupted public officials. When the labor department had sent a mediator to Rockefeller's office, Rockefeller had refused to meet him. After the massacre, Rockefeller had approved the slimy propaganda campaign masterminded by his publicity agent.[27]

In a second, more brutal session, Walsh confronted Rockefeller with all this evidence.[28] In the eyes of Walsh and those who agreed with him, Walsh had convicted Rockefeller of complicity in the events that resulted in the Ludlow massacre. In the eyes of others, that mean uncouth lawyer had browbeaten poor Mr. Rockefeller.

Rockefeller had publicly announced his intention to establish a center for industrial relations within the Rockefeller Foundation and had hired William Lyon MacKenzie King, the former Canadian Minister of Labor as director. To Walsh, this looked like an effort to undercut the committee's work. King confirmed that suspicion when he proposed employee representation schemes as a substitute for union recognition.

And Walsh was justified—if mistaken—in his questioning of the correspondence between Rockefeller and McCarthy. According to McCarthy's friend and biographer, McCarthy had feared that his old friend, with absolutely no working class experience, might innocently do harm, and so McCarthy had tried to dissuade him. The letters do not substantiate the claim that McCarthy had tried to dissuade Rockefeller—or "Junior" as he was called. But they reveal McCarthy's fear that Junior might innocently do harm. Rather McCarthy had recommended an advisory board with union representatives. But Junior had rebuffed McCarthy. He had not consulted union leaders; he had hired King.

When McCarthy's dismissal became irreversible, John R. voted for Basil Manly to replace him. Manly, from an accomplished Southern family, had attended Washington and Lee University and had studied on a fellowship at the University of Chicago before going in 1908 to work for the Bureau of Labor Statistics (BLS) where he had met and married one of John R.'s former students, Marie Bradley.[29] Manly thus became an honorary member of the Washington club of John R.'s ex-students.

In a letter thanking John R. for an expense reimbursement, Helen Sumner had mentioned that she "had dinner tonight at the Manlys with Mr. and Mrs. Stevens."[30]

Manly wrote the staff report. Walsh did not seek comments on a preliminary draft, but sent the final version to commission members for signatures. He was blindsided when Florence Harriman refused to sign. She complained that the final draft was completed without consulting her or the management representatives and that it used language to which she objected. She assumed that the labor representatives had previously seen it. There is no indication that they had, but they signed it.

Even before Manly wrote his report, though, John R. had planned to write a dissent as this exchange with Helen Sumner makes clear. "We had quite a blow up in our Commission and they turned down McCarthy and me which means that practically all of the stuff I had selected to write and work up the reports, recommendations and constructive program will have to go within a week or two. Both employers and employees were against me and I stood alone, but I'm going to stick it out till the end of the Commission's life, which is August 23rd."

Sumner responded: "I hope you will issue a minority report and tell the country in it what you wanted the Industrial Relations Commission to do and why. It seems to me you owe yourself and your friends and your country some public repudiation of the methods and the final fiasco so far as constructive results are concerned of that body. Don't you!"[31]

On May 6, Sumner wrote again: "Are you going to have a minority report? Mrs. Harriman seems to be bestirring herself about women and children and has approached us through Miss Abenauer for a conference . . . Miss Lathrop is unwilling to have anything to do with any report required by Mr. Walsh."

On May 11, John R. apparently rejected any notion of collaborating with Florence Harriman. She had, after all, voted against him in the final showdown.

> It is my present idea to prepare my own minority report without asking, or indeed accepting cooperation or joint signature of any other member of the commission. I intend to be present at the sessions, and it may be that I shall modify this or that arrangement in some particulars, though I do not think it possible, as I have no confidence whatever in investigations or findings controlled by Mr. Walsh. I am writing this confidentially for your advice because I do not intend to make any public criticism of his character as I do not wish to place

> any obstacles whatever in the way of his accomplishing whatever he is able to do by his methods.
>
> My greatest emphasis in my separate report will be on administration of labor laws, and I am quite anxious to secure as early as possible publications which your bureau is getting out on administration of child labor laws. I feel that it is of very little value to agitate or adopt further legislation until we have canvassed the subject of administration and reached some understanding as to whether laws are to be enforced or to be more a bluff for the use of politicians.[32]

In spite of his original intention of working alone, John R. eventually allowed Florence Harriman to join his dissent. (The staff report and the dissent are discussed in appendix A.)

Earlier, before this exchange with Helen Sumner, on May 3, 1916, in a letter to John R. about a chart for the forthcoming interpretive history, Henry Farnam had added, "I have just purchased your *Principles of Labor Legislation*, and am beginning to read it with interest. I do not see how you ever got the time to write this book in addition to all the other things that you have on your hands."[33] There were at least three possible answers to Farnam's question. First, John R. worked incredibly long hours. Second, John Andrews made a significant contribution, as did some other students. And third, the book owed a debt to ten years of research and debate within the American Association for Labor Legislation.

In addition to John R. and the Wisconsin contingent, the AALL included economists such as Paul H. Douglas and Henry Seager, legal scholars such as Ernst Freund, liberal employers such as Henry Dennison, and social insurance experts such as the larger-than-life physician-sociologist, I. M. (Max) Rubinow. To some extent the book owed a debt to all these people and others who had participated in ten years of research, debate, and discussion within the AALL, much of it published in the *American Labor Legislation Review*.

The *Principles of Labor Legislation* (hereafter the *Principles*) may have been John R.'s most successful book. It was favorably, if critically, reviewed.[34] Critics cited an absence of abstract theory and inadequate analysis. But criticisms were almost always imbedded in high praise. "College teachers who have been referring their students to a dozen books for acquaintance with the world's chief laws will be deeply grateful for this volume. Some of the laws have been nowhere so effectively described. There is generally a history of the steps of legislation, the provisions of important laws are stated with elaboration, and the more important court interpretations are invariably given."[35]

The *Principles* became a standard text in many colleges for the next twenty years. It would go through four editions, and each edition would be changed to reflect advances in the content of reforms debated within the AALL.

There were chapters on the legal basis of labor law, individual bargaining, collective bargaining, safety and health, and social insurance. The chapters were divided into sections, and each section began with a description of programs in the United States and a historical survey of programs in other countries followed by a critical analysis of cultural and legal obstacles to adapting similar programs to the United States.

Some passages in the *Principles* provide a background for understanding skimpy allusions in John R.'s dissent, and—surprisingly— concrete proposals in the dissent clarify some abstract vagueness in the *Principles.*

The dissent devoted only a few sentences to issues on which the *Principles* spent entire chapters. The *Principles* consequently placed the dissent in the context of an ambitious agenda that included labor law reform, political reform, health insurance, unemployment insurance, and old age insurance. On the other hand, the dissent provided concrete details sometimes missing in the *Principles.*

In his critical, but ultimately favorable, review of the *Principles*, George Barnett of Johns Hopkins had faulted the authors for failing to give details about the structure of any commission that would fulfill the requirements for their principle of "representation of interests."[36] The dissent corrected for that fault. John R. devoted over half of the dissent to describing the organization and structure of state and federal industrial commissions and to answering objections against the proposal.

The time spent on his dissent was not the major unanticipated cost of John R.'s role as a commissioner—that cost was related to Walsh's decision to fire the staff and destroy all the reports. John R. had recruited an outstanding and talented staff. Their work was now just a pile of papers destined for a furnace in Washington, DC—an outcome that distressed the staff members, some more than others.[37]

Robert Hoxie, a labor economist who had worked on an analysis of Frederick Taylor's managerial science, was seriously distressed.

Hoxie had grown up on a cattle farm in Upstate New York, had attended Cornell briefly, had received his PhD from Chicago, and was teaching at Chicago when John R. recruited him for the USCIR staff. Walton Hamilton described Hoxie's intellectual hegira as "conscientious

The Commission on Industrial Relations

tarrying and restless wandering."[38] But Hoxie's conscientious mind was a curse. "He found it almost impossible to meet his own standards."

John R. described Hoxie's visit after Walsh had fired the staff. "[H]e came to me at Madison, with all of his manuscripts, his notes, and his outline. He was in a nervous and incoherent state of mind. I was immediately alarmed. I went over all his material with him, explaining that he had the first really scientific study of scientific management, and it would be a serious misfortune if he did not publish as much of it as was already prepared. I promised to get a publisher for him but he was worried about the share of costs imposed upon him . . . He went home seemingly cheerful . . . I think I made a mistake."[39]

According to Hamilton, John R. did make a mistake. Hoxie did not really want to publish his work on scientific management. It was in what he considered an incomplete state. On June 22, 1916, Robert Hoxie committed suicide.

Later, Lucy Hoxie came to see John R., bringing with her all of her husband's unpublished work. John R. looked through the manuscripts and selected a set that he thought would make a fine book. It became Hoxie's *Trade Unionism in the United States*, with a note of thanks to John R. in the preface.

On June 19, in response to a letter from Henry Farnam, John R.'s assistant, David Saposs wrote that "Professor Commons has gone into the woods for a month or so."[40] For the rest of the summer Saposs answered all letters with the statement that "Professor Commons was in the woods." These responses are most consistent with the episode that Mark Perlman described.

> At one point Mrs. Commons called my father up and asked him to dig up immediately all the other students anyone whom he could find. John R. had left the house and was running in the fields. He was "out of his mind." . . .
>
> Commons lived about four or five miles from the University. I think the group took the street car to the end of the line, and then walked. When they arrived at the house, Mrs. Commons was in a great state and said, without going into details, that Commons had been behaving strangely, and was running in the fields. So the students broke up, each going out looking over the fields and farm land. The area is now built up, but in those days, even when I was a boy, it was all farm land.[41]

On September 20, Saposs informed Helen Sumner that John R. was now reading correspondence and would be back sometime in October.[42]

157

John R. was present at the meeting of the Carnegie collaborators on October17. In *Myself* John R. wrote that he spent those months at a cabin on Lake Tenderfoot until the snow began to fall, then he went to Mount Vernon and stayed with his sister Clara, returning to Madison on February 1, 1917. He reflected on his experiences with the USCIR.

> Thus ended, with Hoxie's suicide, a series of tragic events in my academic life. I had been compelled to separate myself from my labor friends and from the aggressive and astute lawyer whom I admired in his espousal of labor's interests. I had participated in the confused beginnings of a world-wide conflict that would end in class war and a war of nations. I saw then dimly, and without much experimentation to go by, that which eventually I saw vividly as the clash of politics, unionism, fascism and communism. I saw the initial suppression, and even death of academic economists, with their futile appeals for reason in a din of mass conflict over scarcity of the world's resources.[43]

Notes

1. Graham Adams, *The Age of Industrial Violence: The Activities and Findings of the United States Commission on Industrial Relations 1910–1915* (New York: Columbia University Press, 1966), 1.
2. Ibid., 8. Gompers had reasons. During a strike in 1903, Pinkerton detectives had been discovered planning to derail a train and blame unions. See Foner, *History of the Labor Movement*, vol. 3, 394.
3. Adams, *The Age of Industrial Violence*, 28–31, *The Survey*, 27 (December 30, 1911).
4. *The Survey* (December 30, 1911), 1430–31.
5. Adams, *The Age of Industrial Violence*, 30–33.
6. Commons, *Myself*, 166. Because Wilson never considered John R. for the chairmanship, Adams concluded that such a telegram never existed, implying that John R. either misremembered or made the episode up. However, John R. wrote that the telegram came not from Wilson, but from La Follette who may have been thinking about suggesting his name.
7. Ibid., 167.
8. Joseph McCartin, *Labor's Great War: The Struggle for Democracy and the Origins of Modern Industrial Relations* (Chapel Hill: University of North Carolina Press, 1997), 21–24.
9. Adams, *The Age of Industrial Violence*, 55–74.
10. Florence Harriman, *From Pinafores to Politics* (New York: Henry Holt, 1923).
11. Commons to Andrews, Sumner, and Hoagland, June 17, 1913, John R. Commons, *Papers* (Madison: State Historical Society of Wisconsin, 1982), microfilm, reel 2, frames 641–43.
12. Paul U. Kellogg, "Industrial Relations Statistics or Program," *The Survey* 3(November 8, 1913): 152–53.
13. Commons to Sumner, December 28, 1913; Commons Papers, microfilm, reel 2, frame 868.

The Commission on Industrial Relations

14. United States Commission on Industrial Relations, *Industrial Relations: Final Report and Testimony Submitted to Congress by the Act of August 23, 1912*, vol. 1 (Washington, DC: Government Printing Office, 1916) 173–398.

15. Ibid., vol.2, 1027–61.

16. Ibid., 1034.

17. Ibid., vol.3, 2411–65.

18. John Reed, "War in Paterson," *The Masses* (June, 1913), accessed January 19, 2017, https://www.marxists.org/archive/reed/1913/masses06.htm. Reed's life was the subject of the award winning film *Reds* directed by Warren Beatty. Some rankings list it among the ten best films of the twentieth century.

19. Adams, *The Age of Industrial Violence*, 205–6, Leon Fink, *Progressive Intellectuals and the Dilemma of Democratic Commitment* (Cambridge, MA: Harvard University Press, 1997), 86.

20. Leon Fink, "A Memoir of Selig Perlman and His Life at the University of Wisconsin, Based on an Interview of Mark Perlman Conducted by Leon Fink," *Labor History* 32 (Fall 1991), 517–18.

21. George S. McGovern and Leonard M. Guttridge, *The Great Coalfield War* (Boston, MA: Houghton-Mifflin, 1972), Thomas G. Andrews, *Killing for Coal, America's Deadliest War* (Cambridge, MA: Harvard University Press, 2010). There are many versions of this story. The basic facts can be deduced by comparing the National Guard version in Leon Stein and Philip Taft, *Massacre at Ludlow* (New York: Arno Press 1971) 5–119 with that of Mrs. Pearl Jolly, a nurse in the camp at the time. United States Commission on Industrial Relations, *Report* vol.7, 6347–55. There is even a Woody Guthrie song, "Ludlow," http//woodyguthrie.org/Lyrics/Ludlow Massacre.htm.

22. USCIR, *Report* vol.7, 6348.

23. John A. Fitch, "The Steel Industry and the People of Colorado," *The Survey* 27 (February 3, 1912): 1707.

24. Clifford Kuhn, *Contesting the New South Order: The 1914–1915 Strike at Atlanta's Fulton Mills* (Chapel Hill: University of North Carolina Press, 2001).

25. Hoagland to Commons November 17, 1914, Commons Papers, microfilm reel 2, frames 999–1002. Commons to Hoagland, November 20, 1914, ibid., frame 1004.

26. USCIR, *Report*, vol.8, 7265–895.

27. Stuart Ewan, *A Social History of Spin* (New York: Basic Books, 1996), 78–81.

28. USCIR, *Report*, vol.8, 8592–715.

29. Marie Bradley Manly, "To My Posterity," http//squareknotdesign.com /history/to posterity/page 1,htm. Retrieved October 21, 2009. *Who's Who in the Nation's Capital 1921–1922* (Washington, DC: The Consolidated Publishing Company, 1921), 259.

30. Sumner to Commons, February 26, 1913, Commons Papers, microfilm, reel 2, frame 488.

31. Commons to Sumner March 17, 1915, ibid., frame 1025. Sumner to Commons March 21, 1915, Ibid, reel 2, frame 1029.

32. Sumner to Commons May 6, 1915 ibid, frame 1035; Commons to Sumner, May 11, 1915, ibid. frame 1038.

33. Farnam to Commons, May 3, 1916, Commons Papers, microfilm, reel 3, frame 22.

34. George Barnett, "Review of *The Principles of Labor Legislation* by John R. Commons and John B. Andrews," *American Economic Review* 6 (September 1916): 654–58, Lindley L. Clark, "Review of *Principles of Labor Legislation* by John R. Commons and John B. Andrews," *Review of Political Economy* 24(November 1916): 903–6.
35. Robert, Foerster, "Commons and Andrews' *Principles of Labor Legislation*," *Quarterly Journal of Economics* 30 (May 1916): 566.
36. Barnett, "Review of the *Principles*," 657.
37. Walsh had recommended incineration of the staff reports over the objections of the Secretary of Labor, William B. Wilson. When Congress ordered the incineration, Wilson salvaged as many reports as he could and kept them in the offices of the Bureau of labor Statistics. John R. also salvaged as many as he could and stored them among the files of the Wisconsin Historical Society. Labor historians have since retrieved documents that escaped destruction, and University Microfilms has copied them. They are available in many libraries. See Melvin Dubofsky, Randall Boehm, and Martin Schipper, *U.S. Commission of Industrial Relations 1912–1913 Unpublished Records of the Division of Research and Investigation Reports, Staff Studies, and Background Research Materials* (Ann Arbor: University Microfilms, 1985).
38. Walton H. Hamilton," Robert Franklin Hoxie," *Dictionary of American Biography*, ed. Dumas Malone (New York: Scribner's, 1932) vol.9, 316–17.
39. Commons, *Myself*, 179.
40. Secretary to Farnam June 19, 1916. Commons Papers, microfilm, reel 3, frame 93.
41. Fink, "A Memoir of Selig Perlman," 533.
42. Secretary to Sumner September 20, 1916, Commons Papers. Microfilm, reel 3, frame 144.
43. Commons, *Myself*, 181–82.

13

Shattered Illusions

The war scare was on and I was certainly scared—Myself

After his breakdown in June, 1916, John R. had retreated to a cabin on Lake Tenderfoot in Northern Wisconsin on the Michigan border. When snow had begun falling, he had traveled to his sister's house in Mt. Vernon, New York, and he returned to Madison in February 1917—to a year of world changing events. On January 31, Germany had announced unrestricted submarine warfare. On March 8, International Women's Day, a hundred thousand women poured through the streets of St. Petersburg shouting and crying for food, peace, and an end to autocracy. A week later, Czar Nicholas II abdicated. On April 6, Woodrow Wilson asked Congress to declare war on Germany, bringing America into the era of "great illusions."[1] On October 25, during "ten days that shook the world," Bolsheviks occupied the Winter Palace in Petrograd and toppled the interim government that Prime Minister Alexander Kerensky had declared to be Russia's short-lived socialist republic.[2] On March 3, 1918, Lenin accepted harsh German peace terms at the Treaty of Brest-Litovsk.

After Lenin signed that treaty, Winston Churchill, Britain's war minister, told the allies that they should send troops to North Russia to rescue a Czech legion stranded on the Trans-Siberian railroad, to reclaim Allied war supplies, and to support White Russians fighting the Bolsheviks.[3] Though Wilson opposed the idea, he eventually allowed American troops to participate—with reservations. They could reclaim supplies and rescue the Czechs—but they could not meddle in Russia's internal affairs.

John R.'s son Jack, now twenty-six, volunteered for the army and was commissioned a second lieutenant in Company K 339th infantry regiment, 85th Division—the "Polar Bear regiment" composed mostly of troops from Michigan and Wisconsin. On September 4, 1918, the

"Polar Bears" landed at Archangelsk. Wilson's reservations meant nothing. The 339th was under British command, and the British were there to fight the Bolsheviks. Before the Americans arrived, the British had won some battles, penetrating far inland. But, contrary to Churchill's illusion, Russian peasants never welcomed them, and, with supply lines stretched thin, they were retreating when the Americans landed. Troops would remain there past the Armistice on November 11. Morale was low. They had signed up to fight the Germans, and they did not know why they were in Russia. Jack would not return to Madison until August, 1919, a captain in Company K.

A private in Company K recalled "two days and nights in battle with the Bolsheviks lying on top of four feet of snow, and it was 47 below zero. We lost a hundred men in about two hours on New Year's night. . . . A boy that has seen service in Russia sure has seen service in hell, for they were starving there and I have cried lots of times while I was there over being hungry."[4]

The British gave Jack the Military Cross, and the White Russians gave him the Cross of St. Stanislaus. The document that accompanied the medal explained why. "On October 13, 1918 on the Kadish front, Archangel, Russia [Captain Commons] with Lieut. Chas. B. Ryan also Co. 'K,' and 15 men, armed only with rifles, after everyone else had retreated, held an advance post against a large force of Bolsheviks armed with machine guns. . . . They routed the enemy, saved the situation, and prevented the annihilation of American forces at Kadish."[5]

And Jack came home physically whole, but with psychic wounds unseen by John R. at the time. John R. was immensely proud of his son and wanted him on his team of graduate students and colleagues, but Jack's psychic wounds would impose a cost.[6]

The war imposed another cost. John R. lost a friend—Senator Robert La Follette who had opposed US entry into the war, and who in the face of abusive opposition had led the fight against the Espionage and Sedition Acts. He had endured some of that abusive opposition in Madison. Richard T. Ely had organized the Wisconsin Loyalty League to work for La Follette's political defeat.[7] John R. had signed the faculty resolution condemning La Follette's opposition to the war.[8] And John R. had confronted La Follette in a way that complicated what had been a close relationship. John R.'s account reveals a puzzling failure to appreciate "Fighting Bob's" political courage in opposing the Espionage and Sedition Acts—even though those acts had resulted in long prison terms for many people that John R. admired. For John R., the strained relationship was simply a personal tragedy.[9]

But in spite of all that, in spite of the war, and in spite of the personal tragedies, the postwar years marked a sort of professional milestone in John R.'s life. In 1917 his fellow economists elected him president of the American Economic Association (AEA). With his "Commons team," he would complete the long-delayed interpretive history. The team would develop a "Madison branch" of former students who shared John R.'s commitment to "constructive research" and who remained at Madison. And, in two books, John R. would try to sell his "machinery of collective democracy" to the American management class.

The Madison Team

John R.'s "full team" included graduates who shared John R.'s commitment to "constructive research." Most had left Madison. John Andrews had left for New York to become executive secretary of the American Association for Labor Legislation (AALL). Helen Sumner was in Washington, DC, assistant chief of the Children's Bureau. On the other hand, there were Wisconsin graduates on the Madison faculty who were not on John R.'s "team." William Kiekhofer, the department chairman after 1916, for example, was a Wisconsin graduate who devoted most of his energies to economic literacy. (Ely had stepped down in 1911. Kiekhofer had replaced Ely's successor in 1916.)

Selig Perlman was the first former Wisconsin student who shared John R.'s perspective and who remained in Madison. Perlman may have owed his job to John R.'s wife Nell and the sociologist Edward Alsworth Ross. Perlman received his PhD in 1916 while John R. was recovering from his breakdown at Tenderfoot Lake. Perlman encountered flagrant anti-Semitism in the job market outside of Madison.[10] Nell and Ross campaigned for him within the department. What they actually did is not clear, but Perlman felt that he owed his job to John R.'s wife Nell and the sociologist Edward A. Ross.

Perlman was followed in the next two years by three others: Edwin Witte, Don D. Lescohier, and Arthur Altmeyer.

Witte grew up on a farm in a Moravian community near Ebenezer, Wisconsin. According to his biographer, Witte was gentle, unexcitable, and physically awkward. "Combs, inkwells and his own feet were his natural enemies."[11]

Witte's outward slowness concealed a quick mind, and in high school he had been the "go to" resource for math problems that stumped everybody else. As an undergraduate at Wisconsin, Witte had joined the Athenian Society, a social and debating club, and in a 1908 debate he had drawn the task of defending the Supreme Court decision that fined the Danbury Hatters for boycotting the products of their employers. As Witte studied the court decision, he grew convinced that his side was wrong, and he started a life-long crusade against anti-labor injunctions.[12]

As an undergraduate, Witte had majored in history. When he graduated, his mentor Frederick Jackson Turner, who was leaving for Harvard, had told him that John R. was the best historian on the campus. So in graduate school, Witte had majored in economics with an assistantship from John R.[13]

Between 1912 and 1915, Witte had worked on the staff of Senator John Nelson of Madison. While on Nelson's staff, Witte had written a prophetic critique of the labor protections in the Clayton Anti-Trust Act. Then, on the staff of the United States Commission on Industrial Relations (USCIR), he had written a seminal work on injunctions and had suggested that the United States should enact a law similar to Britain's Trades Disputes Act. John R. and Basil Manly had both accepted this suggestion.[14]

After Frank Walsh had fired the USCIR staff, Ely had hired Witte to teach a course on labor legislation and to help Ely revise some of his books. In 1917 Witte took a job as secretary for the Wisconsin Industrial Commission, but he continued teaching in the department as an unpaid part-time lecturer.

Don D. Lescohier may have owed his position at Madison to war time attacks on the University for its inadequate "Americanism"—in spite of Madison's record liberty bond purchases and in spite of its record for sending a high percentage of its graduates into the military.[15] John R. and Ely also campaigned for "Americanism." John R. gave speeches urging new laws that would require English in the schools.[16] The university instituted an Americanization program, and Ely and Commons searched fruitlessly for a director until they found Don D. Lescohier—at that time the chief statistician for Michigan's labor department.

Lescohier's father, a Detroit stove molder and an active union member, had worked with two of the most prominent union leaders of the nineteenth century—William Sylvis, president of the National Labor Union, and Terence Powderly, president of the Knights of Labor. Lescohier had graduated from Wisconsin in 1908–09 and had been hired as Michigan's chief statistician where he had supervised the implementation of that state's workers' compensation law.

In his new role Lescohier created extension courses in English and history and worked with public school teachers on programs for immigrant children. If John R. and Ely suffered from unwarranted assumptions of Anglo-Saxon superiority, they got better than they deserved in Lescohier.

> Perhaps the fact that my own Catholic grandparents on my father's side knew no English when they came to the United States in the 1850's, attended a church using the Flemish language, used prayer books they brought over from Belgium, and settled in Belgian neighborhoods in Detroit, gave me a more sympathetic understanding of the problem in terms both of the individual foreign-born, non-English-speaking folk, and of their institutions in the United States, particularly their churches, parochial schools, lodges, and neighborhood life. At any rate I was strongly opposed to the use of force in any form in the Americanization program.[17]

But Lescohier, like Perlman, moved beyond his original duties to a whole set of unique contributions to the labor studies program. Over time, he developed new courses covering labor markets and personnel administration, and he consulted with firms that wanted better relations with their employees.

The next member of the "Madison team," Arthur Altmeyer, had been working in his uncle's law office when he came across a pamphlet on the Wisconsin Industrial Commission that kindled an interest in John R. and the university. Altmeyer enrolled at Madison, graduated with a bachelor's degree in 1914, got a job teaching school, and rose to the position of principal. In 1916, he married his former history teacher, Ethel Thomas, and in 1918 he returned to Madison as a graduate assistant to John R. The job almost killed him.

> I discovered that Commons had no idea of the amount of effort required to carry out an idea of his, and he had many ideas every day . . . So instead of working one-fourth time, I'd say I worked more than eight hours a day on work for Professor Commons. I worked down at the State Tax Commission . . . from 8 till 12. So there were 12 hours, I'd say, out of the day. Then I was taking full graduate work. I had to do that at night, and I recall many times I'd tumble into bed at maybe 2 or 3 o'clock in the morning.[18]

So 1917 and 1918 marked a new direction at Madison, not strictly because of anything that John R. did, but because Perlman, Witte, and Altmeyer became the first members of his "Madison team." Together with John R., they created the sometimes praised, sometimes demonized "Wisconsin School" of labor studies with its labor seminars—and its Friday night suppers.

Nell seems to have originated the suppers—inviting all of John R.'s students to Ho-Chee-Ra every Friday night. Mark Perlman remembered Nell as "a mid-western motherly type" and a skillful manager who recruited the graduate student wives to help with the Friday night suppers. Most suppers would start with a rambling, sometimes mystifying, discourse by John R. Then, one or two students would report on their research. The routine would be interrupted now and then by guest speakers or by an interesting letter from a graduate "in the real world." According to Mark Perlman, his father, Selig, could not stand the suppers. Students would heap praise on John R. in ways that Selig found nauseating.[19]

In any case, the suppers bound faculty and students together. Former "Friday Nighters" would organize "Friday night clubs" in Washington, New York, and other cities where Wisconsin labor graduates would gather for camaraderie and fond remembrances.

The History

If the postwar years marked the beginning of one era in the labor studies program, 1918 marked the end of another. Delays and excuses ended when the long-delayed two-volume "interpretive history" rolled off the presses.

The title of both volumes—*History of Labour in the United States*—was misleading. It was not meant to be a history of labor, or even of labor organizations. As John R. explained in the introduction, the two volumes were written to identify and trace the influences that shaped American "labour philosophies and labour movements," to understand the forces that shunted American labor movements down tracks not traveled by similar movements in Europe.[20]

John R. identified seven such forces. Following the thesis of his colleague Frederick Jackson Turner, he made the frontier—before it disappeared—the first such force; it gave American workers an escape hatch unavailable to European workers. Second, white male suffrage—almost universal in the United States by 1830—gave American white workers the early, and ultimately disappointing, option of political rather than economic organization. Third, American markets covered far more space than European markets. Here, John R. repeated the thesis of the "American Shoemakers"—that market expansion over this vast area had created a complicated supply system, with workers and farmers at the producing end, and ultimate consumers at the retail end. This distance had replaced the bargain between producer and consumer with a complicated string of bargains in which workers bargained with employers on one end and consumers bargained with retailers on the other. Businesses along this vast supply system needed credit to operate as they awaited revenue from distant sales. Their need for credit increased the power of the banker capitalists. As a result, the system destroyed the bargaining power of individual workers and increased the bargaining power of banker capitalists. The fourth feature distinguishing the United States from most European countries was the delegation in the United States of police power to individual states so that this vast market had no central authority creating and enforcing uniform laws and regulations. The federal government could intervene only on proof that some issue was subject to the interstate commerce clause of the constitution—a clause strictly interpreted by the courts.

John R. emphasized the fifth force that shaped the evolution of American unionism—the legal supremacy of courts. Unlike European systems where parliaments have the last word, the American Constitution gave the Supreme Court veto power over executive and legislative branches of the government. Moreover, most Supreme Court Justices came from "dominant" classes in American society. "At the same time, the courts, blocking the way of a new aggressive class with precedents created to protect a dominant class, have had in this country, a high authority unknown in other lands. By vetoing the laws which labour in its political struggles has been able to secure, the courts have excluded or delayed labour from legislative influence."[21] Thus, the early right to vote had created a false hope; and American labor organizations were forced to seek by economic means what workers in other countries gained by legislation.

Sixth, unlike worker organizations in other countries, American unions had to cope with successive waves of immigrants unfamiliar with American institutions and unable to communicate in English. Finally, America's chaotic banking system made business cycles and their effects more severe in the United States than in European countries.

Partially to stress different aspects of these forces and partially to mark political or economic events, John R. and his collaborators divided American history into six periods. David Saposs covered the period from early colonial days to Andrew Jackson's presidency; Helen Sumner, the period from Jackson's presidency to the panic of 1837;

Edward Mittleman, the "humanitarian period" from the panic of 1837 to the Civil War; John Andrews, from the Civil War to the railroad strike of 1877; and Selig Perlman, from the railroad strike of 1877 to about 1910, or the "present" from their point of view.

The system for crediting individual authors reflected a compromise between the Carnegie Foundation's insistence that John R. be the official author and John R.'s original plan for students to write monographs published separately. Authorship of volumes was attributed to Commons and Associates. But within the covers, individual authors received full credit for the long sections that they wrote; John R. was credited only with the introduction.

George Barnett of Johns Hopkins wrote the most glowing review. He was the only reviewer to praise the students. Each section, Barnett wrote, presented "the most complete and authoritative narrative account of the period with which it deals."[22]

Ira Cross also praised both volumes. Barnett and Cross faulted the history for lack of unity and for its failure to tie more tightly the interpretive core to the narrative details. Cross would have preferred a history written entirely by John R.[23]

But a modern reader, more aware of the subsequent career trajectories of the students, might be happy that John R. allowed them so much leeway. David Saposs, for example, probably the most radical of the group—though never a communist in spite of later accusations—started his section by minimizing the difference between John R.'s theory of market extension and Karl Marx's emphasis on technical change. Helen Sumner devoted a number of paragraphs to the status of women and children in the 1820s and 1830s. Selig Perlman reviewed the philosophical background of various European revolutionary movements and linked this background to the influence on intellectual debates within the American labor movement of refugees from the failed revolutions of 1848. These perspectives might have been missing in a volume written only by John R.

Industrial Goodwill

A year after publication of the *History of Labor*, John R.'s *Industrial Goodwill* appeared. The title includes a word with three possible meanings.

Goodwill can mean a bookkeeping entry of the type that made the news when J.P. Morgan paid Andrew Carnegie three hundred million dollars for plant and equipment valued at seventy-five million dollars.

To balance the books, the difference—three hundred twenty five million dollars was recorded as goodwill value—even though Morgan simply wanted to remove a competitor so he could fix the price of steel.[24] Goodwill, in this sense, was an accounting concept condemned both by mainstream economists and by Thorstein Veblen.[25]

Goodwill can also mean a type of property that can be bought or sold, such as a trademark or some other characteristic related to a loyal customer base. Finally, Goodwill can mean a management strategy employed to gain consumer loyalty or to gain employee loyalty and reduce turnover.[26] Henry Ford is often cited as an example of the latter strategy for introducing a wage of $5.00 for an eight-hour day on January 5, 1914. He had been paying $2.34 an hour for a nine-hour day.

He did it to reduce labor force turnover at his River Rouge plant where workers were quitting at a pace that drove the turnover rate to 416 percent per year. To counter the myth that Ford granted the eight-hour day from some high-minded motive, the labor historian David Montgomery pointed out that four days after he granted the eight-hour day, Ford fired 900 workers for celebrating Eastern Orthodox Christmas.[27]

John R. adapted the management meaning of goodwill to make the case to employers for his "machinery of collective democracy." He wanted to persuade them because he did not see how they could be compelled to bargain in good faith.[28]

He sorted employers into three classes. The first class adopts labor policies that respond to market conditions; they raise wages and offer extra benefits when hiring is difficult and they reduce wages and benefits when widespread unemployment makes hiring easy. Such employers deal with workers the same way that they deal with commodities—cotton or hog bellies; they hold the "commodity" view of workers. The second class of employers tries to motivate employee behavior with piece work payment, merit pay, and bonuses. Merit pay and bonuses perform the same functions for people as levers and buttons do for machines. These employers hold the "machine" view of workers.

Of course no employer can ignore market conditions or employee motivation. But employers whose vision is limited to commodity and machine views will eventually alienate their employees and pay higher turnover costs.

Finally, employers of the third class think about workers in the same way that they think about customers. Just as managers seek to build a loyal customer base, so employers of the third class try to build a loyal cadre of workers. These employers can reap the rewards: lower turnover costs and the higher productivity of loyal employees. Thus employee goodwill becomes "a valuable asset," a source of future profits to which one can attach a monetary value.[29]

John R. devoted a number of chapters to policies pioneered by employers of the third class. In general, they showed that they cared about their employees. They reduced layoffs by sequencing activities to provide productive work when demand was slack and by training employees for different jobs so that if need for some jobs should decline, employees could move to other jobs within the company. They showed concern for employee welfare by offering group health and life insurance. And, of course, they showed concern in their wage and hour policies. Such policies were consistent with what has been called welfare capitalism, and the chapters that advocated them were praised.

John R., though, was not proposing welfare capitalism but the "machinery of collective democracy," and this machinery required active participation by the state and by free independent trade unions.

John R. gave the state three functions in this "machinery of collective democracy": First, the state must control what Henry Carter Adams had called the "competitive menace"; second, it must correct deficiencies in labor market information; and third it must protect and foster the nation's human resources.

By enforcing minimum standards, the state protects "forward looking" employers from the "competitive menace" of "backward employers" who can gain market share by slashing wages and prices—forcing all others either out of business or down to their level.[30] With minimum standards enforced, the benefits of worker goodwill—loyalty and lower turnover—would enable more humane employers to produce results superior to those of their less ethical competitors who simply hew to the minimum. Here John R. introduced his "ratchet principle" for public policy evolution. Once forward-looking employers prove that they can survive in market conditions, the minimum can be raised forcing all employers to that higher standard. Then forward-looking employers move again beyond the new minimum which can then be raised and so forth.

The state can correct information imbalances in labor markets by creating employment offices. Employers usually know more about labor markets than workers. This knowledge gives employers a bargaining edge. But employers themselves sometimes suffer from ignorance when they look for certain types of skilled workers. Government employment offices can inform workers about wage scales and job opportunities, and they can also help employers find workers with special skills.

Next John R. argued from two perspectives—a legal perspective and an economic perspective—that the state was responsible for the health of its citizens.

His legal argument rested on reasoning in two Supreme Court decisions: *Holden v. Hardy* and *Muller v. Oregon.*[31] In Holden, the court upheld a Utah law limiting hours of work in mines and smelters. The majority decision gave the state responsibility for the health of the workers because their weak bargaining position deprived them of the ability to protect their own health.

In *Muller v. Oregon*, Louis Brandeis and his sister-in-law, Josephine Goldmark, had designed the famous "Brandeis Brief" to defend an Oregon minimum wage law for women. The first part of the brief, written by Josephine Goldmark (110 pages), proved that long hours damaged the health of women. The second part (two pages), written by Brandeis, showed the legal grounds for protecting the health of women.[32] To this legal argument that the state had a responsibility for worker health, John R. added an economic human resource argument.

> Somebody must pay for the conservation of the nation's resources. If left to demand and supply, the most valuable resources are not conserved. For labor is both the source of demand for products and the source of supply of the same products. A nation of sick, ignorant, or rebellious workers produces enough products to keep them sick, ignorant, and unpatriotic. Demand-and-supply goes in a circle when the thing demanded is the supply of health, intelligence and the qualities of citizenship.[33]

Employers, he continued, never pay the full cost of their skilled workers. Most of that cost was paid by families and schools long before employers saw the workers. They should not be allowed to "use up" those human resources. John R. cited European writers who described workers returning from the United States broken in health and spirit from piece-work, merit-pay pressure, accidents, and sickening vapors. And so, while individual employers seeking goodwill can gain a competitive advantage by offering their employees life and health insurance, "backward" employers might not only force others down to their level, but, in the process, they might damage the nation's human resources, and for this reason, John R. advocated universal compulsory health and life insurance.[34]

And John R. gave free independent trade unions a role in his "machinery of collective democracy." First, without some type of employee representation, employers cannot maintain employee goodwill. John R. recounted the puzzlement of Chicago garment manufacturers when workers walked out right after they had received a generous wage increase. The workers had walked out to protest unpleasant and degrading aspects of their work environment that had been invisible to upper management. John R. drew the lesson that employers cannot keep the goodwill of their workers without giving them a voice in the workplace—and a chance for due process when accused of wrong-doing. The best way to give workers this voice would be to recognize a free and independent trade union. As a second best alternative, John R. accepted employee representation plans. He recognized union opposition to such plans, but he held to his position that they were better than nothing and he seemed to think that employee representative organizations would probably evolve into full-fledged unions.[35]

Employee representation plans could not fulfill another role that John R. considered essential to the "machinery of collective democracy." Only free independent trade unions can represent the standpoint of workers in decisions of the democratic state. For an example of how this would work, John R. cited Herbert Hoover's procedure for setting the price of wheat during the Great War. Hoover asked farm and labor organizations to appoint representatives to a committee. The committee settled on a price of $2.20 per bushel—between the $2.50 first proposed by the farm representatives and $1.84 first proposed by the labor representatives. Later Congress tried to impose a price of $2.50. John R.'s comment bore echoes of his earlier critiques of the US election system. "Congress does not directly represent either farmers or consumers. It may be a political democracy, but it is not an industrial democracy. Representative democracy in industry is representation of organized interests."[36]

So employers, the state, and free independent trade unions each play a role in John R.'s "machinery of collective democracy." Employers seek employee goodwill. The state forestalls the "competitive menace" and conserves human resources. Unions represent worker perspectives in the workplace and in the larger society.

The book was well received. The *New York Evening Post* called *Industrial Goodwill* "the most important book for the intelligent employer since Taylor's *Scientific Management*." It was possibly the first academic treatise on the subject, and it introduced the conception of what came to be called the "high performance workplace."[37] *Industrial Goodwill*, as noted, was popular, but some of the popularity may have resulted from reading the book as a "feel good" approach to employee relations while overlooking the roles it gave to the government and to independent trade unions.

Industrial Government

As a supplement to *Industrial Goodwill*, in 1919 John R., financed by a Wisconsin paper manufacturer, led a group of students on a project to find and document "best practices" for gaining employee goodwill. They visited thirty firms with good employee relations. They recorded their results in *Industrial Government.* Students wrote most of the chapters after extensive group discussions. John R. wrote only one.[38] One of the students was John R.'s son, Jack.

While nothing in the study shook his belief in "collective democracy," some experiences undermined his optimism. John R. estimated that between 10 percent and 25 percent of employers offer working conditions that are better than anything that legislation could impose or that a union could obtain, but the other 75 percent or 90 percent "are backward, either on account of inefficiency or greed, and only the big stick of unionism or legislation can bring them up to the level of the 10 percent or 25 percent."[39] His sponsor's comment further damaged his hope that employers might "see the light" and convert. When he reported his results, the paper manufacturer that had financed the study said "that the best way to beat the unions was 'to beat them to it.' The conclusion startled me. I had not expected it."[40] This was disappointing, and it indicated the beginning of a disappointing decade.

Notes

1. Norman Angell, *The Great Illusion: A Study of the Relation of Military Power in Nations to Their Economic and Political Power* (1909; reprint, New York: Gardner Publications, 1972), Thomas Fleming, *The Illusion of Victory, America in World War I* (New York: Basic Books, 2003).
2. John Reed, *Ten Days That Shook the World* (1922; reprint, New York: International Publishers, 1967).
3. Clifford Kinvig, *Churchill's Crusade: The British Invasion of Russia 1918–1920.* (London: Humbledon Continuum, 2006), Richard M. Doolen, *The Polar Bears: America's Expedition to North Russia* (Ann Arbor: University of Michigan Press, 1965).
4. Pfc. Samuel Herbert Darrah Company K, 339th Regiment, 85th Infantry Division. www.wwvets.com/Siberia.html. Retrieved January 3, 2015.
5. *Capital Times (Madison)* (December 9, 1919), 8.
6. Commons, *Myself,* 184.

A Worker's Economist

7. Benjamin Rader, *The Academic Mind and Reform: The Influence of Richard T. Ely in American Life* (Lexington: University of Kentucky Press, 1966), 181–88.

8. Robert Lampman, ed., *Economists at Wisconsin 1892–1992* (Madison: Board of Regents of the University of Wisconsin System 1992), xxiii.

9. Commons, *Myself*, 185–86.

10. According to Mark Perlman Ely had hired Selig Perlman to revise the *Labor Movement in America*, but when Perlman gave him the revision, Ely had declared it unsuitable, fired Perlman, and canceled his stipend. Then, after Perlman ran into open anti-Semitism on the job market John R.'s wife Nell with the assistance of the sociologist Edward Alsworth Ross instigated a department revolt, unseated Ely as chairman, and installed William Kiekhofer. The story can be partially verified Perlman was hired by a contract dated February 28, 1916, in Commons Papers, microfilm, reel 3, frames10, 11.12 in which Perlman agreed to revise *The Labor Movement in America* and Ely agreed to a stipend and a permanent faculty position. Other parts of the interview seem in error. Ely had not been chairman since 1911. The sociology department did not split off until 1929. See Lampman, *Economists at Wisconsin*, 35 and Appendix table A13. So one might conclude that Nell and Ross intervened for Perlman, but how they did so is not clear.

11. Theron Schlabach, *Edwin Witte Cautious Reformer* (Madison: State Historical Society of Wisconsin, 1969), 9.

12. Ibid., 15.

13. Edwin Witte, "Institutional Economics as Seen by an Institutional Economist," *Southern Economic Journal* 21 (October 1954): 131.

14. Schlabach, *Edwin Witte*, 55–57.

15. Curti and Carstensen, *The University of Wisconsin*, 115.

16. Commons papers, microfilm, reel 22, frame 9. The history of their search is in a set of letters in the microfilm edition of Commons's papers, between June 21 and July 18, 1918, reel 21, frames 179–87.

17. Don D. Lescohier, *My Story for the First Seventy-Seven Years* (Madison, WI: Air Brush Creations, 1960), 54.

18. Quoted in Larry DeWitt, *Never a Finished Thing: A Brief Biography of Arthur Joseph Altmeyer—The Man FDR called Mr. Social Security* (Suitland, MD: Social Security Administration, 1997), www.ssa.gov/history/bioaja.html, accessed July 24, 2014.

19. Fink, "A Memoir of Selig Perlman," 514–15.

20. John R. Commons, "Introduction," in *History of Labour in the United Sates*, John R. Commons, David J. Saposs, Helen L. Sumner, E. R. Mittleman, H.E. Hoagland, John B. Andrews and Selig Perlman, eds. (1918;reprint. New York: Augustus M. Kelley, 1966), vol.1 of 2, 3–21.

21. Ibid., 9.

22. George Barnett, "*History of Labour in the United States* by John R. Commons and Associates" *American Economic Review* 9 (June, 1919): 340–42.

23. Ira Cross, "Review of the *History of Labour in the United States*," *Quarterly Journal of Economics* 32 (August 1918): 667–73.

24. John R. Commons, *The Economics of Collective Action* (New York: Macmillan, 1950), 63.

25. A.M. Endres, "Veblen and Commons on Goodwill: A Case of Theoretical Divergence," *History of Political Economy* 17 (1985): 637–48.
26. Magnus Alexander, "Hiring and Firing: Its Economic Waste and How to Avoid It," *Annals of the American Academy of Political and Social Science* 65 (May, 1916): 128–44.
27. David Montgomery, *The Fall of the House of Labor: The Workplace, the State, and American Labor Activism* (New York: Cambridge University Press, 1987), 231, 234, 236.
28. John R. Commons, *Industrial Goodwill* (1919; reprint, New York: Arno Press, 1969), 111.
29. Ibid., 26.
30. Ibid., 28.
31. Ibid., 31, 169 U.S. 366 (1898), 208 U.S. 412 (1908).
32. Peter Irons, *A People's History of the Supreme Court* (New York: Penguin Group, 1999), 249, 256, 258.
33. Commons, *Industrial Goodwill*, 129.
34. Ibid., 90–97.
35. Ibid., 111.
36. Ibid., 40.
37. Cited in Bruce Kaufman, *The Global Evolution of Industrial Relations: Events, Ideas, and the ILRA* (Geneva: International Labor Office, 2004), 143.
38. John R. Commons and Others, *Industrial Government.* (1919; reprint, New York: Arno, 1969), 263–72.
39. Ibid., 263.
40. Commons, *Myself*, 189.

14

The Dominant Class

At the same time, the courts, blocking the way of a new aggressive class with precedents created to protect a dominant class, have had, in this country, a high authority unknown in other lands—History of Labor Volume 3.

On December 10, 1917, in the case of *Hitchman Coal and Coke Co. v. Mitchell*, the US Supreme Court decided that union organizers could not talk to employees who had signed "yellow dog contracts" (contracts in which workers promised that they would not join a union). This decision, John R. complained, changed the debate about unions. The question was "no longer, Shall unions be prohibited from committing violence," but rather, "Shall they be prohibited from even persuading non-unionists to join?"[1] The Hitchman decision was not the only threat to John R.'s vision of industrial democracy. After the Armistice on November 11, 1918, the National Association of Manufacturers (NAM) resumed its open-shop campaigns.

And the NAM campaign got an unintended boost in 1919 when striking shipyard workers appealed to the Seattle Labor Council for help, and the council responded by calling a city-wide sympathy strike on February 6.[2] The strike was short—five days—peaceful, well organized, and nonviolent. The council maintained all essential services. But wild literature covered the streets, convincing journalists of a nascent Bolshevik plot. Seattle's mayor, Ole Hanson, resigned and went on a speaking tour to warn the nation about the imminent threat of a Bolshevik takeover. Thus began the nation's first "red scare."[3] Taking advantage of the "red scare," the Associated Industries of Seattle named their open-shop campaign: the "American Plan" and sold it as a courageous defense of American values against unions controlled by "Bolshevists, aliens, and European radicals." Open-shop campaigns across the nation adopted this patriotic slogan, and unions continued to lose.[4]

Back in Madison, in 1918, John R. had inaugurated a new course called "values and valuation," returning to his interest in the connections between ethics, economics, and law.[5] The course would range widely, picking up issues such as the Hitchman case, wage rates, cyclical instability, and unemployment, an issue about which John R. was growing more concerned after the rounds of inflation and unemployment that followed the end of the Great War. Two quick business cycles drove the estimated unemployment rate to almost 8 percent in1920 and to 16 percent in 1921. Unemployment was still 12 percent in 1922.[6]

Unemployment and Unemployment Compensation

There was also, surprisingly, growing concern about unemployment within the administrations of the Stalwarts Warren Harding and Calvin Coolidge—not so much because of Harding or Coolidge—but because of their secretary of Commerce, Herbert Hoover, a man of humane instincts deeply concerned about the economic waste and human suffering caused by a shortage of jobs. Hoover wanted a high-wage high-efficiency fully employed economy.[7]

To find out how to encourage such an economy, Hoover, on September 26, 1921, convened the President's Commission on Unemployment. John Andrews was there with a large contingent from American Association for Labor Legislation (AALL). "For the first time in the history of the United States," wrote Andrews, "a high government official had fixed unemployment in the public mind as not only a social problem but also a Problem of Industry" (capitals in original).[8] The influence of the AALL's "Practical Program for the Prevention of Unemployment" was evident in the commission's recommendations.[9]

But the recommendations also reflected Hoover's associationism which resembled, in at least one respect, John R.'s vision of constructive democracy. Hoover believed in giving all interested parties a voice in the public decisions that affected them.[10] Unlike John R., though, Hoover did not recognize an inevitable conflict of interest over the distribution of income. And Hoover held stronger convictions about the limits of government activity. For Hoover, the government should facilitate and coordinate activity, but it should act within a strictly limited sphere.

Hoover established a Business Cycle Committee and a Committee on Seasonal Operations to develop cooperative relations with private sector construction companies and state governments. During the

1920–21 depression he supported private groups that lobbied Congress for construction projects. Hoover also encouraged private unemployment insurance provided by companies and unions. His philosophy did not, however, permit him to find an explicit government role in unemployment compensation. The proposals for such a role would come from the AALL and from John R. and his students.

In July, 1920, the Wisconsin Federation of Labor invited John R. to address its annual convention.[11] John R.'s address was all about universal health insurance. But union delegates wanted to talk about unemployment compensation. They appointed a committee, charged it with presenting an unemployment compensation bill to the next session of the legislature, and asked John R. for help. John R., assisted by a graduate student, Allen B. Forsberg, wrote a first draft based on a bill that John Andrews had submitted to the Massachusetts legislature in 1916. That bill had proposed contributions from employers, the state, and employees. The union representatives, however, wanted to start with Wisconsin's worker compensation bill; it required contributions only from employers.[12] Union men argued that if employers were forced to bear the costs of unemployment, they would have an incentive to reduce turnover. They did not need to argue much; John R. was already thinking along those lines. He had been encouraged by the "safety first" campaigns that followed the introduction of workers' compensation, and he knew that some firms had been able to reduce or eliminate seasonal unemployment and turnover.[13]

So John R. wrote a bill that established a mutual insurance company financed by premiums based on the unemployment record of each employer. Since employers as a group would own this mutual insurance company, they would receive dividends whenever revenues exceeded expenditures. Consequently, the financing system embodied a collective incentive to reduce unemployment. In addition the bill prescribed experience-rated compensation premiums, so that firms with higher turnover would pay higher premiums. The bill was introduced into the Wisconsin State Legislature by Senator Henry Huber.

John R. and his student assistant, Allen Forsberg (also a union carpenter), traveled the state trying to whip up support for the Huber bill. Every business organization in Wisconsin lobbied against it, and it failed in 1921. But some form of the Huber bill would be introduced at every legislative session over the next decade.

In the meantime, some unions and employers were sponsoring private unemployment compensation schemes. One such scheme—worked out between the Associated Clothing Manufacturers of Chicago and the Amalgamated Clothing Workers—would involve John R.[14]

The president of the Amalgamated Clothing Workers, Sidney Hillman, had floated the idea of unemployment compensation during negotiations in 1920. Over the next three years, union and management representatives had worked out details with the technical assistance of labor economist Leo Wolman. On May 1, 1924, the system began operating. Employers and workers each contributed 1.5 percent of wages to a fund from which unemployed workers could receive benefits up to a maximum of 40 percent of their wages. There were three such funds, one for Hart, Schaffner & Marx, one for the B. Kuppenheimer Company, and a third for the smaller companies. Each was administered by a separate board of trustees. Union and management representatives agreed to ask John R. to chair all three boards.[15]

Contrary to John R.'s statement in *Myself*, this plan was not quite the same as the one he had written for Senator Huber.[16] The Chicago plan provided for contributions from workers. John R.'s plan did not. John R.'s plan pooled premiums in an employer-owned Mutual Insurance Company. The Chicago plan gave each company its own fund. In the future John R. would stick to his principle that only employers should pay. But he would drop his mutual insurance company and adopt company-specific funds as more acceptable to employers.

John R. laid out his argument for "preventive compensation" in *The Survey*.[17] He traced unemployment to three causes: labor turnover, seasonal demand, and the credit cycle. He argued that employers could control all three. They could reduce turnover by making the workplace more attractive. They could reduce seasonal unemployment by sequencing tasks and by training workers to do more than on job. They could reduce cyclical unemployment by controlling the tendency to over expand in boom times, thus preventing the bust of cyclical unemployment. This article alone could give the impression that John R. held employers responsible for all unemployment including cyclical unemployment, but that impression would be mistaken.

That impression that he held employers responsible for cyclical unemployment can be corrected by considering John R.'s support for the AALL program, by his work with Irving Fisher's stable money movement, and by his analysis of business cycles in his values seminar.

The AALL's five-part program included, in addition to unemployment compensation, public works and government employment offices—all called for only on the assumption that individual firms cannot alone compensate for cyclical unemployment.

Money and the Business Cycle

John R. also participated in Irving Fisher's stable money movement. Fisher, like John R. and many other economists, had been dismayed by the monetary mess created at Versailles—a mess worsened when American presidents rebuffed allies seeking lenient terms for repayment of war debts. It was worsened further by inept central bank policies. To prevent the inevitable collapse, Fisher had convened a group of likeminded citizens to find and promote more intelligent policies.

The group changed its name and reorganized a number of times until it emerged in 1922 as the National Monetary Association with John R. Commons as president and Norman Lombard as its energetic executive secretary.[18] John R. wrote three papers with the group.[19] He contested the conventional belief of central bankers that their policies had little influence on prices—which, they claimed, rose and fell mainly in response to "real" events such as droughts, wars, famines, and periodic fits of mass psychology. He argued that postwar business cycles proved that central bank policies do in fact influence prices. He pointed to the "enormous inflation" that followed the sale of US treasuries at below-market interest rates in 1919 and to the response of the general price level to every other central bank policy change since the Great War. To refute the objection that monetary policy had little effect on business behavior because interest costs were just a fraction of total costs, he pointed to the effect of interest rates on expectations. If interest rates rise, managers expect hard times and cut back on production. If interest rates fall, managers expect better times and increase in production. Over time, John R. would develop a stronger argument.

He brought the business cycle into his values seminar where, as shown in an article he wrote with two students, Harlan McCracken and William Zeuch, he sought a theoretical basis for explaining how capitalist economies, in their normal operations, generate business cycles. The article focused on competing value theories represented in the famous debate between Ricardo and Malthus who argued about the causes of the "Glut" that began in 1815, the depression that ended the Napoleonic wars.[20] Ricardo's value theory represented "embodied" theories that based value on something "real"—labor or land or the cost of production. Malthus's theory represented "commanded theories" that based values on market prices determined by supply and demand. Using these two categories, John R. and his two students sorted all economic value theories into either "embodied" or "commanded" categories. Next they examined how each of these theories would handle three types of economy: barter, metallic money, and credit. They concluded that a "commanded" value in a credit economy was the only one that could generate endogenous business cycles—business cycles that result from the ordinary operations of the economy, and not just from "accidental" events such as wars, droughts, or famines.

They finished by defining value as a figure found by discounting future income with an interest rate, and they related that interest rate to a modification of Knut Wicksell's "natural rate of interest"—the rate at which the amount of money that savers plan to lend would equal the amount of money that borrowers plan to spend. The other rate, the actual rate, is the rate maintained by the central bank.

The article illustrated the way that John R. worked with his students. It also illustrated his desire to understand business cycles and to blunt their devastating impacts on the lives of workers.

He assigned the business cycle as a dissertation topic to one of his best students, Alvin Hansen. For the entire cycle that lasted from 1902 till 1908, Hansen analyzed monthly statistics in the United States, Britain, and Germany looking for patterns and correlations.[21]

And, during the Great Depression, both McCracken and Hansen would make significant contributions to the effort to understand and alleviate the consequences of that economic disaster. McCracken's contribution would go largely unacknowledged until recently.[22] Hansen would become recognized for explaining John Maynard Keynes's theories to Americans.[23] A psychic looking back at Madison in the 1920s might sense that in some odd way, the department was preparing, not just in research, but in institutional structures for the challenges that would come in 1929.

The Death of Charles McCarthy and the Expansion of "the Team"

A tragedy initiated changes that, like the paper with McCracken and Zeuch, and like the dissertation of Alvin Hansen, seemed eerily designed to prepare John R.'s team for the challenges of the Great Depression.

The tragedy was the passing of Charles McCarthy. He had not looked well for some time, and his friend from the Irish Free State movement, Sir Horace Plunkett, had persuaded him to visit Plunkett's friend,

Dr. Pritchett at the Battlecreek, Michigan, clinic. Dr. Pritchett could not do much because McCarthy would not let him examine anything below his chest. Pritchett advised rest in a warm, dry climate, and McCarthy left Madison on March 12, 1921, for Prescott, Arizona, where he died two weeks later, the day after Good Friday.

Edwin Witte replaced McCarthy as the official Legislative Reference Librarian.[24] Arthur Altmeyer replaced Witte as the secretary of the Wisconsin Industrial Commission—just in time to let Altmeyer catch up on his sleep. The new full-time job was less demanding than Altmeyer's part-time job as John R.'s assistant. Witte and Altmeyer would gain political and administrative skills that they would employ fifteen years later in Washington, DC.

In addition, two new students came to Wisconsin: Paul Raushenbush and Elizabeth Brandeis. Raushenbush, son of the eminent social gospel theologian, Walter Raushenbusch, came from Amherst College in 1922 (Paul seems to have dropped the "c" from his name). Elizabeth Brandeis, the daughter of the famous jurist, came from Washington, DC, in 1923. She came to study law, but upon arrival, she discovered that all the action in which she was interested was happening around John R., so she changed to economics. Everybody called her EB. After she earned her MA in 1924, Smith College offered her a job which her father thought she should take. But, John R. convinced her to stay at Madison and work toward a PhD.

John R. claimed another cupid credit when, on July 2, 1925, EB and Paul Raushenbush were married in a private ceremony in Chicago.[25] In 1926 Swarthmore offered both EB and Paul teaching positions. Again, John R. persuaded them to stay in Madison. EB would receive her PhD in1928 and remain in Madison as a full-time faculty member. Paul would remain with the Wisconsin Industrial Commission and serve as a part-time lecturer in the department.

The NBER and the NCL

In a way, John R. was better at keeping EB and Paul Raushenbush in Madison than he was at keeping himself there. Friendships and connections from his exile years and from the Pittsburgh Survey exercised a pull that he could not ignore.

One friendship that he could not ignore was the one he had forged with N (Nahum) I. Stone in the first insecure days of the American Bureau of Economic Research when he and Stone had created a pioneering price index.

Later, in 1916, Stone and another statistician, Malcolm Rorty, had conceived of a politically neutral organization that would collect and analyze statistics using the most up-to-date methods.[26] The organization would preserve neutrality with a board of trustees composed of competent researchers representing a broad spectrum of political positions. Stone and Rorty had consulted with John R. from the beginning, and John R. had served on the initial advisory board in 1917.[27] In 1920 Stone and Rorty got their National Bureau of Economic Research (NBER) up and running. They asked John R. to serve on the new advisory board. John R.'s friend, Wesley Clair Mitchell became the organization's first research director.

Three years later, on November 8, 1923, another old Friend, Florence Kelley, asked John R. to serve as president of the National Consumers' League (NCL).[28] John R. had worked on the Pittsburgh Survey with Kelley, the daughter of William (Pig Iron) Kelley, the high tariff congressman from Pennsylvania. She had graduated from Cornell and had studied law in Zurich. With her three children, Kelley had later fled from an abusive husband to Hull House and Jane Addams in Chicago. She had joined the Hull House anti-sweatshop campaign that persuaded Governor John P. Altgeld to sponsor a strong set of factory acts. She so impressed Altgeld that he appointed her the first female factory inspector in US history. In addition, while at Hull House, Kelley had earned a law degree from Northwestern University, and when Altgeld's factory laws were challenged in court, she had written the defense brief. With Jane Addams and Josephine Lowell, Kelley had founded the NCL in 1899, and she served as its executive secretary and guiding light until her death in 1932.

The league encouraged its members to patronize firms for which it issued white labels—symbols of good working conditions. But white labels were only the beginning. Until her death, Kelley led the league into almost every progressive campaign that ever happened. She was present at the formation of the National Association for the Advancement of Colored People (NAACP). She supported campaigns for a children's bureau, the socialist party, eight-hour laws, and minimum wages. Most significantly, she supported the State of Oregon and the Brandeis Brief.

When the State of Oregon's ten-hour law for women was challenged in court, Kelley hired Louis Brandeis as additional counsel for the State of Oregon. (Hired is a strong word. Brandeis worked pro bono.) Under Brandeis's guidance Josephine Goldmark, the NCL's labor coordinator, wrote 113 pages of the famous 115 page "Brandeis Brief" that won unanimous Supreme Court approval for the law.[29] The 113 pages summarized practically all the existing evidence and proved that long hours damage the health of women. The last two pages used precedents to show that the court admitted health benefits as a reason for interfering with freedom of contract.

A similar strategy did not work as well during John R.'s presidency. Congress, in 1918, had established a minimum wage board for the District of Columbia. After sponsoring a set of household surveys to estimate the cost of a minimum living standard, the board had set the minimum wage. Washington Children's Hospital sued, arguing that the law deprived its employees of the freedom to contract for lower wages.[30] The bill's opponents employed the tactic of finding a "victim"— an elevator operator, Willie Lyons, who duly swore that the law limited her freedom to contract for low wages.

Kelley followed the successful *Muller v. Oregon* strategy. Felix Frankfurter replaced Brandeis who was now a Supreme Court Justice. On April 9, 1923, the court by a five to three majority found Washington's minimum wage law unconstitutional because it deprived women of freedom of contract under the Fifth Amendment. (Brandeis, now a Supreme Court Justice, had recused himself). The decision, written by Justice George Sutherland, a Harding appointee, was long, detailed, and notable only because it drew famous dissents from William Howard Taft and Oliver Wendell Holmes.

The *Adkins v. Children's Hospital* decision created a problem. It was now a precedent for other minimum wage laws. John R. contributed to a brief defending California's minimum wage by emphasizing how different it was from the DC law.[31]

The Adkins decision incited outrage. In its May 15, 1923, issue, *The Survey* ran a cartoon in which a portly judge informs a thin little woman that he has just given her the right to starve. In the same issue, Paul Kellogg printed a number of citizen comments. John R. commented that it seemed "unfitting" that five men should be able to undo a decision approved by the entire Congress and the President. He suggested a law requiring a majority of seven for any opinion that overturned laws passed by Congress.[32]

Florence Kelley was stronger.

> Although the life, health, and happiness of women and girls are at stake, no woman has participated in the minimum wage case in any

of its stages, and against this unnatural and unreasonable circumstance public opinion has not protested until the catastrophe is now upon us. The Supreme Court of the United States has by the votes of five men affirmed in 1923 the inalienable constitutional right of American women to starve, as it affirmed in 1918, also by the votes of five men and in 1922 by the votes of eight men, the inalienable constitutional right of hundreds of thousands of American children to be illiterate, overworked, and bereft of the equal protection of the law. . . .

The next appointee to the Supreme Court of the United States and also the next appointee to the Court of Appeals of the District of Columbia should be the first of a series of able women of modern mind, to share the duty of *interpreting and not vetoing* necessary industrial and social statutes.[33]

The Pittsburgh Plus Case

Unlike N. I. Stone and Florence Kelley, the attorney generals of four Midwestern states—Illinois, Iowa, Minnesota, and Wisconsin—were not old friends of John R. They may have considered him their own "Midwestern economist." At any rate, in 1923, they asked him to help them in their case before the Federal Trade Commission.[34] They wanted the commission to stop the US Steel Corporation from continuing a practice it had followed since 1902—of adding the cost of freight from Pittsburgh to the cost of any rolled steel that it sold—no matter where that steel was produced. For example, if a Chicago customer bought steel from a Chicago steel mill, the freight bill would be the same as if the steel had traveled all the way from Pittsburgh. This practice went unchallenged until the Great War when the War Labor Board ordered steel companies to bill actual shipping costs. The order stood for a short time— until Judge Elbert Gary, president of US Steel, convinced the board to reinstate the Pittsburgh Plus System. These sudden changes alerted customers to the costs of this system. On August 1, 1919, the Western Association of Rolled Steel Consumers and the city of Duluth, Minnesota, petitioned the Federal Trade Commission to issue a complaint against US Steel for the Pittsburgh Plus method of billing for rolled steel. US Steel deployed its staff of lawyers, and in July, 1920, the FTC rejected the complaint by a vote of three to two.

A new attorney for the association, H. G. Pickering of Duluth, requested a rehearing.[35] In 1923 four Midwestern states—Illinois, Iowa, Minnesota, and Wisconsin—joined the plaintiffs and appropriated

$55,000 to defray further legal expenses. Twenty-eight other states officially supported the plaintiffs.

The attorneys general of the four states asked that the hearing be postponed from May to December, 1923, to give them time to consult economists. They asked John R. to help them and paid him to spend a semester in Washington. John R. called on two old friends—Frank A. Fetter and William Z. Ripley. He had known Fetter since their days together at the University of Indiana. And he had worked with Ripley, the transportation expert for the United States Industrial Commission (USIC) on the commission's final report in the house that Nell had managed. The three economists gave their testimony in December 1923. On July 21, 1924, the FTC, by a majority of four to one, voted a cease and desist order for the Pittsburgh Plus system. John R. gave major credit for the victory to Ripley and Fetter, perhaps a little more to Fetter who expanded his argument in *The Masquerade of Monopoly*.[36]

The Legal Foundations of Capitalism

Before Pittsburgh Plus, before the National Consumers' League, at the same time as the article with McCracken and Zeuch, in 1922, John R. had sent his friend, Wesley Clair Mitchell, drafts of an article and a book, both on law and economics.[37] Mitchell had liked them, but he made two comments about the book. First, he thought that John R.'s approach was so original, that the book might not be appreciated until after a lapse of time. Second, Mitchell found the book too long. He suggested splitting it into two volumes. John R. sent the article to the *Yale Law Journal* which published it in 1924, and, following Mitchell's suggestion, he divided the original manuscript. The first volume, the *Legal Foundations of Capitalism* (hereafter referred to as *Foundations*), was published in 1924. The second volume would be revised so many times that a completely different book would appear ten years later.

Mitchell's prediction about delayed appreciation was only partially correct. Mitchell of course praised the book.[38] Legal realists in the Yale Law School were so impressed that they asked John R. to teach a summer course there. Beyond that, though, the contemporary reviews of the *Foundations* were mixed. Friend and foe alike criticized John R.'s terminology. R.H. Tawney, the British author of *Religion and the Rise of Capitalism*, in an otherwise favorable review, commented that "Technical economic language is bad, and technical legal language is worse. Some of the terms used by the author suggest that he determined to beat economists and lawyers at their own game."[39]

Negative reviewers accused John R. of straying outside his field and making elementary errors in legal reasoning.[40]

In perhaps the most insightful—though somewhat critical—review, the British economic historian, Sir William Ashley, deftly related John R.'s *Legal Foundations of Capitalism* to Ely's *Property and Contract in Relation to the Distribution of Wealth*. Ashley commented on the way that Anglo-Saxon individualism, especially as it was incorporated in the US Constitution, hindered intelligent responses to the damaging side effects of industrial progress. In a passage almost as dense as those he criticized in the *Foundations*, Ashley summarized John R.'s entire argument in a single lapidary passage.

> The adaptation of law to social needs might conceivably be brought about by definitions which limit property rights. But ever since the Roman law with its sharp conception of "dominium" began to influence the modern mind, the trend of legal interpretation has been towards the recognition of the completest right of individuals to make use of themselves and of forms of wealth under their control. It has preferred to think rather of "absolute" property subject to some right of another—subject to "servitude" to that extent—rather than of two persons each, but in different senses "owning" its property.[41]

In this final sentence, Ashley uncovered the central argument of the book. John R. made his argument in three parts—not necessarily covered in three distinct places. There was a theoretical part on transactions and going concerns, a historical part on the creation and definition of property rights, and a final argument that the courts had failed to adapt laws surrounding the wage bargain to the human realities of an industrial society, or, in Ashley's terminology, the courts had redefined the meaning of property to protect the absolute right of employers to wealth but they had not redefined the meaning of the wage bargain in a way that would protect the right of workers to jobs or decent wages. And, in this way, John R. responded to the Supreme Court's decisions that concerned the wage bargain, and especially to its Hitchman decision. A more extended treatment of the *Legal Foundations of Capitalism* has been relegated to appendix B.

Notes

1. John R. Commons, "Introduction," in *Civil War in West Virginia*, ed. Winthrop D. Lane (New York: Huebsch, 1921), 7.

2. Melvyn Dubofsky, *The State and Labor in Modern America* (Chapel Hill: North Carolina University press, 1994), 211–20.
3. Murray Levin, *Political Hysteria: The Democratic Capacity for Repression* (New York: Basic Books, 1971); Robert Murray, *Red Scare: A Study in National Hysteria 1919–1920* (New York: McGraw-Hill, 1974).
4. Philip S. Foner, *History of the Labor Movement in the United States, The T.U.E.L. and the End of the Gompers Era*, vol. 9 (New York: International Publishers, 1994), 173.
5. Lampman, *Economists at Wisconsin*, 38.
6. Stanley Lebergott, *Manpower in Economic Growth* (New York: McGraw-Hill, 1964), 512, Susan B. Carter et al., *Historical Statistics of the United States: Earliest Times to Present*, vol.2 (New York: Cambridge University Press, 2006), 82–83.
7. Ellis W. Hawley, "Herbert Hoover, the Commerce Secretariat and the Vision of the 'Associative State,'" *Journal of American History* 61(June, 1974): 116–40. William Barber, *From New Era to New Deal: Herbert Hoover and American Economic Policy 1921–1933* (New York: Cambridge University Press, 1985), 15–22.
8. John B. Andrews, "The President's Conference on Unemployment Success or Failure?," *American Labor Legislation Review* 11 (December, 1921): 307–10.
9. At its annual meeting in 1914, the AALL had worked out a program with four major components and six suggestions. The four components were establishment of unemployment exchanges; systematic distribution of public works; regularization of industry (this meant encouraging firms to schedule work in a way that reduces seasonal unemployment), and unemployment insurance. The six suggestions were industrial training; agricultural revival; "constructive" immigration policy; abolition of child labor; reduction of working hours; and constructive care of the unemployable. This last suggestion included health insurance, old age insurance, "segregation of the feeble minded," and work camps, John Andrews, "A Practical Program for the Prevention of Unemployment," *American Labor Legislation Review* 5 (June, 1915): 171–92.
10. Hawley, "Herbert Hoover, the Commerce Secretariat and the Vision of an 'Associative State,'" 131–33.
11. Daniel Nelson, "Unemployment Insurance in Wisconsin," *Wisconsin Magazine of History* (Winter 1967–1968): 109–21.
12. Ibid., 117.
13. Dennison Manufacturing Corporation, Personnel Division, "Plan in Use by an American Corporation for Combatting Unemployment," *American Labor Legislation Review* 11 (March 1921): 53–58.
14. Harry A. Millis, "Unemployment Insurance in the Men's Clothing Industry in Chicago," *The University Journal of Business* 2 (March 1924): 157–68.
15. Ibid., 167n.
16. Commons, *Myself*, 198.
17. John R. Commons, "Unemployment Compensation and Prevention," *The Survey* 47 (October 1, 1921): 5–9.
18. J. Dennis Chasse, "The Economists of the Lost Cause and the Monetary Education of John R. Commons," *Journal of the History of Economic Thought*

36 (June, 2014): 193–214. Irving Fisher and Hans R.L. Cohrssen, *Stable Money: A History of the Movement* (New York: Adelphi Co., 1934).

19. John R. Commons, "Price Level Changes through Changes in the Rate of Discount and Rediscount," "Bank Credit," "Inflation and Deflation," all in Commons Papers, microfilm, reel 10, frames 572–627.

20. John R. Commons., H.L. McCracken, and W E. Zeuch, "Secular Trends and Business Cycles," *The Review of Economics and Statistics* 4 (October, 1922): 244–63.

21. Alvin Hansen, *Cycles of Prosperity and Depression in the United States, Great Britain, and Germany 1902–1908* (Madison: University of Wisconsin Press, 1921).

22. When the depression struck, McCracken resigned his position as president of Penn College and returned to research on business cycles. He wrote two books, one of which "seemed to influence the treatment of Say's law in the *General Theory.*" See Steven Kates, "A Letter from Keynes to Harlan McCracken Dated 31st of August 1933 Why the Standard Story on the Origins of the General Theory Needs to Be Rewritten," *History of Economics Review* 47 (Winter, 2008): 39–42.

23. Alvin Hansen, *A Guide to Keynes* (New York: McGraw-Hill, 1953).

24. Schlabach, *Edwin Witte, Cautious Reformer*, 33.

25. Urofsky, Melvin. *Louis D. Brandeis: A Life* (New York: Pantheon Books, 2009), 663–64.

26. N.I. Stone, "The Beginnings of the National Bureau of Economic Research," in *The National Bureau's First Quarter Century* (New York: National Bureau of Economic Research, 1945), 5–11; Solomon *Fabricant "Toward a Firmer Basis for Economic Policy: The Founding of the National Bureau of Economic Research (New York: NBER, 1984),* ww.nber.org/nberhistory/sfabricantrev. *pdf*, accessed November 14, 2013.

27. Dorfman, Joseph, "The Mutual Influence of Mitchell and Commons," *American Economic Review* 48, no. 3 (June, 1958): 405–8.

28. Commons, *Myself*, 181.

29. Muller v. Oregon 208 U.S, 412 (1908).

30. Adkins v. Children's Hospital 261 U.S.525 (1923).

31. Felix Frankfurter, Molly Dawson, and John R. Commons. *State Minimum Wage Laws in Practice* (New York: National Consumers' League, 1924).

32. John R. Commons, "Restore the Balance of Power," *The Survey* 50, no. 4 (May 15, 1923): 261.

33. Florence Kelley.1923. "Women on the Bench." Ibid., 222.

34. Samuel Schneider, *Three American Economics Professors Battle against Monopoly and Pricing Practices: Ripley, Fetter, and Commons: Three for the People* (Lewiston, NY: Edward Mellen Press, 1998).

35. Frank A. Fetter, *The Masquerade of Monopoly* (New York: Harcourt Brace and Company, 1931), 145–55.

36. Fetter and Ripley both wrote books. Ripley created a meme, *Main Street and Wall Street* (Boston, MA: Little Brown and Company, 1927).

37. Joseph Dorfman, "Prefatory Note," in *Legal Foundations of Capitalism* (1924; reprint, New York: Augustus M. Kelley, 1974), 5–11.

38. Wesley Clair Mitchell, "Commons on the Legal Foundations of Capitalism," *American Economic Review* 14 (June 1924): 240–51.

39. R.H. Tawney, "Legal Foundations of Capitalism: Review," *Economica* 13 (March, 1924): 104–5.
40. Gerard C. Henderson, "Legal Foundations of Capitalism Review," *Harvard Law Review* 7 (May, 1924): 923–27; David Lillienthal, "An Economist Strays Outside His Field," *The Nation* (September 21, 1924): 782–83.
41. William. J. Ashley, "*Legal Foundations of Capitalism* by John R. Commons: Review," *Economic Journal* 36, no. 141 (March, 1926): 84–88.

15

Croaking Cassandras

*Here are Collected . . . the croakings of a Cassandra who
could never influence the course of events in time.*
—J.M. Keynes, Essays in Persuasion

On December 6, 1924, in Mexico City, Samuel Gompers, president of the American Federation of Labor, collapsed from a heart attack. When he regained consciousness, he asked to be placed on a train heading north so he could die on the soil of his adopted country. He died a week later, in San Antonio, Texas. The train kept on to New York, and, wherever it stopped crowds gathered. "Up from the humble places of the earth," wrote the A.P. reporter, "came a host of men and women to honor the memory of Samuel Gompers." At Fort Worth an Osage Indian chief boarded the train, raised his hand, and intoned the Osage prayer for the dead. At other stops the train was delayed until the "laboring men" could be persuaded to leave so the train could continue.[1]

The editors of *Current History* asked John R. for an article about Gompers.

He wrote a glowing tribute.[2] He likened Gompers to the great leaders of history—Jefferson, Hamilton, Washington, Lincoln. Admitting that many on the left and on the right would disagree with this comparison, he defended it—first indirectly by noting that disagreement is natural over leaders who take principled stands in fields of social conflict; then directly by pointing out how Gompers learned from failed strikes and collapsing unions to develop organizations and tactics that could survive attacks from hostile capitalists and judges. Though hardnosed and tough, Gompers never grasped at dictatorial power. He "never had the power to call a strike or make a settlement of a strike, or control the funds of any nationally organized body of labor." His power was only "moral." He understood how far workers could go, and he limited his goals to their goals—decent wages and working conditions—and freedom from arbitrary and capricious treatment in the workplace. He sought common ground with people he disliked, and for this reason he retained his membership in the National Civic Federation.

Dark Clouds

In praising Gompers, John R. did not allude to the symbolism of his death. The mourners that assembled at the train crossings may have been mourning something more than the death of a single union leader. For, neither Gompers nor anyone else had been able to preserve unions or their influence in the years following the Great War. Buffeted by open shop campaigns, hamstrung by what the labor lawyer Donald Richberg called "the vast wreckage of judge-made law," and vilified in the "Red Scare," unions had been unable to keep their wartime gains.[3] Membership had fallen from a peak of about five million in 1919 to about three and half million in 1925, and membership kept falling—not good news for John R.'s dream of collective democracy.

At first glance, though, workers seemed not the worse for it. Average wages were rising. With a host of inventions, including the invention of installment buying, and with the economies of mass production, families could buy vacuum cleaners, washing machines, radios—even automobiles. But the apparent prosperity was deceptive. Rising wage averages masked a wide gap between the salaried on the one hand and the hourly and piece-work wage-earners on the other. There was want and hunger in big city slums and there was outright desperation on farms where postwar recessions had never ended.

Less noticed on the national level, but perhaps as symbolic and as large a loss for the American working classes was the death on June 18, 1925, of John R.'s old patron, Robert M. La Follette. In lists of great senators, La Follette is generally ranked near the top with Henry Clay and John Calhoun.[4] To replace him, the people of Wisconsin elected his son, Robert M. La Follette Jr. But the son could not compensate for the seniority and influence of his crusty old father.

And an ominous economic cloud overshadowed the western world— more ominous because political elites could not even see it. People can debate whether John Maynard Keynes had been technically correct in the *Economic Consequences of the Peace.* But his prophecy—that the Treaty of Versailles would shred the social and economic fabric of Europe—even if it contributed to its own fulfillment—was proving true. The 1923 German inflation was only one symptom of a wildly unstable international monetary structure. And the situation was worsened by

President Coolidge's refusal to grant more lenient terms to US allies for repayment of war-induced debts— worsened further by inept central bank policies. Keynes's warnings had no effect on the conduct of Britain's policy elites, leading him to call himself a "croaking Cassandra."

The Paradoxes and the Rise of Labor Economics

But there were also croaking Cassandras in the United States. In the field of labor, Joseph Dorfman and Paul McNulty called attention to a paradox. Just as unions were declining, wrote Dorfman, a "new labor specialty" was growing. "Almost without exception," these new labor specialists "were steadfast supporters as well as vocal public defenders of the main goals of organized labor," and they argued for the benefits of a high wage economy.[5] The year 1925 saw the first text explicitly titled *Labor Economics*. And in the same year, Paul Douglas, in *Wages and the Family*, argued on the basis of John Bates Clark's marginal productivity theory for a family allowance.[6] If a worker's marginal productivity does not generate enough income to support his family, Douglas argued, the state's responsibility for the common welfare implies that it should provide a family allowance so that the worker's family can care for children, fulfilling the family's role as the cradle for the nation's human resources.

And Wisconsin hosted its own paradoxes in the middle 1920s. Richard T. Ely, the champion of labor studies, departed, and without him labor studies did not contract; they expanded. Then, toward the end of the decade, John R. joined the croaking Cassandras, attempting vainly to avoid an impending economic disaster.

And, paradoxically again, Ely's departure for Northwestern University resulted, not from persecution by his old political enemies but from attacks by progressives. La Follette had easily won reelection in 1922, and his coattails brought his progressive allies into power in Wisconsin. They remembered that the university faculty had voted to censure La Follette for his opposition to the war and that Ely had campaigned to defeat him. And "Fighting Bob La Follette" had a habit of attributing the worst possible motives to his opponents. So, six months before he died he wrote about: "Our universities and colleges and other educational institutions . . . cringing and fawning for the favors of predatory wealth."[7]

As if to support La Follette's charge, Ely had been busily seeking funds for his land institute—gaining generous contributions from large real estate firms and utility companies.[8] At the same time, an association founded on Henry George's ideas, the Manufacturers and

Merchants Federal Tax League, had introduced a bill for a national site-value tax, the Ralston–Norton bill. The big real estate and utility companies mounted a vigorous campaign to defeat that bill, and Ely also publicly attacked it.

The League responded with seven articles in its *Bulletin* connecting the donations to the land institute and Ely's opposition to the bill. The articles portrayed Ely as the evil genius behind big business attacks on site value taxation.[9] Ely asked John R. to defend him—creating something of a problem for John R. who had helped write the Ralston–Norton Bill.[10] But John R. could defend Ely's integrity. He showed that Ely had opposed single taxes before he received all those donations, and consequently the donations had not affected his position.

Still, with progressives attacking the University for "cringing and fawning for the favors of predatory wealth," Ely decided to move his land institute to a private university where large donations would not be questioned.

Ely's departure coincided with a recognized turning point in John R.'s role at Madison; perhaps more accurately, it was a turning point for the "Commons team" at Madison.[11] Between 1926 and 1935 John R. would supervise thirty-three PhD dissertations, 72 percent of all that he supervised since his arrival in 1904, and the number of labor studies courses increased. It might improve accuracy to give more credit, especially for the increase in courses, to the "Madison team," allowing for what Harold Groves called John R.'s "genius at team work."[12]

The Team

The Workers' School offers a case study of this "team work." In 1924 Mary Anderson of the Madison YWCA asked Don D. Lescohier if he could create a special summer school for eight working girls.[13] Lescohier worked out a curriculum and set up an oversight committee chaired by Selig Perlman who almost immediately envisioned possibilities that did not seem apparent to Lescohier or anyone else—especially since the first summer school flopped. The girls were not ready for college level courses; they could not adapt to the lecture system. Perlman responded by reforming both curricula and methods to fit the backgrounds and interests of the students. At Perlman's suggestion, boys were admitted, and some courses were extended beyond summers—to entire years.

Then, in 1925, John R. promoted a display in the Madison Armory. He sent letters to all graduates asking them for photographs and information about their jobs.[14] The resulting display showed what Wisconsin graduates had done—on union staffs, in government agencies, and in corporate personnel offices. David Saposs, who was teaching at the Brookwood Labor College in Katonah, New York, sent pictures along with a description of the curriculum and classes at Brookwood.[15]

By 1926, the little summer program had grown into a full-blown Workers' School within the university's Extension Department. John R. introduced the school and described its rationale at the annual meeting of the Wisconsin Federation of Labor on April 10, 1926.[16] He pointed out that university curricula were not designed to give union leaders the skills they needed for organizing or managing union affairs. As a result, future union leaders in a standard university program might waste time on irrelevant courses. Some potential leaders might even be drawn away to other careers. Moreover, many union members lacked high school diplomas; the semester pattern was too rigid for people with full-time jobs. A workers' school located in the extension branch could overcome these problems. Courses could be any length and offered at any time—in evenings, during summers, or on weekends, and methods could be adapted to student backgrounds.

The Workers' School introduced what was arguably the first industrial relations program in the United States.[17] And, though writers credit John R. for its creation, it was really a team effort, originating with Don D. Lescohier and developed with significant leadership from Selig Perlman who advocated the first expansions and who seemed to devote most energy to maintaining the Workers' School and improving its quality.

While the Workers' School offered a case study of teamwork, Ed Witte, in 1927, illustrated the individual initiative of "Madison team" members. John R. had encouraged Witte's interest in court injunctions and in 1927 Witte got his first chance to have an effect.

In that year Senator Henry Shipstead of Minnesota introduced a bill to prevent judicial injunctions by narrowly defining the meaning of property.[18] The bill was sent to a subcommittee composed of Senators John Blaine of Wisconsin, George Norris of Nebraska, and Thomas Walsh of Montana.[19] They liked Shipstead's goal—to limit anti-labor injunctions—but they doubted the effectiveness of his approach.

Senator Blaine, who as Wisconsin's Governor, had worked with Witte in the Legislative Law Library, asked him for help. On Witte's advice, the Senators called in four lawyers: Felix Frankfurter and Francis Sayre of Harvard, Herman Oliphant of Columbia, and Donald Richberg, a Chicago labor lawyer. The four lawyers huddled with Witte in an empty

Senate office. Witte brought notes and documents that he had been collecting since his years on the undergraduate debate team.[20]

They debated strategy—whether to attack the assumptions that legitimated the injunctions or to create a blizzard of unquestionably constitutional obstacles to issuing them. The final bill did a little of both. It did not, for example, outlaw Yellow Dog Contracts, but declared them "not in the public interest," hence unenforceable in the courts. Then the law defined a limited number of unusual circumstances under which *ex parte* restraining orders could be issued, and it limited the duration of such orders to five days (an *ex parte* judicial proceeding is one conducted for the benefit of only one party). Injunctions of any kind could not be issued before hearing oral arguments from both sides. Anyone charged with contempt could ask for a jury trial under a judge different from the one that issued the injunction, and the law specified further conditions that limited the ability of judges to issue injunctions. For example, it decreed that no injunction should be issued if the party seeking it had not first made a reasonable effort to settle the dispute through negotiation or with the aid of "any available government machinery of mediation."[21] The Full Senate Committee rejected the bill at that time, and it seemed that Witte's work had been futile. But it was not.

The Age of Stability—Or Instability

For his part, John R. was continuously revising his unfinished volume on reasonable value and investigating the business cycle in his values and valuations seminar. He had come to believe that cyclical instability posed the greatest current threat to worker welfare. "In the long run nothing," he told an audience of locomotive engineers in 1923, "is more important to organized labor than the stabilization of the business cycle."[22]

He placed cyclical stability in a larger context when he wrote an article on Karl Marx.[23] He gave Marx credit for improving David Ricardo's labor theory of value. Ricardo had based his theory on an assumed natural right to private property. Marx had realized that property rights were not natural and were, in fact, created by the state. Ricardo had made profits the dynamic force in economic evolution and had considered high wages to be obstacles to capitalist accumulation. Marx had made high wages a necessary condition for continued capitalist expansion because wages permitted workers to buy everything that they produced.

But Marx was obviously wrong in 1847 when he predicted the collapse of capitalism. He would have been correct if capitalism had not changed in ways he could not have foreseen. He could not have foreseen the passage of laws limiting working hours and setting minimum wages or the creation of social insurance systems, or the rise of trade unions or widespread stock ownership, innovations that short-circuited the process that Marx had predicted. Then, John R. drew a lesson. Marx had shared a fundamental error with Hegel. "The outstanding characteristic of both Hegel's and Marx's philosophy was the idea of an impelling force that worked out its evolution regardless of the will of man. The individual was helpless to push it on or hold it back. Consequently, in both cases, the actual historical evolution of collective wills was overlooked."[24]

John R. did not find capitalism's redemption in individual initiative, but in "the historical evolution of collective wills"—in the democratic processes of states, cities, trade unions, and stockholder meeting. He then outlined three stages in the evolution of capitalism to show how this "evolution of collective wills" had worked. First there was a period of scarcity, and then came a period of abundance, and finally a period of stabilization. In the early period of scarcity, merchants and manufacturers organized gilds and developed their own courts. Then, the steam engine ushered in the era of abundance, and in the name of individualism the common law courts destroyed the gilds. Instability following the destruction of gilds led to corrective collective action—minimum wages and maximum hour laws, social security, and trade unions. Finally, by calling the current age "the age of stability," John R. made cyclical instability the limiting factor preventing any further solution to capitalism's problems.

This article is noteworthy because John Maynard Keynes cited it in a lecture at the Academy of Sciences in Moscow in September of 1925.[25] Keynes agreed with John R.'s optimism as well as with his conviction that cyclical instability posed the greatest threat to capitalist democracies. "But England is now entering the third era, which Professor Commons has called the period of stabilization and has truly characterized it as the actual alternative to Marxian communism . . . The extremes of this epoch in the realm of government are Fascism on the one side and Leninism on the other For my part I accept neither."

Joining the "Croaking Cassandras"

John R.'s concern about cyclical stability had motivated his work at the National Monetary Association. And in 1927, he joined the "croaking

Cassandras" warning about the dangers of central bank and international financial policies.

In 1927, Congressman James Strong of Kansas asked John R. to testify in favor of a bill that Strong had introduced in the House of Representatives—to make price stability a statutory goal of the Federal Reserve System.[26]

All officials of the Federal Reserve System opposed the bill. Most, like Adolph Miller, the only academic member of the Board of Governors, rejected any goal of price stability. Miller stressed two principles laid down in the Federal Reserve Board's 1923 report on open market policy.[27] The first set of principles defined a quality standard: the central bank should lend to member banks only for productive activities, not for speculation. The second set established a quantity standard: the central bank should use a large number of indicators to monitor the total amount of credit in the economy. These principles, Miller argued, would be undermined by a rule forcing Fed officials to focus on the general price level. He argued further that many factors—other than central bank policy—influence general price levels and that these other factors had played the major role in the wild price swings of the early 1920s. Finally, he objected to all price indexes. Both price weights and components are matters of judgment, he argued, and indexes measure past prices—not the current needs of commerce and industry. Good monetary policy depends on intuition. A rigid stable price goal would deprive Fed officials of the ability to use their intuitions in responding to current and unpredictable situations.

But Benjamin Strong (unrelated to the Congressman), Governor of the New York Fed and the country's de facto central banker, had drifted from party dogma.[28] The plight of farmers in the 1919–20 deflation had troubled Strong more than he admitted. Massive gold inflows had forced him into sterilization measures to prevent price increases. Because member banks could borrow with treasury bonds as collateral and then lend any way they wished, Federal Reserve officials could not possibly monitor the credit worthiness of the funds that they made available to the banking system. By December 13, 1922, Strong had implicitly accepted the goal of price stability.[29] Still, he objected to the bill.[30] He feared that people would blame the Fed for relative price changes. He was particularly adamant in rejecting responsibility for farm prices that were falling at the time. To achieve the goal of price stability Benjamin Strong placed his faith in universal adoption of a free gold system. But, even though he opposed the bill as it was written, he sympathized with its objectives, and he offered some hope to the bill's advocates.

> If I could find it possible to frame language which would accomplish this very desirable purpose that you have described, and which I stated at the first hearing by saying I thoroughly agreed with, I would not hesitate to do it, and with the approval of my associates, because I am simply one element in the system—one bank—I would not hesitate to do it, and I do not know but what it may be possible to devise some language. Frankly, I would avoid the use of the words 'inflation' and 'deflation.' 'Stability' is a less objectionable word from my point of view. We all want stability of prices and conditions of all kinds, and I wish I might be able to write the words. I will try if you would like to have me.[31]

John R. was the last witness on February 4, 1927.[32] He explained the concept of the general price level and introduced a chart relating measures of Federal Reserve actions to an index of wholesale prices.[33] He showed that prices as measured by this index had responded to every Fed initiative since the Great War. Inflation had ensued when Fed officials held down interest rates to support treasury borrowing in 1919. A recession had followed when, to control the inflation, the Fed had driven up interest rates. Then, in the final months of 1921, all twelve reserve banks, anxious to increase their earnings, had independently bought treasury securities. By May 1922, their security holdings had increased by $400 million, but, paradoxically, their total earning assets had decreased—just as they were trying to increase them.

John R. explained how this happened. The Federal Reserve banks bought securities from bond dealers who deposited the proceeds in member banks. The new deposits reduced the need for member banks to borrow from the Fed while simultaneously increasing their ability to lend. The increased lending drove down interest rates and initiated another inflationary spiral. The combination of lower interest rates and reduced borrowing by member banks resulted in a reduction rather than an increase in reserve bank earnings. The Fed overreacted causing another recession. In each case, the wholesale price index responded to Federal Reserve decisions. In these cases, at least, central bank actions had affected the general price level. John R.'s testimony impressed everyone, especially the Chairman of the House Committee on Banking and Currency, Representative, Louis McFadden.[34]

Governor Strong's willingness to contribute to a new bill had, however, changed the dynamics of the debate. Negotiations now focused on a second "Strong Bill" acceptable to the Governor of the New York Fed.

And John R. changed his focus from Congress to the public. He wrote up his testimony for an article in the *Annalist*, a weekly magazine published by the *New York Times*.[35] He also wrote two articles on the farm problem for the *North American Review*.[36] The farm articles went beyond his testimony to Congress. There were no footnotes, but the articles reflected the latest advances in agricultural economics. John R. argued that price instability hurt farmers more than other producers. Corporations could maintain their prices by restricting production. Farmers could not because "they must feed their families." Unorganized and scattered across the land, farmers were incapable of such tactics as price leadership or other methods by which corporations maintained their prices. Thus, in deflations, prices of the things that farmers sold fell faster than the prices of the things that they bought. Consequently general price volatility affected farmers more than other producers. The economic power of the banking industry also worked against farmers. The Fed, as the "bankers' bank," was more attentive to bankers' interests. And bankers worried more about inflation. But farmers suffered more from deflation. And farmers suffered because of policies followed by the United States and its allies after the Great War.

The allies had imposed a Carthaginian peace with consequences that, as Keynes had famously argued, would shred the economic and social fabric of the Western World.[37] President Coolidge had made things worse by refusing to grant lenient terms of debt repayment to former allies, strengthening their insistence on draconian reparations from Germany in order to pay their debts to the United States. John R. now explained how this affected American farmers and argued for forgiveness of the sovereign debts.

He distinguished war debts from reconstruction debts.[38] Reconstruction debts generate surpluses that enable loan repayments with interest. War debts do not generate such surpluses. To repay war debts, European governments must tax their citizens, thus reducing their ability to buy American farm products. The inflation–deflation cycle of 1919–20 aggravated the European debt problem.[39] Loans incurred during war and postwar inflations came due after prices had fallen. So, like farmers, Europeans repaid debts with sales at deflated prices, further reducing their income to buy US farm products. John R. concluded with three proposals.

First, Congress should reduce the rates of the Fordney–McCumber tariffs so that European export industries could employ and pay more workers—a departure from his habitual high tariff position.[40] "A lower American tariff would help feed and clothe impoverished and unemployed Europe whose very impoverishment and unemployment are an important cause of American farmers' reduced markets."

Second, the central banks of the world should hold gold prices steady. A tariff reduction would be useless if prices fell. It is not true that no one would be worse off if all prices fell. Farmers incur relatively large debts in sowing seasons and repay them when crops are sold. If prices should fall after they borrowed and before they sold their crops, they would pay higher commodity prices for debts fixed in terms of gold. "It is on account of taxes, interest, debts and the violence of agricultural price changes that farmers need both stabilization of the value of money and 'orderly marketing' of crops; for it is not the high or low value of gold in itself that hurts the farmer. Changes from a high to a low value demoralize him, or from a low to a high value damage him."

Third, the United States must forgive European war debts. Then European governments would no longer need to tax their people to pay these debts. As a result of lower taxes, European disposable incomes would increase and these higher disposable incomes would enable Europeans to buy more US farm products.[41]

He sent copies of his *Annalist* article to Gustav Cassel, John Maynard Keynes, and Reginald McKenna, the president of the Midland Bank and former Chancellor of the Exchequer. Cassel and Keynes answered with encouragement. Keynes's response has become well known. "I would very much like to have some conversations with you on this and other matters. Judging from limited evidence and at great distance, there seems to me to be no other economist with whose general way of thinking I feel myself in such genuine accord."[42]

As negotiations for a "Second Strong Bill" began, an anonymous donor contacted Norman Lombard, executive secretary of the National Monetary Association, offering financial support if John R. would spend the spring semester helping Congressman Strong write the new bill.[43] John R. never learned the donor's identity. But that donor was Irving Fisher.[44]

John R. accepted the offer; he looked forward to the trip; and Nell looked forward to going with him. They talked about spending time together in Washington, DC, and about perhaps going to England when the work was done. It was not to be. Nell was hospitalized for a pulmonary infection during the fall semester. John R. seems to have believed that the illness was serious but temporary. He still looked forward to Nell's companionship in Washington and perhaps to a summer together in England. She had an early operation that did not turn out well, but she was scheduled for a second operation, and John R. still hoped that his daughter Rachel would bring her to Washington after she recovered.[45] The second operation seemed successful. Nell seemed to be improving, then she died suddenly on December 31, 1927.[46] Nell had been not only a tower of strength and a loving companion, but a highly intelligent and talented writer. She had written three plays and two short stories while managing Ho-Chee-Ra and supporting John R.'s fragile ego. It is hard to overstate his loss.

John R. still went to Washington with his daughter Rachel and his secretary, Myrtle Starr.[47] He took full advantage of Benjamin Strong's offer. He visited the New York Fed. He interviewed members of the Federal Reserve Board in Washington. He lectured at the Brookings Institute. In the final rewriting of the bill, John R. added provisions reflecting his belief that Fed deliberations should be public and that its processes should include feedback and revision, and he qualified the goal of price stability with the hope of responding to Benjamin Strong's objections to the original bill. Then, John R. and the Congressman took the penultimate draft of the bill to the central banker.[48] Strong praised sections that John R. had added and left them intact, but he marked up the section dealing with price stabilization. Strong added the goal of maintaining the gold standard and to John R.'s goal of a stable price level, and Strong added goals of stability of commerce, industry, and employment .[49]

Even though the bill now met his approval, Strong warned that he could not publicly support it without Reserve Board approval. So, after the board's Governor, Roy A. Young, announced the board's opposition to the bill, Strong testified against it.[50] He was able to do so honestly. He honestly disagreed with the quantity theory. He placed his trust in an international free gold standard. Finally, he expressed fear that some committee might change the bill's wording. To which the chairman of the House committee commented that Strong must be thinking of the Senate. Laughter followed.[51]

204

The second Strong Bill did not pass. Given the subsequent sequence of events, it is worth quoting Meltzer's history of the Federal Reserve System.

> It is an understatement to say that it was a missed opportunity. If the mandate for price stability had been passed and followed, the Federal Reserve could not have permitted deflation during the Great Depression of 1929–33 or the inflation of 1965–80. Possibly a recession would have occurred in 1929, but the United States would have avoided the deflationary policy and its consequences.[52]

No one has commented on John R.'s argument that the United States should have forgiven the sovereign debts of its former allies, indeed that all sovereign debts should have been forgiven. No one has commented on his plea for a reduction in the Fordney–McCumber tariff. And one might ask what the path of the world economy might have been if all these suggestions had found willing ears. But they did not. Like Keynes, Fisher, and Cassel, John R. was a "croaking Cassandra." No one knows when the depression started or how the complex of bad policies combined to produce it or how the missed opportunities might have mitigated it. This does not make them any less missed opportunities.

Notes

1. "Gompers Rites at New York at 9 A.M. Thursday: Route of Funeral Train Lined with Mourners," *Chicago Tribune*, 15 December 1924.
2. John R. Commons, "The Passing of Samuel Gompers," *Current History and Forum* (February 1925), 670–76. This was a eulogy, so John R. ignored disagreements. Gompers had opposed almost every government program that John R. had advocated. Gompers was less friendly to industrial unions than John R. So the statement that he considered himself a "follower of Gompers" requires some qualification. He admired Gompers and considered him a friend, but he did not agree with all of Gompers's positions.
3. The quotation is from Irving Bernstein, *The Lean Years: A History of the American Worker 1920–1933* (Boston: Houghton, 1960), 190.
4. http://www.senate.gov/artandhistory/history/common/briefing/Famous_Five_Seven.htmhttp://www.electoral-vote.com/evp2014/Info/greatest-senators.html, accessed May 27, 2015.
5. Joseph Dorfman, *The Economic Mind in American Civilization*. vol.5 (New York: Viking Press, 1949), 515; Paul McNulty, *The Origins and Development of Labor Economics: A Chapter in the History of Social Thought* (Cambridge, MA: MIT Press, 1980), 158.
6. Solomon Blum, *Labor Economics* (New York: Henry Holt and Company, 1925); Paul H. Douglas, *Wages and the Family*. (Chicago, IL: University of Chicago Press, 1925).

A Worker's Economist

7. Rader, *The Academic Mind*, 213, quoting an unsigned editorial in *La Follette's Magazine* 17 (January-February 1925): 2–3, 19–20.
8. Ibid., 206–9.
9. Ibid., 209–10.
10. John R. Commons, "A Progressive Tax on Bare Land Values," *Political Science Quarterly* 37 (March 1922): 41–68.
11. Malcolm Rutherford, *The Institutionalist Movement in American Economics, 1918–1947* (New York: Cambridge University Press, 2011), 204–5. Many of John R.'s students had left Madison without degrees before 1925. Rutherford cites David Saposs who attributed their departure to Ely's hostility toward many of them.
12. Harold Groves to Charles M. Sullivan, February 11, 1957, Harold M. Groves Papers, Wisconsin Historical Society, Madison, Box 3, folder 16.
13. Don D. Lescohier, *The Story of My Life For the First Seventy-Seven Years* (Madison, WI: Air Brush Creations, 1960), 55–56.
14. John R. Commons Papers (Madison: State Historical Society of Wisconsin, 1982), microfilm reel 22, frames 843–943.
15. Saposs to Commons, March 22, 1925, ibid., reel 22, frame 903.
16. John R. Commons, "Workers' Education and the Universities," *American Federationist* (April, 1927), ibid.; reel 20, frames 177–79.
17. Bruce Kaufman, *The Origins and Evolution of the Field of Industrial Relations in the United States* (Ithaca, NY: Cornell Studies in Industrial Relations, 1993), 10, 54. Glen G. Cain, "Labor Economics," in *Economists at Wisconsin*, ed. Robert Lampman (Madison: Regents of the State University System of Wisconsin, 1993), 237.
18. Schlabach, *Edwin Witte Cautious Reformer*, 63.
19. Walsh, from Two Rivers, WI, had graduated from the University of Wisconsin and from its law school, so two of the three Senators were Wisconsin graduates.
20. Witte laid out his reasoning in *The Government in Labor Disputes* (1932; reprint, New York: Arno Press, 1959).
21. John R. Commons and John B. Andrews, *Principles of Labor Legislation*, 4th edition (1936: reprint, New York: Augustus M. Kelley, 1967), 415–16.
22. Commons Papers, microfilm; reel 19, frame 364.
23. John R. Commons, "Marx Today: Capitalism and Socialism," *Atlantic Monthly* 136 (November, 1925): 682–93.
24. Ibid., 690.
25. John Maynard Keynes, "The Economic Transition in England," in the *Collected Writings of John Maynard Keynes Activities 1922–1929 The Return to Gold and Industrial Policy*, ed. Donald Moggridge, vol. 19 (London: Cambridge University Press, 1981), 438–42.
26. Irving Fisher and H, Cohrssen, *Stable Money: A History of the Movement* (New York: Adelphi Company, 1934), 170, Allan H. Meltzer, *A History of the Federal Reserve 1913–1951* vol. 1 (Chicago, IL: University of Chicago Press, 2003), 182.
27. U.S. House of Representatives, *Hearings before the Committee on Banking and Currency of the House of Representatives 69th Congress 1st Session on H.R. 7895 February 4, 1927* (Washington, DC: Government Printing Office, 1927), 633–74, 791–906.

28. Lester Chandler, *Benjamin Strong Central Banker* (Washington, DC: Brookings Institution, 1958), 51, 199.
29. Ibid., 199–201.
30. U. S House of Representatives, *Hearings before the Committee on Banking and Currency on H.R. 7895*, 290–397, 421–580, Meltzer, *History of the Federal Reserve*, 184–85.
31. Ibid., 553, Fisher and Cohrsson, *Stable Money*, 165.
32. U.S. House, *Hearings on H.R. 7895*, 1074–121.
33. This is covered more completely in J. Dennis Chasse, "The Economists of the Lost Cause and the Monetary Education of John R. Commons," *Journal of the History of Economic Thought* 36 (June 2014): 193–214.
34. James Frear to John R. Commons, Commons Papers, microfilm, reel 4, frame 378.
35. John R. Commons, "Price Stabilization and the Federal Reserve System," *The Annalist* 29 (April 1, 1927): 450–67.
36. John R. Commons, "Farm Prices and the Value of Gold I," *The North American Review* 225 (January 1928): 27–41; "Farm Prices and the Value of Gold II," Ibid. (February 1928), 196–211.
37. John Maynard Keynes, *The Economic Consequences of the Peace* (New York: Harcourt, Brace, and Jovanovich, 1920).
38. Commons, "Farm Prices and the Value of Gold II," 201.
39. Ibid., 202.
40. John R. Commons. "Tariff Revision and the Protection of American Labor," *Annals of the Academy of Political and Social Science* 32 (September 1908): 315–20, Yngve Ramstad, "Free Trade versus Fair Trade: Import Barriers as a Problem of Reasonable Value," *Journal of Economic Issues* 21(March, 1987): 5–32.
41. Commons, "Farm Prices and the Value of Gold II," 197–99.
42. Keynes to Commons, April 27, 1927, Commons Papers, microfilm; reel 4, frame 448.
43. Lombard to Commons, October 24, 1927, Ibid.; reel 4, frame 579.
44. Commons, Myself, 183, Meltzer, *History of the Federal Reserve*, 289, n.2.
45. Commons to Morehouse, November 28, 1927, Commons Papers, microfilm; reel 4, frame 631.
46. Lombard to Commons December 14, 1927, Ibid.; reel 4, frame 631, Commons to Robert Barr, December 31, 1927, ibid., reel 4, frame 671.
47. Commons to M.E. Graham, December 13 and 28, 1927, ibid., reel 4, frames 630 and 639.
48. Fisher and Cohrsson, *Stable Money, A History*, 170–71.
49. Ibid., 227–28. I have reproduced the original and the revision in Chasse, "Economists of the Lost Cause."
50. U.S. House of Representatives, *Hearings before the Committee on Banking and Currency of the House of Representatives, 1928, 70th Congress, 1st Session on H.R. 11806* (Washington, DC: Government Printing Office, 1928), 12–28.
51. Ibid., 17.
52. Meltzer, *History of the Federal Reserve*, 192.

16

The Social Statesman and His Team

I was trying to save capitalism by making it good—Myself

Herbert Hoover did his best, but he was no match for the depression, and persistent "hard times" sparked political changes that set the "Commons team" to work on long-sought reforms. So, as John R. aged into social statesman status and finished his book on reasonable value, he might have felt some satisfaction as his students worked on programs that he had been advocating for decades, but any such satisfaction was marred by the tragedy of the depression, and even more for John R. by a personal tragedy.

On August 1, 1930, his son, Jack, drove off with the family car, leaving his wife, Ellen, and their daughter Anne in Madison.[1] John R. who was deeply attached to Jack, broke down again. A physician friend tried to explain the nature of what we now call post-traumatic stress disorder. John R. did not seem to fully understand and insisted on calling it amnesia.

His breakdown did not keep him from responding to a friend who asked him to investigate the impact on farmers of the Smoot–Hawley tariff. The bill had fulfilled one of President Hoover's campaign promises—to raise tariffs on agricultural goods. John R.'s friend, William T. Rawleigh, an importer and patent medicine salesman, doubted that an agricultural tariff would help farmers, and he offered to fund an investigation, supervised by John R., to find out what its effects would be. John R. recruited two faculty assistants: Benjamin Hibbard from the agriculture department and Walter Morton from commerce. They set the project up in the form of monographs written by graduate students.[2] Two accidental features gave the project a place in the history of American economic thought. One of the graduate students,

Theodore W. Schultz, later received the Nobel Prize in economics, and the project generated a heated debate about methods between Walter Morton and Henry Schultz of the University of Chicago.[3]

The Wisconsin Idea Returns

Then, in November, 1930, Wisconsin voters elected a new governor, Philip La Follette, a son of "Fighting Bob" who brought back the "Wisconsin Idea"—with mixed results for John R.'s sense of equilibrium. On the one hand La Follette welcomed John R. back to the capitol. A huge headline proclaimed John R. the leader of La Follette's cabinet.[4]

On the other hand, John R. had supported a 1927 bill that established a system of small loan firms licensed to charge a maximum monthly interest rate of 3.5 percent (an annual compound rate of 51 percent). A household budget study—with his name attached as supervisor—had persuaded him that, until credit unions could be formed, the system offered the best alternative for working families with cash flow problems.[5] Pawn shops, for example, charged higher rates.[6] His argument did not impress the progressive legislators. They discovered that one of the study's authors had worked for a small lenders association in Georgia.

Henry Huber who had introduced John R.'s unemployment bill in 1921 was now Lieutenant Governor, and when he summoned John R. to testify before a senate committee, he was no longer friendly. "But meanwhile Governor Huber went after me in a terrifying examination before the senate committee. Was not the Russell Sage Foundation an association of big capitalists? Did I receive any compensation from the Foundation or from the loan companies? How much was my university salary and how much did I earn outside my salary? He believed me when I said I received no compensation whatever for services in anything I had done on this bill. The money, about $3,000, went to pay expenses and compensation for investigators, and came from the loan companies".[7]

John R. defended himself and continued to defend the bill. The Lieutenant Governor was not appeased; neither were the progressive legislators who quickly repealed the bill.

The Social Statesman

The small loan debacle did not impede John R.'s progress toward social statesman status. In 1931 the university conferred an honorary degree.[8] John R. confessed to the chairman of the Committee on

Honorary Degrees that he did not own an academic gown to wear for the ceremony. Someone loaned him a gown and he was awarded the degree on June 22. The university president, Glenn Frank, devoted his McClure newspaper column for July 14, 1931, to the argument that John R. deserved the title of "social statesman." Then, in the fall, Governor Philip La Follette sent a telegram to the "Friday Nighters" declaring October 13 an official Wisconsin Holiday—Commons Day.[9]

Congressmen and Senators cemented John R.'s social statesman status by seeking his advice about their proposed cures for the Great Depression.[10] No matter what the politicians proposed, John R. always stressed the money problem, the need to raise prices to 1926 levels, and the need to abandon the gold standard. John R. also feared that unless something was done about the gold standard, deficit financing might drive up interest rates. Nevertheless, he expressed sympathy for deficit spending proposals.

He gave the clearest indication of his own thinking when Congressman Samuel Pettengill asked about the wisdom of a bill introduced by Representative Wright Patman from Texas. Wright's bill would have used Congressional powers to create $2.4 billion to pay veterans' bonuses.[11] In his response to Pettengill, John R. wrote that he liked Patman's idea, but added that he was "probably more radical than you or Mr. Patman." He continued that the country should leave the gold standard and that Congress should create enough new money to raise prices back to 1926 levels.[12]

Two years earlier, during the 1930 meeting of the American Economic Association, three former students had gathered in a hotel room to plan a birthday party for John R. The three—John B. Andrews, executive secretary of the American Association for Labor Legislation, Meredith Givens, director of the Social Science Research Council, and Donald Montgomery, consumer advocate in the Department of Agriculture—contacted as many former students as they could.[13] There was considerable back and forth before the plan was solidified.

When the day came, November 18, 1932, 235 former students showed up to celebrate John R.'s seventieth birthday.[14] Other guests included the former president of the University of Wisconsin, E. A. Birge, Governor Phillip La Follette, Henry Ohl, president of the Wisconsin Federation of Labor, and Samuel Levin of the Amalgamated Clothing Workers of Chicago (where John R. had chaired the board of trustees for the labor-management unemployment compensation scheme). Thirty Syracuse University students signed a letter that said they were sorry that

John R. was not celebrating there.[15] There were many speeches. Thomas S. Adams announced that John R. would not go to heaven because he would not be happy unless there were some evils to attack.

Alvin Hansen read an insightful paper on the economic significance of John R.'s thought.[16] Hansen recognized, as few have, the influence of Henry George along with that of Richard Ely on John R.'s earliest thought. He paid attention to the introductions that John R. had written for the volumes in the *Documentary History of American Industrial Society* and in the *History of Labor.* While praising these massive publications for their historical scholarship, Hansen added that John R. was not satisfied with "pure description," but that he made two theoretical contributions in those volumes. First, he showed the relation between the extension of markets and bargaining power of different classes. Second, he related price changes to changes in the business cycle and in economic organization "long before Earl J. Hamilton and John Maynard Keynes presented their studies." In the area of policy, John R. had thrown himself with "vigor" into the formulation of an industrial constitution that would replace the age of industrial violence. Hansen concluded. "Professor Commons has not always been right—that would be too much to expect of a courageous innovator—but besides being always a live wire and giving impetus to an amazing variety of social experimentation, he has contributed to American economics a solid body of constructive research which will stand the test of careful scrutiny and analysis."

John R. responded. "I didn't know until tonight what sort of a fellow I am. I didn't know until this evening that I was so smart."

The Team Takes Over

All this attention may have been good for John R.'s fragile ego. But the policy successes of his former students—now colleagues—must have been better. Harold Groves, Ed Witte, Elizabeth Brandeis, Paul Raushenbush, and Arthur Altmeyer carried his principles to the state capitol and beyond.

Groves and Philip La Follette had been undergraduate classmates. La Follette had gone on for a law degree and Groves for an economics PhD. When, in 1930, La Follette decided to run for governor, he asked Groves to run for the state assembly.[17] After consulting with a few friends, Groves decided to try. The night before the election, at a noisy rally in a packed gymnasium, John R. was slated to introduce Groves. "The old man was a little nervous and completely forgot the microphone into which he was supposed to talk. He got in front of it and his introduction was entirely lost to the radio audience."[18]

Groves won, and he began thinking about John R.'s 1920 unemployment compensation bill. He brought the bill up while hiking in the Wisconsin River region with Paul Raushenbush, Elizabeth Brandeis, and two other "Friday Nighters," Alfred and Hazel Briggs.[19] They were enthusiastic. Raushenbush suggested a few changes, and on February 8, 1931, Groves introduced the bill. It sailed through the State Assembly. The State Senate sent it to a committee. Everyone was afraid of employer opposition. Paul and EB raised funds, organized a committee, and barnstormed the state to drum up public support.[20] The next year, the committee recommended passage. And on January 28, 1932, Governor Phillip La Follette signed the first unemployment compensation bill in the United States—with Groves, Brandeis, Raushenbush, Witte, and John R. looking on.

Groves explained the bill's intellectual sources.

> We have been asked not infrequently about the intellectual sources of the ideas involved in our unemployment compensation act. Some of them were indigenous and grew out of the state of the economy and of Wisconsin politics at the time. As to literary sources, we were impressed by A. C. Pigou's *Economics of Welfare* and J. M. Clark's *Economics of Overhead Cost*, both of which introduced the idea of externalities, that is the social costs that are associated with some businesses and are ignored in the determination of prices in the market place. On the prevention side, we were influenced by Professor Commons's experience with workmen's compensation which might be described as a small tax on industrial accidents, one purpose of which was to reduce their numbers.[21]

The bill was not universally praised. Many liberal social insurance advocates rejected the Wisconsin hypothesis about prevention. They stressed the need to spread the cost of unavoidable social risks as widely and as progressively as possible, and they emphasized adequate compensation. For them, a payroll tax only on employers would not generate the funds needed for adequate compensation—and segregating funds by employer introduced uncertainty. If an employer's fund ran out, there was a danger that the compensation payments could cease.[22] For opponents on the business side, the bill imposed an unfair cost and made Wisconsin business uncompetitive.

For Phil La Follette, though, this was just the beginning. In 1932, he called a special session of the state legislature. In that session, the

A Worker's Economist

legislature passed and La Follette signed Ed Witte's anti-injunction law, the first in the United States. Pennsylvania followed almost immediately, and fourteen other states followed Pennsylvania.[23] Senator George Norris of Nebraska resubmitted the bill in the Senate, and Representative Fiorello LaGuardia of New York introduced it in the House. It passed in both. President Hoover signed the Norris–LaGuardia Act on March 23, 1932. The bill achieved its purpose. It halted the flood of judicial injunctions. Yellow dog contracts ceased. The Hitchman decision was effectively neutered.[24]

John R. retired in 1932. Ed Witte, until then, an unpaid lecturer, quit his full-time job as Legislative Librarian and replaced John R. on the faculty.[25] John R. would continue to teach his courses on values and valuation, but Witte, though now full-time on the faculty, was about to be pulled to Washington, DC, along with Arthur Altmeyer.

The Team in Washington

Groves had drafted the first unemployment compensation law in the country, but it was unlikely that other states would follow. Thomas Eliot, the Labor Department's Assistant Solicitor, explained why.

> Every day if you were driving from Chicago to Madison, you'd meet a big truck filled with office furniture. Obviously, a big office was being moved. And on the outside there would be a sign saying, 'Forced to leave Wisconsin by La Follette's program of unemployment compensation.' If you went up Monday, you'd see it; if you went up Tuesday, it was still being forced to leave Wisconsin at the same hour. While this was a political trick if it actually happened, it does illustrate one of the great difficulties that faced each State—even those State legislatures that were most anxious to take steps of economic reform within their borders. You do lose business.[26]

On the other hand, the Constitution seemed to rule out a national system because the Tenth Amendment reserved to the states any powers not explicitly granted to the federal government. The Supreme Court at that time interpreted the major exception to this amendment—the commerce clause—strictly.

Elizabeth Brandeis and Paul Raushenbush presented the problem to her father, the Supreme Court justice. He referred them to the decision in *Florida v. Mellon*.[27] In that case the Supreme Court had upheld a federal inheritance tax that included an offset for any state inheritance taxes. Raushenbush together with Eliot and Frances Perkins, the secretary of Labor, then wrote a bill that imposed a 5 percent excise tax on

214

all firms with more than ten employees; it included an offset for state taxes that supported unemployment compensation. Senator Robert Wagner of New York introduced the bill in the Senate and Representative David Lewis of Maryland introduced it in the House. Then President Roosevelt asked Lewis to delay the bill because Roosevelt wanted a bigger program. That program would bring Arthur Altmeyer and Edwin Witte to Washington.

Altmeyer had become acquainted with Frances Perkins, the secretary of Labor, during his trips to Washington as secretary for the Wisconsin Industrial Commission.[28] In 1933 she had put him on a committee to reorganize the Labor Department. After six months, he had returned to Madison, but upon arrival, he found a telegram from Perkins requesting his immediate return. As soon as he arrived back, Perkins asked him to write the first draft of a memo for President Roosevelt—the famous memo of June 8, 1934, reading in part: "If as our Constitution tells us, our Federal Government was established among other things 'to promote the general welfare,' it is our plain duty to provide for that security upon which welfare depends. . . . [to] provide at once security against several of the great disturbing factors of life—especially those which relate to unemployment insurance and old age."[29] And, on June 8, Altmeyer took the oath of office as assistant secretary of Labor. Then Altmeyer prepared the first draft of Executive Order No. 6757 of June 29, 1934.[30] By that order Roosevelt created the Committee on Economic Security to "study problems related to the economic security of individuals" and to "report to the President not later than December 1, 1934." Perkins appointed a small advisory group to draw up a plan. That group, Meredith B. Givens, Arthur Altmeyer, and Bryce Stewart, a Canadian labor-relations specialist, drew up plans for a committee staff. Perkins wanted Witte to be executive director of that organization and Altmeyer to be chairman of its technical board. The next months were filled with crises and conflicts, both within the committee and in the charged political atmosphere without. Witte gamely defended the final imperfect product before Congress and then went home to Wisconsin where he began working on ways to improve social security. "FDR, Altmeyer, Perkins, and Witte If we wanted to establish the Hall of Fame for Social Security, these would be the first four names."[31]

Another Wisconsin student, Wilbur Cohen, had accompanied Witte to Washington. Like Altmeyer, Cohen remained in Washington as Altmeyer's legislative assistant. Altmeyer became chairman of the Social Security Board from 1937 till 1946, and Social Security

Commissioner from 1946 till 1952. President Roosevelt would call him Mister Social Security. Cohen would eventually become secretary of Health Education and Welfare. President Johnson would call Cohen Mr. Social Security.

While Witte and Altmeyer were struggling against a December deadline in Washington, two long slow intellectual developments were converging on Madison and in the mind of John R. One had started in 1924 when John R. had decided to delay publication of his volume on reasonable value. He had agonized over it, repeatedly rewritten it, and broadened its scope. He had dropped the original title, *Reasonable Value*. He had had tried and abandoned a succession of other titles and was influenced in his final choice by another intellectual process.

The other intellectual process dated from two sessions at the 1918 meeting of the American Economic Association (AEA). Economists at those sessions had explored the relation between social psychology and economics. In one session, Walton Hamilton of Amherst College had listed five desirable characteristics for what he called an "institutional approach" to economic theory. It should: (1) "unify economic science" (2) "be relevant to modern problems of control"; (3) accept institutions as subject matter; (4) "be concerned with matters of process;" and (5) "be based upon an acceptable theory of human behavior."[32] Thus began the much debated, much criticized, and much misunderstood "institutionalist movement" in the history of American economic thought.[33] Research programs based on Hamilton's principles flourished in many of the nation's universities—not without controversy.

Because of the controversy the American Economic Association (AEA) sponsored a number of conferences and roundtables. One such conference was scheduled for the 1931 meeting of the AEA, and Ernest L. Bogart, the president, invited John R. to present a paper.

John R. wrote the paper, but he wrote Bogart that he could not afford to attend the conference.[34] Bogart responded that he did not like papers read in absentia and asked John R. if he could suggest a substitute.[35] John R. suggested John M. Clarke or Walton Hamilton.[36]

Institutional Economics, The History of Labor, Principles of Labor Legislation

The paper that John R. had written for the conference was published in the *American Economic Review*.[37] After listing many meanings of the word "institution," the paper proposed John R's definition: "collective action in control, liberation and expansion of individual action." The article expanded on that definition and defended it. It briefly reviewed arguments of the *Legal Foundations of Capitalism* and anticipated the main drift of a coming book called *Institutional Economics.*

The explanation for the definition started with David Hume's insight into the reality that resources are scarce, that competing claims to resources generate conflicts, and that societies develop customs, or "rules of conduct" to prevent these conflicts from becoming destructive. To enforce these rules, societies exercise three kinds of power over individuals. Each kind of power controls with its own sanctions: "moral power" with sanctions of custom and public opinion; "economic power" with sanctions of "profit and loss"; and "political power" with sanctions of physical violence. For example, custom controls the way businesses pay bills. In John R's day, the moral power of custom forced most business owners to pay their bills with checks. A business owner who insisted on cash would face a moral sanction imposed by other business owners. But, while controlling the behavior of business owners, the same controlling power expanded their capabilities by putting the resources of the banks at their disposal. Thus, while sanctions control individuals' behavior, they simultaneously liberate and expand their capabilities. The same laws that impose duties create rights. People can call on officers of the state to protect their rights by enforcing duties on others. By enforcing such duties, the state liberates its citizens from undue coercion, duress, and discrimination. The controls of collective action also expand individual powers. Thus the state gives people power of controlling events after their death by calling on the state to enforce their will. And, state diplomacy enables citizens to securely engage in transactions in foreign countries. So, an institution is collective action in control, liberation, and expansion of individual action.

Beyond defending this definition of collective action, the article repeated the reasoning of the *Legal Foundations of Capitalism* that made transactions rather than individuals the smallest units of analysis, and it replaced the psychology of "economic man" with "negotiational psychology," based on observing the behavior of participants to transactions. The article also anticipated John R's coming book by classifying transactions in a new way.

In the *Legal Foundations*, John R. had distinguished "authorized" from "authoritative" transactions, with the state as a mere observer in the first type and as an active participant in the second. John R. may have spotted the logical inconsistency in this distinction or he may simply have wanted a different framework.[38]

Here, he defined three types of transactions: bargaining, managerial, and, rationing. Bargaining transactions transfer rights between legal equals. Outcomes of bargaining transactions depend on a negotiational psychology—personal skill—and on economic power. Managerial transactions take place between a legal superior and a legal inferior. Outcomes are determined by a negotiational psychology of command and obedience. Rationing transactions determine the distribution of the costs and benefits of collective action. The relations are between a collective superior and an individual inferior. The collective superior could be a legislature, a corporate board of directors, or a union–management bargaining session. The negotiational psychology of the rationing transaction is one of pleading and argument. John R. added that bargaining in a rationing transaction would be condemned as a form of corruption.

The article served as prelude to two books, *Institutional Economics* and *Myself*. These books would initiate a small surge in Wisconsin's book production—volumes three and four of the *History of Labor* in 1935 and in 1936 and the fourth edition of *Principles of Labor Legislation* in 1936.

Volume three of the *History*, after John R.'s introduction, was written by Don D. Lescohier and Elizabeth Brandeis. Lescohier covered labor markets: the labor force composition, wages, working conditions, unemployment, and employer personnel policies; Elizabeth Brandeis reviewed the history of labor legislation. Selig Perlman and his student Philip Taft wrote volume four which brought the interpretive history of labor movements up to what was then the present. In their conclusion, Taft and Perlman gave two reasons for the decline of unions during the 1920s. First, they emphasized the hostility of American employers.

> American employers were endowed by America's history with a will to power unrivaled for persistence and effectiveness by employers in other countries. American employers were steeled in their opposition to unionism and at the same time enabled to make their opposition effective by the extraordinary strength of the institution of private property in a country which was occupied and settled by laboring pioneers, creating property for themselves as they went along and holding it in small parcels. For, unionism, however conservative its objectives, is still a campaign against the absolute rights of the private property of the employer.[39]

Second, Perlman and Taft advanced the thesis that workers in the United States were harder to organize because they were less class conscious and more "job conscious" than workers in Europe. They gave a number of reasons.[40] Availability of free land had undermined the notion of a "settled" wage-earning class. Universal suffrage had given workers a political power that workers in other countries lacked. Successive waves of immigrants had imposed ethnic divisions that undermined notions of class solidarity.

Many "new" labor historians would build their reputations by challenging this Perlman–Taft thesis that American workers were "job conscious" rather than "class conscious." Whether the "new" labor historians actually made their case is another question.

The fourth edition of the *Principles* was up to date, thoroughly revised, and rearranged. The 1916 edition had started with the basis of labor law. The 1936 edition started with employment and unemployment, followed by an extended discussion of minimum wages. The 1916 edition had covered social insurance in chapter eight. The 1936 edition covered it in chapter five. The *Principles of Labor Legislation* was the only one of John R.'s books that ever sold in large numbers. John R. and John Andrews had assigned all the royalties to American Association for Labor Legislation.[41] The *Principles of Labor Legislation* is largely ignored today. Scholars interested in John R.'s thought generally pay more attention to the *Legal Foundations of Capitalism*, *Institutional Economics*, and perhaps *Myself*. But the *Principles* probably exercised a greater influence over his students.

John R. called *Myself* his autobiography. It might better be called a memoir. As John R. put it, "I do not write this story as a chronology. It is the genesis of my ideas."[42] And *Myself* remains a fine introduction to his ideas—short, easily understandable, and almost fun to read.

Institutional Economics, on the other hand, at nine hundred pages, is not short and not much fun to read. The reviews were mixed. Three institutionalists panned the book.[43] Raymond Bye of the University of Pennsylvania gave the book a mixed review combining praise and criticism.[44] He criticized the language and the organization, but he wrote in his conclusion. "It is hoped that that someday one of his disciples will give us the gist of his philosophy in more readable form, and weld it more coherently into the existing body of politico-economic theory."

Frank H. Knight, a strident critic of institutionalism, spent most of his review attacking institutionalists in general and complaining about John R.'s terminology. But, he concluded as follows. "For all that—and all that—and whatever one may think of any detail or particular aspect of the work, it is not merely 'curious and interesting' but extremely suggestive and valuable for any student of economic phenomena. . . . if they will take it in the right spirit, minds trained in orthodox economic theory and devoted to clarity, definiteness and 'system' are the very ones to read it with great profit."[45]

Mitchell praised the book and, as he had in the case of the *Legal Foundations of Capitalism*, provided its best introduction and a key to understanding it. He suggested first reading *Myself*, where John R. connected his ideas with his life experiences. Then he added another suggestion that embodied a slight criticism.

> [The candid reader] may feel that the ripe scholar who writes this book has much in common with the young instructor who failed when he tried to give a systematic course of lectures at Wesleyan in 1890. But the discursive writer of today is also the teacher who became keenly stimulating when he began to make his students participate in his own investigations. That is the opportunity which Professor Commons offers in *Institutional Economics*. The reader must do his own systematizing of the rich materials put before him, but the result will amply reward the effort.[46]

In spite of Mitchell's support and in spite of the positive endorsement of Knight, however, John R. seemed disappointed in his book's reception. So partly at the urging of students, he began work on a book that would answer critics of *Institutional Economics* and explain in simpler language what he had tried to communicate there.[47] This book would have a convoluted history initiated in part by John R.'s next personal tragedy.

Notes

1. Commons, *Myself.*, 184. John R. supported Jack's wife Ellen, through a sociology degree at Madison. She earned a fellowship for graduate study at NYU. John R. and his daughter, Rachel, cared for Anne while Ellen was in New York. Ellen eventually became head librarian for the Social Security Administration.
2. Ibid., 188.
3. Robert Baldwin, "International Economics and International Development," in *Economists at Wisconsin*, ed. Robert Lampman (Madison: Board of Regents of the University of Wisconsin System, 1993), 210–13.
4. "Commons Heads Cabinet," *Wisconsin State Journal*, January 6, 1931.
5. Barr Blackburn and Margaret Pryor, *Wisconsin Study of the Uniform Small Loan Law.* (Madison: University of Wisconsin 1929), Commons Papers, microfilm, reel 21, frames 715ff.
6. John R. Commons, "The Small Loan Problem," *The Milwaukee Sentinel* (April 1, 1931).

7. Commons, *Myself*, 147.
8. Commons papers microfilm;, reel 21, frame 420, Commons to Paxson, May 8, 1931, reel 22, frame 209, Wilkinson to Commons, June 25, 1932; reel 21, frames 117–18.
9. Ibid; reel 21, frames 426 and 434.
10. Ibid; all on reel 5 Blaine to Commons May 8, 1931, frame 91, Commons to Blaine May 15, 1931, frame 95, Wagner to Commons April 20, 1932 frames 305–6, Commons to Wagner April 25, 1932, frame 310.
11. In 1924 Congress had established a trust fund that would have paid veterans' bonuses in 1945. Veterans were allowed to borrow up to 22.5 percent of the bonuses. Patman's bill would have used the power granted in article 1, section 8, paragraph 5 of the Constitution to create money to pay the bonuses immediately. Patman's bill inspired the bonus march on Washington.
12. Commons to Pettengill, April 15, 1932, Commons Papers, microfilm; reel 5, frames 295–96.
13. Many of the letters between students are reproduced on reel 22 of the microfilm edition of the Commons papers between frames 215 and 289. Many objected to the goal of raising $20,000 during the depression. The goal was reduced to $1,300 with the order that John R. use it for a trip to England.
14. "The Seventieth Birthday," Leiserson papers Box 9, folder 1, Archives The State Historical Society of Wisconsin, Madison, Wisconsin.
15. "Professor Commons at Seventy," *The Survey* 68 (December 15): 674.
16. Alvin Hansen. "The Contributions of John R. Commons to American Economics," The papers of Alvin Hansen. Harvard University Library Archives Call Number HUGEP 3.42, Box 1.
17. Harold Groves, *In and Out of the Ivory Tower* (Madison: Wisconsin Historical Society, 1969), 67–68.
18. Ibid., 141–42.
19. Ibid., 144.
20. The Supreme Court Justice and his wife were bursting with pride when they learned that their daughter had been called "a real rabble rouser." Melvin Urofsky, *Louis D. Brandeis: A Life* (New York: Pantheon Books, 2009), 730.
21. Groves, *In and Out of the Ivory Tower*, 148 addendum.
22. Theron Schlabach, in *Edwin Witte Cautious Reformer* (Madison: State Historical Society of Wisconsin, 1969), 74–97 summarizes the "twisted" intellectual roots of the controversy which was deeper and angrier than indicated here. The American Association for Labor Legislation broke apart over it. Friends became enemies. Contrary to conventional wisdom at the time, there was division at Madison. John R.'s colleague, Walter Morton attacked the plan publicly. John R. answered Morton in *Institutional Economics*, 840–49. Paul H. Douglas, though still John R.'s friend, continued to oppose the plan. See *In the Fullness of Time, The Memoirs of Paul H Douglas* (New York: Harcourt, Brace, and Jovanovich, 1971), 388–89.
23. John R. Commons and John B. Andrews, *Principles of Labor Legislation*, 4th ed. (New York: Macmillan, 1936), 415.
24. New Negro Alliance v. Sanitary Grocery Co.303 U.S. 552 (1938).
25. According to Mark Perlman, John R. had offended his father Selig by saying that if Witte was not replacing him, he would have needed to replace him

A Worker's Economist

with Selig. This is hard to interpret. Both John R. and Selig held full-time positions in the department. Witte did not. John R. did not hold any official position that another full-time faculty member could inherit. His full-time position could be taken only by someone like Witte who did not previously hold a full-time position. John R. must have said something that Selig interpreted as anti-Semitic. It is doubtful that John R. intended such a thing, though he probably said something carelessly and Selig Perlman who from Bialystok on had experienced real anti-Semitism may have over-reacted.

26. Thomas E. Eliot, *The Legal Background of the Social Security Act* (delivered at a general staff meeting at Social Security Administration Headquarters, Baltimore, Maryland, on February 3, 1961), www.ssa.gov/history/eliot2.html, accessed October 9, 2014.

27. Florida v. Mellon 273 U.S. 12 (1927).

28. Larry DeWitt, *Never a Finished Thing: A Brief Biography of Arthur Joseph Altmeyer—the Man FDR Called "Mr. Social Security,"* www.ssa.gov/history/bioaja.html, accessed July 24, 2014.

29. Larry DeWitt, Daniel Belano, and Edward Berkowitz, eds., *Social Security: A Documentary History* (Washington, DC: Congressional Quarterly Press, 2008), 49.

30. The Executive Order can be found in Witte, *Development of the Social Security Act*, Appendix I, 201. The committee members were Frances Perkins, Secretary of Labor, Henry Morgenthau Jr., Secretary of the Treasury, Homer Cummings, Attorney General, Henry Wallace, Secretary of Agriculture, and Harry Hopkins, Federal Emergency Relief administrator.

31. Dewitt, *Never a Finished Thing*. Fairness should include the names of Barbara Nachtrieb Armstrong and Douglas Brown who wrote the Old Age parts of the bill. They did not get along very well with Witte and Altmeyer, largely because of misunderstandings—especially of the political maneuverings behind the scenes. The final bill would have been better if more of their suggestions could have been politically feasible.

32. Walton Hamilton, "The Institutional Approach to Economic Theory," *American Economic Review* 9 (March, 1919): 309–18.

33. Malcolm Rutherford, *The Institutional Movement in American Economics 1918–1947*. (New York: Cambridge University Press, 2011).

34. Commons to Bogart, August 29, 1931, Commons Papers (microfilm), reel 5, frame 184.

35. Bogart to Commons, September 17, 1931, ibid., reel 5, frame 192.

36. Commons to Bogart, September 19, 1931, reel 5, frame 193.

37. John R. Commons, "Institutional Economics," *American Economic Review* 21 (December, 1931): 648–57.

38. For the logical inconsistency, see Vincent Ostrom, "John R. Commons's Foundations for Policy Analysis," *Journal of Economic Issues* 10 (December, 1976): 830–57.

39. Selig Perlman and Philip Taft *History of Labor in the United States, 1896–1932*, vol.4 ed. John R. Commons. 1935. Reprint (New York: A.M. Kelley, 1966), 621.

40. Ibid., 622.

41. Parsons to Chasse, personal letter, October 22, 1987.

42. Commons, *Myself*, 5.

43. Willard E. Atkins, "Institutional Economics of John R. Commons, A Review," *International Journal of Ethics* 45 (July, 1935): 474–76; Morris A. Copeland, "Commons's Institutionalism in Relation to Problems of Social Evolution and Social Planning," *Quarterly Journal of Economics* 30 (February, 1936): 333–46; Clifford James, "Commons on Institutional Economics," *American Economic Review* 27 (1937): 61–76.

44. Raymond Bye, "Review of *Institutional Economics* by John R. Commons," *Annals of the American Academy of Political and Social Science* 178 (March, 1935): 200–2.

45. Frank H. Knight, "Institutional Economics: Its Place in Political Economy," *Columbia Law Review* 35 (May, 1935): 805.

46. Wesley Clair Mitchell, "Commons on Institutional Economics," *American Economic Review* 25 (December 1935): 642–43.

47. This comes out in a number of letters on reel 5 of the microfilm of Commons's papers. See James Madden to Patricia Adams, July 30, 1936, frame 662, Commons to Jean Barr, October 16, 1936, frame 684.

17

The Trailer Park and the Last Book

Now I go further than I did twenty-five years ago and contend that the preservation of the American economic system against a totalitarian world and against its own internal disruptions consists mainly in the collective bargaining between organized capital and organized labor
—The Economics of Collective Action.

On April 22, 1936, twelve-year-old Mark Perlman picked up the phone, and he heard John R. on the other end. John R. was sobbing and repeating "I need Selig."[1] Selig was not home, but Mark knew where he was. He caught a bus to the Memorial Union where Selig was attending a meeting and relayed John R.'s message. Selig went immediately to John R.'s home and stayed with him all through the night. John R.'s daughter Rachel had died that afternoon—a most wrenching loss.

She was all that was left of John R.'s Madison family. Nell had died in 1927. Jack had disappeared in 1930, and efforts to locate him had failed. Jack's wife, Ellen, and her daughter Anne were in Washington, DC. John R.'s half-sister, Anna who had come to share his old age, had died in an automobile accident. That left Rachel, dead now, perhaps a suicide. John R. may have hit bottom. He probably destroyed many of his papers, and he offered Selig Perlman his entire library.[2]

But, his sister Anna's daughter, Bertha Best, was also there at the time. With Bertha's assistance, John R. sold Ho Chee Ra, the home with the cheerful Winnebago name. They bought an Airstream trailer, and because his doctor did not think that John R. could take another Wisconsin winter, they left Madison in November 1936 and drove to a trailer park in Fort Lauderdale, Florida.[3] When they arrived, the friendly "trailer folk" revived his spirits, and he thought of working again—teaching a course on values and valuation and writing a book that would respond to the criticism of *Institutional Economics*.[4]

The New Routine

Letters flew back and forth between John R. and Witte, now department chairman, and after some dickering, and academic politicking, they managed to work out the schedule that John R. would follow for the next four years. He would travel to Madison late in the spring and teach a course on values and valuation followed by a short series of lectures at the beginning of October. Then he would return to Florida where he would write book reviews and articles—mostly working papers for his continually changing book.[5] He would write book reviews, but compose only one major article—warning about what he considered dangerous implications of "structuralist" explanations for the Great Depression.

Former students would come to help, the first being Theresa McMahon. She and her husband Ed had come to Madison in 1906 from Seattle, Washington. She had received her PhD in 1909 with a dissertation on women in industry.[6] Ed, a historian, had never finished a dissertation, possibly because Frederick Jackson Turner had left Madison in 1910. Both McMahons taught at the University of Washington.

With their outspoken support for labor rights, they had become a problem for the university trustees. Theresa had taken students to Central Labor Council meetings—including the meeting that called the general strike of 1919—the one condemned as a Bolshevik plot.[7] In 1936, the trustees passed a nepotism rule that made it impossible for two members of the same family to serve on the faculty. Theresa was forced to retire.

When he learned what had happened, John R. wrote immediately. "I had a letter from Professor Witte speaking most highly of your students and of your work at Seattle, and his regrets that you felt compelled to resign your position, though he recognizes you will have a much better opportunity for your research work."[8]

John R. then asked if she would be willing to look at his manuscript and to see it through to publication if he should die too soon. "I hope to be able to finish it, but, in case I cannot, you are the only person in whom I feel confidence that the book would come through in proper shape." She responded that she would be glad to comment on his manuscript and that she would work to see the book through if he should die first, but she was certain that he would live to see it published. "Next time I write I will send you a picture of myself in my new vocation as an unskilled laborer."[9]

McMahon must have suggested an elementary text because John R. wrote that: "I begin to feel that it will be very difficult for me to write out elementary economics for beginners. I am so much concerned with the advanced and unsettled problems and with squaring myself with the various criticisms as well as taking into account various theories which I am writing up and comparing with my own that I cannot get down to writing something introductory."[10] At that time, he seems to have told McMahon that he was thinking of calling the book "Administrative Economics."[11]

He worked on the book by writing working papers and sending them to students and colleagues for criticism—but not for publication or wide dissemination. He specifically rejected proposals for publishing his paper on Lionel Robbins's *An Essay on the Nature and Significance of Economic Science.*[12]

New Deal legal issues drew him away from any intention of merely answering critics or simplifying what he had already written. Since many of his students were now working in New Deal agencies, he could consult them for information and advice. This seems to have been the case for another piece that seemed to circulate continuously—on the Agricultural Adjustment Act.[13]

Martin Glaeser, a former student and colleague, now chief economist for the Tennessee Valley Authority, invited John R. to stop over during one of his annual trips South.[14] The visit became the occasion for an article in the *Survey Graphic*, a page in the ultimate book—and John R.'s first airplane ride.

The Last Major Article

John R. disturbed this routine once. He wrote Witte that he was "accumulating stuff" to write an article in response to a Brookings study.[15] John R. was referring to two books advancing the structuralist view of the Great Depression.[16] This view attributed the depression to inefficiencies created by large firms and unions—special interests that maintain prices by restricting production, and thus sabotaging a "natural progression" from innovation to falling prices to expanding markets to increased employment. The solution, according to Harold Moulton, the author, lay in some form of indicative planning that would encourage firms to reduce prices and wages. To John R., this looked like the old argument that deflation was the natural and desirable result of technical progress.

His response revealed that he had remained up-to-date on the literature—especially on the writing of the Swedish economist Bertil Ohlin and Stockholm School, and that he had read John Maynard Keynes's *General Theory of Employment, Interest, and Money*.[17] (Though the correspondence seems lost, there are some indications that John R. also corresponded with Ohlin.) In any case, John R.'s article revealed familiarity with the latest writings both of Stockholm and of Keynes.

He started with a principle that they all shared—that monetary authorities should commit to stable, slightly rising prices. He contrasted this principle with what seemed to him to be Moulton's toleration for deflation, and he contrasted the proven success of Sweden's "experiment in collective action" with the untried nature of Moulton's prescription.

He adapted his going concern theory to a fundamental insight shared by Keynes and the Swedes—the insight that planned saving (defined as income not spent on consumer goods) might not equal planned spending by borrowers on currently produced goods and services—with the result that reduced total demand will result in reduced income and hence in reduced actual saving and spending.

He praised Moulton for realizing that capitalist economies do not necessarily tend toward full employment equilibrium and for realizing that credit was not a neutral medium in economic transactions. Following Thorstein Veblen's distinction between pecuniary and real assets, Moulton had distinguished two uses for savings: one, pecuniary, the purchase of credit instruments, such as stocks, bonds; the other productive, the purchase of buildings, equipment, and inventories. John R. started there, but he replaced the pecuniary–real distinction with the notion of bubbles. He pointed out that in both stock and commodity markets ownership is distinct from possession of the physical products. Speculators can bid up the prices of stocks or of hog bellies without taking possession of either. Repeated sales of hog bellies can, until delivery, exceed the number of actual hog bellies. So anticipated savings can be channeled into stock and commodity bubbles. John R. added that all transactions create debts equal to the credits.

Next John R. moved to the managers of the going business as they decide how much to borrow in order to fund future production. These managers must make legally binding commitments without knowing precisely how much they will be able to sell. Their decisions rest in part on assumptions about future price levels.

At this point, John R. interrupted his chain of thought to criticize Moulton's notion of profits as a share in the aggregate economy, and he substituted the notion of the short-run margin of profit that he had developed in *Institutional Economics*, emphasizing, as he had there, the tininess of this margin as a constraint on management decisions. If managers anticipate falling prices, hence falling profit margins, they reduce their production plans. As a result their planned borrowing will fall short of the anticipated savings that had been bidding up prices in credit and commodity markets. The managers of the going businesses would be more likely to borrow and spend if they could anticipate rising prices. So while Moulton concluded to the benefits of gradually falling prices, John R. concluded to the benefits of gradually rising prices.

In addition to arguing for a rising rather than a falling general price level, John R. attacked the assumption that a scientific analysis must avoid value judgments. John R. presented two arguments—one toward the beginning of his article; the other toward the end.

Toward the beginning, he noted that Moulton, like Keynes and Fisher, had proposed polices to achieve "an avowed public purpose," something that would have been considered unscientific by the classical economists. Then he added that the science of medicine is not considered unscientific because it has an avowed ethical purpose—the health of the human person. Policy sciences, he continued, resemble medicine in this respect. Medicine diagnoses the causes of physical illnesses and proposes solutions. Policy sciences diagnose the causes of social illnesses and propose solutions. If medicine, guided by the purpose of physical health, is recognized as a science then policy sciences, guided by the purpose of common welfare, should be so recognized.

Then, toward the end of his article, he returned to the question of ethics. First he attacked the adequacy of consumer satisfaction as the major rule for guiding economic policy. His attack was a little complicated. People earn the incomes to consume as producers, mostly as wage-earners. But their jobs depend on the decisions of businessmen who make those decisions on the basis of anticipated profits. An anticipation of falling prices creates an anticipation of falling profits and an increased subjective probability of insolvency. "[W]hen the businessman gets scared about insolvency he slashes right and left regardless of others." And when the businessman slashes, incomes and consumption ability to fall. On the other hand, anticipation of rising prices makes the businessman more likely to respond to appeals of "labor unions and charities." So, he concludes. " The policy of gradually raising the general price level yields what our Francis A. Walker seventy years ago named a 'fillip to industry,' by which was meant a fillip to profits. It gradually enlarges the business man's capacity to pay debts. Ohlin's exposition shows it experimentally at work on a credit basis."[18]

Finally, John R. pointed out the inconsistency between Moulton's pose of offering "value-free" policy advice and his statements such as "raising the level of material well-being . . . is the ultimate purpose of an economic system." "The underlying purpose of business is to serve the people; indeed only as it serves people can it serve its own interests."[19]

This article, in a way, broke John R.'s practice of writing book reviews and papers that circulated only among students and friends, but it fit in well with a routine that depended on his niece Bertha. She drove him north to Madison in the summer for his seminar on value and valuation, and she drove him South to Fort Lauderdale in the winter where he wrote and worked on his book. She stayed with him in both places and supported him emotionally. But Bertha's silent support ended late in 1941 when she died of cancer.

The Routine Breaks Down

Fortunately, a family that Bertha had known for six years, the Carpenters, brought John R. into their home. A graduate student, Chester Meske, assigned as John R.'s assistant, came, stayed, and helped with the book.

William Leiserson offered to come down for ten days or so.[20] When Leiserson got there, John R. told him that he did not think that he could stay in Florida and suggested a room at the University Union at Madison.[21] By June 1942, John R. was living at the University Union in Madison, but Ed Witte was worried.

> I am not at all sure that Professor Commons's coming to Madison this early will work out satisfactorily. He complains that he cannot sleep and is very much dissatisfied. He has a nice room at the University Club, but, after all, a Club is not very homelike and Professor Commons is a man who has always had to have people look after him—particularly women. The last months in Florida he seems to have had a pretty fair arrangement because a Mrs. Carpenter, who brought him to Madison, looked after his welfare. Here in Madison there is no one who takes her place. Most of Professor Commons's old friends are of course gone, and his former students, like myself, have a lot of other things to do.[22]

In July 1942, Chester Meske left Madison to work as an organizer for the CIO.[23]

230

The Carpenters took John R. back to their home in Florida. In October, he suffered a stroke that paralyzed his left arm, and fearing again that he might die before the book was completed, he contacted Kenneth Parsons who had written an article on his point of view.[24] Parsons received a grant that enabled him to go to Florida in June 1944. He spent five weeks with John R. They went through the first chapters of the book, and Parsons returned to Madison with the completed manuscript.

Jack Is Found

In that same summer of 1944, William Kiekhofer, while in Hartford, Connecticut, on business, noticed something familiar about a laundry truck driver. He asked the police to investigate. On July 15, 1944, the police confirmed that the laundry truck driver was indeed John R.'s long lost son Jack. He remembered who he was. He remembered Madison, and he seemed anxious to restore old bonds. The following Monday, Jack left for Fort Lauderdale where he spent four days with John R. who was so elated that he almost collapsed.[25]

A year later, in April 1945, Kenneth Parsons sent John R. the final typed revision of his manuscript. John R. approved and prepared to move from Fort Lauderdale.

The Carpenters, who had cared for him since Bertha's death, were leaving for Massachusetts. John R., his sister, Clara, and his son Jack decided that they would live together in Raleigh, North Carolina. Jack quit his job in Hartford and went to Raleigh to look for a home. John R. arrived in the beginning of May.[26] He found old friends old students at the University of North Carolina and at Duke. Kenneth Parsons wrote that "in the university atmosphere he was young again for a few days; and then the little canter at the end of the race was over."[27] On the afternoon of May 10, John R. suffered a stroke and lapsed into unconsciousness. He never regained consciousness, and he died the next day on May 11, 1945.

Jack came to the funeral at Madison, the following Monday, May 14, 1945. Clara was too weak. John R.'s granddaughter Anne insisted on coming—alone, on the long train ride with changes at Chicago. John R. and Rachel had cared for her after 1930 when her father had disappeared and her mother had gone to New York on a fellowship.[28]

President Roosevelt had died on April 12. Germany had surrendered on May 7 or May 8. Battles raged in the Pacific. So it was understandable that when Ed Witte visited Harvard for a conference that summer, he found that the attendees, many of whom considered John R. a friend, had not heard of his death.

After John R.'s death, Jack and Clara rented a house in Roseville, a suburb of Raleigh, North Carolina. Jack supported them with his veteran's pension and income from odd jobs. Over time, the people of Roseville came to accept Jack as a respected local character—good-natured, helpful, and a little odd in a nice way. He cared for Clara even as she became a complete invalid and descended into dementia. He kept her from a nursing home until her very last days. She died on March 3, 1951.[29]

In January and again in April, 1957, Jack suffered heart attacks. He never fully recovered from the second, and he died on September 4. He was buried with full military honors on September 10 in the National Cemetery in Raleigh.[30]

But the story of John R., his other family, and his team, of course, did not end with his death or with the passing of his sister and son.

Notes

1. Leon Fink, "A Memoir of Selig Perlman and His Life at the University of Wisconsin: Based on an interview of Mark Perlman, Conducted and Edited by Leon Fink," *Labor History* 32 (Fall 1991): 503–21. According to Karl Smith MD, she was suffering from a pulmonary infection, Commons Papers. Microfilm reel 5, frame 656. According to John R., she died on Wednesday, July 22 at 4 PM. Commons to Professor Fay Cooper Cole July 24, 1936 ibid., frame 659. His students seemed to think that she committed suicide.
2. He may have destroyed his papers at that time, See guide for John R. Commons *Papers* (Madison, WI: State Historical Society of Wisconsinn), p.17. Mark Perlman told Leon Fink that Commons offered his entire library to Selig Perlman, but that Selig took only five books, Fink, "A Memoir of Selig Perlman," 524.
3. Commons to Witte January 18, 1937, Commons Papers, microfilm, reel 5, frames 728–29.
4. Kenneth Parsons, "Introduction," in *The Economics of Collective Action*, ed. John R. Commons (New York: Macmillan, 1950), 5; James Madden to Patricia Adams, July 30, 1936 and Commons to James Barr, October 16, 1936, Commons Papers, microfilm, reel 5, frames 663 and 684.
5. Commons to Witte, January 3, 1937. Commons Papers, microfilm; reel 5, frames 719–20.
6. Theresa McMahon, *Women and Economic Evolution: or the Effects of Economic Evolution on the Evolution of Women. University of Wisconsin Bulletin no. 496 of Economics and Political Science Series* (Madison: University of Wisconsin, 1912).
7. Geraldine Clifford, *Lone Voyagers Academic Women in Coeducational Universities 1870–1937* (New York: City University of New York, 1989), 230.

The Trailer Park and the Last Book

8. Commons to McMahon, August 30, 1937, Commons Papers, microfilm, reel 5, frame 841.
9. McMahon to Commons, September 12, 1937, Ibid., frame 854.
10. Commons to McMahon, October 22, 1937, Ibid., frame 886.
11. Witte to Parsons June 12, 1945, Witte Papers Box 9.
12. Commons to Herbert Black, September 4, 1937, Commons Papers, microfilm; reel 4, frame 846.
13. Morton to Commons March 17, 1937, Commons to McMahon, October 22, 1937, ibid., frames 757–58 and 841.
14. Glaeser to Commons, September 9, 1937, Commons to Glaeser September 25, 1937, ibid., frames 857 and 860. Commons, "What I Saw in the Tennessee Valley." *Survey Graphic* 27 (May, 1938), 279; *Economics of Collective Action*, 87.
15. Commons to Witte, February 28, 1937, Commons Papers, microfilm, reel 4, frame 746.
16. Harold Moulton, *The Formation of Capital* and *Income and Economic Progress* (Washington, DC: The Brookings Institution, 1935). For the structuralist view, see William Barber, *Designs within Disorder, Franklin Roosevelt, the Economists, and the Shaping of American Economic Policy 1933–1945* (New York: Cambridge University Press, 1996), 5–10, 29–32.
17. John R. Commons, "Capacity to Consume, Capacity to Produce," *American Economic Review* 27(December 1937): 680–97, Bertil Ohlin, "Some Notes on the Stockholm School of Saving and Investment," *Economic Journal* (March 1937): 53–69. The fall 1981 issue of the *History of Political Economy* is devoted to the Stockholm School.
18. Commons, "Capacity to Consume, Capacity to Produce," 694.
19. Ibid., 696.
20. Leiserson to Commons, February 2, 1941, Leiserson Papers, Madison, State Historical Society of Wisconsin, Box 9, Folder 1.
21. Leiserson to Witte May 12, 1942, ibid., Box 45.
22. Witte to Leiserson, June 5, 1942, ibid.
23. Lee Brown with Robert L. Allen, *Strong in my Life, Struggles of a Black Activist* (Oxford: Rowman and Littlefield, 2001), 55. Meske became business agent and organizer for the International Longshoremen and Warehousemen's Union.
24. Parsons, "Introduction," *Economics of Collective Action*, vi.
25. John R. Commons to Ellen Commons, August 2, 1944, Commons Papers, microfilm, reel 5, frame 955.
26. Witte to Perlman, April 6, 1945, Witte Papers, Madison, Historical Society of Wisconsin, Box 9.
27. Parsons, "Editor's Preface," Economics *of Collective Action*, viii.
28. Edwin Witte to Theresa McMahon, June 11, 1945, Witte Papers, Box9.
29. Tom Holland to Edwin Witte and Selig Perlman September 11, 1945, Commons Papers, microfilm, reel 5, frame 960.
30. Ibid., frames 961–62.

18

The Team's Last Stand

The real decision to be made is the choice of alternatives between self-governing labor unions and militaristic government. The unions may not be 'conservative' from the standpoint of bargaining power, but they are conservative from the standpoint of representative government.—Economics of Collective Action.

In 1950 Kenneth Parsons saw John R.'s last book through to publication.[1] He called it *The Economics of Collective Action*, and he wrote that it should be "the first book" for anyone interested "in understanding Commons' thought."[2] It should be the "first book," he might have added, not just for Commons's text but for Selig Perlman's memorial preceding it and for Parsons's article following it, the article endorsed by John R. himself (Note 1).

The Book

Perlman's memorial added a personal context in his description of John R. conducting an interview.

> Commons' intellectual democracy perhaps showed clearest when he was interviewing. His was no "technique of modesty" or a simulated ignorance to appeal to the other's ego and thus evoke information. It was a genuine groping, questions without any ultimate goal—a mere stabbing in this direction and in that. What kept the conversation from degenerating into a boring experience to the person interviewed was Commons' deep earnestness and his unmistakable assumption that the latter's problems were not just his own private worries, but of general concern and deeply instructive to any serious minded interrogator. And then, sometimes after hours had elapsed, a question or series of questions would come forth which not only touched the nerve of the whole situation but as if by sleight- of-hand made the earlier groping appear as an orderly quest with little waste motion.[3]

Allen Gruchy cited this passage in criticism. The book, he wrote, read like the "stabbing . . . groping somewhat directionless way of the interviewer."[4] Gruchy was partially correct, but he missed something—the possibility that some "stabbing and groping" is unavoidable in the real world of public policy making, that the "stabbing and groping" can be purpose driven. John R. indicated as much after he contrasted his "comparative method" with the deductive method of "orthodox economics."

"The conflict between deductive and comparative reasoning becomes evident when economists are required to work with public administrators—in public commissions or action agencies." They may be speaking different languages. The language of the economist assumes that a proper policy can be deduced from spare assumptions: "that all individual cases are similar." But the administrator speaks a language of the unique case looked at from many points of view.[5]

In other words, realistic policy analysis must involve some "stabbing and groping," but it is not "directionless," and in *The Economics of Collective Action* John R. maintained that the "direction" is best discovered in disciplined democratic inquiry.

> These are the subject matters set forth for investigation in this book. The assumption is that whatever is "reasonable" is constitutional, and that reasonableness is best ascertained in practice when representatives of conflicting organized economic interests, instead of politicians or lawyers, agree voluntarily on the working rules of collective action in control of individual action. This is not logical, neither is it revolutionary. It is the discovery, through investigation and negotiation of what is the best practicable thing to do under the actual circumstances of conflicting economic interests, organized as they are, to impose their collective will on individuals and each other.[6]

John R. was thinking concretely of his advisory committees, and he emphasized that they were an idea that had not been tried, even though critics might object that they had been tried and had not worked. The critics were thinking of advisory committees appointed by the politicians in power. John R. was thinking of advisory committees appointed not by politicians but by the interested groups, and he invoked the organization of the Wisconsin Industrial Commission in 1911. He wanted something that would approach an "occupational legislature instead of the territorial legislatures." He wanted an advisory board whose recommendations would be "adopted by the legislature and the commission, regardless of political changes in the administration itself."[7]

In the field of labor relations, this implied that labor representation would be more adequate if labor leaders were responsible to more workers. And the leaders would represent more workers if all workers were required, as a condition of employment, to support their unions. This was an argument for closed or union shops. For John R., the closed shop would exemplify collective action in control, liberation, and expansion of individual action. It would control workers by enforcing a duty corresponding to the right of citizenship in an industrial society.[8] It would liberate workers by freeing them from the arbitrary and capricious actions of the corporation, and it would expand their powers by putting the bargaining power of the union at their disposal.

Indeed, John R.'s defense of unions in this book went beyond anything in the *Legal Foundations of Capitalism* or in *Institutional Economics*. He argued that trade unions constitute the strongest defense of representative government against various forms of authoritarianism, and he warned that a decline in union strength would remove one of the most effective bulwarks against the authoritarianism that had overthrown so many democracies in the 1920s and 1930s. Strong unions transform their members from subjects to industrial citizens with rights, duties, liberties, immunities, and above all dignity.[9]

The growing power of corporations added urgency to the need to bolster the capabilities of representative processes—including those provided by unions. John R. cited a long passage from *The Modern Corporation and Private Property* by Adolph A. Berle and Gardiner C. Means summarized in this statement: "The rise of the modern corporation has brought a concentration of economic power which can cope on equal terms with the modern state."[10]

The Times

Ironically, three years before John R.'s argument for the closed shop appeared in print, the Taft–Hartley Act had outlawed the closed shop. Nelson Lichtenstein has argued that the Taft–Hartley Act was the main factor in the decline of union membership since 1950 and that economists at the time did not understand how it effectively denied freedom of assembly.[11] He was partly right. Union membership stagnated for a few years after 1950 and then began its steady decline, and the Taft–Hartley Act offers the most obvious explanation.

But Lichtenstein was only partly right. Harry Millis, a Commons student, and Emily Clark Brown clearly understood the consequences of the act. They called it an "omnibus" measure that involved "a historically unprecedented extension of federal power" over workers and unions.[12]

Taft–Hartley reinstituted the injunction, annulling, in part, the Norris–LaGuardia Act. It placed onerous and expensive reporting requirements on unions. It outlawed secondary boycotts. It inserted a "free speech" clause that allowed employers to force employee attendance at "informational meetings" and at one-on-one "counseling meetings" where they were harangued with anti-union propaganda. At the same time the courts enforced property rights that denied union representatives any meaningful right to respond to such propaganda. The act flatly denied supervisors the right to form unions.

Labor leaders called it a "slave labor" law. Millis and Brown rejected that label, but they added their own: "it was too much a strait-jacket, a strait-jacket which we believe proved a misfit at many points."[13]

The bipartisan support for the Taft–Hartley Act reflected the political climate of the years surrounding the publication of John R.'s final book. In 1946, Joseph McCarthy had replaced Robert M. La Follette Jr., "Fighting Bob's" son, as Wisconsin's senator. McCarthy voted for the Taft-Hartley Act and won a sort of infamy in the second red scare.

The political climate was also changing in some graduate schools. John R.'s old friend Paul H. Douglas who had enlisted in the Marine Corps and had been badly wounded on Okinawa returned from the war to the University of Chicago.

> Teaching was enjoyable after all those years, and I was honored by election to the presidency of the American Economic Association— the highest distinction my profession could accord. Nevertheless, I was disconcerted to find that the economic and political conservatives had acquired an almost complete dominance over my department and taught that market decisions were always right and profit values the supreme ones. The doctrine of noninterference with the market meant, in practice, clear the track for big business. Inequalities of bargaining power, knowledge and income were brushed aside, and the realities of monopoly, quasi monopoly, and imperfect competition were treated as immaterial or nonexistent.[14]

Douglas left the University of Chicago in 1948 and spent the rest of his life representing the State of Illinois in the US Senate.

The Last Act of the Tradition

The political climate made 1950 a bad year to publish *The Economics of Collective Action*. Nevertheless, it was an oddly significant year for the John R. Commons tradition. That tradition rested less on the theories in the *Legal Foundations of Capitalism* or *Institutional Economics*, than on the tradition of "constructive research" which his students, Perlman, Witte, Groves, and Glaeser had absorbed by working with him. And they passed this tradition on to their best students.

In 1950, one such student, Robert Lampman, graduated with a dissertation on collective bargaining by West Coast sailors. He turned his attention immediately to income distribution, publishing articles that questioned accepted beliefs—that poor families had more children than rich families and that the income distributions became more equal in late stages of capitalist development.[15] He wrote a literature review on egalitarianism as a value and on the causes and consequences of inequality.[16] In an article about institutions and the income distribution, he explored the effects of urbanization and technical change on the ability of families to protect their members from the tremors of capitalist instability, concluding that the decline of the three-generation family threw the burden on other institutions— corporations, unions, and states. He noted that unions have an equalizing effect on the upper half of the income distribution, but that they have no effect on the lower half. He also noted that exemptions and deductions in income taxes create a sort of inconsistent and arbitrary family allowance.[17]

In 1959, Senator Paul H. Douglas, chair of the Joint Economic Committee of Congress, asked Lampman to write a paper on the effects of aggregate demand on poverty. Douglas was concerned about John Kenneth Galbraith's argument that the rising tide of economic growth would not lift all boats. Lampman concluded, on the basis of the last two censuses, that economic growth would lift most boats. Then he agreed with Galbraith that growth would not lift some boats, though he disagreed somewhat about which boats would not rise. Galbraith had listed two types of poverty. The first he called "island poverty" created by the failure or inability of families to move when income opportunities decline in an area; the second, "case poverty"—"some quality peculiar to the individual or family involved—mental deficiency, bad health, inability to adapt to the discipline of modern economic life, excessive procreation, alcohol, insufficient education, or perhaps a combination of several of these handicaps."[18] Lampman did not see a statistical argument for area poverty. As for case poverty, he moved from ethical to statistical descriptions. Past economic growth had not increased the incomes of female-headed families or of families headed by elderly people or of single persons over the age of fifty-five. The incomes of non-whites had increased, but not by as much as the incomes of whites. As for "excessive procreation," Lampman's previous work had raised questions about that piece of conventional wisdom. Finally, Lampman did not have evidence on mental or physical disability, but he still agreed with Galbraith that the boats of people with mental or physical disability would not rise with the tide of economic growth.[19]

And, in 1956 there was a seemingly unremarkable job change. Wilbur Cohen, a former "Friday Nighter" had come to Washington with Ed Witte and had stayed as assistant to Arthur Altmeyer. When Altmeyer had resigned in 1950, Cohen had moved to the research branch of the Social Security Administration. Then in 1956, Cohen moved to the University of Michigan.

In that same year, 1956, Senator John F. Kennedy, running for reelection, asked his legislative aide, Theodore Sorensen, to develop a Social Security proposal. Sorensen had once worked for the Federal Security Administration where he had come to know Wilbur Cohen. So, Sorensen turned to Cohen who understood all the minutiae of Social Security—and all the political pitfalls—and all the ramifications of poorly conceived proposals. Kennedy was so impressed with Cohen's advice that when he became president in 1960, he told Cohen to pick his own job. Cohen, who liked to work with Congress, chose the job of assistant secretary for Legislation in the Department of Health, Education, and Welfare.

Kennedy also asked Walter Heller to serve as chair of the Council of Economic Advisors. Heller, though most noted for post-Keynesian fiscal policies, was also a Wisconsin graduate, a former assistant for Harold Groves. Kennedy also asked Heller to look into the problem of poverty, and Heller brought Lampman to the staff of the Council of Economic Advisors.[20]

So, with Cohen in the Department of Health, Education, and Welfare (HEW), and with Heller and Lampman in the Council of Economic Advisors the tradition of John R. Commons returned to Washington, DC.

Since the Commons tradition stressed teamwork and avoidance of taking credit, it is difficult to isolate a specific Wisconsin influence in the mass of legislation produced in the 1960s. For example, Medicare and Medicaid were designed by health professionals who had been lobbying for national health insurance since 1912.[21] But Wilbur Cohen wrote the bill.

Similarly, Robert Lampman worked with two other CEA staff members, William Capron and Burton Weisbrod, and with some economists from the Bureau of the Budget. But Lampman wrote the second chapter of the 1964 *Economic Report of the President.* This was the chapter that laid out the rationale for what came to be called the "War on Poverty."

The term "war on poverty" has been applied in different ways. Sometimes it is applied only to the Economic Opportunity Act.[22] And sometimes it is applied to all the initiatives proposed by President Johnson in 1964, including the HEW proposals.[23] Cohen who worked on the HEW proposals did not like the Economic Opportunity Act. He thought the term "War on Poverty" was over the top and raised expectations that could not be fulfilled. So it seems unfair to lump HEW proposals together with the Economic Opportunity Act.[24] It created the Office of Economic Opportunity (OEO), which clearly resembled a design on principles of John R.'s "constructive democracy" and "constructive research"—experimentalism with a recognition that some experiments will fail.[25] There were two job training programs, funds set aside for local experiments, and the most controversial of its provisions established the Community Action Program in Part A of Title II which began with a three-paragraph definition.

The first paragraph defined a community action program as one that mobilizes community resources in an attack on poverty. The second paragraph stipulated that such a program would provide "services, assistance and other activities of sufficient scope and size to give promise toward elimination of poverty of a cause or causes of poverty through developing employment opportunities, improving human performance, motivation and productivity, or bettering the condition under which people live, learn, and work."[26] The third part of the definition created the most controversy. It defined a community action program as one "which is developed, conducted, and administered with the maximum feasible participation of the areas and members of the groups served."[27]

Critics attributed the phrase "maximum feasible participation," to sociologists influenced by the Ford Foundation's Gray Areas program and by Saul Alinsky's Industrial Areas Foundation.[28] Carl Brauer showed that the OEO was designed by economists, not sociologists. Alinsky's program was never mentioned.[29] It is worth noting, however, that the requirement was strikingly consistent with the central theme of *The Economics of Collective Action*: "that reasonableness is best ascertained in practice when representatives of conflicting organized economic interests, instead of politicians or lawyers, agree voluntarily on the working rules of collective action in control of individual action."[30]

Once the OEO began operating, its implementation of the doctrine of "maximum feasible participation" drew the most fire, illustrating another of John R.'s principles— that scarcity and conflict will characterize every search for reasonable values.[31] Moreover, the "maximum feasible participation" component seemed to threaten a new interest group—a group of elite liberal policy professionals who became neoconservatives.

Heller and Lampman both left Washington before the OEO began operation. When President Johnson expanded defense spending for the Vietnam War, Heller told him that he needed to raise taxes to stave off inflation. When Johnson failed to do so, Heller resigned on November 15, 1964. In discussions about the poverty program it had been decided that anything like a family allowance would be politically infeasible, and Lampman left Washington for Wisconsin to found the Institute for Research on Poverty where he initiated the negative income tax experiments.

In 1965, Lampman wrote an optimistic article about poverty, its causes, and its cures. He proposed a three-prong strategy.[32] First, fiscal policy must drive the unemployment rate to 4 percent and it must be accompanied by some form of family allowance to support the disabled and prevent families from suffering the psychological damage of extremely low income. Second, barriers must be broken down, barriers that prevent people from escaping poverty—employment and housing discrimination, segregated schools, absence of affordable housing or recreation, and public health facilities. And third, educational opportunities must be expanded, beginning with prenatal care, continuing through preschool all the way up to training of young adults. This three-prong approach, Lampman confidently predicted, could eliminate poverty in a generation.

One might call Lampman naïve, or one might say as Ramirez said of John R.'s dissent or as Meltzer said of the Strong Bill which John R. defended that an opportunity was missed.

Wilbur Cohen was the last of the three Wisconsinites to leave Washington. In 1968 President Johnson appointed him secretary of Health, Education, and Welfare, and he earned the title "Mr. Social Security." "When civil rights laws were discussed, he was there. When legislation to protect farm workers was considered, his views were sought. He shaped training programs, child welfare standards and aid to the aging and handicapped. He supported federal aid to education, health insurance and medical research."[33] But even as Cohen was winding up his term in Washington, dark clouds were gathering.

242

In 1969, in an influential book, with what proved to have prophetic name, *The End of Liberalism*, Theodore Lowi, a political scientist at Cornell attacked the notion of interest group democracy. Lowi did not mention John R. Commons. But Mancur Olson, an economist, did mention him in *The Logic of Collective Action* which explicitly attacked interest group liberalism. More accurately Olson attacked a distorted caricature beyond recognition of anything that Commons ever believed or taught.[34] Though the Lowi–Olson theses have since been questioned, the title of Lowi's book proved prophetic for the subsequent course of public policy.[35]

Heller, Lampman, and Cohen had to endure a public discourse that threatened everything they believed in. Cohen helped found an organization, Save Our Social Security (SOS). And one could find, if one looked at news photos, a little man, almost bald, the few strands of hair on his head now white, the once Mr. Inside, now outside of public buildings, a dwarf beside taller placard bearers protesting cuts to social security and welfare programs. Cohen and Heller died a month apart in 1987, Cohen on May 17, Heller on June 15. Robert Lampman died in 1997.

Lampman's fellow classmate, another former student of Witte, Groves, and Perlman, Eugene Genovese, wrote a brief memorial for his friend, Robert Lampman.

> It is the recent passing of this last great pillar of the third generation of the Wisconsin School—the fourth to carry the burden imposed by Henry George on that school to contribute to the elimination and alleviation of poverty that necessitates the writing of this article . . . as the historical wheel turns slowly with regressions, in the recent times he [Lampman] had to watch attacks on antipoverty programs, indeed, on the very idea of helpful compassion and the need for an economic system that more equally distributed income and a social system that allowed broadened access for all citizens "regardless of race, religion, or national origin" and including the weak, the poor, the halt, and the lame. But the wheel will continue to turn.[36]

Notes

1. Commons and Parsons had discussed titles such as "Investigative Economics" or "Administrative Economics," but they had not settled on a specific title before Commons died. Parsons chose "The Economics of Collective Action." Kenneth Parsons, "Editor's Preface," in *The Economics of Collective Action*, ed. John R. Commons (New York: Macmillan, 1950), x. There are references to discussions about the title in Witte to Parsons, June 12, 1945, Witte Papers, State Historical Society of Wisconsin, box 9.
2. Parsons, "Introduction," in *The Economics of Collective Action*, 10.

A Worker's Economist

3. Selig Perlman, "John Rogers Commons 1862–1945," in ibid., 5.
4. Alan G. Gruchy. "Review of *The Economics of Collective Action*," *Journal of Farm Economics* 33 (May 1951): 264.
5. *Economics of Collective Action*, 124–25.
6. Ibid., 25.
7. Ibid., 257.
8. Ibid., 269.
9. Ibid., 117,130, 267–70.
10. Adolph A. Berle and Gardiner C. Means, *The Modern Corporation and Private Property* (New York: Macmillan, 1932), 357, cited in *Economics of Collective Action*, 58.
11. Nelson Lichtenstein, *State of the Union: A Century of American Labor.* (Princeton, NJ: Princeton University press, 2002), 117–22.
12. Harry A. Millis and Emily Brown, *From the Wagner Act to Taft Hartley* (Chicago, IL: University of Chicago Press, 1950), 395. Millis was a former Commons student from Indiana.
13. Ibid., 398.
14. Paul H. Douglas, *In the Fullness of Time: the Memoirs of Paul H. Douglas* (New York: Harcourt, Brace and Jovanovich 1972), 271.
15. Dean A. Worcester, Jr. and Robert Lampman, "Ability and Size of Family in the United States," *Journal of Political Economy* 58 (October 1950): 430–44, Robert Lampman, "Recent Changes in Inequality Reconsidered," *American Economic Review* 44 (June 1955): 251–68.
16. Robert Lampman, "Recent Thought on Egalitarianism," *Quarterly Journal of Economics* 71 (May 1957): 234–66.
17. Robert Lampman, "The Effectiveness of Some Institutions in Changing the Distribution of Income," *American Economic Review: Papers and Proceedings of the Sixty-Eighth Annual Meeting* 47 (May 1957): 519–28.
18. John Kenneth Galbraith, *The Affluent Society* (Boston, MA: Houghton-Mifflin, 1958), 374. This was in the context of Galbraith's main argument that the nation spends too much on private goods and too little on public goods.
19. Robert Lampman, "The Low Income Population and Economic Growth," in *Study Papers Nos. 12 and 13. Materials Prepared in Connection with Study of Employment, Growth and Price Levels for Consideration of the Joint Economic Committee, Congress of the United States.* 86th Congress 1st Session (Washington, DC: Government Printing Office), 1–34.
20. Carl Brauer, "Kennedy, Johnson, and the War on Poverty," *The Journal of American History* 69 (June 1982): 98–119.
21. J. Dennis Chasse, "The American Association for Labor Legislation and the Institutionalist Tradition in National Health Insurance," *Journal of Economic Issues* 28 (December 1994): 1063–90.
22. U.S. House of Representatives *Economic Opportunity Act of 1964* Public Law 88–420 August 20, 1964 70 Stat. 508–34.
23. The HEW initiatives were summarized by Wilbur Cohen and Robert M. Ball, "Social Security Amendments of 1965: Summary and Legislative History," *Social Security Bulletin* 28 (September 1956): 1–21. They included Medicaid for recipients of welfare payments, increased federal payments within

the welfare categories—aged, disabled, blind, and dependent children, and expanded benefits for maternal and child health. They created Medicare; expanded social security benefits for children aged eighteen to twenty-one who are still attending schools; expanded social security payment of benefits to widows; liberalized requirements for eligibility for persons aged seventy-two and over; expanded social security coverage to self-employed physicians and to tip workers. The bill also increased the payroll tax to finance these benefits.

24. Edward Berkowitz, *Mr. Social Security: The Life of Wilbur Cohen* (Lawrence: University of Kansas Press, 1995), 196–97.

25. The law established an Office of Economic Opportunity responsible to the White House (Title VI), a number of youth programs including a Job Corps and a Neighborhood Youth Corps to give youths in poor neighborhoods job experience, VISTA (Volunteers in Service to America), a sort of domestic Peace Corps, a work-study program that would finance students working their way through college with campus jobs (Title I), and a Work Experience program to develop pilot studies on programs to provide work experience for unemployed men (Title V). It authorized the director to make loans for rural area development (Title III) and to provide business incentives for small businesses (Title IV). In addition, it set aside funds for experimental programs of which Head Start was one of the first. The two job programs give the experimental philosophy away. The OEO designers were trying to find programs that would work.

26. U.S. House of Representatives, *Economic Opportunity Act of 1964*, 516.

27. Ibid. 156.

28. Daniel Patrick Moynihan, *Maximum Feasible Misunderstanding* (New York: Free Press, 1969).

29. Brauer, "Kennedy, Johnson, and the War on Poverty," 109.

30. Commons, *The Economics of Collective Action*, 25.

31. The literature on the history of the OEO is voluminous. Much of this literature was nicely summarized by Alice O'Connor, *Poverty Knowledge: Social Science, Social Policy, and the Poor in the Twentieth Century U.S. History* (Princeton, NJ: Princeton University Press, 2001), 166–95. For a strong statistical defense of these programs, see John E. Schwarz, *America's Hidden Success*, revised edition (New York: W.W. Norton, 1988). For example, the poverty rate was cut in half between 1965 and 1969.

32. Robert J. Lampman, "Approaches to the Reduction of Poverty," *American Economic Review* 55 (March, 1965): 521–29.

33. Washington Post, 1987 cited in Larry DeWitt, "Cohen, Wilbur J," in *Social Welfare History Project* 2010, http//www.socialwelfarehistory.com/people/cohen-wilbur, accessed September 12, 2015.

34. J. Dennis Chasse, "John R. Commons and the Special Interest Issue: Not Really Out of Date," *Journal of Economic Issues* 31 (December 1997): 933–49.

35. For the latest debunking of Olsen's thesis, see Gunnar Trumbull, *Strength in Numbers: The Political Power of Weak Interests* (Cambridge, MA: Harvard University Press, 2012).

36. Frank C. Genovese, "In Memoriam: Robert J. Lampman, 1920–1997," *American Journal of Economics and Sociology* 57 (January 1998): 115–18.

Appendix A to Chapter 12: Report and Dissent at the USCIR

The first volume of the USCIR report contained Basil Manly's staff report and all the dissents. The report and the dissents have often been analyzed from the perspective of the conflict that marred the commission's final days—a conflict about methods—research versus hearings—not about issues or reforms. Consequently, both the report and the dissent raise issues and propose reforms that remain relevant and unappreciated. John R., it will be recalled, decided to write his dissent before Manly started on the staff report. So it is a mistake to assume that John R. was primarily interested in criticizing Manly's report. Rather he wanted to insist on something that he thought would be left out.

The report and the dissent do reflect different interpretations of the commission's charge: to uncover "the underlying causes of dissatisfaction in the industrial situation."[1] Walsh wanted to assign blame and, to some extent, Manly agreed with Walsh. John R. wanted to find out what was wrong with the system and to propose ways to fix it. But Manly also wanted to fix the system. So, from the standpoint of "fixing the system," the reports are better viewed as complementary, with Manly's as the main report and the Commons–Harriman dissent as a supplement.

Manly's Report and Areas of Agreement

Manly's report opened with the first reliably estimated poverty rate ever calculated for the entire United States—one-third of the nation ill-fed, ill-housed, and ill-clothed. That estimate rested on budget studies conducted by Edgar Sydenstriker—later, the nation's leading medical statistician. Manly supplemented and verified Sydenstriker's work with data previously collected by the immigration commission (21–24). In response to the Committee's basic charge, Manly listed four causes of industrial unrest: "Unjust distribution of wealth and income; Unemployment and denial of opportunity to earn a living; Denial of justice; Denial of right to organize." But, in his extended explanations, Manly focused on a single fundamental cause—the corporate organization of major American industries. Stockholders nominally own corporations. Boards of directors control them and represent the interests only of dominant shareholders (26–29, 80–86). Dominant shareholders and boards of directors are usually financiers. They do not understand the technical operation of their companies, and they make decisions on the basis of their own financial self-interest. Managers answer to these financial elites, by keeping wages low and working conditions hazardous. Workers, on the other hand, deal with foremen and superintendents. So there is a complex system of stages connecting workers with the putative owners, the stockholders. "The crux of the whole question of industrial relations is: Shall the workers for the protection of their interests be organized and represented collectively by their chosen delegates, even as stockholders are represented by their directors and by the various grades of executive officials and bosses" (27–28).

John R. could not possibly have disagreed with this. In fact, though he started his dissent with statements on specific issues of disagreement—about assigning blame and about effective administration—he also indicated a general agreement about the nature of the problems and of the solutions. "From our personal experience we agree with many of the alleged findings and with the objects intended to be accomplished by the enactment of the proposed laws, but we consider that it is not worthwhile to propose any more laws until we have provided methods of investigation, legislation, and administration which can make the laws enforceable" (171).

His term "alleged" reflected his position that the "findings" could be accepted only after consideration of all the facts from all points of view—after giving all members of the commission a chance to comment on the rough draft. So the term "we agree" meant what it said. Thus John R., at the start, indicated that he would not disagree with Manly's report but would supplement it by focusing on "methods of investigation, legislation, and administration which can make laws enforceable." He did, in fact, agree with many of Manly's positions.

Like Manly, he argued that workers without unions were so disadvantaged in the wage bargain that they needed extensive legal protection.[2] Like Manly, he advocated policies designed to reduce land speculation,

Appendix A to Chapter 12

tenant farming with absentee landlords, and Texas latifundia. Like Manly, he supported a law patterned after the British 1906 Trade Disputes Act (91, 214). When Manly recommended the creation of industrial courts, he referenced the US Bureau of Labor Bulletin No. 98. Helen Sumner wrote that bulletin. It was a massive five-hundred-page study of every industrial court system in the world at that time. In their *Principles of Labor Legislation* John R. and John Andrews recommended industrial courts and referred to the same study.[3]

Both Manly and John R. suggested an inheritance tax with the revenues earmarked for social welfare expenditures including education, sickness insurance, and social security. Their justifications differed in ways that are instructive. Manly gave three reasons: (1) "to adjust on the basis of compensation approximating the service actually performed, the existing inequalities in the distribution of wealth and income"; (2) "to check the growth of a hereditary aristocracy, which is foreign to every concept of American Government and menacing to the welfare of the people and the existence of the Nation as a democracy"; and (3) to "leave no large accumulation of wealth to pass into the hands which had no share in its production." These three reasons reflect an exploitation theory of income distribution and a labor theory of value. Consequently, Manly proposed a graduated inheritance tax that would confiscate all funds above a certain limit (in a footnote, he suggested a million dollars).[4]

John R. proposed a less confiscatory graduated inheritance tax, and he justified it with a different theory of income distribution. John R.'s tax rates were those recommended by his Wisconsin colleague, Thomas S. Adams who advised President Wilson on income and inheritance tax proposals. John R.'s justification for an inheritance tax rested not on an exploitation theory of income distribution, but on a theory of social production in which relative shares are determined by bargaining power. "The great majority of wage earners cannot provide in advance for future contingencies when they will get no income"—for two reasons: "(1) Inability in bargaining for wages to take into account future contingencies and future cost of living"; . . . "(2) Lack of thrift and habits of saving, owing in part to their own fault, and in part to contingencies which eat up their savings and bring discouragement."

Inheritances grant shares in a social surplus to heirs who did not contribute to its creation. "Inheritances are the principal means by which owners, without effort or thrift on their part, secure titles to wealth and to its future continuous income. Consequently, for the

249

Government to take a part of large inheritances to devote the proceeds to the purpose of making incomes more nearly continuous for those who are not able, under existing conditions, to do it for themselves appeals to the sense of justice" (222–223).

The list could go on. Manly's report was more detailed. The Commons–Harriman report expressed some disagreement to account for Florence Harriman's objection to Manly's report, but it was most complete and detailed in what John R. considered a necessary supplement.

Manly's rhetoric offended Florence Harriman. But, if his report had been circulated to the committee before release, he might have found a way to make his points without antagonizing her. For example, he compared Rockefeller to Louis XVI (34).

Manly, like Frank Walsh, believed that the philanthropy of the rich threatened the political integrity and social fabric of the nation by extending the power of irresponsible oligarchs beyond the economy into all areas of public life (80–86). Manly developed this position at length, noting that state charters did not limit foundation activities; that foundations paid no taxes; that their endowments were invested in securities; and that the welfare of corporations whose securities the endowments held must at least "color" the decisions of the people who controlled the foundations. Manly cited instances of foundation control of municipal affairs in New York City and of teaching in universities, referring without name to the infamous case in which the University of Pennsylvania fired Scott Nearing, a Christian socialist after he had testified before the committee.

For Manly, John D. Rockefeller Jr.'s interference in the work of the USCIR was a notorious case of oligarchic domination; the industrial relations center was a ploy to keep unions out of Rockefeller's mines. But, after describing what he considered a threat to representative democracy, Manly proposed surprisingly mild solutions—stricter licensing of foundations and a Congressional investigation.

Since John R. was currently working on a project funded by the Carnegie Foundation, one might discern a conflict of interest. On the other hand, John R.'s Syracuse experience verified Manly's charge about oligarchic control over university faculty and curricula. Commons and Harriman cited the "beneficial effects" of charitable organizations— that charitable organizations could notice and respond to problems more quickly than governments and that they could pioneer activities later taken up by governments. But Commons–Harriman proposed the same corrective as Manly. Like Manly, they recommended a thorough investigation and licensing of foundations. They also argued against any direct collaboration between governments and private foundations. Such collaboration would create too many opportunities for corruption. Rather government should compete with foundations (220–221).

The Dissent

Commons and Harriman gave three reasons for their refusal to sign Manly's report. (1) Representatives of affected interests were not given the opportunity to comment on preliminary drafts before the report was issued in final form. (2) Manly's diagnosis of causes paid too much attention to scapegoats and too little attention to the system. (3) The report suggested laws without paying enough attention to whether the laws could attain their objectives or were enforceable or constitutional (171–173). The first objection was common to both John R. and Florence Harriman. The second objection reflected Harriman's concern. The third reflected the concerns of John R.

To deal with this third concern, John R. proposed a federal commission composed of three commissioners appointed by the President and approved by the Senate. He also proposed similar state commissions. The commission's staff would be selected and governed on merit according to civil service rules.

He stressed the importance of making the commission legally responsible to an advisory council composed of the secretary of Labor, the secretary of Commerce, and thirty representatives appointed and financially supported by nongovernmental organizations—ten appointed by labor unions; ten by management organizations; and ten by organizations concerned with the welfare of unorganized workers—organizations such as the National Consumer Federation and the American Association for Labor Legislation. There should be no lawyers on the council; it was to be a deliberative body, not a debating forum. The council should operate independently with its own secretary and staff—able to initiate and direct research on any subject it might select. It should have subpoena powers. Except for emergencies, no action of the commission would be legal unless first presented to the advisory council for comment, but the council would have no veto power over commission decisions. This single commission would replace a jumble of agencies that had grown up over the years to enforce different categories of labor laws.

John R. summarized his argument that the governing institutions of the United States—the legislative, judicial, and executive branches—were not designed to cope with conflicts of interest created by a technically changing industrial society. To deal with these conflicts, legislatures had created commissions—The Interstate Commerce Commission for conflicts between railroads and shippers; the Federal Trade Commission for conflicts between trusts, their competitors, and their customers; the Federal Reserve System for conflicts between banks and commercial and business classes (182).

Countries with a parliamentary form of government did not need such commissions. Cabinet members in these countries must answer questions from representatives of the opposing party on the floor of the Parliament. To avoid embarrassing questions, Cabinet officials who are partisan insist that their subordinates operate in a nonpartisan fashion (187–188). This is not true in the United States, so we create commissions with nonpartisan staffs. But a labor commission cannot be organized precisely like these other commissions because "in none of these cases were the opposing interests strongly organized for aggression and occasional paralysis of business verging on civil war." Both workers and employers must trust the commission, and they will do so more easily if their chosen representatives have a voice in commission decisions.

Labor laws have broken down in this country because the executives in position to administer them have been partisans of one side or the other. Employers have an incentive to use political pressure either to get their own people appointed to those positions or to get weak labor people appointed. Colorado labor laws were as good as those in any state, but they were not enforced, because the Colorado Fuel and Iron Company had purchased the state government. The fact that Colorado's laws were not enforced probably contributed significantly to "the current problems" (187).

The problem in Colorado might have been avoided if there had been an advisory board of the type John R. recommended because nonbusiness members of the board would have noticed, publicized, and checked the failure of enforcement.

Industrial commissions should be responsible for investigating and publishing information on all labor issues—wages, strikes, accidents, minimum wages, and so forth. John R. considered information the most important task of the industrial commissions because the effectiveness of all other activities depends on the accuracy of the information—and

Appendix A to Chapter 12

because effective administration depends on public confidence that the information has been obtained in an unbiased manner.

The dissent turned briefly to the relations of the commission with legislative bodies and courts. Congress and the legislatures should pass general laws leaving development of specific rules and regulations to the commission. The commission itself should initiate only legislation needed for its administrative purposes. People dissatisfied with commission decisions should be free to appeal to the courts, but the courts should accept only testimony previously presented to the commission. The commission should also provide legal aid to individual workers in legal confrontations with employers.

After its lengthy treatment of the commission, the dissent turned to specific issues. It began with the hated private detectives, police departments, and state militias (201–202). The commission should license and regulate detective agencies, requiring companies to hire only licensed agencies. No guards other than watchmen should be armed. To control violence by public authorities, the commission should work with military authorities to formulate rules for military intervention—whether by state National Guards or federal troops—in violent confrontations.

John R. summarized his general views on labor legislation in two sections, one on mediation and minimum wages and the other on trade disputes (206–220).

The commission should appoint a chief mediator and finance the mediator's staff, but once appointed the mediator should be completely independent of the commission. The mediator could appoint an arbitrator, but only if the parties agree. If either party objects to arbitration, the mediator could, with their approval, appoint a board of inquiry. But that is the limit. The mediator's role is that of a persuasive advocate for conciliation. The mediator should not have access to the coercive powers of the state and should not threaten to use them.

John R. distinguished between individual and collective wage bargains. In the case of individual wage bargains, the commission is justified in calling on the coercive power of the state to enforce minimum wages and other legal protections of workers. The justification for state intervention arises from the fact that individual workers have so little bargaining power that their agreement to conditions of employment could almost always be judged as coerced rather than voluntary.

In collective bargaining, however, workers hold a stronger bargaining hand. Any insertion of the state's police power creates an incentive for

253

corporations and unions to struggle for control of political parties in order to turn the state's coercive power against the other party. If one party should succeed in its effort, the government would become corrupted and discredited, and one or both sides would lose confidence in the neutrality of government officials. Moreover, John R. tended to believe that in the long run there was a greater likelihood that corporations would gain control of the state.

John R. did not want the state to interfere in collective bargaining negotiations. But he did want the state to remove legal restrictions that unfairly weakened the bargaining power of unions. Like Manly, Commons and Harriman recommended a US law similar to the British Trade Disputes Act of 1906. That act exempted collective bargaining participants from the common law restrictions against collusion. In trade disputes, any actions considered legal for an individual would also be legal for a group. Thus, the act would legalize boycotts because individuals are free to buy or not buy any product. John R. went further, arguing that unions should be free to adopt any nonviolent tactic—including secondary as well as primary boycotts—as well as nonviolent tactics unions might devise in the future—such as sit-down strikes. John R. considered a vibrant and extensive trade union movement essential for industrial peace and also for the operation of his industrial commissions. But he felt it important to free unions from political interference, and he had some concerns about positive political interference in their affairs.

> It doubtless has appealed to some people who consider the employer's position more powerful than that of the unions, that the employer should be compelled in some way to deal with unions, or at least confer with their representatives. But if the State recognizes any particular union by requiring the employer to recognize it, the State must necessarily guarantee the union to the extent that it must strip it of any abuses that it may practice. The State might be compelled to regulate its initiation fees and dues, its apprentice-ship ratio, its violation of agreements, and all the other abuses on account of which the employer refuses to deal with it. This is exactly what is done through compulsory arbitration, and there is no place where the State can stop if it brings compulsion to bear on employers without also regulating by compulsion the unions. If so, the whole question is transferred to politics, and the unions which attempt to use a friendly party to regulate the employer may find a hostile party regulating them. (212)

Frank Walsh attacked the Commons–Harriman proposal as undemocratic, un-American, impractical, and impossible. It would create

Appendix A to Chapter 12

"unlimited opportunities for graft and corruption." He finished with a flourish

> If the ponderous legal machinery provided for in this report could be put into operation throughout our Nation, it would mean—(a) that the economic condition of the workers of the country would be absolutely subjected to the whim or caprice of an army of officials, deputies and Government employees and (b) the establishment of an autocratic control over the business operations of manufacturers, merchants and other employers, repugnant to American standards of freedom in manufacture and commerce. (157–158)

Walsh offered no evidence for these assertions. More than anything else, Walsh's charges resembled campaign slogans of McGovern's stalwart opponents. These slogans in addition to newspaper attacks on the Wisconsin Idea may well have influenced Walsh. But, the stalwarts changed their tune once they gained control, and the history of industrial commissions in Wisconsin and other states does not bear out Walsh's dire prediction. Indeed, as Barnett noted, in his review of the *Principles*, the industrial commissions, by replacing a hodge-podge of agencies with overlapping jurisdictions, actually simplified government administration.[5]

In any case, while the USCIR probably had a beneficial effect, it also seems probable that the vitriolic ending prevented many people from critically reading the report and the dissent, and so prevented the nation from profiting from the promise contained in both.

Ramirez, one of the few who actually read the report and the dissents, had this to say about John R.'s scheme.

> Clearly Commons's industrial relations scheme was the best that progressive enterprise could offer. It was based on an acknowledgement of the institutional evolution that had occurred in the field of labor and employer's organizations: it was sensitive to the positive function that public opinion could play on the issue of labor–capital relations; and it envisaged a state intervention immunized from the dangers of political partisanship, being solely guided by scientific criteria and administrative expertise.[6]

Notes

1. United States Commission on Industrial Relations, *Report*, vol.1, 6.
2. Ibid., 28–31, 68–70, 80–81, 91, 214–22.
3. Ibid., 89, John R. Commons and John B. Andrews, *Principles of Labor Legislation* (New York: Macmillan, 1916), 68n.

4. USCIR, *Report*, vol. 1, 35–36, 221–24.
5. George Barnett, "Review of *Principles of Labor Legislation* by John R. Commons and John B. Andrews," *American Economic Review* 6 (September, 1916): 656.
6. Bruno Ramirez, *When Workers Fight: The Politics of Industrial Relations 1898–1916* (Westport, CN: Greenwood Press, 1978), 179.

Appendix B to Chapter 14:
The Legal Foundations of Capitalism

At Madison, veteran students would tell newcomers that to fully understand John R.'s lectures one must impose one's own organization on them. If these veteran students could be conjured into the present, they would repeat that advice to anyone opening either one of John R.'s most cited books.

Wesley Clair Mitchell imposed one such organization. American legal historians imposed another. Another can be imposed that links his legal terminology—ridiculed by some reviewers—to the arguments of the final two chapters. Adding this third organization to the other two can be justified on the following grounds: first, it provides rationale for the terminology; second, it calls attention to the argument of the final chapters toward which the entire book seems directed.

First, though, it is necessary to pause at the preface where John R. wrote that he was working out "an evolutionary and behavioral, or rather volitional theory of value." He had started on that task thirty-five years earlier at Johns Hopkins, and, five years after Hopkins, he had made his first attempt in the *Distribution of Wealth* which he considered a failure. He recalled that when he was working with the Wisconsin Industrial Commission, he had been introduced to constitutional law and to the legal concept of reasonable value. He had also been impressed by Thorstein Veblen's argument that economics should be "an evolutionary science."[1] And as he had investigated with his students the relation between economic and legal notions of value, they had stumbled on the legal foundations of capitalism. This was what interested Wesley Clair Mitchell.

Mitchell's Organization

Mitchell, a former student of Thorstein Veblen and a monetary economist, was most impressed by the way that John R. traced the evolution of a money economy, beginning with the laws and customs of a feudal economy where people produced largely what they consumed and arriving at laws and customs that enabled people to produce largely for a market where they bought what they consumed.[2] This was the subject of the sixth and seventh chapters on the rent and price bargains.

John R. started not, as he had in *A Sociological View of Sovereignty*, with hypothetical prehistory, but with 1066 when there was no private property because William the Conqueror owned everything—even the people.

He showed how particular notions of private property emerged over centuries through the operation of three historical forces. First struggles for power between kings, nobles, townspeople, and merchants resulted in shifting alliances as kings, to defend themselves from nobles, strengthened the power of merchants and townspeople. Second, the substitution by kings of standing armies for levies of troops and supplies created a need for money in the royal treasury. And third, the substitution of the kings' courts for those of the nobles created conditions for an evolving common law.

Common law exemplified for John R. a social artificial selection analogous to the physical artificial selection described in the first two chapters of the *Origin of the Species* where Darwin showed how selective breeding fostered desirable traits in plants and animals (375–376). This analogous social "artificial selection" originated in twelfth-century England when King Henry II sent royal judges across the land. The king's courts gradually displaced the nobles' courts. The judges of the king's courts, guided by their belief in the commonwealth or public good, investigated the customs of the people, and when a dispute arose, they condemned customs that they considered bad for the commonwealth and preserved customs that they considered good.

This legal evolution was accompanied by complex power struggles between kings, nobles, and townsmen, struggles that produced a right to land in 1660 when Parliament substituted a fixed excise tax for the king's right to arbitrarily demand tribute. This gave landowners the right to any revenues above and beyond that fixed payment. In other words, it gave them a right to the property. When landowners began evicting

Appendix B to Chapter 14

tenants in the enclosure movement, tenants appealed to common law judges who developed precedents for settling disputes about the law of private property.

Then, just as they had replaced the courts of the nobles, the common law courts began replacing the courts of the gilds. Things did not go smoothly. The common law judges, with their notion of property tied to land, could not understand any reasons for the purchase and sale of debts, such as promissory notes. The equity courts of the Chancery intervened. Debates arose in and between common law courts, equity courts, and parliament, but eventually the notion of property was extended, not just to incorporeal property such as promissory notes, bills of exchange, and bonds, but also to intangible property such as patents, copyrights, and trademarks. A money economy that runs on credit cannot operate without such rights because transactions that involve money must create debts and the debts must be negotiable. This is why a money economy cannot be accurately analyzed using the analogy of a barter economy (240–246).

This insight into the difference between a money economy and a barter economy and into the path of evolution from a feudal economy characterized by barter to a capitalist economy characterized by money and credit was what interested Wesley Clair Mitchell.

Legal Historians

Legal historians were more interested in the constitutional issues analyzed in the second and in parts of the fifth chapter of the *Legal Foundations*. In the second chapter, John R. traced a change in the Supreme Court's interpretation of rights protected by the Fifth and Fourteenth Amendments. The justices started with a conception of property as the right to hold and use something physical and with a definition of liberty as a negative freedom from interference. They ended with a conception of property as the right to anything that has exchange value and with a notion of liberty as a positive right to engage in market transactions.

The Fifth Amendment was part of the original bill of rights. The Fourteenth resulted from Congressional frustration with President Andrew Johnson's failure to protect slaves newly freed in the former Confederate states.[3] The Fourteenth Amendment extended to the states a section of the Fifth Amendment that defined the rights of citizens and persons by limiting the power of the government: "No State shall make or enforce any law which shall abridge the privileges or immunities of citizens of the United States, nor shall any State deprive any person of life, liberty, or property without due process of law; nor deny any person within its jurisdiction the equal protection of the laws."

The first case calling for interpretation of the Fourteenth Amendment arose when the Louisiana legislature responded to a request from a New Orleans city government battling a public health crisis. Butchers were polluting the city's water supply by dumping animal waste in the Mississippi River. Cholera, dysentery, and other water-borne diseases were ravaging New Orleans' citizens. Since many butchers operated beyond the reach of the city government, city officials persuaded the legislature to pass a law requiring all butchers to work in the Crescent City Slaughterhouse, a privately owned monopoly where sanitary disposal of refuse could be assured. John A. Campbell, the butchers' lawyer argued that the law deprived his clients of liberty and property without the due process guaranteed by the Fourteenth Amendment. The case reached the Supreme Court as the *Slaughterhouse Case*.[4]

The butchers lost. Justice Samuel F. Miller, writing for the majority, pointed out that the law did not take away the butchers' tools, but limited their use for the purpose of preserving public health. Consequently, it did not deprive the butchers of liberty or property. Moreover, the legislative purpose of the Fourteenth Amendment was the abolition of slavery and the butchers had never been slaves.

It was not Miller's argument, though, but the argument of the dissent to which John R. called attention. The dissent expanded the meaning of free labor and abandoned the traditional meaning of property as something physical to be held and used.

> Thus Justice Field described slavery as physical coercion and servitude as economic coercion. And Justice Swayne declared "Property is everything which has exchangeable value, and the right to property includes the power to dispose of it according to the will of the owner. Labor is property, and as such merits protection. The right to make it available is next in importance to the rights of life and liberty."[5]

John R. then showed how this minority position became a majority position as the Court worked through the so-called "Granger cases." The Grangers—farmer organizations that often met in local farms or granaries (granges)—had complained about the predatory prices and practices of railroad and grain storage companies. In response, state legislatures had passed laws setting up commissions to regulate railroad and grain storage prices and practices. Corporate lawyers argued

Appendix B to Chapter 14

that these laws deprived corporations, as legal persons, of property and liberty without the due process guaranteed by the Fourteenth Amendment.

The legal historian Morton Horwitz credited John R. with being the first to demonstrate how, in this string of cases, the Supreme Court dropped its analogy for property developed in compensation cases—an expanse of land—and substituted an analogy developed in the Granger cases—the exchange value of anything that could be sold—including incorporeal property such as stocks, bonds, and bills of exchange— and intangible property such as patents, copyrights, trademarks, and customer goodwill.[6]

Legal historians were also interested in John R.'s fifth chapter where he sketched his theory of going concerns. He could not use the standard theory of the firm because he wanted to explicitly consider the role of internal power relations— ignored by the standard theory of the monolithic profit-maximizing firm. So he worked out his own going concern theory from two Supreme Court cases.

In the first case, owners of shares in the New York Bank contested New York State's right to tax their dividends.[7] Since the bank's capital consisted of US Government bonds, the stockholders argued that New York was violating the decision in *McCulloch v. Maryland* which denied the State of Maryland's right to tax notes of federally chartered banks because "The power to tax involves the power to destroy."[8] The court rejected this application of the McCulloch decision, and in so doing, it endorsed the entity concept—that corporations are going concerns distinct from shareholders—and it rejected the nominal concept—that corporations are simply groups of shareholders.[9] The court ruled that stockholders owned not the banks' capital, but the right to income from the bank's operations. The stocks themselves were not, therefore, government property, and hence were taxable at the state level.

The second case grounded John R.'s division of the going concern into two distinct "sub-concerns." This case originated when the Ohio State Board of Assessors calculated the taxable value of the Adams Express company by the following method. First, the assessors estimated the total value of the company from the total market value of its outstanding stocks and bonds. Then they created a fraction. On the bottom of the fraction, they put all of the company's rail mileage in the entire country. On the top, they put the company's rail mileage in the State of Ohio. Then the board multiplied the total estimated value of the company by this fraction. The result of this calculation, $449,377.60, produced the taxable value of the company's property within the state. The company objected that it should be taxed only on the value of its plant and equipment in the state, $23,400. The Supreme Court supported the Board of Assessors.[10] On the basis of this decision John R. divided the going concern into a going plant and a going business. The going plant exists wherever the concern's physical assets exist, and the going business exists wherever the concern engages in transactions.

The value of the going concern, however, is not the value of its physical equipment, but the present value of its income anticipated from future transactions (195–203). Here again, Horwitz credited John R. for being among the first to recognize the correct conception of a corporation's value, to put that conception into a legal framework, and to criticize Supreme Court Justices for reasoning in a circle when they tried to estimate fair prices by relating them to the market value of the corporation which, of course, would be affected by the prices.[11]

Transactions and the Wage Bargain

In addition to his descriptive and legal passages, John R. created a theory fitted to his purpose of analyzing the relations between economics and law. He applied that theory to the wage bargain in his final two chapters, and both the theory and his rationale can be clarified by first summarizing the theory and then watching how he applied it to the wage bargain. He started in the first chapter where he explained why he could not begin at traditional economic starting points—rational self-interested consumers on the demand side and limited resources on the supply side.

Once incentives are known standard economic analysis moves mechanically to necessary results determined by fixed consumer preferences on the demand side and diminishing returns on the supply side. While useful for seeking answers to some questions, this framework was problematic for the questions that John R. wanted to pursue—questions of freedom, coercion, power, ethics, and law. He could pursue these questions only by starting with transactions.[12]

So he started his analysis of transactions with Böhm Bawerk's story about a horse market with eight sellers and ten buyers. Böhm Bawerk showed that the final price in this market depended only on four of the original eighteen participants—the actual buyer, the actual seller, the next alternative buyer, and the next alternative seller.[13] The alternative seller's offer sets a ceiling above which the actual seller cannot go without losing the buyer. The alternative buyer sets a floor below which the final buyer cannot go without losing the seller. Thus alternatives set a range of possibilities within which buyers and sellers bargain. Good alternatives increase negotiating power. Bad alternatives reduce it and, in the limit, they enable economic coercion. To incorporate ethics and law in his analysis, John R. added a fifth participant to Böhm Bawerk's four.

This fifth participant enforces rules and settles conflicts. Buyers want a low price, and sellers, a high price. Differing backgrounds and ethical beliefs can aggravate conflicts. Simple bickering can escalate into arguments, blows, even wars. So, to preserve peace and order, most societies designate for every transaction a fifth participant— a chief, judge, shaman, or governor—empowered to settle disputes. This fifth participant need not intervene or even be physically present. "Working rules" or "laws" developed from settlements of past conflicts carry community influence into the transaction even when no judge is physically present (67).

The wage bargain is, of course, a particular type of transaction. John R. had described its uniqueness in the *Principles of Labor Legislation* where he noted the absence of alternatives and the weak bargaining position of the worker, "if he has no property of his own sufficient to fall back upon, he is under an imperious necessity of agreeing with someone who has [property]." John R. had added there that the wage bargain "involves not only wages, but also hours of labor, speed and fatigue, safety and health, accident and disease, even life itself."[14]

In the final chapters of the *Legal Foundations of Capitalism*, starting with Supreme Court decisions in the Hitchman and yellow dog cases, John R. argued that the courts had failed to address in any realistic way the workers' side of the wage bargain and, as a result, the courts had endangered the nation's human resources.

He opened his chapter on the wage bargain by reviewing some language from the Granger cases in which the justices had affirmed that labor is property to which workers have rights, that any citizen is free to pursue any "calling," or "occupation," anywhere in the United States, and that workers are free to enter into legally binding contracts (283). Then John R. asked whether this really made sense.

To decide whether it all made sense, he turned to the terminology that so irritated his reviewers, terminology systematized by Wesley Newcomb Hohfeld, one of America's most brilliant legal minds. Hohfeld died young, but after his death his colleagues at Yale continued to interpret his system and illustrate its application.[15] Hohfeld wanted to overcome the ambiguous and inconsistent use in legal writings and judicial decisions of such words as "right," "duty," "immunity," and "privilege." Sometimes when judges wrote the word "rights," they meant actual rights, but at other times, they really meant privileges or immunities. The result was sloppy logic and bad decisions.[16]

Rather than defining these terms, Hohfeld tried to clarify their meaning by making two tables, one of opposites and one of correlatives. John R. reproduced and modified Hohfeld's tables.[17]

Jural opposites			
Right	Privilege	Power	Immunity
No right	Duty	Disability	Liability

Jural correlatives			
Right	Privilege	Power	Immunity
Duty	No right	Liability	Disability

The tables become less mysterious when placed in the context of an actual court room trial. Suppose, for example, that Adrienne wants the court to enforce her right to drive through Bart's property to reach her garage. If the judge agrees, the sheriff can compel Bart to unlock his gate so Adrienne can drive through. Adrienne has a right, and Bart has a correlative duty. If the judge does not agree, then Adrienne has "no right," and the sheriff will not force Bart to open his gate. Bart has the privilege of keeping his gate closed, and Adrienne has no right to drive through Bart's property. Note that the table can be interpreted as defining duties for officers of the law. If the judge decrees that Adrienne has a right, then the sheriff has the duty of enforcing Adrienne's right. If not, then the sheriff cannot intrude on Bart's privilege.

Outside of the concrete context of a trial, however, the terms take on a sort of woolly character. The term "no right," for example, was criticized as empty when used in larger jurisprudential contexts. To avoid such criticism, and to adapt the terms to his purposes, John R. substituted the word "limits" for Hohfeld's "opposites." He substituted "exposure" for "no right," and "liberty" for privilege as the correlative of exposure. Rights specify working rules that bring the state to the aid of some citizens by enforcing duties on other citizens. Rights and duties are correlatives. In the case of exposures state officials will not come to the aid of citizens by imposing a duty on someone else. By

264

Appendix B to Chapter 14

not imposing a duty, the state creates a privilege or leaves the citizen at liberty. John R. preferred the term "liberty" to "privilege" because the term "privilege" had a historical connotation of franchises granted by the crown. But he did not stick to his own terminology. He used privilege and liberty interchangeably.

John R.'s revised system looked like this.

Jural opposites			
Right	Liberty	Power	Immunity
Exposure	Duty	Disability	Liability

Jural correlatives			
Right	Liberty	Power	Immunity
Duty	Exposure	Liability	Disability

If the village has no noise ordinance, then Adam has the liberty (or privilege) of playing loud music. And his neighbor, Bertha, is exposed to Adam's loud music. If she calls the police, they will tell her that they cannot do anything about Adam's music. If the village passes a noise ordinance, then the police will support Bertha's right to quiet by enforcing on Adam the duty of ceasing loud music after a certain hour.

Hohfeld's system is now a commonplace in law schools, but Horwitz cited Kennedy and Michelman on its lost context.

> For while it has become "a staple of academic legal culture," Hohfeld's system "survives like a sack of dried beans, unesteemed by those who have lost the recipe for its use . . . By today's law students (not to speak of their teachers), Hohfeld is often envisaged as a chap with a scholastic passion for terminological nicety—at worst a carping bore, at best an authentic, if pedantic exemplar of the academic virtue of precision."[18]

The lost context was Hohfeld's commitment to progressive legislation. He did not want the Supreme Court to gut President Wilson's reforms. The "recipe" was best illustrated by his colleague at Yale, Walter Cook, who used Hohfeld's scheme to deconstruct the majority opinion in the case of *Hitchman v. Mitchell*. By the time Cook was finished, he had reduced the majority opinion to incoherent nonsense. John R. knew the context and "the recipe." He cited Cook's article, and he used Hohfeld's scheme to answer his questions about the wage bargain. Recall that the

Supreme Court had struck down much labor legislation on grounds that it interfered with the workers' freedom of contract. In *Hitchman v. Mitchell*, the Court's majority had ruled that union organizers were attempting to induce workers to violate the terms of a valid contract. In *Adkins v. Children's hospital* the court had ruled that a minimum wage law interfered with an employee's right to contract for low wages.

Now, John R. showed that the abolition of involuntary servitude made it impossible for the wage bargain to be a contract because it was a transaction that could not oblige state officials to enforce rights and duties. If workers quit, state officials could not force them back to work without violating constitutional amendments that outlawed involuntary servitude. Similarly, state officials could not, without violating the employment-at-will doctrine, prevent an employer from firing an employee. The worker can quit anytime and the employer can arbitrarily fire the worker at any time (284–286).

Rather than rights and duties, wage bargains create liberties and exposures. They expose employers to workers' liberty to walk off the job, and they expose workers to employers' liberty to terminate them at will. Since the wage bargain is not a contract, it makes no sense to strike down a law on grounds that it interferes with employees' freedom of contract.

Having established that the wage bargain is not a contract, John R. turned to the conception of freedom and volition in the three "yellow dog" cases: Hitchman, Coppage, and Adair. The courts had followed legal tradition in assuming that workers signed those contracts freely of their own volition. Legal traditions envisaged absence of volition due to coercion, mainly when there was a threat of physical violence (56–59). Since the state holds a monopoly on the incentive of physical violence; judges assumed that the legislative or executive branches of the government would be the usual sources of unconstitutional coercion.

Legal tradition allowed few exceptions. Courts would invalidate a contract on evidence of undue influence by a superior, such as that of a legal guardian who had induced a child to sign away an inheritance. They would invalidate a contract on evidence of duress of person in which an agreement had been forced by threat of physical harm and on duress of goods when something that the party owned was taken away and withheld to force agreement.

In the Coppage and Adair cases, the court had followed this tradition by invalidating state and federal laws that outlawed "yellow dog contracts" (agreements signed as a condition of employment in which employees agreed not to join a union). The majority claimed that, in outlawing these contracts, Congress and legislatures were invalidly using the police power of the state to deprive workers of their right to freedom of contract.

John R. argued that, in these cases, the judges were ignoring another kind of duress that could destroy actual freedom—the duress of economic coercion in which one party to a transaction withholds what the other party needs but does not own. Whether such coercion reaches the point of depriving one party of freedom depends on the alternatives available to the parties.

To show that some judges already recognized this type of coercion, John R. reviewed majority arguments in two cases: *Munn v. Illinois* and *Holden v. Hardy*. The Munn decision resulted from charges filed on June 9, 1872, in Chicago criminal court against Munn and Scott, Inc. for failing to register their "North-Western Elevator" as a grain storage facility and for setting their fees higher than those established by an Illinois law of 1871. Munn's lawyers argued that the state law violated the Fourteenth Amendment by depriving their client of liberty and property without due process. The court ruled for the state, pointing out that farmers could not leave their grain on the ships when they arrived at the Port of Chicago and that the Chicago warehouses colluded to fix prices. The absence of reasonable alternatives for the farmers "clothed" the organized Chicago warehouses with a "public purpose," and this "public purpose" legitimated the state practice of setting reasonable limits on their fees.

In the case of *Holden v. Hardy*, the court upheld a Utah eight-hour law for workers in mines and smelters. John R. cited the majority decision. "The fact that both parties are of full age and competent to contract does not necessarily deprive the state of the power to interfere where the parties do not stand upon an equality, or where the public health demands that one party to the contract shall be protected against himself."[19]

So John R. concluded that, in addition to political power, there is also economic power. In the yellow dog contract cases, judges ignored economic power, even though legislators understood that this power could reach the stage of coercion when the alternatives on both sides of the transaction differed so starkly. "It is this economic coercion upon which is built industrial government, for its extreme penalty and inducement to obedience is that fear of poverty which varies greatly in its many aspects from fear of bankruptcy to fear of unemployment" (304).

In his criticism of the Hitchman decision, John R. picked out another issue that typified the inconsistency of the court in its labor decisions—its selective interpretation of the conspiracy doctrine. In the eyes of the law, the coercive power of a conspiracy lies in the advantage that a group has over a single individual so that what is lawful for an individual is not lawful for a combination of individuals. The justices in the Hitchman case treated the corporation like a single person with full property rights—not an association of individuals—but, then, they treated the union like a conspiracy of individuals "inflicting damage on property."

A balanced view would either treat both corporation and union as conspiracies of individuals or treat them both as single persons. Here John R. referred back to the court's opinions defining labor as property. If the justices really meant that labor is property, then they should have recognized that, if they granted a corporation the right to protect the expected value of its profits, they should have granted to an association of laborers the property right to protect the expected value of their future income (296).

John R. generalized. He argued for a concept of labor as property that would take account of the rules that workers had devised for their survival in a capitalist society.[20] First, he noted that the prerogative courts of the sixteenth and seventeenth centuries could not at first understand the liquidity needs of merchants and manufacturers because they thought of property only in terms of land and rent. Only when they began to grasp the reasons behind the customs of the business classes could they adapt the laws to new realities. So now, judges in the industrial era have been unable to understand the needs of landless workers bargaining for wages because they think of property only in terms of commercial buying and selling. Only when they grasp the reasons behind the customs developed by workers can they adapt the laws to the realities of the wage bargain.

> And while, the courts, when overruling the closed-shop privileges of the gilds, began to take over the fair competition rules of the gilds, yet in nullifying the closed-shop privileges of the unions, they do not take over the protection of labor against the "unfair employer." Apparently a "new equity" is needed—an equity that will protect the job as the older equity protected the business.[21]

Public Purpose

After calling for a "new equity" for workers, John R. needed to respond to still another justification for the Hitchman decision—that unions

Appendix B to Chapter 14

served no public purpose. And, again, John R. made a general argument that went beyond the specifics of the Hitchman case.

He opened his final chapter—on the public purpose—with short sketches illustrating from different perspectives the evolution— "from the time of the Norman Conquest to the Twentieth Century—of customs and their formalization in working rules"—including the evolution of laws governing the wage bargain (313).

Next, he applied his theory of decision making to the question of the public purpose. People cannot think of everything at once. So to make any progress toward goals, they must set priorities and focus on the most important obstacle standing between them and their goals. This most important obstacle is the limiting factor that is holding all the other factors back. For a corporation, the limiting factor could be a bottleneck on an assembly line that holds back all the cooperating factors—the workers and machines idled or hindered by the bottleneck. Once that limiting factor is removed, the cooperating factors can act more efficiently, but another limiting factor appears, and when that limit is removed, attention turns to another, and so people work sequentially going from one limiting factor to the next.

In the case of the state, the goal itself is a matter for sequential decision making. The state as a going concern has evolved not just by removing limiting factors holding back the attainment of the public purpose but also by changing the meaning of the public purpose as the ethical perspectives of new groups make their way into debates about the public purposes and the public welfare.

Earlier, John R. had contrasted majority and minority opinions in the Hitchman case, and he presented the contrast as typical. The majority favored one association of persons, the corporation, over another association of persons, the workers, because the majority held that the union served no public purpose while the corporation did serve a public purpose. The minority had argued that the union did serve a public purpose by strengthening the bargaining power and protecting the living conditions of the workers. The minority view represented the ethical perspective of the working classes, a view that John R. held should be considered in the debates that control the public purpose and the conception of factors limiting its attainment.[22]

Since the time of Elizabeth and Sir Thomas Smith, state officials had held that a shortage of physical capital was the factor limiting the progress of the commonwealth, and so they had accorded special privileges to the classes that controlled physical capital (330). But John R.

appealed to a growing realization that privileges for capitalists had gone too far and that limitations on the welfare of workers now constituted the factor limiting the progress of the commonwealth. The court itself had ruled in *Muller v. Oregon* that the health of women and children was vital to the public welfare. Earlier, the court had placed the health of mine and smelter workers within the public purpose.

And well before the Supreme Court began making decisions Adam Smith had located the factor limiting the progress of the commonwealth within the laboring classes.

> The annual labour of every nation is the fund which originally supplies it with all the necessaries and conveniences of life which it annually consumes, and which consist always either of the immediate produce of that labour, or in what is purchased with that produce from other nations. . . .
>
> The greatest improvement in the productive powers of labour, and the greater part of the skill, dexterity, and judgment with which it is anywhere directed or applied, seem to have been the effects of the division of labour.[23]

Then John R. argued that the Supreme Court, in interpreting the Fourteenth Amendment, had been more solicitous for the rights of corporations than for the rights of the human persons—"the annual labour"—for which the amendment had been intended.

> It [the Court] changed the meaning of due process of law and thus amended the federal and every state constitution. It changed the meaning of property and liberty as used in the Fourteenth Amendment, and thus took over from the states the final determination of what is due process of law in the regulation of property and business. On the other hand, by changing the meaning of due process of law as applied to life and personal liberty, the court left to the states the power to deprive workingmen and others without property of their common law and federal rights of indictment by grand jury, trial by petit jury of twelve, the right to be confronted by witnesses, the right to exemption from self-incrimination, the right to be present throughout the trial, and the right to have federal courts determine whether a state court has been terrified by a mob.[24]

And so, John R. ended this effort to correlate economics, ethics, and law with an attack on judicial customs that were hindering union organization and an accusation—that the courts and the nation had not been as solicitous for the welfare of human persons as they had been for the welfare of artificial persons—corporations and that courts

Appendix B to Chapter 14

had failed to create rules for the wage bargain suitable for preserving the human resources of a capitalistic society and that this failure was limiting progress toward the goals included in the concepts of public purpose and public welfare.

Notes

1. Thorstein Veblen, "Why is Economics Not an Evolutionary Science," *Quarterly Journal of Economics* 12 (July 1898): 373–97.
2. Wesley Clair Mitchell, "Commons on the Legal Foundations of Capitalism," *American Economic Review* 14 (June 1924): 24.
3. See Lea Van der Velde, "The Labor Vision of the Thirteenth Amendment," *University of Pennsylvania Law Review* 138 (December, 1989): 437–504, and Peter Irons, *A People's History of the Supreme Court* (New York: Penguin Press, 2006), 191–95.
4. 83 U.S. 36 (1873), Ronald Lubbé and Jonathan Lurie, *The Slaughterhouse Cases, Regulation Reconstruction and the Fourteenth Amendment* (Lawrence, KS: University of Kansas Press, 2003).
5. Commons, *Legal Foundations*, 12–13.
6. Morton Horwitz, *The Transformation of American Law 1780–1860* (Cambridge, MA: Harvard University Press, 1977), 145–46.
7. Commons, *Legal Foundations*, 174–78, Van Allen v. Assessors 70 U.S. 573 (1866).
8. Irons, *A People's History*, 122–26.
9. Commons, *Legal Foundations*, 174–75, Glen W. Atkinson and Stephen P. Parschall, "Law and Economics an Evolutionary Perspective," Paper Presented at the annual meeting of the Association for Institutional Thought, April 15, 2011.
10. Commons, *Legal Foundations*, 172–73, 200, Adams Express Co. v. Ohio State Auditor 165 U.S. 194 (1897).
11. Horwitz, *The Transformation*, 163.
12. Commons, *Legal Foundations*, 2–8. To show that John R.'s position was close to the mainstream at the time, Yuval Yonay, The *Struggle over the Soul of Economics*, (Princeton, NJ: Princeton University Press, 1998), 33 cited the following passage in which Alfred Marshall criticized Ricardo and the other classical economists.
    "This fault led them astray as to the relations between the different industrial classes. It caused them to speak of labour as a commodity without staying to throw themselves into the point of view of the workman . . . . They therefore attributed to the forces of supply and demand a much more mechanical and regular action than is to be found in real life; and they laid down laws with regard to profits and wages that did not really hold even for England in their own time". Alfred Marshall, *Principles of Economics* 6th ed. (London: Macmillan 1910), 762–63.
13. Commons, *Legal Foundations*, 65–66, Eugen von Böhm Bawerk, *The Positive Theory of Capital*, tr. William Smart (1889, reprint: New York: G.E. Steichert & Co, 1923), 201–9.
14. John R. Commons and John B. Andrews, *Principles of Labor Legislation* (New York and London: Harper and Brothers, 1916), 2.

15. Walter Wheeler Cook, "Privileges of Labor Unions in the Struggle for Life," *Yale Law Journal* 37 (April, 1918): 779–801. Arthur Corbin. "Jural Relations and Their Classification." *Faculty Scholarship Series Paper 2873.1921*, http// digitalcommons.law.yale.edu/fss papers/2873, accessed May 24, 2014.
16. Wesley Newcomb Hohfeld, "Some Fundamental Legal Conceptions as Applied to Legal Reasoning," *Yale Law* (November 1913): 16–59.
17. Commons, *Legal Foundations*, 91–134.
18. Horwitz, *The Transformation*, 132, Duncan Kennedy and Frank Michelman, "Are Property and Contract Efficient?" *Hofstra Law Review* 8 (1980), 751–52. <http//scholarlycommons.law.hofstra.edu/hlr/vol8/iss3/10/> accessed December 28, 2013.
19. Commons, *Legal Foundations.*, 63,Holden v. Hardy 169 U.S. 366 (1898)
20. Ibid., 304–6. For a later development of this argument, see William Forbath, "The Ambiguities of Free Labor and the Law of the Gilded Age," *Wisconsin Law Review* (July-August 1985), 767–825.
21. Commons, *Legal Foundations*, 307.
22. Ibid., 330, Muller v. Oregon 208 U.S. 412 (1907).
23. Commons, *Legal Foundations*, 362, Adam Smith, *An Inquiry into the Nature and Causes of the Wealth of Nation*, ed. Edwin Canaan vol. 1 of 2 (3rd ed. 1784 reprint. London: Methuen & Co., 1923), 1, 5.
24. Commons, *Legal Foundations*, 355.

Appendix C to Chapter 16:
Institutional Economics

Commons's *Institutional Economics* can be a hard sell. Nine hundred pages make it forbidding enough. *The Economics of Collective Action* is a better introduction to Commons's thought—and kinder to readers. And "yet and yet," as Frank H. Knight qualified himself, there are rewards for readers who follow Mitchell's advice and impose their own order on *Institutional Economics*. There is a depth that is absent from *The Economics of Collective Action*, and there are topics and insights that appear nowhere else. This appendix will try to illustrate the depth by tracing Commons's philosophical development of reasonable value, a policy philosophy for muddling through in a representative democracy. It will illustrate insights that appear nowhere else by summarizing the short-run analysis of going concern behavior that led Commons to the concept of the liquidity trap two years before John Maynard Keynes proposed it. (Numbers in parentheses refer to pages in the book.)

Reasonable Value

In the second chapter Commons began his philosophical treatment of reasonable value with John Locke's *Essay Concerning Human Understanding*. Locke wrote it, according to Commons, as "intended for reasonableness in all things" (14). And it turned out to be "not so much a philosophy of skepticism which it was supposed to be" but "a handbook for consensus of opinion in practical affairs" (21).

> Thus if probability, belief, opinion, experience, take the place of certain knowledge, the foundation is laid, not for skepticism, but for distinguishing reason from reasonableness. Reason may give us the immutable laws of God, Nature, Perfection, but Reasonableness gives us mutual assent to the preponderance of probability in the affairs of life. It is Locke's doctrine of Reasonableness, not his degree of Reason that survives. (23)

While Commons accepted this first notion of reasonableness as a "mutual assent to the preponderance of probability," he rejected Locke's notion of natural universally recognized rights to property. That notion was based on two fallacies. First, it assumed an abundance of resources so that artisans could easily find raw materials and thus lay an undisputed property claim to the work of their hands (35–37). Second, Locke committed the "historic fallacy of Inverted Sequence"— projecting backward the customary assumptions of his own time (50). The so-called "self-evident rights" to "life liberty and property" had not been "self-evident" from the beginning of human history; they had been created over a very long time to justify the positions of the dominant classes and to permit merchant classes to buy and sell debts and intangible assets. And, while John R. praised Locke as the apostle of "reasonableness in all things," the man who rescued belief from certainty, he rejected Locke's dualist separation of mind and body, his labor theory of value.

To find more acceptable assumptions, Commons turned—a hundred pages later—to David Hume and Charles S. Peirce (140–157).

Following Hume, he replaced Locke's assumption of abundant resources with scarce resources giving rise to conflicts—the source of property. He also followed Hume in rejecting "economic man." While scarcity engenders conflict, conflict resolution can be a source not only of war and exploitation, but also of virtue and public spirit.

> Yet if we are familiar with modern trade union "ethics" and business "ethics" of industry, commerce and banking, we shall find that it is exactly Hume's Scarcity of opportunities with their resulting conflict of interests that gives rise, out of conflict, to all the economic virtues of honesty, fair-dealing, fair competition, reasonable exercise of economic power, good-will and reasonable value, which subordinate the immediate interests of self to that sharing with others of limited opportunities which makes possible the peaceful conduct of transactions and going concerns. (143)

Of course, conflict has also generated social Darwinist savagery (John R. preferred the term "Malthusian" to "Darwinist") (244–250).

> "Malthus began the disillusionment of the Age of business cycles, overproduction, underproduction, unemployment, mass migrations, tariffs, monopolies, political and economic struggles of landlords, peasants, farmers, capitalists, and laborers . . . an age that brought another world war with its revolutionists, dictatorships, tariffs, impe-

Appendix C to Chapter 16

> rialism, futile American efficiency and drastic American exclusion
> of the overpopulation of Europe—the "melancholy hue" of Malthus
> vindicated and even frightfully overdone. (250)

This was Lester Frank Ward's challenge—to create through the collective intelligence of democratic processes an evolution of reasonable "artificial selection" that protects human beings from the savage effects of conflict and Darwinian or "Malthusian evolution." While Locke and Hume had provided some philosophical background to guide this "artificial selection," they had not, in John R.'s opinion, supported their philosophies with an adequate theory of knowledge and inquiry. For this, he turned to Charles Sanders Peirce.

Peirce, a mathematician, astronomer, physical scientist, logician, and philosopher of science, was not an economist, or even a political philosopher. But Peirce's philosophy of science offered the grounding that John R. sought for his philosophy of reasonable value.[1]

Inquiry for Peirce begins with "the irritation of doubt" and ends with beliefs strong enough to support "habits of action"—but not strong enough to be considered infallible. An "irritation of doubt" may at some later date lead to further inquiry and a rejection or modification of the previous fallible belief and its replacement with a new fallible belief. Nevertheless, Peirce related these fallible beliefs to a notion of truth—"The opinion which is fated to be ultimately agreed to by all who investigate." This notion made truth something to be sought by collective action rather than by the ruminations of a single person. It also advanced a correspondence notion of truth that was compatible with Locke's "mutual assent to the preponderance of probability in the affairs of life." Thus a belief considered reasonable at one time may be reasonably rejected later. Still, behind this notion of fallibilism stood the hope that honest collective inquiry properly conducted would approach ever closer to a reality "whose characters are independent of what anybody may think them to be" (152). So, with Peirce and Hume, John R. completed the philosophical basis for reasonable value—a fallible consensus of competent beliefs on questions that arise from conflicts of interest.

To move beyond philosophy to a capitalist economy in a representative democracy, he brought in efficiency as a way to overcome scarcity—the task of producers. Then, after a long review of economic value theories, he arrived at a point reached by many texts on the history of economic thought, the famous "scissors" of Alfred Marshall in which markets tend toward prices that reflect both the costs of production and the preferences of consumers (386).

But then he questioned the belief that this market outcome is reasonable. Such a belief rests on an absolute conception of ownership; it assumes that everything offered for sale would be purchased; it abstracts from money and credit; it ignores social "forces" of efficiency and scarcity. Efficiency is the source of power over nature, and scarcity is the source of power over others, the power that derives from the ability to withhold what others need but do not possess. John R. did not explicitly mention the actual power exercised by the railroads and warehouses over farmers, or the power exercised by US Steel over its rolled steel customers, or the power corporations exercised over workers in wage transactions. But he alluded to them when he added that it is "in the measurement of these *degrees* of social 'force' that we shall find the problem of Reasonable Value" (387).

From these theoretical considerations of reasonable value, he proceeded to problems of debt and credit, going concerns, and price stability. Then, before returning to his promised "practical examples of the application of a theory of Reasonable Value," he resurrected the legal notion of reasonableness in the Supreme Court decision in *Smith v. Ames*. "Reasonable Value is the evolutionary collective determination of what is reasonable in view of all the changing political, moral, and economic circumstances and the personalities that arise therefrom to the Supreme Court" (683–684). But, still referring to the court, he added a qualifier: "it is more important to know" who the Justices are "than to know what the law is. The Constitution is not what it says it is—it is what the Court says it is." And, just as unquestioned assumptions affect judicial decisions, so the unquestioned assumptions of economic investigators affect the outcomes of their investigations (697).

To illustrate changing habitual assumptions, John R. cited two court cases (700). In the first case, a British court, in 1771, refused to send back to his previous owner James Sommerset, who had been a slave in Jamaica. In the second case, in 1856, the US Supreme Court ruled that Dred Scott, who was living in a free state, should be returned to his owner. Then John R. drew a lesson. "The idea of 'natural' rights in 1856 became 'unnatural' by the proclamation of 1863 and by the sovereignty of the Northern States expressed in the Thirteenth and Fourteenth Amendments in1865 and 1868."

So, in these examples, John R. illustrated the notion of reasonable value as a fallible belief arrived at through a due process. But he also illustrated the role of habitual assumptions in the determination of reasonableness. Whether considering a market price, or an action, or a law, the "reasonable" is found at any time by weighing all the evidence from all points of view. The result of this process, the reasonable value at one time, will be fallible. But the process offers the hope of a convergence over time on some "best" solution.

The two hundred pages explicitly titled "reasonable value" might by some stretch be labeled practical applications of reasonable value, but it would take quite a stretch. The section begins with a critical examination of Veblen's economics, so critical that Veblen's former student, Wesley Clair Mitchell, chided John R. for misinterpreting Veblen.[2]

To restore the practical application context, one might well start with the last two pages of the reasonable value discussion which provide a sort of summary. In these pages, John R. elaborated on his "theory of reasonable value" as a "theory of social progress by means of personality controlled, liberated, an expanded by collective action." He assumed a capitalist system and continued in the vein of an optimistic old labor mediator, fitting his theory to a "Malthusian concept of human nature, starting from the passion, stupidity and ignorance whereby mankind does the opposite of what reason and rationality would prescribe and ending in admiration for the individual who, by initiative, persistence, taking risks, and assuming obligations to others, rises to leadership" (874).

John R. continued, calling to mind the notion of reasonableness that he had developed with the help of Francis Bird: a reasonable level of safety is the highest possible level that can be attained by surviving concerns. Now it could be a reasonable level of anything. This level can be empirically discovered by finding out what the most ethical employers are doing. Once other employers are brought up to that level by regulation, taxes, or some other device, some employers with a higher ethical sense will set a new standard, and since these employers can survive in the "Malthusian" environment of capitalism, they can be models to justify the imposition of higher standards on others and so forth.

The determination of reasonableness included not only empirical data on safety practices in firms but also consideration of the data by an advisory council that represented the viewpoints and habitual assumptions of all interested parties resulting in a fallible decision of what was reasonable at the time. Commons had introduced the advisory council of the Wisconsin Industrial Commission on page 849. So he had expanded the notion of reasonable value beyond the legal context and had applied it to a fallible conclusion reached by a due process of investigation, a chain in a sequence reaching toward the conclusion that would be accepted by all who investigate.

He had explicitly expanded this notion of reasonableness on pages 860–861 where he went beyond safety to include reasonableness as illustrated by "the *best* unions or *best* associations" that can survive the "Malthusian" environment of the capitalist system. "The problem, then, is the limited one of investigating the working rules of collective action which bring reluctant individuals up to, not an impracticable ideal, but a reasonable idealism, because it is already demonstrated to be practicable by the progressive minority under existing conditions" (874).

It must be recalled that in *Principles of Labor Legislation*, his search for best practices had extended to the practices of other countries. And here he mentioned cooperatives and other such ventures. He followed this on page 875 by urging the profit motive as the most "dynamic" and "constructive" motive to be "enlisted in a program of social welfare." So his discussion of reasonable value moved from the philosophical level of uncertainty and fallibilism to his own concrete experiences, and finally to incentives directed at the profit motive. The entire treatment, beginning with John Locke, was a reflection, an effort to make sense of his many "collective activities." And while his notion of reasonable value has received considerable attention, his treatment of the going concern with its application to taxation and the business cycle has received less.

The Going Concern.

Any organization—a family, a church, a government, a fraternal society, or even a baseball team—can be a going concern. But John R., devoted most of his discussions to corporations (53–54, 69). He started, as in the *Foundations,* by dividing the going concern into a going plant and a going business, but then he added details that fit more closely with his emphasis on debt, credit, and power relations.

First, the going business has power over the going plant because the going business is responsible for the continued survival of the going concern. Then, since production must precede sales, the concern must borrow in the short term, giving bankers and other lenders power over the managers of the going business. And all managers make decisions consistent with the limitations of the human mind. People cannot think of everything at once; so they depend on habitual assumptions for

Appendix C to Chapter 16

routine decisions and they focus strategic attention on limiting factors that seem to pose the greatest obstacle to the attainment of their goals.

In the short run, the limiting factor for the going business is the margin for profit, defined as the net income remaining after the deduction from revenues of taxes, interest, and operating expenses (526–528). A persistent zero margin for profit would threaten the concern's survival. And bankers make credit and interest decisions on the basis of an expected margin for profit. Hence, managers will slash production plans if they anticipate threats to the profit margin. This centrality of profit margins led John R. to conclusions about taxes and interest rates.

He argued against corporate profit taxes while continuing to support progressive income and inheritance taxes. Anything that reduces anticipated profit margins creates an incentive for managers to cut production plans. Thus, progressive corporate profit taxes can "defeat the social purpose of capitalistic civilization which uses the profit motive to increase the efficiency of production" (586).

His margin of profit analysis supported his argument against deflation because falling prices threaten both short-term margins of profit and the ability of going concerns to borrow. In the limit, the anticipation of falling margins of profit can render managers unwilling or unable to borrow and banks unwilling to lend. Combining this consideration with Irving Fisher's risk discount, John R. reasoned to what three years later John Maynard Keynes would call the liquidity trap—a situation in which lending and borrowing—even at zero interest rates—would be so curtailed as to generate declining production and high unemployment.[3]

For such a situation, John R. proposed a solution that harked back to the platform of the old Populist Party's invocation of Article 1, Section 8 of the constitution, the section that gave Congress the power to coin money and regulate its value.

> The purchasing power of all classes, whether expended as savings or expended for consumption, furnishes the same employment for labor, barring temporary difficulties of adjustment. In order to increase the purchasing power of labor the unemployed must be put to work by *creation of new money*, not by *transferring* the existing purchasing power of taxpayers to laborers as Malthus proposed, nor by borrowing money by government which *transfers* investments but does not augment them.
>
> This new money cannot be issued by bankers, either in commercial investment, or central banks, because, in a period of depression, the margins for profit have disappeared, and there are no business borrowers willing to cooperate with bankers in creating new money.

279

In order to create the *consumer demand* on which business depends for sales, the government itself must create the new money and go completely over the head of the entire banking system by paying it out directly to the unemployed either as relief or for construction of public works as it does in times of war. Besides, this new money must also go to farmers, the business establishments, and practically all enterprises, as well as to wage-earners, for it is all of them together that make up the total of consumer demand. (589–590)

Thus, his model of the going concern, like his notion of reasonable value, was expanded and applied far beyond the legal context in which he first proposed those conceptions. And these two themes—reasonable value and going concern—offer a glimpse into the insightful originality of *Institutional Economics*.

Notes

1. Charles Sanders Peirce, *The Essential Peirce: Selected Philosophical Writings*, edited by Nathan Houser and Christian Kloesel, vol. 1 of 5 (Bloomington and Indianapolis: Indiana University press, 1992), 137–39.
2. Wesley Clair Mitchell, "Commons on Institutional Economics," *American Economic Review* 25 (December, 1935): 647-8n.
3. For a more thorough treatment of the relation between Keynes and Commons with an emphasis on the liquidity trap, see Charles Whalen, "John R. Commons and John Maynard Keynes on Economics, History, and Policy: The 1920s and Today," *Journal of Economic Issues* 27 (March 2008): 225–42; Eric Tymoigne, "Keynes and Commons on Money," *Journal of Economic Issues* 37 (September 2003): 527–45.

Chronology

1755	William and Sarah Scarlett Commons come to Chester County, PA, with their son, Robert, age 7.
1780	Robert Commons marries Ruth Hayes.
1785	Isaac Commons is born.
1802	Isaac Commons leaves Randolph County, NC, for Wayne County, IN.
1809	Isaac Commons marries Mary Townsend.
1818	John A. Commons is born.
1826	Clarissa Rogers is born on March 16.
1856	John A. Commons opens his harness shop.
1860	John A. Commons marries Clarissa Rogers on June 27.
1862	John R. Commons is born on October 13.
1873	During the panic of 1873, John A. Commons trades his harness shop for the *Union City Times*.
1877	A railroad strike starts in Martinsburg, WV, on July 14 and spreads across the country.
1878	John A. Commons trades the *Union City Times* for the *Winchester Herald*. The family moves from Union City, a railroad town, to Winchester, IN.
1881	John R. Commons graduates from Winchester High School.
1882	John R. Commons enters Oberlin College.
1888	He graduates from Oberlin.
1888	He enters Johns Hopkins.
1890	He leaves Johns Hopkins for a lectureship at Wesleyan.
1890	John R. Commons marries Ella Brown (Nell) Downey on Christmas day.
1891	He leaves Wesleyan for a faculty position at Oberlin.
1891	John Alvin Commons is born on September 13 (named for his grandfather).
1892	John R. Commons leaves Oberlin for the University of Indiana at Bloomington.

1893	Sidney Robert Commons is born on June 1 and dies on August 6.
1893	John R. attends the founding session of the League for Proportional Representation.
1893	*The Distribution of Wealth* is published.
1894	He becomes secretary for the Institute of Christian Sociology.
1894	He is in Chicago on May 11 when the Pullman strike begins. He had previously interviewed Eugen V. Debs.
1895	He accepts the chair in Sociology at Syracuse University.
1896	*Proportional Representation* is published.
1897	Julia Margaret Commons is born on March 26.
1899	A series of articles on "A Sociology of Sovereignty" seem intended for a book, as do two articles —1900 on the George Junior Republic.
1899	In March Chancellor James Roscoe Day fires Commons.
1899	In the summer, funded by George Shibley, a silver advocate, John R. Commons, Edward W. Bemis, and N.I. Stone establish the Bureau of Economic Research and begin producing index numbers. They collect other information, and their bulletins contain digests of the latest research on index numbers. Contrary to Shibley's assumption, they find rising prices.
1899	Rachel Sutherland Commons is born on July 26.
1900	In September, George Shibley removes funding from the Bureau of Economic Research.
1900	John R. Commons testifies before the United States Industrial Commission and is hired by Jeremiah Jenks.
1901	Julia Margaret Commons dies on March 7 .
1901	On September 6, Leon Czolgosz shoots President McKinley, and Theodore Roosevelt is sworn in as president.
1902	The United States Industrial Commission completes its work and Commons goes to work for the National Civic Federation.
1902	On May 12, miners in Western Pennsylvania begin a strike in which Commons becomes a participant observer. Under the alias of Campbell, Commons interviews miners and merchants for the National Civic Federation (NCF).
1903	On March 10, Ella Brown Commons bears twins, one dies immediately, the other on July 4.
1904	Ely brings Commons to Wisconsin and in March they sign the contract establishing the American Bureau of Economic Research.

Chronology

1905   In the spring, Commons suggests publishing a documentary history and Ely agrees.

1906   In the summer Commons goes to England with the National Civic Federation's committee investigating public utility ownership and operation.

1907   In the summer Commons with William Leiserson, John Fitch, and another student participates in the Pittsburgh Survey.

1910   *A Documentary History of American Industrial Society* is published.

1910   Commons, together with some students, begins work on the Bureau of Economy and Efficiency for the city of Milwaukee.

1911   Commons begins two-year term as commissioner on the Wisconsin Industrial Commission.

1913   *Labor and Administration* is published. It includes articles on "constructive democracy" and "constructive research."

1913   June 27 Commons is appointed to the United States Commission on Industrial Relations.

1914   June 28 Archduke Francis Ferdinand, Crown Prince of Austria, is assassinated initiating World War I. On August 1 Germany declares war on Russia. On August 3 Germany declares war on France.

1916   The *Principles of Labor Legislation* is published. The Commission on Industrial Relations ends in controversy. The entire research staff is fired. Robert Hoxie commits suicide. Commons suffers a complete breakdown in June.

1917   Commons returns to Madison in February. Is elected president of the American Economic Association. On April 2 President Wilson asks Congress to declare war.

1918   On September 4 Jack Commons lands with American troops in Northern Russia. They will be in battle past the armistice.

1918   The first two volumes of the *History of Labor in the United States* are published.

1919   The end of World War I ushers in an inflation followed by a depression.

1919   *Industrial Goodwill* is published.

1920   Commons becomes president of the National Consumers' League.

1920   N.I. Stone and Malcolm Rorty establish the National Bureau of Economic Research. Commons serves on advisory board. Wesley Clair Mitchell becomes research director.

1920	Commons writes an unemployment compensation plan that is introduced in the Wisconsin Legislature, but it does not pass. He chairs the board of trustees for a union-management insurance plan in the Chicago garment industry.
1921	*Industrial Government* is published.
1921	September 26, Commerce Secretary Herbert Hoover convenes the President's Conference on Unemployment, making unemployment a matter of federal concern, even though Hoover held strong views about the limits of government.
1922	Commons becomes president of the National Monetary Association.
1923	Commons chairs boards of trustees for the unemployment compensation plan of the Amalgamated Clothing Workers and the Chicago Associated Clothing Manufacturers.
1923	Commons becomes president of the National Consumers' League.
1923	John R. Commons, Frank A. Fetter, and William Z. Ripley testify before the Federal Trade Commission in the Pittsburgh Plus case. Their arguments prevail.
1924	*Legal Foundations of Capitalism* is published.
1927	Commons testifies before Congress for the Strong Bill that would make price stability a goal of the Federal Reserve System.
1927	Ella Brown Commons dies on December 31.
1928	From January till June Commons works on the second Strong Bill for the House Committee on Banking and Currency. He testifies in Congress again, becomes deathly ill from a pulmonary disease.
1929	March 15, President Hoover calls special session of Congress to deal with the economic crisis, especially the plight of farmers.
1929	October 29, Black Tuesday, stocks in free fall.
1932	Commons retires.
1934	*Institutional Economics* and *Myself* are published.
1935	Last two volumes of *History of Labor in the United States* and the fourth edition of *Principles of Labor Legislation* are published.
1936	In July, his daughter Rachel dies. In November with his niece, Bertha, he drives to a trailer camp in Fort Lauderdale.
1945	May 11 John R. Commons dies.
1950	His last book, *The Economics of Collective Action* is published.

Abbreviations

American Association for Labor Legislation AALL
American Bureau of Economic Research ABER
American Bureau of Industrial Research ABIR
American Economic Association AEA
Chicago Civic Federation CCF
Colorado Fuel and Iron Corporation CFI
National Civic Federation NCF
United States Commission on Industrial Relations USCIR
United States Industrial Commission USIC

Bibliography

Adams, Graham. *The Age of Industrial Violence 1910–1915: The Actions and Findings of the United States Commission on Industrial Violence.* New York: Columbia University Press, 1966.

Adams, Henry Carter. *Relation of the State to Industrial Action and Economics and Jurisprudence.* Edited by Joseph Dorfman. New York: Columbia University Press, 1954.

Adams, Thomas, Sewall and Helen L. Sumner. *Labor Problems: A Textbook.* New York: Macmillan, 1905.

Albert, Alexa, and Yngve Ramstad. "The Social Psychological Underpinnings of Commons's Institutional Economics I: The Significance of Dewey's *Human Nature and Conduct.*" *Journal of Economic Issues* 31 (December, 1997): 881–916.

Albert, Alexa, and Yngve Ramstad. "The Social Psychological Underpinnings of Commons's Institutional Economics II: The Concordance of George Herbert Mead's 'Social Self' and John R. Commons's 'Will.'" *Journal of Economic Issues* 32 (March, 1998): 1–46.

Alexander, Magnus. "Hiring and Firing: Its Economic Waste and How to Avoid it." *Annals of the American Academy of Political and Social Science* 65 (May, 1916): 128–44.

Almeder, Robert. *The Philosophy of Charles S. Peirce: A Critical Introduction.* Totowa, NJ: Rowman and Littlefield, 1980.

American Association for Labor Legislation, *Proceedings of the Second Annual Meeting: Madison Wisconsin, December 30–31, 1907.* Madison: University of Wisconsin, 1908.

American Social History Project. "The Omaha Platform: Launching the Populist Party." In *History Matters: The U.S. Survey Course on the Web.* New York and Fairfax, VA: CUNY Graduate Center and George Mason University, 1998 historymatters.gmu.edu/d/5361. Accessed September 4, 2012.

Andrews, John, B. *American Bureau of Industrial Research: Leaflet no. 3.* Madison, WI: American Bureau of Industrial Research, January, 1907. (Commons microfilm reel 1, frames 168–173).

———. "A Practical Program for the Prevention of Unemployment." *American Labor Legislation Review* 5 (June, 1915): 171–92.

———. "The President's Conference on Unemployment—Success or Failure?" *American Labor Legislation Review* 11 (December, 1921): 307–10.

Andrews, Thomas. *Killing for Coal, America's Deadliest War.* Cambridge, MA: Harvard University Press, 2010.

Angell, Norman. *The Great Illusion: A Study of the Relation of Military Power in Nations to their Economic and Political Advantage.* 1909. Reprint. New York: Gardner Publications, 1972.

Ashley, William. *"Legal Foundations of Capitalism* by John R. Commons: Review." *Economic Journal* 36 (March, 1926): 84–88.

Atkins, Willard, E. "Institutional Economics by John R. Commons Review." *International Journal of Ethics* 45(July, 1935): 474–76.

Atkinson, Glen, W., and Stephen P. Parschall. "Law and Economics an Evolutionary Perspective." Paper Presented at the annual meeting of the Association for Institutional Thought, Salt Lake City April 15, 2011.

Baldwin, James, Mark. *Social and Ethical Interpretations in Mental Development.* 1897. Reprint. New York: Arno Press, 1973.

Baldwin, Robert, J. "International Economics and Economic Development." In *Economists at Wisconsin 1892–1992,* 210–13. Edited by Robert Lampman. Madison, WI: Board of Regents of the Wisconsin University System, 1993.

Barbash, Jack. "The Legal Foundations of Capitalism and the Labor Problem." *Journal of Economic Issues* 10 (December, 1976): 799–810.

Barber, William. *From New Era to New Deal: Herbert Hoover and American Economic Policy, 1921–1933.* New York: Cambridge University Press, 1985.
_____. *Designs within Disorder. Franklin Roosevelt, the Economists and the Shaping of American Economic Policy 1933–1945.* New York: Cambridge University Press, 1996.

Barbour, Hugh, and J. William Frost. *The Quakers.* New York: Greenwood Press, 1988.

Barnard, John. *From Evangelicalism to Progressivism at Oberlin College 1866–1917.* Cleveland: Ohio State University Press, 1969.

Barnett, George E. "Review of *Principles of Labor Legislation* by John R. Commons and John B. Andrews." *American Economic Review* 6 (September, 1916): 654–58.
———. "History of Labor in the United States by John R. Commons, David. J. Saposs, Helen L. Sumner, E. B. Mittelman, H. E. Hoagland, John B. Andrews, and Selig Perlman with an introductory note by Henry W. Farnam." *American Economic Review* 9 (June, 1919): 340–42.
———. "American Trade Unionism and Social Insurance." *American Economic Review* 23 (March, 1933): 1–15.

Barthel-Bouchier, Diane, L. *Amana: From Pietist Sect to American Community.* Lincoln: University of Nebraska Press, 1984.

Bergquist, Harold, E. "The Edward Bemis Controversy at the University of Chicago." *AAUP Bulletin* (Winter, 1972): 384–93.

Berkowitz, Edward. *Mr. Social Security: The Life of Wilbur Cohen.* Lawrence: University of Kansas Press, 1995.
———. and Kim Mc Quaid. *Creating the Welfare State: The Political Economy of Twentieth-Century Reform.* New York: Praeger Publishers, 1980.

Berle, Adolph, A and Gardiner C. Means. *The Modern Corporation and Private Property.* New York: Macmillan, 1932.

Bernstein, Irving. *The Lean Years: A History of the American Worker 1920–1933.* Boston, MA: Houghton, 1960.

Bibliography

Blackburn, Barr and Margaret Pryor. *Wisconsin Study of the Uniform Small Loan Law.* Madison: University of Wisconsin, 1929 (Commons Microfilm Reel 21, frames715ff).

Blum, Solomon. *Labor Economics.* New York: Henry Holt and Company, 1925.

Bogart, Ernest, L. "Reviewed Work: A Documentary History of American Industrial Society. Volumes III and I Labor Conspiracy Cases, 1806–1842 by John R. Commons, Eugene A. Gilmore." *Economic Bulletin* 3, no. 2 (June, 1910): 149–51.

Böhm Bawerk, Eugen von. *The Positive Theory of Capital.* 1889. Reprint New York: G.E. Steichert Company, 1923.

———. *Karl Marx and the Close of His System*, 1898. Reprint. Edited by Paul Sweezy. Philadelphia, PA: Orion Publications, 1984.

Boulding, Kenneth. 1957. "A New Look at Institutionalism." *American Economic Review* 47 (May, 1957): 1–12.

Brandeis, Elizabeth. "Labor Legislation." In *History of Labor in the United States* 1896–1932, edited by John R. Commons, 399–697. Reprint. New York: Augustus M. Kelley, 1935.

Brandt, Nat. *The Town that Started the Civil War.* Syracuse, NY: Syracuse University Press, 1990.

Brauer, Carl. "Kennedy, Johnson, and the War on Poverty." *The Journal of American History* 69 (June, 1982): 98–119.

Brent, Joseph. 1993. *Charles Sanders Peirce: A Life.* Bloomington: University of Indiana Press.

Broda, Philippe. "Conflict Resolution: A Key to the Interpretation of John R. Commons's Intellectual Journey." *Journal of Economic Issues* 47 (December, 2013): 855–72.

Brody, David, *Steelworkers in America.* Cambridge, MA: Harvard University Press, 1960.

———. *Labor in Crisis: The Steel Strike of 1919.* Philadelphia, PA and New York: J.P. Lippincott and Company, 1965.

———. "The Old Labor History and the New." *Labor History* 20 (Winter 1974): 111–26.

———. "Reconciling the Old Labor History and the New." *Pacific Historical Review* 62 (February, 1993): 1–18.

Brown, John, H. "Jeremiah Jenks: A Pioneer in Industrial Economics." *Journal of the History of Economic Thought* 26 (March, 2004): 69–89.

Brown, Lee with Robert L Allen. *Strong in the Struggle: My Life as a Black Activist.* London: Rowman and Littlefield, 2001.

Brubacher, John, S., and Willis Rudy. *Higher Education in Transition an American History: 1636–1956.* New York: Harper and Brothers, 1958.

Burnham, John. *Bad Habits, Smoking, Taking Drugs, Gambling, Sexual Misbehavior, and Swearing in American History.* New York: NYU Press, 1993.

Bye, Raymond, T. "Review of *Institutional Economics* by John R. Commons." *Annals of the American Academy of Political and Social Science.* 178 (March, 1935): 200–2.

Casebeer, Kenneth. *At Will Employment.* University of Miami Legal Studies Research Paper No. 2008–28, 2008. Accessed April 9, 2013. http://papers.ssrn.com/sol3/papers.cfm?abstract_id=1131275.

Cain, Glen, G. "Labor Economics." In *Economists at Wisconsin.* Edited by Robert J. Lampman, 234–46. Madison, WI: Board of Regents of the University of Wisconsin System, 1993.

Calhoun, Charles. "Fire in the Rear." *Reviews in American History* 35 (December, 2007): 530–37.

Carlton, Frank, T. "History of Labor in the United States by John R. Commons and Associates." *Journal of Political Economy* 26 (December, 1918): 981–83.

Carter, Susan, B Scott Sigmund Gartner, Michael B. Haines, Alan C. Olmstead, Richard Such, and Gavin Wright. *Historical Statistics of the United States: Earliest Times to the Present.* New York: Cambridge University Press, 2006.

Chambers, Clark, A. *Seedtime of Reform: American Social Service and Social Action 1918–1933.* Minneapolis: University of Minneapolis Press, 1963.

Chamberlain, Neil "The Institutionalism of John R Commons." In *Institutional Economics: Veblen, Commons and Mitchell Reconsidered* by Joseph Dorfman, C. E. Ayres, Neil W. Chamberlain, Simon Kuznets, and R. A. Gordon. Berkeley and Los Angeles: University of California Press, 1963. 1–44, (p. 1.), 1963: 63–94.

Chandler, Alfred. *Scale and Scope: The Dynamics of Industrial Capitalism.* Cambridge, MA: Belknap Press, 1990.

Chandler, Lester. *Benjamin Strong, Central Banker.* Washington, DC: Brookings, 1958.

Chase, Stuart. *Prosperity: Fact or Fiction.* New York: Boni Press, 1929.

Chasse, J. Dennis. "John R Commons and John Maynard Keynes: Two Philosophies of Action." *Journal of Economic Issues* 25 (June, 1991): 441–48.

———. "The American Association for Labor Legislation: An Episode in Institutionalist Policy Analysis." *Journal of Economic Issues* 25 (September, 1991): 799–822.

———. "The American Association for Labor Legislation and the Institutionalist Tradition in National Health Insurance." *Journal of Economic Issues* 28 (December, 1994): 1063–90.

———. "John R. Commons and the Special Interest Issue: Not Really Out of Date." *Journal of Economic Issues* 31, no. 4 (December, 1997): 933–49.

———. "John R. Commons and His Students: The View from the End of the Twentieth Century." In *The Institutionalist Tradition in Labor Economics,* edited by Dell P. Champlin and Janet Knoedler, 50–74. Armonk, NY: M.E. Sharpe, 2004.

———. "The Economists of the Lost Cause and the Monetary Education of John R Commons." *Journal of the History of Economic Thought* 36 (June 2014): 193–214.

Clark, John, Bates. 1965. *The Distribution of Wealth.* 1899. Reprint. New York: A.M. Kelley, 1965.

Clark, Lindley, D. "Review of *Principles of Labor Legislation* by John R. Commons and John B. Andrews." *Journal of Political Economy* 24 (November, 1916): 903–6.

Bibliography

Clark, Norman. *Deliver Us from Evil: An Interpretation of American Prohibition.* New York: W.W. Norton, 1976.

Clifford, Geraldine. *Lone Voyagers: Academic Women in Coeducational Universities 1870–1937.* New York: City University of New York, 1989.

Clarke, Thomas, D. *Indiana University: Midwestern Pioneer. Volume I. The Early Years.* Bloomington and London: Indiana University Press, 1970.

Cohen, Wilbur, J. "Edwin E. Witte (1887–1960) Father of Social Security." *Industrial and Labor Relations Review* 14 (October 1960): 7–9.

———and Robert M. Ball. 1965. "Social Security Amendments of 1965: Summary and Legislative History." *Social Security Bulletin* 28, no. 9 (September, 1965): 1–21.

Committee on Social Insurance. "Health Insurance Tentative Draft of an Act." *American Labor Legislation Review* 6 (June, 1916): 239–67.

Commons, Clarissa." Introduction: Sunday School Department." *Union City Times* 4 (March 25, 1875): 2.

Commons, John, A. "Faith in People." In *Industrial Government*, edited by John R. Commons. 1921. Reprint, 13–25. New York: Arno Press, 1969.

Commons, John, R. "Political Economy." *Oberlin Review* (December 20, 1887).

———. "Abstract Studies and the World." *Oberlin Review* (February 7, 1888).

———. "Preparation for Life's Work." *Oberlin Review* (April 3, 1888).

———. "The Educated Man in Politics." *The Indiana Student* 19 (March 1893): 6–11.

———. "How to Abolish the Gerrymander." *Indiana Student* 19 (April 1893): 3–8.

———. "What Should Congress Do About Money?" *Review of Reviews* 7 (August, 1893): 153.

———. "Bullion Notes and an Elastic Currency." *Annals of the American Academy of Political and Social Science* 4 (September 1893): 99–101.

———. *The Distribution of Wealth.* 1893. Reprint. New York: A.M. Kelley, 1963.

———. "American Institute of Christian Sociology." *The Congregationalist* 88 (July–December 1893): 32.

———. *Social Reform & the Church.* 1894. Reprint. New York: A.M. Kelley, 1967.

———." Progressive Individualism." *The American Magazine of Civics* (June, 1895): 562–74.

———. "The Junior Republic I." *American Journal of Sociology* 3 (November, 1897): 281–96.

———. "The Junior Republic II." *American Journal of Sociology* 3 (January, 1898): 433–48.

———. *Truths for Our Time, Series A. Good Citizenship.* New York: United Charities of New York, 1898.

———. "Sociology." In *Extension Department Syllabus 74.* Albany, NY: University of the State of New York (June 1898). (Commons microfilm Reel 15).

———. "The Right to Work." *The Arena* 21 (February, 1899): 140–41.

———. "Discussion on the President's Address." *Economic Studies: Supplement* 4, no. 2 (April, 1899): 111–12.

———. "Its Dangers." *The Independent* 54 (May 1, 1902): 1040–45.

———. "The Personal Relations of Employer and Employee." *The Independent* 54 (May 29, 1902): 1319–20.

———. "The Anthracite Coal Strike Award." *The Independent* 55 (March 26, 1903).

———. "The Anthracite Coal Strike Award." *Monthly Review of the National Civic Federation.* 1 (April, 1903): 12–15.

———. "Combinations of Capital and Labor." *The National Civic Federation Review* 3 (September, 1903): 113–14.

———. "Causes of Union Shop Policy." *American Economic Association: Papers and Proceedings of the Seventeenth Annual Meeting, December 28–30, 1904,* 140–59. New York: Macmillan, 1905.

———. *Races and Immigrants.* 1907 Reprint. New York: A.M. Kelley, 1967.

———. "Tariff Revision and the Protection of American Labor." *Annals of the American Academy of Political and Social Science* 32 (September 1908): 315–20.

———. "Horace Greeley and the Working Class Origins of the Republican Party." *Political Science Quarterly* 24, no. 5 (September 1909): 466–88.

———. "Economists and Class Partnership." *Papers and Proceedings of the Twelfth Annual Meeting of the American Economic Association Ithaca N. Y.* December 27 1899, 63–80. New York: Macmillan, 1900.

———. "American Shoemakers, 1648–1895: A Sketch of Industrial Evolution." *Quarterly Journal of Economics* 34 (November, 1909): 39–84.

———. "Economic Reconstruction: Foreign and Domestic Investments: Annual Address of the President." *American Economic Review: Supplement, Papers and Proceedings of the Thirtieth Annual Meeting of the American Economic Association* 8 (March 1918): 5–17.

———. "Introduction." In *History of Labour in the United States,* by John R. Commons, David J. Saposs, Helen L. Sumner, E. R. Mittelman, H. E. Hoagland, John B. Andrews, and Selig Perlman. 1918. Reprint. New York: Augustus M. Kelley, 1966. V.I: 3–21.

———. "Unemployment Compensation and Prevention." *The Survey* 47 (October 1, 1921): 5–9.

———. *Industrial Goodwill.* 1919. Reprint. New York: Arno, 1969.

———. *Industrial Government.* 1921. Reprint. New York: Arno, 1969.

———. "Introduction." In *Civil War in West Virginia,* edited by Winthrop. D. Lane. 1921 Reprint. New York: Arno Press, 1969, 7–10.

———. "Labor in 1922, A Review." *Locomotive Engineers' Journal* (January, 1922) (Commons Microfilm Reel 19 frame 364).

———— John, R. 1922. "A Progressive Tax on Bare Land Values." *Political Science Quarterly* 37, no. 1 (March, 1922): 41–68.

———. "Price Level Changes through Changes in the Rate of Discount and Rediscount." In *John R. Commons Papers.* Madison. WI: State Historical Society of Wisconsin, 1923 (microfilm edition) Reel 10 frames 572–80.

———. "Bank Credit." In *John R. Commons Papers.* Madison. WI: State Historical Society of Wisconsin, 1923 (microfilm edition) Reel 10, frames 585–90.

———. "Inflation and Deflation." In *John R. Commons Papers.* Madison. WI: State Historical Society of Wisconsin, 1923 (microfilm edition), Reel 10, 624–27.

———. *Legal Foundations of Capitalism.* 1924. Reprint. Clifton, NY: A.M. Kelley, 1974.

Bibliography

———. "The Passing of Samuel Gompers." *Current History and Forum* (February, 1925): 670–76.

———." Stabilization of Prices and Business." *American Economic Review* 15 (March, 1925): 43–52.

———. "Marx Today: Capitalism and Socialism." *Atlantic Monthly* 136 (November, 1925): 682–93.

———. "Price Stabilization and the Federal Reserve System." *The Annalist* 29 (April 1, 1927): 459–62.

———. "Workers' Education and the Universities." *American Federationist* (April 1927). (Commons Microfilm Reel 20 frames 177–79).

———. "Farm Prices and the Value of Gold I." *North American Review*. 225 (January, 1928): 27–41.

———. "Farm Prices and the Value of Gold II." *North American Review* 225 (February, 1928): 196–211.

———. "The Small Loan Problem." *Milwaukee Sentinel* (April 1, 1931).

———. "Institutional Economics." *American Economic Review* 21, no. 4 (December, 1931): 648–57.

———. *Myself: The Autobiography of John R Commons*, 1934 Reprint. Madison: University of Wisconsin Press, 1964.

———. *Institutional Economics.* 1934. Edited by Malcolm Rutherford. Reprint New Brunswick, NJ: Transactions Press, 2003.

———. "Capacity to Produce, Capacity to Consume, Capacity to Pay Debts." *American Economic Review*. 27, no. 4 (December, 1937): 680–97.

———. "What I Saw in the Tennessee Valley." *Survey Graphic* 27 (May, 1938): 279.

———. *The Economics of Collective Action.* New York: Macmillan, 1950.

———. *John R Commons Papers.* Madison, WI: State Historical Society of Wisconsin, microfilm, 1982.

———., and J. W. Sullivan. "Labor and Politics." In National Civic Federation. *Municipal and Private Operation of Public Utilities: Report of the National Civic Federation on Public Ownership and Operation.* Vol 2, 1–112. New York: National Civic Federation, 1907.

———, Ulrich B. Phillips, E. A. Gilmore, H. L. Sumner, and J. B. Andrews. *A Documentary History of American Industrial Society.* 10 vols. Cleveland: The Arthur H. Clark Company, 1910–1911.

———, and Helen L. Sumner. "Introduction to Volumes 5 and 6." Vol. 5 of *A Documentary History of American Industrial Society.* Edited by John R., 19–43. Commons and Associates. Cleveland, OH: Arthur Clarke and Company, 1910.

———, and John B. Andrews. "Introduction to Volumes 9 and 10." Vol. 9 of *The Documentary History of American Industrial Society.* Edited by John R. Commons and Associates, 19–51. Cleveland, OH: Arthur H. Clarke and Company, 1910.

———with William Leiserson. "Wage-Earners of Pittsburgh." In *Wage-Earning Pittsburgh*, edited by Paul U. Kellogg, 113–88. 1914. Reprint, 113–188. New York: Arno Press, 1974.

———, and John B. Andrews. *Principles of Labor Legislation.* New York: Harper Brothers, 1916.

———, and Florence J. Harriman. "Report of Commissioners John R Commons and Florence J. Harriman." In *Final Report of the Commission on Industrial Relations*. Senate Document No. 415. 64th Congress, 1st Session. 1916, 169–120. Washington, DC: Government Printing office, 1916.

———, H. L. McCracken, and W. L. Zeuch. "Secular Trends and Business Cycles." *The Review of Economics and Statistics* 4 (October, 1922): 244–63.

Cook, Walter, Wheeler. "Privileges of Labor Unions in the Struggle for Life." *Yale Law Journal* 27 (April 1918): 779–801.

Copeland, Morris, A. "Commons's Institutionalism in Relation to Problems of Social Evolution and Economic Planning." *Quarterly Journal of Economics* 30 (February 1936): 333–46.

Corbin, Arthur. "Jural Relations and Their Classification." *Faculty Scholarship Series. Paper 2873.* 1921. Accessed May 24, 2014. http://digitalcommons. law.yale.edu/fss_papers/2873.

Cornell, Robert *The Anthracite Coal Strike of 1902.* 1957. Reprint. New York: Russell & Russell, 1971.

Cross, Ira. "Review: *History of Labor in the United States.*" *Quarterly Journal of Economics* 32 (August, 1918): 667–73.

Crunden, Robert, M. *Ministers of Reform: The Progressive Achievement in American Civilization 1899–1920.* New York: Basic Books, 1982.

Curti, Merle, and Vernon Christensen. *The University of Wisconsin 1848–1925; a history*, vol. 2. Madison: University of Wisconsin, 1949.

Curtis, Susan. *A Consuming Faith: The Social Gospel and Modern American Culture.* Baltimore, MD and London: Johns Hopkins University Press, 1991.

Dawson, John, P. "Economic Duress: An Essay in Perspective." *Michigan Law Review* 45 (January 1947): 253–90.

Denis, Hector. *Histoire des Systèmes Économiques et Socialistes.* Brussels: C Rosez; Libraire Éditeur, 1897.

DeWitt, Larry. *Never a Finished Thing: A Brief Biography of Arthur Joseph Altmeyer—The Man FDR Called "Mr. Social Security,* 1997." Accessed July 24, 2014. www.ssa.gov/history/bioaja.html.

———. "Cohen, Wilbur, J." In *Social Welfare History Project.* 2010. Accessed September 12, 2015. http://www.socialwelfarehistory.com/people/ cohen-wilbur-j/.

———, Daniel, Béland, and Edward Berkowitz. *Social Security: A Documentary History.* Washington, DC: Congressional Quarterly Press, 2008.

Dimand, Robert. W., and John Geanakoplos. *Celebrating Irving Fisher: The Legacy of a Great Economist.* Malden, MA: Blackwell, 2005.

Dodge, Esther. *Genealogy of John Rogers of Boxford Mass.* Online book contributed by Allen County Public Library (An updated version first compiled by Mrs. C.R. Commons in 1882), 1907. Accessed September 9, 2010. http:// www.archive.org/details/genealogyofjohnr00dodg.

Dombrowski, James. 1936. *The Early Days of Christian Socialism in America.* 1936 Reprint. New York: Octagon Press, 1966.

Doolen, Richard, M. *Polar Bears: The American Expedition to North Russia.* Ann Arbor: U of Michigan Press, 1965.

Bibliography

Dorfman, Joseph. *The Economic Mind in American Civilization.* 5 vols. New York: Viking Press, 1949.

———. "The Mutual Influence of Mitchell and Commons." *American Economic Review* 48 (June, 1958): 405–8.

———. "The Background of Institutional Economics." In *Institutionalism Reconsidered* edited by Joseph Dorfman, C. E. Ayres, Neil W. Chamberlain, Simon Kuznets, and R. A. Gordon, 1–44. Berkeley and Los Angeles: University of California Press, 1963.

———." Prefatory Note." In *Legal Foundations of Capitalism* by John R. Commons, 5–11. 1934. Reprint. Clifton, NJ: Augustus M. Kelley, 1966.

Doubleday, Douglas A. *Slavery by Another Name: The Enslavement of Black Americans from the Civil War to World War II.* New York: Doubleday, 2008.

Douglas, Paul, H. *Wages and the Family.* Chicago, IL: Chicago University Press, 1925.

———. *The Theory of Wages.* 1934. Reprint New York: Kelley and Millman, 1957.

———. *In the Fullness of Time: The Memoirs of Paul H. Douglas.* New York: Harcourt, Brace and Jovanovich, 1971, 1972.

Downey, Kirstin. *The Woman Behind the New Deal.* New York: Doubleday, 2009.

Dubofsky, Melvin. *We Shall Be All: A History of the Industrial Workers of the World.* Chicago: Quadrangle Books, 1969.

———. Randolph Boehm and Martin Schipper. *U.S. Commission on Industrial Relations 1912–1915 Unpublished Records of the Division of Research and Investigation: Reports, Staff Studies, and Background Research Materials.* Ann Arbor, MI: University Microfilms, 1985.

———, and Foster Rhea Dulles. *Labor in America: A History.* Wheeling, IL: Harlan Davidson, 2010.

Dugger, William, M. "The Reform Method of John R. Commons." *Journal of Economic Issues* 13 (June, 1979): 369–81.

Durand, E. Dana. "The United States Industrial Commission: Methods of Government Investigation." *Quarterly Journal of Economics* 16 (August, 1902): 564–86.

———. *Memoirs of E. Dana Durand.* Washington, DC: Durand, 1954.

Eastman, Crystal. *Work Accidents and the Law.* New York: Charity Publications Committee, 1910.

Eichengreen, Barry. *Golden Fetters: The Gold Standard and the Great Depression, 1919–1939.* New York: Oxford University Press, 1992.

Ekelund, Robert B., Jr. and Robert F. Hébert. *A History of Economic Theory and Method.* New York: McGraw-Hill, 1990.

Eliot, Thomas, E. *The Legal Background of the Social Security Act (delivered at a general staff meeting at Social Security Administration Headquarters, Baltimore, Maryland, on February 3, 1961).* Accessed October 9, 2014. www.ssa.gov/history/eliot2.html.

Ely, Richard, T. "Past and Present of Political Economy." *Overland Monthly* II (September 1883): 225–35. Accessed October 29, 2010. http://quod.lib. umich.edu/cgi/t/text/pageviewer-idx?c=moajrnl;cc=moajrnl;rgn=full%20 text;idno=ahj1472.2-02.009;didno=ahj1472.2-02.009;view=∂image;se-q=257;node=ahj1472.2-02.009%3A1;page=root;size=100;frm=frameset.

———. "Pullman: A Social Study." *Harper's New Monthly Magazine* 70 (February 1885): 452–66.

———. *The Labor Movement in America*. New York: Thomas Y. Crowell & Company, 1986.

———. "The Founding and Early History of the American Economic Association." *American Economic Review Supplement Papers and Proceedings* 26 (March 1936): 141–50.

———. *Richard T. Ely Papers*. Madison, WI: State Historical Society of Wisconsin. Microfilm, 1986.

———, Edwin R. A. Seligman, Edmund J. James, F. W. Taussig, Simon Newcomb, and others. *Science Economic Discussion*. New York: Science, 1886.

Endres, A. M. "Veblen and Commons on Goodwill: A Case of Theoretical Divergence." *History of Political Economy* 17 (1985): 637–49.

Ewen, Stuart. *A Social History of Spin*. New York: Basic Books, 1996.

Ezechial, Mordecai. "Studies of the Effectiveness of Individual Farm Enterprise." *Journal of Farm Economics* 8 (January, 1926): 86–101.

Fabricant, Solomon. *Toward a Firmer Basis for Economic Policy: The Founding of the National Bureau of Economic Research*. New York: NBER, 1984. Accessed November 14, 2013. www.nber.org/nberhistory/sfabricantrev.pdf.

Fels, Rendig. "The Long-Wave Depression, 1873–1897." *The Review of Economics and Statistics* 31 (February, 1949): 69–73.

Fetter, Frank, A. *The Masquerade of Monopoly*. New York: Harcourt Brace and Company, 1931.

Fink. Leon. *Progressive Intellectuals and the Dilemma of Democratic Commitment*. Cambridge, MA: Harvard University Press, 1997.

———. "A Memoir of Selig Perlman and His Life at the University of Wisconsin: Based on an Interview of Mark Perlman Conducted and Edited by Leon Fink." *Labor History* 32 (Fall 1991): 503–25.

Finney, Charles, G. *The Memoirs of Charles G. Finney: The Complete Restored Text*, edited by Garth M. Rosell and Richard A. G. Dupuis. 1876. 1975. Reprint. Grand Rapids, MI: Zondervan Press, 1989.

———. *Lectures on the Revival of Religion*. Cambridge, MA: Harvard University Press, 1960.

Fiorito, Luca. "John R. Commons, Wesley N. Hohfeld and the Origins of Transactional Economics." *History of Political Economy* 42 (Summer 2010): 267–95.

Fisher, Irving. *Booms and Depressions: Some First Principles*. New York: Adelphi Company. 1932.

———. *100% Money Designed to Keep Checking Banks 100% Liquid to Prevent Inflations and Deflations, Largely to Cure or Prevent Depressions and to Wipe Out Much of Our National Debt*. New York: Adelphi, 1935.

———, and Cohrssen, H. *Stable Money: A History of the Movement*. New York: Adelphi Company, 1934.

Fisher, Irving Norton. 1956. *My Father Irving Fisher* New York: Cornet Press.

Fitch, John, A *The Steelworkers*. 1910. Reprint. New York: Arno Press, 1969.

Bibliography

———. "The Steel Industry and the People of Colorado." *The Survey* 27, no. 18 (February 3, 1912): 1706–22.

———. "Law and Order: The Issue in Colorado." *The Survey* 33, no. 10 (December 5, 1914): 241–58.

Fleisher, Alexander "Review of Labor and Administration." *Annals of the American Academy of Political and Social Science* 52 (March, 1914): 244–45.

Fleming, Thomas. *The Illusion of Victory America in World War I.* New York: Basic Books, 2003.

Foner, Philip. *History of the Labor Movement in America.* 10 vols. New York: International Publishers, 1947–1994.

Forbath, William. "The Ambiguities of Free Labor: Labor and the Law in the Gilded Age." *Wisconsin Law Review* (July–August, 1985): 767–825.

Foerster, Robert. "Commons and Andrews' Principles of Labor Legislation." *Quarterly Journal of Economics* 30, no. 3 (May, 1916): 566–75.

Fox, Henry Clay. *Memoirs of Wayne County and the City of Richmond Indiana.* 1912. Reprint. La Crosse, WI: Brookhaven Press, 2004.

Frankfurter, Felix, Molly Dewson, and John R. Commons. *State Minimum Wage Laws in Practice.* New York: National Consumers' League, 1924.

Furner, Mary, O. Advocacy and Objectivity: A Crisis in the Professionalization of American Social Science 1865–1905. Lexington: University of Kentucky Press, 1975.

———." Knowing Capitalism." In *The State and Economic Knowledge: The American and British Experience.* Edited by Mary O. Furner and Barry Supple, 241–86. New York: Woodrow Wilson International Center for Scholars and Cambridge University Press, 1990.

Galbraith, John Kenneth. *The Affluent Society.* Boston, MA: Houghton-Mifflin, 1958.

Gasparini, Innocenzo. "Approaches to the General Theory of Wage Rates." In *The Theory of Wage Determination: Proceedings of a Conference held by the International Economic Association*, edited by John T. Dunlop, 39–47. New York: St. Martin's Press, 1964.

Gehring, Wes, G. "Kin Hubbard's Abe Martin: A Transition in American Humor." *Indiana Magazine of History* 78 (March 1982): 26–37.

Genovese, Frank, C. "In Memoriam: Robert J. Lampman 1920–1997." *American Journal of Economics and Sociology* (January 1998): 115–18.

George, Henry. *Progress and Poverty.* 1879. Reprint New York: Walter J. Black, 1941.

Gephart, W. F. "The Stabilization of Prices and Business: Discussion." *American Economic Review* 15 (March, 1925): 66–67.

Getze, George. "Second Reprieve Saves Youth 17." *Pittsburgh Courier* (May 18, 1946): 1, 4.

Gitelman, Howard. *The Legacy of the Ludlow Massacre: A Chapter in American Industrial Relations.* Philadelphia: University of Pennsylvania Press, 1988.

Gonce, Richard, A. "The New Property Rights Approach and Commons's *Legal Foundations of Capitalism." Journal of Economic Issues* 10, no. 4 (December 1976): 765–97.

———. "John R. Commons's Five Big Years 1899–1904." *Journal of Economics and Sociology* 61, no. 4 (October 2002): 755–77.

Green, James. *Death in the Haymarket.* New York: Pantheon Books, 2006.

Green, Marguerite. 1956. *The National Civic Federation and the Labor Movement 1900–1925.* Washington, DC: Catholic University Press.

Gregory, T. F. "What do Central Banks Really Do?" *American Economic Review* 15 (March, 1925): 53–59.

Groves, Harold. *In and Out of the Ivory Tower.* Madison: Wisconsin Historical Society, 1962.

Gruchy, Alan G. "Review of *The Economics of Collective Action.*" *Journal of Farm Economics* 33 (May, 1951): 263–65.

Hamilton, Walton, H. "Hoxie Robert Franklin." In *Dictionary of American Biography*, Vol. 9, edited by Dumas Malone, 316–17. New York: Scribners, 1932.

———. "The Institutional Approach to Economic Theory." *American Economic Review* 9 (March, 1919): 309–18.

Handy, Robert, T. "George D. Herron and the Kingdom Movement." *Church History* 19 (June 1950): 97–115.

———. *The Social Gospel in America 1870–1920.* New York: Oxford University Press, 1966.

Hanes, Christopher "Price and Price Indexes." In *Historical Statistics of the United States Millennial Edition*, edited by Susan B. Carter, Scott Sigmund Gartner, Michael R. Haines, Alan L. Olmstead, Richard Sutch, and Gavin Wright. Vol. 3 of 5,, pp. 3-147-3-157. New York: Cambridge University Press, 2006.

Hansen, Alvin. *Cycles of Prosperity and Depression in the United States, Great Britain, and Germany 1902–1908.* Madison: University of Wisconsin Press, 1921.

——— "The Effect of Price Fluctuations on Agriculture." *Journal of Political Economy* 33 (April, 1925): 196–216.

———. "Contributions of Professor John R. Commons to American Economics." Alvin Hansen Papers. Harvard University Archives, HUGFP-3.42 Box 1.

———. *A Guide to Keynes.* New York: McGraw-Hill, 1953.

Hansen, Bent. "Unemployment, Keynes, and the Stockholm School." *History of Political Economy* 13 (Summer, 1981): 257–77.

Hansen, W. Lee, James F. Bryce, and Jan Levine Thai. *Unemployment Insurance the Second Half Century.* Madison: University of Wisconsin Press, 1990.

Harriman, Florence. *From Pinafores to Politics.* New York: Henry Holt, 1923.

Harrod, Roy. *The Life of John Maynard Keynes.* New York: Basic Books, 1963.

Harter, Lafayette, G. *John R. Commons: His Assault on Laissez-Faire.* Corvallis: Oregon State University Press, 1962.

Hawkins, Hugh. *Pioneer: A History of the Johns Hopkins University 1874–1889.* Ithaca, NY: Cornell University Press, 1960.

Hawley, W. Ellis. "Herbert Hoover the Commerce Secretariat and the Vision of an Associative State." *Journal of American History* 61 (June, 1974): 116–40.

Heiss, William, C. *Abstracts of Records of the Society of Friends in Indiana.* Indianapolis: Indiana Historical Society, 1962.

Henderson, Gerard, C. "Legal Foundations of Capitalism Review." *Harvard Law Review* 37 (7) (March, 1924): 923–27.

Bibliography

Henderson, John, P. "Political Economy and the Service of the State: The University of Wisconsin." In *Breaking the Academic Mould: Economists and American Higher Learning in the Nineteenth Century*, edited by William J. Barber, 318–39. Middlesex, CT: Wesleyan University Press, 1988.

Herbst, Jurgen. *The German Historical School in American Scholarship: A Study in the Transfer of Culture.* Ithaca, NY: Cornell University Press, 1965.

Hicks, John R. *The Theory of Wages.* 1932. Reprint. New York: St. Martin's Press, 1966.

Hinshaw, Gregory. *Indiana Friends Heritage 1821–1996. The 175th Anniversary History of Indiana Yearly Meeting of Friends (Quakers)*, 1995.

Hoag, Clarence Gilbert and George Harvey Hallett. 1926. *Proportional Representation.* New York: Macmillan.

Hohfeld, Wesley, Newcomb. "Some Fundamental Legal Conceptions as Applied to Legal Reasoning." *Yale Law Journal* 23 (November 1913): 16–59.

Holland, Thomas Erskine. *Elements of Jurisprudence.* 7th ed. London: Clarendon Press, 1895.

Hoover, David. *Memoir of David Hoover, Pioneer of Indiana.* 1854 Reprint Edited by Isaac H. Julian. Richmond, IN: James Elder, 1967.

http://www.mrlinfo.org/history/dhoover/index.htm.

Hopkins, C. Howard. *The Rise of the Social Gospel in American Protestantism 1865–1915.* New Haven, CT: Yale University Press, 1967.

Horwitz, Morton. *The Transformation of American Law 1780–1960.* Cambridge, MA: Harvard University Press, 1977.

———. *The Transformation of American Law 1870–1960.* New York: Oxford University Press, 1992.

Howe, Florence. "Practical in Her Theories Theresa McMahon 1878–1961." In *Lonely Voyagers Academic Women in Coeducational Universities 1870–1937.* Edited by Geraldine Clifford, 223–80. New York: Feminist Press at CCNY, 1989.

Hoxie, Robert, F. *Trade Unionism in the United States.* 1923. Reprint. New York: Russell & Russell, 1966.

Hovenkamp, Herbert. "Labor Conspiracies in American Law 1880–1930." *Texas Law Review* 66 (April, 1988): 919–65.

Hudson, Winthrop. *Religion in America: An Historical Account of the Development of American Religious Life.* New York: Charles Scribner's and Sons, 1973.

Hunt, George, L. *Calvinism and the Political Order: Essays Prepared for the Woodrow Wilson Lectureship of the National Presbyterian Center.* Washington, DC: Philadelphia, PA: Westminster Press, 1965.

Indiana Public Media. "A Fledgling Historian Takes on Reconstruction." Accessed August 27, 2012. Indianapublicmedia.org/momentsofindianahistory/fledglinghistorian-tsakes-on-reconstruction.

Indiana Student. 19 (February, 1893) Bloomington: University of Indiana.

Irons, Peter. *A People's History of the Supreme Court.* New York: Penguin Press, 2006.

Isserman, Maurice. "'God Bless our American Institutions': The Labor History of John R. Commons." *Labor History* 17 (Spring 1976): 310–28.

Hoover, David. 1857. *Memoirs of David Hoover.* Richmond, Indiana, James Elder, Publisher http://www.mrlinfo.org/history/dhoover/index.htm.

James, Clifford. "Commons on Institutional Economics." *American Economic Review* 27 (March, 1937): 61–75.

James, J., and M. Thomas. "Romer Revisited Changes in the Cyclical Sensitivity of Unemployment." *Cliometrica* 11 (2007): 19–40.

Jenks, Jeremiah. "The Trust: Facts established and Problems Unsolved." *Quarterly Journal of Economics* 15 (1900): 46–74.

Jo, Tae Hee and John Henry. "The Business Enterprise in the Age of Money and Capitalism." *Journal of Economic Issues* 29, no. 1 (March, 2015): 23–46.

Johns Hopkins University. *Johns Hopkins University Circulars.* Volume 8 No. 68 (November, 1888). Accessed November 4, 2010. https://jscholarship. library.jhu.edu/handle/1774.2/32721.

Johns Hopkins University 1889. *Johns Hopkins University Circulars.* Volume 9 No. 79 (November, 1889). Accessed November 4, 2010. https://jscholarship. library.jhu.edu/handle/1774.2/32721.

Jones, Rufus, M. *Later Periods of Quakerism.* 2 vols. London: Macmillan, 1921.

Jordan, Ryan, P. *Slavery and the Meetinghouse: The Quakers and the Abolitionist Dilemma 1820–1865.* Bloomington and Indianapolis: Indiana University Press, 2007.

Kates, Steven. "A Letter from Keynes to Harlan McCracken Dated 31st of August 1933 Why the Standard Story on the Origins of the General Theory Needs to Be Rewritten." *History of Economics Review* 47 (Winter, 2008): 39–42.

Kaufman, Bruce. *The Origins and Evolution of the Field of Industrial Relations in the United States.* Ithaca, NY: Cornell Studies in Industrial Relations, 1993.

———. *The Global Evolution of Industrial Relations: Events, Ideas, and the IIRA.* Geneva: International Labor Office, 2004.

Kellogg, Paul. U. "Conservation and Industrial War." *The Survey* 27 (December 30, 1911).

———. "Industrial Relations Statistics or Program." *The Survey* 31, no. 6 (November 8m 1913): 152–53.

———. "Editorials." *The Survey* 33 (October 10, 1914): 51–54.

Kemp, Thomas. *Progress and Reform: The Economic Thought of John R. Commons.* Saarbrucken: VDM, 2009.

Kennedy, Duncan, and Frank Michelman. "Are Property and Contract Efficient." *Hofstra Law Review* 8, no. 3 (1980): 718–70. Accessed December 28, 2013. http://scholarlycommons.law.hofstra.edu/hlr/vol8/iss3/10/.

Kerr, K. Austin. *Organized for prohibition: A New History of the Anti-Saloon League.* New Haven, CT and London: Yale University Press, 1985.

Keynes, John, M. *The Economic Consequences of the Peace.* New York: Harcourt, Brace and Howe, 1920.

———. "The Economic Transition in England." In *Activities 1922–1930 the Return to Gold and Industrial Policy* Vol. 19 pt.1 of *The Collected Writings of John Maynard Keynes: Activities.* Edited by Donald Moggridge, 438–42. 1925 Reprint. London: Macmillan Cambridge University Press for the Royal Economic Society, 1981.

Bibliography

———. *Essays in Persuasion*. Edited by Donald Moggridge. 1931.Reprint. New York: Cambridge University Press, 2013.

———. *The General Theory of Employment, Interest, and Money*. 1936. Reprint. Amherst, New York: Prometheus Press, 1997.

Kimeldorf, Howard. "Bringing Unions Back In (Or Why We Need a New Old Labor History)." *Labor History* 32, no. 1 (Winter 1991): 29–104.

Kinvig, Clifford. *Churchill's Crusade: The British Invasion of Russia 1918–1920*. London: Humbledon Continuum, 2006.

Knight, Frank, H. "Institutional Economics: Its place in Political Economy." *Columbia Law Review* 35 (May, 1935): 803–5.

Kocurek, Albert. "The Hohfeld System of Fundamental Legal Concepts." *Illinois Law Review* 15 (May 1920): 24–39.

Kuhn, Clifford, M. *Contesting the New South Order: The 1914–1915 Strike at Atlanta's Fulton Mills.* Chapel Hill: University of North Carolina Press, 2001.

LaFollette, Robert, M. *LaFollette's Autobiography*. 1911&1913. Reprint. Madison: University of Wisconsin Press, 1960.

Lamoreaux, Naomi, P. *The Great Merger Movement in American Business, 1894–1904.* New York: Cambridge University Press, 1985.

Lampman, Robert. 1954. "Recent Changes in Inequality Reconsidered." *American Economic Review* 44 (June, 1955): 251–68.

———. 1957a. "Recent Thought on Egalitarianism." *Quarterly Journal of Economics* 71 (May, 1957): 234–66.

———. 1957b. "The Effectiveness of Some Institutions in Changing the Distribution of Income." *American Economic Review: Papers and Proceedings of the Sixty-Eighth Annual Meeting of the American Economic Association* 47 (May, 1957): 519–28.

———. 1959 "The Low Income Population and Economic Growth." In *Study Papers Nos. 12 and 13. Materials Prepared in Connection with Study of Employment, Growth and Price Levels for Consideration of the Joint Economic Committee Congress of the United States.* 86th Congress 1st Session, 1–34. Washington, DC: Government Printing Office, 1959.

———. "Approaches to the Reduction of Poverty." *American Economic Review* 55 (March, 1965): 521–29.

———, ed. 1992. *Economists at Wisconsin 1892–1992*. Madison: Board of Regents of the University of Wisconsin System.

Lebergott, Stanley. 1964. *Manpower in Economic Growth*. New York: McGraw-Hill, 1964.

Lee, R. Alton. 1966. "The Eradication of Phossy Jaw: A Unique Development of Federal Police Power." *The Historian* 29 (November): 1–21.

Lescohier, Don, D. "Working Conditions." In *History of Labor in the United States, 1896–1932*, Edited by John R. Commons and Associates, 3–396. 4 vols. 1935. Reprint. New York: Augustus M. Kelley, 1966.

Lescohier, Don, D. *My Story for the for the First Seventy-Seven years*. Madison, WI: Air Brush Creations, 1960.

Levin, Murray. *Political Hysteria in America: The Democratic Capacity for Repression.* New York: Basic Books, 1971.

Lichtenstein, Nelson. *State of the Union: A Century of American Labor.* Princeton, NJ: Princeton University Press, 2002.

Lindley, D. Clark. "Review of *Principles of Labor Legislation* by John R. Commons and John B. Andrews." *Journal of Political Economy* 24 (November, 1916): 903–6.

L. H. "The IWW on Trial." *The Outlook* 19 (July, 1918): 448–50.

Link, Arthur, S. "Federal Reserve Policy and the Agricultural Depression of 1920–1921." *Agricultural History* 20, no. 3 (July, 1946): 166–73.

Link, Arthur, S. "What Happened to the Progressive Movement." *American Historical Review* 64 (July, 1959): 833–51.

Llewellyn, Karl. "The Effect of Legal Institutions upon Economics." *American Economic Review* 15, no. 4 (December 1925): 665–83.

Lobdell, Robert, A. "Helen Laura Sumner Woodbury (1873–1933)." In *A Biographical Dictionary of Women Economists*, edited by Robert W. Dimand, Mary Ann Dimand and Evelyn L. Forget. Northampton, MA: Edward Elgar, 2000.

Lonergan, Bernard. *Insight: A Study of Human Understanding.* New York: Harper and Row, 1978.

Lowi, Theodore. *The End of Liberalism.* New York: Norton, 1969.

Lubbé, Ronald, and Jonathan Lurie. *The Slaughterhouse Cases. Regulation, Reconstruction and the Fourteenth Amendment.* Lawrence: University of Kansas Press, 2003.

Madison, James. *The Indiana Way: A State History.* Bloomington and Indianapolis: Indiana University Press, 1986.

Manly, Basil, M. "To the Editor." *The Survey* 33, no. 11 (December 12, 1914): 304.

Manly, Marie Bradley. "To My Posterity." Accessed October 21, 2009. http://squareknotdesign.com/history/to posterity/ page1.htm.

Marshall, Alfred. *Principles of Economics.* 6th ed. London: Macmillan, 1910.

———. *Principles of Economics.* 8th ed. Philadelphia, PA: Porcupine Press, 1920.

Martin, Mary. *The Corpse on Boomerang Road Telluride's War on Labor 1899–1908.* Montrose, CO: Western Reflections Publishing Company, 2004.

Mayhew, Ann, and Gary Dymski. "John R Commons in the Twenty-First Century: Introduction." *Journal of Economic Issues* 48 (December, 2014).

Mazzini, Giuseppe." The Duties of Man." In *The Duties of Man and Other Essays* edited by Joseph Mazzini, 7–122. 1907. Reprint. New York: E.P. Dutton, 1961.

McCarthy, Charles. *The Wisconsin Idea.* New York: Macmillan, 1912.

McCartin, Joseph, A. *Labor's Great War: The Struggle for Industrial Democracy and the Origins of Modern Industrial Relations.* Chapel Hill and London: University of North Carolina Press, 1997.

McCracken, Harlan, L. *Value Theory and Business Cycles.* Binghamton, NY: Falcon Press, 1933.

———. *Keynesian Economics in the Stream of Economic Thought.* Baton Rouge, LA: Louisiana University Press, 1961.

McGovern, George, S., and Leonard M. Guttridge. *The Great Coalfield War.* Boston, MA: Houghton-Mifflin, 1972.

Bibliography

McMahon, Theresa. *Women and Economic Evolution; or The Effects of Industrial Changes on the Evolution of Women. Bulletin of the University of Wisconsin no. 496.of Economics and Political Science Series.* Madison: University of Wisconsin, 1912.

———. "My Story," 1958 Reprinted in *Lone Voyagers.* Edited by Geraldine Jonich Clifford. New York: The Feminist Press at The City University of New York, 1989.

McNulty, Paul, J. *The Origins and Development of Labor Economics: A Chapter in the History of Social Thought.* Cambridge, MA: MIT Press, 1980.

Miller, Adolph, C. "*The Distribution of Wealth.* By John R. Commons." *Journal of Political Economy* 2 (June 1894): 462–64.

Meltzer, Allan, H. *A History of the Federal Reserve 1913–1951.* Vol. 1. Chicago, IL: University of Chicago Press, 2003.

Miller, Harold, L. "The American Bureau of Industrial Research and the Origins of the 'Wisconsin School' of Labor History." *Labor History* 25 (Spring 1984): 165–88.

Miller, John, E. "From South Dakota Farm to Harvard Seminar: Alvin H. Hansen, America's Prophet of Keynesianism." *Historian* 64 (Spring/Summer 2002): 603–22.

Millis, H. A. "Unemployment in the Men's Clothing Industry of Chicago." *The University School of Business* 2 (March 1924): 157–68.

———, and Emily Clark Brown. *From the Wagner Act to Taft-Hartley.* Chicago, IL: University of Chicago Press, 1950.

Milwaukee Journal. "Urges Teaching Only of English: Prof. J.R. Commons Favors Re-enacting Law Making This Mandatory." *Milwaukee Journal* (May 4, 1918) Commons Papers, Microfilm Reel 22, frame 9.

Misak, Cheryl. *Truth, Politics, Morality.* New York: Routledge, 2000.

Mitchell, Wesley Clair. "Commons on the Legal Foundations of Capitalism." *American Economic Review* 14 (June 1924): 240–51.

———. "Commons on Institutional Economics." *American Economic Review* 25 (December, 1935): 635–52.

Monroe, James. *A Journey to Virginia, 1859. A Thursday Lecture.* www.oberlin.edu/external/EOG/History/monroe.html Extracted September 5, 2010.

Montgomery, David. "To Study the People: The American Working Class." *Labor History* 21 (Fall, 1980): 495–512.

———. *Beyond Equality: Labor and the Radical Republicans 1862–1872:* Urbana: University of Indiana Press, 1981.

———. *The Fall of the House of Labor: The Workplace, the State, and American Labor Activism, 1865–1925.* New York: Cambridge University Press, 1987.

Montrose, Mary Joy. *The Corpse on Boomerang Road: Telluride's War on Labor 1899–1908.* Montrose, CO: Western Reflections Publishers, 2004.

Moore, Joel R., Harry H. Mead, and Lewis E. Jahns. *The History of the American Expedition fighting the Bolsheviki in North Russia 1918–1920.* Detroit, MI: Polar Bear Publishing, 1920.

Moorhead, James, H. "Charles Finney and the Modernization of America." *Journal of Presbyterian History* 62 (Summer, 1984): 95–110.

Morris, Clair. "Ely's Rivalry with James L. Laughlin." In *Economists at Wisconsin 1892–1992*. Edited by Robert Lampman. Madison: The Board of Regents of the University of Wisconsin System, 1993.

Morris, J. Brent. *Oberlin, Hotbed of Abolitionism*. Chapel Hill, NC: University of North Carolina Press, 2014.

Morton, Walter, A. "The Aims of Unemployment Insurance with Especial Reference to the Wisconsin Act." *American Economic Review* 23 (September, 1933): 395–412.

Moss, David, A. *Socializing Security: Progressive Era Economists and the Origins of American Social Policy*. Cambridge, MA: Harvard University Press, 1996.

Moulton, Harold. *The Formation of Capital*. Washington, DC: The Brookings Institution, 1935.

_____. *Income and Economic Progress*. Washington, DC: The Brookings Institution, 1935.

Moynihan, Daniel, P. *Maximum Feasible Misunderstanding*. New York: The Free Press, 1969.

Murphy, Bruce, Allen. *The Brandeis/Frankfurter Connection: The Secret Political Activities of Two Supreme Court Justices*. New York: Oxford University Press, 1982.

Murray, Robert. *Red Scare: A Study in National Hysteria 1919–1920*. New York: McGraw-Hill, 1964.

Nelson, Daniel. "The Origins of Unemployment Insurance in Wisconsin." *The Wisconsin Magazine of History* 51(Winter 1967–1968): 109–21.

[Newcomb, Simon]. "Dr. Ely and the Labor Movement." *The Nation* (October 7, 1886): 293–94.

Newman, Daisy. *A Procession of Friends: Quakers in America*. Garden City, NY: Doubleday & Co, 1972.

Ohlin, Bertil. "Some Notes on the Stockholm Theory of Saving and Investment." *Economic Journal* 47, no. 185 (March 1937): 53–69.

Olson, Mancur. *The Logic of Collective Action*. 2nd ed. Cambridge, MA: Harvard University Press, 1971.

Ortiz. Stephen, R. "Rethinking the Bonus March: Federal Bonus Policy, the Veterans of Foreign Wars, and the Origins of the Protest movement." *The Journal of Policy History* 18 (July, 2006): 275–303.

Ostrom, Elinor. *Governing the Commons: The Evolution of Institutions for Collective Action*. New York: Cambridge University Press, 1991.

Ostrom, Vincent. "John R. Commons's Foundations for Policy Analysis." *Journal of Economic Issues* 10 (December, 1976): 839–57.

Papke, David, Ray. 1999. *The Pullman Case: The Clash of Labor and Capital in Industrial America*. Lawrence: University of Kansas Press.

Parsons, Kenneth. "John R. Commons Point of View." *Journal of Land and Public Utility Economics* 18 (August, 1942): 245–66. Reprinted in *The Economics of Collective Action* by John R. Commons. New York: Macmillan: 341–75.

———. "Editor's Preface." *The Economics of Collective Action*, edited by John R. Commons. New York: Macmillan, 1950: v-x.

———. "Introduction." In *The Economics of Collective Action*, edited by John R., 9–18. Commons. New York: Macmillan, 1950.

Bibliography

Perlman, Mark. *The Character of Economic Thought, Economic Characters and Economic Institutions.* Ann Arbor: University of Michigan Press, 1996.

Perlman, Selig. 1918. "Upheavals and Reorganization." In *History of Labor in the United States Volume II.* Edited by John R. Commons and others, 195–501. Reprint. New York: Augustus M. Kelley, 1966.

———. "John Rogers Commons 1862–1945." *American Economic Review* 35 (September 1945): 782–86.

———. "John Rogers Commons 1862–1945." In *The Economics of Collective Action,* edited by John R. Commons, 1–7. New York: Macmillan, 1950.

Peirce, Charles Sanders. *The Essential Peirce: Selected Philosophical Writings.* Edited by Nathan Houser and Christian Kloesel. 5 vols. Bloomington and Indianapolis: Indiana University press, 1992.

Plummer, John, T. 1957. *Reminiscences of the History of Richmond.* Richmond, Indiana: R.O. Domer and W.R. Holloway. Extracted March 22, 2015. http://www.mrlinfo.org/history/plummer/plummer1.htm.

Potts, David, P. *Wesleyan University 1831–1910.* New Haven, CT and London: Yale University Press. 1992.

"Prof Commons." *Indiana Student* 19 (February, 1893): 18–19.

Prof John R. Commons. *Indianapolis News* (January 3, 1894): 5.

"Professor Commons at Seventy." *The Survey* 68, no. 17 (December 15. 1932): 674.

Rader, Benjamin, G. *The Academic Mind and Reform: The Influence of Richard T. Ely in American Life.* Lexington: University of Kentucky Press, 1966.

Ramirez, Bruno. *When Workers fight: The Politics of Industrial Relations in the Progressive Era, 1898–1916.* Westport, CT and London: Greenwood Press, 1978.

Ramstad, Yngve. "Fair Trade versus Free Trade: Import Barriers as a Problem of Reasonable Value." *Journal of Economic Issues* 21 (March 1937): 5–32.

———. "Reasonable Value' versus 'Instrumental Value." *Journal of Economic Issues* 23 (September, 1989): 761–77.

———. "John R Commons's Reasonable Value and the Problem of the Just Price." *Journal of Economic Issues* 35 (June, 2001): 252–77.

Reed, John. *Ten Days that Shook the World.* 1922; Reprint. New York: International Publishers, 1967.

Richards, Lawrence. *Union-Free America: Workers and Antiunion Culture.* Urbana and Chicago: University of Illinois Press, 2008.

Ripley, William, Z. *Main Street and Wall Street.* Boston, MA: Little Brown and Company, 1927.

Robbins, Lionel. *An Essay on the Nature and Significance of Economic Science.* 2nd ed. London: Macmillan, 1936.

Robinson, Joan. *The Economics of Imperfect Competition.* London: MacMillan, 1933.

Romer, Christina. "Spurious Volatility in Historical Unemployment Data." *Journal of Political Economy* 94, no. 1 (February 1986): 1831–958.

Ross, Edward, A. *Social Control: A Survey of the Foundations of Order.* 1901 Reprint Cleveland, OH: Case Western Reserve University, 1969.

———. *Seventy Years of It: An Autobiography.* New York and London: D. Appleton-Century Company, 1936.

Ross, Dorothy. *The Origins of American Social Science.* New York. Cambridge University Press, 1991.

Rutherford, Malcolm. "J.R. Commons's Institutional Economics." *Journal of Economic Issues* 17 (September, 1983): 721–44.

———. "Wisconsin Institutionalism: John R Commons and His Students." *Labor History* 47, no. 2 (May, 2006): 161–88.

———. "Did Commons Have Few Followers? Continuing My Conversation with Yngve Ramstad." *Journal of Economic Issues* 43 (June 2009): 441–49.

———. 2011. *The Institutionalist Movement in American Economics, 1918–1947.* New York: Cambridge University Press.

———, and Warren Samuels. *John R. Commons Selected Essays.* New York: Routledge, 1996.

Sandoz, Ellis. *The Voegelinian Revolution: A Biographical Introduction.* Baton Rouge: Louisiana State University, 1982.

Saposs, David, J. "The American Labor Movement Since the War." *Quarterly Journal of Economics* 49 (February 1935): 236–54.

Schlabach, Theron. *Edwin E. Witte Cautious Reformer.* Madison: State Historical Society of Wisconsin, 1969.

Schneider, Samuel. *Three American Economics Professors Battle against Monopoly and Pricing Practices: Ripley, Fetter, and Commons: Three for the People.* Lewiston, NY: Edward Mellen Press, 1998.

Schumpeter, Joseph, A. *History of Economic Analysis.* New York: Oxford University Press, 1974.

Schwarz, John, E. 1988. *America's Hidden Success.* Revised Edition. New York: W.W. Norton.

Shambaugh, Bertha, H, 1908. *Amana: The Community of True Inspiration.* Reprint. Iowa City, IA: Penfield Press, 1988.

Skocpol, Theda and John Ikenberry. "The Road to Social Security." In *Social Policy in the United States: Future Possibilities in Historical Perspectives.* Edited by Theda Skocpol. Princeton, NJ: Princeton University Press, 1995.

Seager, Henry, R. *Labor Problems: A Text-Book*, edited by Thomas Sewall Adams and Helen L. Sumner, *Political Science Quarterly* 20 (September, 1905): 562–65.

———. *Social Insurance.* New York: Macmillan, 1910.

Simon, Herbert. *Models of My Life.* New York: Basic Books, 1992.

Smith, Adam. *An Inquiry into the Nature and Causes of the Wealth of Nations*, 3rd ed. 1784. Reprint. Edited by Edwin Canaan. London: Methuen & Co. 2 vols. 1922.

Smith, John, L and Lee L. Driver. *Past and Present of Randolph County.* Indianapolis, IN: A.L. Bowen, 1914.

Smith, Richmond, Mayo "*The Distribution of Wealth* by John R. Commons." *Political Science Quarterly* 9 (Septembers 1894): 568–72.

Smith, Sir Thomas. *De Republica Anglorum A Discourse on the Commonwealth of England,* edited by L. Alston. Cambridge: Cambridge University press, 1906. Accessed June 19, 2014. http://www.mindserpent.com/American_History/books/Smith_Thomas/1583_smith_commonwealth_of_england.pdf.

Bibliography

Starbuck, Dana. 2001. *The Goodriches.* Indianapolis. Library of Liberty— Online version. Accessed September 29, 2010. app.libraryofliberty.org/ option=com&staticfile=show.php%Ftitle=1065& chapter=1.

Starr, Paul. 1962. *The Transformation of American Medicine.* New York: Basic Books.

Steeples, Douglas W. and David O. Whitten. *Democracy in Desperation: The Depression of 1893.* Westport, CN: Greenwood Press, 1998.

Stein, Leon and Philip Taft. 1971. *Massacre at Ludlow.* New York: Arno and New York Times Press.

Steffens, Lincoln. 1911. "An Experiment in Good Will." *The Survey* 27, no. 13 (December 1911): 1434–36.

Stone, Katherine, V. W. 2010. "John R. Commons and the Origin of Legal Realism; or the Other Tragedy of the Commons." In *Transformations in American Legal History: Law, Ideology, and Methods: Essays in Honor of Morton Horwitz*, Vol. II; 326–43. Cambridge, MA: Harvard University Press, 2010.

Stone, N. I. "The Beginnings of the National Bureau of Economic Research." In *The National Bureau's First Quarter Century*, 5–11. New York: NBER, 1945.

Strum, Phillippa. *Louis D. Brandeis.* Cambridge, MA: Harvard University Press, 1984

Sullivan, James, W. "Labor." In National Civic Federation. 1907. *Municipal and Private Operation of Public Utilities: Report of the National Civic Federation on Public Ownership and Operation.* Vol. 1, 60–87. New York: National Civic Federation, 1907.

Syracuse University. *The University Forum* 4 Vols. Syracuse, NY: Syracuse University, 1895–1898.

Syracuse University. *Trustees' Minutes February 22–24 1870-June 6, 1907.* Syracuse, NY: Syracuse University Press, 1909.

Sullivan, James, W. "Labor." In National Civic Federation. 1907. *Municipal and Private Operation of Public Utilities: Report of the National Civic Federation on Public Ownership and Operation.* Vol. 1 of 3, 60–87. New York: National Civic Federation, 1907.

———. *Municipal and Private Operation of Public Utilities; Relative to the Report of the National Civic Federation Commission on Public Ownership and Operation.* New York: Bible House, 1908.

Taft, Philip. *Organized Labor in American History.* New York: Harper & Row, 1964.

———. "Selig Perlman as a Teacher and Writer." *Industrial and Labor Relations Review* 29 (January 1976): 249–57.

Taylor, Alonzo, E. "The Decline of Prices in Cereals." *Journal of Farm Economics* 4 (October, 1922): 193–208.

Tawney, R. H. "Legal Foundations of Capitalism: Review." *Economica* 13 (March, 1924): 104–5.

Tead, Ordway. "Trade Unions and Efficiency." *American Journal of Sociology* 22 (July, 1916): 30–37.

Trelevan, J. E. "The Milwaukee Bureau of Economy and Efficiency." *Annals of the American Academy of Political and Social Science* 41 (May, 1912): 270–78.

Trumbull, Gunnar. *Strength in Numbers: The Political Power of Weak Interests.* Cambridge, MA: Harvard University Press, 2012.

Tucker, Ebenezer. 1882. *History of Randolph County, Indiana with Illustrations and a Biographical sketch of its Prominent Men and Pioneers to Which Are Appended Maps of Several Townships.* Chicago: A.G. Kingman 1882. Reprint. Knightstown, IN: Eastern Indiana Publishing Co., 1967.

United States Bureau of Labor. *Bulletin, No. 98* "Industrial Courts in France., Germany, and Switzerland," by Helen L. Sumner. Washington, DC: Government Printing Office, 1912.

United States Commission on Industrial Relations (USCIR). *Industrial Relations: Final Report and Testimony Submitted to Congress by the act of August 23, 1912.* Washington, DC: Government Printing Office, 1916.

United States Industrial Commission (USIC). *Report of the Industrial Commission*, 19 vols. Washington, DC: Government Printing Office, 1902.

U.S. House of Representatives. *Hearings before the Committee on Banking and Currency of the House of Representatives 69th Congress, 1st Session on H.R, 7895 February 4, 1927.* Washington, DC: Government Printing Office, 1927. Accessed May 7, 2012. http://babel.hathitrust.org/cgi/pt?id=mdp.39015038790534.

U.S. House of Representatives. *Hearings before the Committee on Banking and Currency of the House of Representatives, 1928. 70th Congress, 1st Session on H. R, 11806.* Washington, DC: Government Printing Office, 1928. Accessed May 17, 2012. http://babel.hathitrust.org/cgi/pt?u=1&num=22&seq=9&view=image&size=100&id=mdp.39015038790559.

U.S. House of Representatives. 1964. *Economic Opportunity Act of 1964.* Public Law 88–420 August 20, 1964. 70 Stat. 508–534.

U.S. Office of the President. *Economic Report of the President* Washington, DC: U.S. Government Printing Office, 1964.

Urofsky, Melvin. *Louis D. Brandeis: A Life.* New York: Pantheon Books, 2009.

Van der Velde, Lea. "The Labor Vision of the Thirteenth Amendment." *University of Pennsylvania Law Review* 138 (December, 1989): 437–504.

Veblen, Thorstein. "Why Is Economics Not an Evolutionary Science." *Quarterly Journal of Economics* 12 (July, 1898): 373–97.

———. *The Theory of Business Enterprise.* 1904. Reprint. New York: A.M. Kelley, 1965.

Viner, Jacob. "Legal Foundations of Capitalism." *Illinois Law Review* 19 (April, 1925): 710–12.

Voegelin, Eric. *On the Form of the American Mind.* Vol. 1 of *The Collected Works of Eric Voegelin*, translated by Ruth Hein. 1928, Reprint. Baton Rouge: Louisiana University Press, 1995, 205–82.

Walling, William English. "The Race War in the North." *The Independent* 65 (September 3, 1908): 529–34.

Ward, Lester, Frank. Review of *What Social Classes Owe Each Other* Man IV (1884)1–4. Reprinted in *Lester Ward and the Welfare State.* Edited by Henry Steele Commager, 78–82. Indianapolis: Bobb-Merrill, 1967.

Warren, George. "The Agricultural Depression." *Quarterly Journal of Economics* 38 (February 1924): 183–213.

Bibliography

Washington Post "Wilbur Joseph Cohen." May 19, 1987. A19.

Waugh, Joanna. Florence Kelley and the Anti-Sweatshop Campaign of 1892–1893. *UCLA Historical Journal*, 3(1982). ucla_history_historyjournal_14752. Retrieved from http://escholarship.org/uc/item/6kw872sz.

Weber, Jennifer. *Copperheads: The Rise and Fall of Lincoln's Opponents in the North.* New York: Oxford University Press, 2006.

Weeks, Stephen, B. *Southern Quakers and Slavery: A Study in Institutional History.* 1896. Reprint. Baltimore, MD: Johns Hopkins University Press, 1968.

Weir, David. "A Century of Unemployment 1890–1990." In *Research in Economic History*, edited by Roger L. Ransom, Richard Such, and Susan Carter, 341–42. New York: Jai press, 1992, Table D5.

Wells, Herman, B. *Being Lucky: Reminiscences and Reflections.* Bloomington: Indiana University Press, 1980.

Westbrook, Robert, B. *Democratic Hope: Pragmatism and the Politics of Truth.* Ithaca, NY and London: Cornell University press, 2005.

Westmeyer, Paul. *A History of American Higher Education.* Springfield, IL: Charles C. Thomas, 1985.

Whalen, Charles. "John R Commons and Endogenous Money: A Comment on Niggle." *Journal of Economic Issues* 26 (September 1992): 904–7.

———. "Saving Capitalism by Making It Good: The Monetary Economics of John R Commons." *Journal of Economic Issues* 27 (December 1993): 1115–79.

Wheeler, Kenneth, H. "How Colleges Shaped a Public Culture of Usefulness." In *The Center of a Great Empire; The Ohio Country in the Early Republic.* Edited by Andrew R. L. Cayton and Stuart D. Hobbs, 105–21. Athens: Ohio University Press, 2005.

Who's Who in the Nation's Capital 1921–1922. Washington, DC: The Consolidated Publishing Company, 1921.

Wiebe, Robert. *The Search for Order 1877–1920.* New York: Hill and Wang, 1967.

Williamson, Oliver. *Markets and Hierarchies.* New York: Free Press, 1975.

———. *Economic Organization: Firms, Markets, and Policy Control.* New York: New York University Press, 1986.

Wilson, George. "Education Column." *Jasper (Indiana) Weekly Courier* (April 27, 1894): 1.

Witte, Edwin, E. *The Government in Labor Disputes.* 1932 Reprint. New York: Arno Press, 1969.

———. "An Historical Account of Unemployment Insurance in the Social Security Act." *Law and Contemporary Problems* 3 (January 1936): 157–69.

———. "Institutional Economics as Seen by an Institutional Economist." *Southern Economic Journal* 21 (October, 1954): 131–40.

———. *The Development of the Social Security Act.* Madison: University of Wisconsin, 1962.

Wolfe, A. B. "Institutional Reasonableness and Value." *The Philosophical Review* 45 (March, 1936): 192–206.

Woodburn, James, A. *American Politics, Political Parties, and Party Problems in the United States.* 2nd ed. New York and London: G.P. Putnam, 1914.

Woodburn, James, A. *History of Indiana University.* Bloomington, IN: University, 1940.

Worcester, Dean, A. Jr., and Robert Lampman. "Ability and size of Family in the United States." *Journal of Political Economy* 58 (October, 1950): 430–42.

Wunderlin, Clarence, E. *Visions of a New Industrial Order: Social Science and Labor Theory in America's Progressive Era.* New York: Columbia University Press, 1992.

Yonay, Yuval. *The Struggle over the Soul of Economics.* Princeton, NJ: Princeton University Press, 1998.

Young, Andrew. *History of Wayne County, Indiana from Its First Settlement to the Present Time with Biographical and Family Sketches.* 1872. Reprint. Knightstown: Eastern Indiana Publishing Co., 1967.

Zinn, Howard. *A People's History of the United States.* New York: Harper Collins, 2003.

Index

Adams, Henry Carter 50, 84, 101
Adams, Herbert, Baxter, 30
Adams, Thomas Sewall: Wages, bargaining theory 114–15
Addams, Jane 54, 184
Adkins v. Children's Hospital 185–6
Altgeld, John, Governor 44
Altmeyer, Arthur 3, 165, 184, 214–15
Amana Community 45
American Association for Labor Legislation (AALL) 3, 178; founding, 113–14
American Bureau of Economic Research (ABER) 72–3, 75
American Bureau of Industrial Research (ABIR) 97–8
American Commonwealth 32
American Economic Association 31, 43
American Institute of Christian Sociology 43
American Proportional Representation League 46
American Shoemakers 101–4
Andrews, Irene Osgood 114
Andrews, John Bertram 98–9, 107; executive secretary of AALL 114, 146, 168; unemployment 178–9
Anthracite Strike of 1902 85–9
Anthracite Commission 89
Anti-Saloon League: roles of Clarissa and John R, 24
Archbold, John D.: Syracuse trustee, 53
artificial selection 57–8, 258, 275
Ashley, Sir William: review of *Legal Foundations of Capitalism* 188
Ashtabula, Ohio 14
Austin, John 60

Baldwin, Mark: child psychologist 62
Barnett, George 156, 168–9, 255
Belgian Superior Labor Council 132
Bemis, Edward W. 54, 72
Best, Anna Commons (half-sister) 9, 12, 23
Best, Bertha (Niece) 225; death of 230
Bird, Francis 147, 277, 131
Bisno, Abram 76
Blaine, John, Senator: anti-injunction bill 197
Bogart, Ernest 216
Böhm-Bawerk, Eugen 4, 39, 47–8; horse market story 262–3
Brandeis, Elizabeth 184, 213, 218,
Brandeis, Louis 148; Brandeis Brief 171, 184
British Trade Disputes Act: Manly, Commons, and Harriman on 254
Brook farm 106
Brown, Emily Clark 237–8
Brown, John, Jr. 25
Bryan, William Jennings 42, 84
Bryce, James: Hopkins lectures 32

capital income 47
Capron, William 240–1
Carlyle, Elizabeth (first wife of John A. Commons) 11
Carnegie Foundation 91
Carnegie, Andrew 44, 168
Cassel, Gustav: letter to Commons 203
Chamberlain, Edward 49
Chautauqua Institute 33, 43
Chicago Civic Federation 83
Churchill, Winston 161–2
Claghorn, Kate: immigration report 76; "Progress of the Nation" 77
Clark, John Bates 92
Cleveland Herald 22
Cleveland, Grover 42–4, 83

Cohen, Wilbur 215–16; advisor on poverty and social security 240, 242–3
collective action: control, liberate, expand 59, 106, 199, 216–18, 236–7
Colorado Fuel and Iron Company (CFI) 151–2
Commission on Industrial Relations (USCIR) 144–9
Commons, Alvin (brother) 12, 22; family crisis, 25
Commons, Anne (granddaughter) 209, 231
Commons, Clara (sister) 12, 71, 99, 231; family crisis, 24–5
Commons, Clarissa Rogers (mother) 11–14, 22, 23; arthritis and family crisis, 24–5
Commons, Ella Brown Downey (Nell) (wife) 71, 112, 117; marriage 37; house manager for USIC staff 77; Perlman advocate 163–4; death 204
Commons, Ellen Holland (daughter-in-law) 209
Commons, Frank (son): death 71
Commons, Isaac (grandfather) 10
Commons, John A. (father), 10–11, 23; financial problems, 16–17
Commons, John A.(Jack)(son) 39, 71; Polar Bear regiment 161–2; disappearance 209; reunion 231
Commons, John R. 12–17, 33–4, 37; advisory councils 75, 236, 251–3, 277; agreement with USCIR staff report 248–50; on alleged violence in anthracite strike 87; anthracite interviewer as "Campbell," 86–7; American Shoemakers 101–4; breakdowns 22–3, 157–8 closed shop, case for 138, 236–7; commissioner on industrial commission 133; conflict with Ely 99; constructive democracy 104–7; contract with ABIR 97–8; corporate profit taxes, opposition to 279; defense of small loan bill 210; on dysfunctional legislatures 59; economic power 79–80; correspondence with Sumner on dissent 152–5; education financed by Monroe 27–8; fired from Syracuse, 66–7; fired from Wesleyan 38; on freedom and economic coercion 266–7; on George Junior Republic 56–7; going concern 261–2, 278–80; going plant, going business 278; habitual assumptions 17, 276–8;

Henry George influence, 1–2, 26–7, 32, 46–9; Hohfeld tables modified 264–5; job, right to 49, 65, 268; labor party proposal 137; Legal realism, 49; letters to James Monroe, 31–5; machinery of collective democracy 170–3; Marx Yesterday and Today 198–9; Monetary theory 43; NCF Municipal Utility Study 111–13; NCF work with Easley, 84; order and right, checks on sovereign power 62–4; president of AEA 163; president of National Monetary Association 181; private property, origin 258; property, incorporeal and intangible 259; reaction to George Herron and Amana Community 45; reasonable Value 129–32, 134, 198, 236, 242, 273–8; reflections on "Five Big years" 71–2; research 3, 57–8, 138–9; response to Hadley 66; rights, source of, 48, 61, 274 social statesman and honorary degree 210–12; on structuralist depression views 227–30; student cooperative at Syracuse 54–5; summer with Ward and Dewey 57–8; as teacher 2–3, 39, 41, 54–55, 115–18; testimony before USIC 74–6; testimony on first stable money bill 199–200; tribute to Gompers 193–4; at UMW "industrial parliament" 77; unemployment compensation bill 179; wage bargain 89, 203–4, 212, 225; workers'school 296–7; worker welfare as public purpose 270–1
Commons, Julia Margaret (daughter) death 71
Commons, Mary Townsend (grandmother) 10
Commons, Rachel (daughter) 9, 71, 225
Commons, Robert Sidney (son) death 42
Commons, Robert (great-grandfather) 10
Commons, Rose (daughter) death 71
Commons, William and Sarah Scarlett, Irish immigrant ancestors 9
Company of Shoemakers (Boston) 102
competitive menace 101; defined 84, 170
constructive democracy 104–7
constructive research 134–5
Contraction Act of 1865 42
Cook, Walter: deconstruction of Hitchman v. Mitchell 265–6
Coolidge, Calvin 178, 195
Copeland, John A., Harper's Ferry Raid 25

Index

copperhead 13, historians disagree 19n20
Cordery, Richard 88
Cournot, Auguste 49
Coxey's Army 44
Cross, Ira 117, 168
Crunden, Robert: on Clarissa's influence on John R 17

Darrow, Clarence 44, 89, 143–4: Anthracite report "cowardly" 90
Davidson, James (Yim), Governor 130
Debs, Eugene, V. 15, 44
Dennison, Henry 155
DeTarde, Gabriel 62
Dewey, John: on Austin's theory of sovereignty 60–1
Distribution of Wealth, The 46–9
Documentary History of American Industrial Society 100
Dorfman, Joseph 34, 49; on labor economics, beginning 195
Douglas, Paul H. 155, 238–9; family allowance proposal 195
Dred Scott 276
Durand, E. Dana: secretary USIC 73–4
Durkheim, Émile 62

Easley, Ralph 83–4
Eastman, Crystal 118–19, 130–1, 147
Eliot, Thomas 214
Ely, Richard T. 29, 30, 38, 57, 90–1, 111, 114; book proposal with Commons and Ross 33; conflict with Commons 99; contract with ABIR 97; departure from Wisconsin 195–6; La Follette critic 162; *The Labor Movement in America* 24, trial 50; USIC report comments 77
Emmot, George Henry 33
employee representation plans 172

Fairchild, James 21
Farnam, Henry 99–100, 114, 15
Federal Trade Commission 186–7
Fetter, Frank A. 50, 54; *Masquerade of Monopoly* 187
Finney, Charles G. 12; on usefulness, 21
Fisher, Irving: stable money movement 181, 204–5
Fitch, John, A. 115–16, 119–20, 152
Flynn, Elizabeth Gurley 139, 148
Ford, Henry 169
Fort Lauderdale, FL 225

Fourier, Charles 106
Foxe's Book of Martyrs 13, 17
Frankfurter, Felix: anti-injunction bill 197
Freund, Ernst 155
Fugitive Slave Act 14

Galbraith, John Kenneth 240
Gary, Elbert 186
Genovese, Eugene 243
George Junior Republic 55–7
George, Henry 1, 26–7, 32, 46, 66, 108, 243
George, William Reuben 55
Gilman, Daniel Coit 29–30
Givens, Meredith 211, 215
Glaeser, Martin 113, 227
Goldman, Emma 76
Goldmark, Josephine 171; Brandeis Brief 184–5
Gompers, Samuel 84, 139, 143–4; Death 193–4
Gonce, Richard 92
Goodrich, James Putnam 15–16
Granger cases 260–1
Great Merger Wave 73, 81n13
Greeley, Horace 105–7
Green, Shields: Harper's Ferry Raid 25
Greenback Party 42, 108
Groves, Harold 117; unemployment compensation bill 212–13
Gruchy, Alan 235–6

habitual assumptions 276–7, 278–9
Hadley, Arthur Twining 49–50, 66
Hagerty, Reverend Thomas 139
Hamilton, James: Syracuse associate of Commons 54
Hamilton, Walton: on Hoxie 156–7; on institutional economics 216
Hanna, Mark 84, 87
Hansen, Alvin 82, 212
Harding, Warren 178
Harnack, Adolph 22
Harriman, Florence 146; conflict ending USCIR 154–5
Harter, Lafayette 3, 29
Haymarket Affair, 23–4
Haywood, Big Bill 139, 148
Heller, Walter: Economic Opportunity Act 240–1; Washington departure 241
Herron, George 43, 45, 50

313

Hibbard, Benjamin: investigation of Smoot-Hawley 209
Hill, Joe 139
Hillman, Sidney: president of Amalgamated Clothing Workers 180
History of Labour in the United States 166–8
Hitchman Coal and Coke v. Mitchell 177
Hohfeld, Wesley Newcomb: legal terminology system 263–4; uses 265
Holden V. Hardy 171, 267
Holland, Thomas 47, 60
Homestead Act 106–7
Homestead PA: Lockout 44
Hoosier: defined 15
Hoover, David: Quaker Aristocracy 10
Hoover, Herbert: 178–9; 209
Hopkins, Johns: will interpretation 29
Horowitz, Morton: Commons on property evolution credited 261
Hoxie, Robert 156–7
Huber, Henry Senator and Lt. Governor: unemployment bill 179; critic of small loan bill 210
Hull House 54, 76, 184
Hume, David 274–5

immigration 73, 76–7, 120
institutions 61, 63–5, 144, 216, 252; Commons's article on 216–18; Lampman on 239
Industrial Goodwill 168–72
Industrial Government 173
inheritance tax 249
Institutional Economics 219–20
International Workers of the World (IWW) (Wobblies) 139
Iyenaga, Toyokichi 31

Jackson, Andrew: negative democracy 105
James, William 62
Jenks, Jeremiah 50, 74, 83, 92
Johnson, Lyndon, B, President 241
Jolly, Mrs. Pearl: Ludlow Massacre witness 151

Kelley, Florence 118–19, 184–6
Kellogg, Paul U. 119, 185–6; petition for USCIR 144
Kemp, Thomas 6n5
Kennedy, John F. 240

Keynes, John, Maynard 203, 228; *Economic Consequences of the Peace* 195; liquidity trap 279; Marx Yesterday and Today cited 199; letter to Commons expressing agreement 203
Kiekhofer, William 163; Jack Commons found by 231–2
King, William Lyon Mackenzie 153
Knights of St. Crispin 103
Kinley, David 32
Knight, Frank H. 219–20, 273

La Follette, Philip: "Wisconsin idea" returns 210, 212–14
La Follette, Robert M. (Fighting Bob) 97, 129–30, 145, 162; opponent of war and Espionage and Sedition Acts 162–3; death 194–5
La Follette, Robert M, Jr. 238–9
Labor and Administration 134–8
Labor Movement in America, The. See Ely, Richard, T.
LaGuardia, Fiorello, Representative 214
Lampman, Robert 239; design of Economic Opportunity Act 240–1; negative income tax experiments 242
Lauck, W. Jett 147–8
Legal Foundations of Capitalism 187–8, 217, 257–71
Leiserson, William115–16, 119, 149, 230
Lescohier, Don 164–5, 218; workers' school 196
Lewis, David, Representative 215
Lichtenstein, Nelson 237
limiting factor and cooperating factors 269, 279
Lincoln, Abraham 106
Lloyd, Henry Demarest 89
Locke, John 273–4
Lombard, Norman 203
Los Angeles Times 143
Lowell, Josephine 184
Lowi, Theodore: *The End of Liberalism* 243
Ludlow massacre 150–1

Mace, William, H., 53; Syracuse historian recommended Commons 50–1
Madison Team 163–5
Maine, Sir Henry 60
Manly, Basil: causes of industrial unrest 247–8; staff director of USCIR 153–4

314

Index

Marshall, Alfred 4, 39, 47–8, 274–6
Marx, Karl 66, 101, 106, 108, 116, 168; article "Marx Today" 198–9
maximum feasible participation 241
Mazzini, Giuseppe, 58–9
McCarthy, Charles 127–9 148; clash with Frank Walsh in USCIR 152–3; influence on Commons 129–31; death 182–3
McCarthy, Joseph 238
McCracken, Harlan: co-author "Secular Trends and Business Cycles" 181–2; influence on J.M. Keynes 190n22
McGovern, Francis, Governor 130–4
McKenna, Reginald 203
McKinley, William 84
McMahon, Theresa 117, 226
McNamara, John and James 143–4
McNulty, Paul: bargaining theory 115; beginning of labor economics 195
Meltzer, Allan 205
Meske, Chester 231
Mill, John Stuart 47
Miller, Adolph 49; opposition to Strong bills 200
Millis, Harry 237–8
Mitchell, John 89; anthracite strike 85–87; before Roosevelt 88; before commission 89
Mitchell, Wesley Clair 184, 187, 220, 258, 277
Mittleman, Edward 168
Monroe, James, Professor: background 25–6; letters from Commons 31–5; suggests Oberlin position 38
Montgomery, Donald 211
Morgan, J.P. 50, 73, 79, 88, 136, 146, 168–9
Morton, Walter: investigation of Smoot-Hawley 209–10, 221, opponent of unemployment plan 221 n22
Mother Jones aka Mary Harris Jones 87–8
Muller v. Oregon 171, 185, 270
Munn v. Illinois 267
Myself 219

National Association of Manufacturers (NAM) 84; American Plan 177; open shop campaigns 136–7
National Bureau of Economic Research: founding 184
National Civic Federation (NCF) 83–4; Municipal Utility Study 111–13

New York State Court of Appeals: on Worker Compensation Law 130–1
Newcomb, Simon 24, 30
"new" economists, vs. "old" economists 30–1
Norris, George, Senator 214; anti-injunction bill 197
Norris-LaGuardia Act 238; background 197–8

Oberlin College: changes 21–2
Oberlin Rescue 14–15
Oberlin Review 22
Ohlin, Bertil 228
Oliphant, Herman: anti-injunction bill 197
Olson, Mancur: *The Logic of Collective Action* 243
Omaha Platform. *See* People's Party
Otis, Harrison, Gray 143

Panic of 1893 44
Parsons, Kenneth 231, 235
Patman, Wright, Representative: veterans' bonus bill 211
Peirce, Charles Sanders 30, 275
People's Party (Populists) 42, 279
Perkins, Francis 214–15
Perlman, Mark 117–8, 157, 166, 225
Perlman, Selig 115–18, 139, 149, 163, 168; workers' school 196–7; labor history 218–19, 225 Commons as interviewer 235
Pettengill, Samuel, Senator 211
Philanthropy: Manly and Commons on 250–1
Phillips, Thomas Wharton, Representative 72–3; dissent on USIC report 78
Phillips, Ulrich 100
Pittsburgh Plus 186–7
Pittsburgh Survey 118–119
Principles of Labor Legislation 155–6, 219
Progress and Poverty. See George, Henry
Proportional Representation 60–1
Public Purpose 48, 58–9, 61–2, 91, 229–30, 267; worker welfare in 268–71
Pullman Strike 33–4, 83

Quakers: Southern exodus, 10

Races and Immigrants 119–22
Ramirez, Bruno 73; comment on Commons-Harriman dissent 255

Raushenbush, Paul 184, 214
Rawleigh, William T.: Smoot-Hawley investigation, 209
Raymond, Bradford 37
reasonable value. See Commons, John R.
Red Scare 177
Reed, John 148
Rent: income unearned from land 26; from legal opportunities 47
Richberg, Donald 194; anti-injunction bill 197
Riley, James Whitcomb, Hoosier poet 15, 16
Ripley, William Z. 187
Robbins, Lionel 227
Robinson, Joan 49
Rockefeller, John D., Jr. 128, 151; Ludlow massacre 151–3
Rockefeller, John D. Sr. 73, 79, 250
Roosevelt, Franklin Delano 148, 215
Roosevelt, Theodore: anthracite strike intervention 88–9; significance of 90
Rorty, Malcolm: founding of NBER 184
Ross, Edward Alsworth 32, 33; Perlman advocate 163
Rubinow, I.M. (Max) 155
Russell, Howard 24

Saposs, David 115–16, 167; workers' school 197
Sayre, Francis: anti-injunction bill 197
Schultz, Theodore W.: Smoot-Hawley investigation 210
Schumpeter, Joseph 31
Seligman, E.R.A. 83
Shaw, Albert 43
Sheffield Scientific School 29
Sheridan, Lewis: Harper's Ferry 25
Sherman Silver Purchase Act 43
Shibley, George 72
Shipstead, Henry, Senator: anti-injunction bill 197
site-value taxation 27, 47, 196
Slaughterhouse Case 260
Smith, Adam 66, 270
Smith, Hoke, Senator 147
Smith, Richmond Mayo 49–50
Smoot-Hawley Tariff investigation 209–10
Social Reform and the Church 45–6
Society of Master Cordwainers 102
Sociological View of Sovereignty 60–6

Somerset, James 276
Sorenson, Theodore 240
Specie Resumption Act 42
Spencer, Herbert 61
St. John, Vincent 139
Stead, William 83
Steward, Ira 108
Stewart, Bryce 215
Stone, N.I (Nahum, Isaac) 72, 183–4
Strong, Benjamin: Governor New York Federal Reserve Bank 200; on second Strong Bill 204
Strong, James, Representative: author of Strong bills 200
Sullivan, J.W. 112
Sumner, Helen Laura 98, 104, 115, 146; industrial courts report 49
superior labor councils in France, Belgium and Austria 75
surplus value 47
Swain, Joseph: president of University of Indiana 50, 53
Sydenstrikcer, Edgar: poverty rate estimate 247

Taft, Philip 218–19
Taft, William Howard 44; USCIR petition 144
Taft-Hartley Act 237
Tawney, R.H: review of Legal Foundations of Capitalism 187–8
Temperance Herald 24
Tresca, Carlo 148
Thoreau, Henry David 106
transactions 188, 228, 274, 276; wage bargain 262–8; classifications 217–18; participants 263
Turner, Frederick Jackson 100, 166

U.S. Steel Corporation 73, 78, 119, 136, 186, 276
Union City Times, 12–13
United Beneficial Society of Journeymen Cordwainers 102
United Mine Workers (UMW) 77, 149–51; "industrial parliament" 84–5
United States Industrial Commission (USIC), 73–9

Van Hise, Charles 97, 99, 100, 115
Veblen, Thorstein 91–2, 169, 228, 257–8, 277

Index

Voegelin, Eric: democratic presuppositions of John R 10, 17

Wagner, Adolph 47
Wagner, Robert, Senator 215
Walker, Francis, A.: race suicide thesis 120
Walling, William English, 80, 116, 149; race blindness 149
Walsh, Frank 145–6; cross-examination of Rockefeller Jr. 152; comment on Commons-Harriman dissent 254–5
Ward, Lester Frank 57–8, 61, 275–8
Watson, James, Eli, 15–16
Webb, Sidney and Beatrice, *Industrial Democracy*, 92
Weisbrod, Burton: design of Economic Opportunity Act 240–1
Wesleyan University 34
West, Max 77
Western Reserve 13
Weyl, Walter 86, 89

Wicksell, Knut 182
Wilkinson, Charlotte 54
William the Conqueror 258
Wilson, Woodrow, 37, 161; Hopkins lectures on government, 32
Winchester Herald, 12–13
Wisconsin Industrial Commission 130–4; law creating it 132
Wisconsin workers' school 196–7
Witte, Edwin 3, 118, 163–4, 184, 215–16, 226; anti-injunction bill 197–8; Norris-LaGuardia Bill 214
Wolman, Leo: garment workers' unemployment scheme 180
Woodburn, James, A. 32, 42
Wright, Carroll, D. 100; USIC plan 74
Wunderlin, Clarence 2; *Visions of a New Industrial Order* 72

Zeuch, William co-author of "Secular Trends and Business Cycles" 181–2

CPSIA information can be obtained
at www.ICGtesting.com
Printed in the USA
BVHW072116071218
535054BV00010B/180/P